Diver's Guide to Underwater America

Revised Edition

Diver's Guide to Underwater America

Revised Edition

by Kate Kelley & John Shobe

illustrated by Jeff Brundege

cartography by Carolyn Kelley
book design and layout by John Shobe and Jeff Brundege
research writing by Kate Kelley
proofreading by Shelly Ogle

Diving Accident Network at Duke University

EMERGENCY HOTLINE: 919-684-8411

First Edition, © 1982

ISBN 0-9611522-3-0 hardcover

ISBN 0-9611522-2-2 paperback

Typeset electronically from computer disk by Candlelight Type-Print Incorporated, Austin Texas

Printed by Communication Specialists Inc., Austin, Texas

Divesports Publishing, P.O. Box 1397, Austin, Texas 78767

HOW TO USE THIS BOOK

* For ease of use, the United States is broken into twelve regions — see the Table of Contents for breakdown of states within each region.

* Each section has a different illustrative key (manatee for Florida, kelp for California, etc.) in the upper right corner of right-hand pages. These built-in bookmarks help you locate sections by flipping the pages.

* All states are listed alphabetically within each section.

* An index in the back has all dive sites listed alphabetically by state.

* Maps for each state are intended to give a general idea of where sites are located. If many sites are within a small area, a single number shows on the map, with sites listed below.

* State laws concerning diving are listed at the end of the coverage of each state. This is intended only to give you a idea of activities permitted. In many cases license requirements are not specified — assume a license will be required for any food-gathering activity. Check locally.

* For more information on dive sites, consult the Dive Store Directory in the back of the book, which is organized regionally within each state.

TABLE OF CONTENTS

Acknowledgements . . . . *ix*
Introduction . . . . *x*

Hawaii
Oahu 4
Maui 10
Hawaii 14
Kauai 18

Pacific Northwest
Alaska 21
Oregon 25
Washington 29

California
Northern 47
Central 55
Southern 63
Channel Islands 77
Inland 95

The West
Arizona 98
Colorado 99
Idaho 104
Montana 106
Nevada 110
New Mexico 112
Utah 113
Wyoming 115

The Gulf States
Alabama 118
Louisiana 120
Mississippi 121
Texas 122

The Midwest
Arkansas 134
Iowa 138
Kansas 140
Missouri 140
Nebraska 145
North Dakota 145
Oklahoma 146
South Dakota 147

The Great Lakes

Illinois 150
Indiana 152
Michigan 157
Minnesota 167
Ohio 170
Wisconsin 172

Appalachia

Kentucky 182
Tennessee 184
West Virginia 185

New England

Connecticut 188
Maine 192
Massachusetts 198
New Hampshire 208
Rhode Island 210
Vermont 213

The Middle Atlantic

Delaware 216
Maryland 218
New Jersey 222
New York 226
Pennsylvania 234
Virginia 236

The Southeast

Georgia 240
North Carolina 241
South Carolina 251

Florida

East Coast 254
Keys 271
Gulf Coast 285
Inland 299
Cave Diving 315

Dive Store Directory 318

Index

ACKNOWLEDGEMENTS

A book of this scope couldn't be completed without help from many people. Special thanks go to:

Laurie Kuhr and the Montana Dive Council — Montana

Harry Truitt — Washington

Charles Hoffman — Texas

Joanie Follmer — Florida Keys

Bob Widmann — Alaska

Rod Farb — North Carolina

Tom Fitzpatrick — New Jersey

Rich Onesty — New Jersey

Bruce Good — California

Barbara Brundage — Hawaii

Paul Rollins — Maine

Bruce at The Diving Locker — Connecticut

Jon Hardy — Catalina

Dave Mitchell — Florida

Doug at West End Diving — Missouri

Wes Skiles — Florida springs

Carol Rose — central California

In addition, thanks to Steve Gerrard, Merlin Hilmoe, Steve Klem, Lola Huitt, Dave Farrar, Carolyn Kelley, Phil Buterbaugh, the Austin Chronicle, William Roston, Don Peterson, Ruth and John Kelley, Dave Lang, Pauline and Dale Brown, and — especially — Jeff Brundege.

INTRODUCTION

The *Diver's Guide to Underwater America* is designed to acquaint you with the incredible variety of diving found within the United States. Every possible attempt has been made to verify the information presented and make it as complete as possible. However, this book is not meant to stand alone as the sole information a diver needs to visit a new area. We have included a Directory of Dive Stores so you can check with professionals for current conditions. All depths, altitudes, and visibilities are approximations, and should not be used to compute bottom time. Since water isn't a stable element, conditions at a dive site can change overnight. It should be obvious to every diver that each new dive experience should be discussed beforehand with local professionals.

HAWAII

OAHU   MAUI   MOLOKINI   LANAI

To really understand Hawaiian diving, you need to take a look at a map of the Pacific Ocean floor. The Hawaiian Islands are only the tips of gigantic volcanoes that plunge to abyssal depths. In fact, if measured from its true base on the seabed, Mauna Kea, on Hawaii, is actually the world's highest mountain, with its origin in a crack in the sea floor over 19,000' below sea level.

The underwater realm reflects that volcanic history in a number of ways. For one thing, no other locale offers the amazing undersea lavascape of Hawaii. When the lava came pouring out of the craters and met the water with a giant hiss, it formed some of the most bizarre shapes possible. All the islands have at least a few sites with either lava arches, caves, pinnacles, or tubes, and some islands, like Hawaii and Lanai, are full of them. Hollow lava tubes were formed when a column of hot flowing lava plunged into the sea. The outer layer quickly cooled and hardened, leaving the hot core still flowing. You can swim into many of these big "straws." Lights will add immensely to diving in Hawaii, since you need to peer into dark crannies and cave ceilings to see many of the spectacular residents like slipper lobster and nudibranches.

Another reflection of Hawaii's volcanic origin can be found in the fish life. Little continental shelf exists around these sea mountains. As a consequence, diving in Hawaii reveals many large open-ocean rovers like sea turtles, jacks, and eagle rays, as well as a spectacular abundance of reef tropicals. Parrotfish, clownfish, filefish, butterflyfish, 2'-long imperial angels, hawkfish, goatfish, scorpionfish, wrasses, damsels and squirrelfish — the list is endless. No one has yet come up with a satisfying scientific theory that really explains the gaudy color schemes of these fish. It's hard to believe they aren't engaged in some form of one-upmanship when you see the staggering variety of color and patterning.

The corals, too, have developed in response to the peculiar conditions imposed by perching on the edge of the abyss. The huge breakers that Hawaii is famous for have limited the numbers of soft corals and huge sponges, so don't expect a Caribbean-style reef of elkhorn. Instead, small hard corals and brilliant encrusting growth adorns the craggy lava rock. Since Hawaii approaches the northern limits of the coral realm, the reefs are more developed on the southern islands.

Diving varies tremendously amongst the islands, and even at different sites on each individual island. While there are spots so calm and easy that they're perfect for beginners, a few — including some of the most rewarding — call for precise pre-dive planning. On Oahu, for instance, the north shore may be calm and easy in summer, only to be battered by 30' surf all winter. It's essential to check with local divers. Besides surf, currents can be present. And if you're not aware of them, you could end up like the couple who fell asleep on their rubber raft just off one of Maui's idyllic beaches, only to find themselves washed up on Lanai the

MOLOKAI   HAWAII   KAUAI

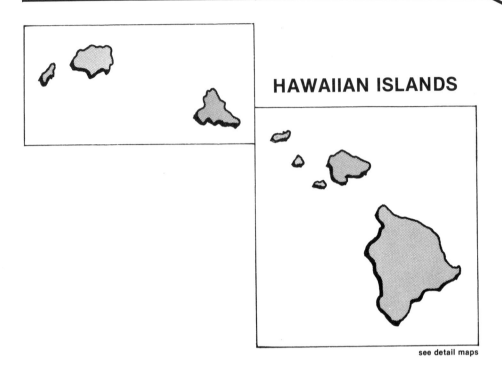

HAWAIIAN ISLANDS

see detail maps

next day, or the buddy team who thought a certain spot on Oahu's southeast shore looked great, so they jumped in and found themselves ten miles out to sea in a hurry.

Luckily, the currents and surf operate in predictable fashion, so a little checking around is all it takes to prevent these scenes from happening.

Hawaiian diving can also be strongly affected by the tradewinds, with divers seeking out the lee side of the islands. Since the tradewinds often build up in the afternoon, morning is the best time to attempt a dive in a less protected site. Hawaii also has its version of the odd winter wind that upsets the normal routine. Like California's Santa Ana winds, Hawaii's Kona wind comes very rarely, usually in January, and reverses the normal tradewinds so that what was lee is now unprotected, and vice-versa. You can always tell when the Kona is blowing, because all those windward areas that are inaccessible over 90% of the year are suddenly packed with divers.

Another unique aspect of diving Hawaii is lava rock entries. Lava rock, as many a scraped diver will attest, surely takes the prize for the most abrasive substance known to humanity. Boat diving eliminates this problem.

To many divers, shells are one of the best things about Hawaii. Our island state has the most exotic shells in the country, but a couple of the 24 species of cone

shell are highly poisonous. The cones, who catch their prey by extending a proboscis and injecting a poison similar to the cobra's, are predators on other mollusks. Many cause only a mild reaction, but the striated cone (4") and the textile cone (3" — also called cloth-of-gold cone) are known to be poisonous to people, so don't pick up cones unless you can identify them.

Hawaiian waters are warm to those of us used to submerging in temperatures of 60° or less. The water temperature averages 72°, + or −3°, year-round. No thermoclines exist. Most people wear a wetsuit top or shorty to make extended dives more comfortable. Water clarity averages 100'.

OAHU — Leeward and South Shore

Since Oahu has the largest population and receives more visitors than all the outer islands put together, naturally it also sees the majority of diving activity. But despite all this intense human pressure, exciting diving still exists around Oahu. While it might not be the best place to find lobster, Oahu offers plenty of opportunities for photography and sightseeing in beautiful coral reefs and lava formations.

Hanauma Bay, only 20 minutes from Waikiki, is the most popular dive site on the island, with showers, a picnic area, and a lifeguard. Sheltered from practically all weather, Hanauma is usually calm when the rest of the leeward shore is off-limits due to Kona winds. Also adding to its popularity is the fact that Hanauma Bay has been a state Marine Life Conservation District since the 1960's. You can now see a wide range of fish including blue-stripe and long-nose butterflyfish, red soldierfish, schooling convict tangs, eagle rays, moray eels, and even an occasional sea turtle. Even sought-after food fish seem to realize they're safe here, and might accept food from the diver's hand.

Hanauma also appeals to the coral fancier, since the bay is home to one of the best developed remaining coral reefs on Oahu. The bay is actually the crater of a dormant volcano, which blew its side out and filled with water during its last eruption over 20,000 years ago. Coral communities found the lava rock of the crater a perfect home, and today the reefs start in water as shallow as 15', making Hanauma a great site for snorkelers or novice divers. More experienced divers follow a steel cable which winds out through the channel into deeper water around the mouth of the cove, where clarity improves to 100'. Wreck fans can find a submerged airplane outside the mouth of the bay. Returning to shore through the wash of the reef requires caution.

Another good diving site along the southeast stretch of coastline is known as **Portlock Point**. You enter the water over a lava rock ledge, which is easy as far as lava rock entries go. The bottom quickly drops off to around 50', with rocky ledges and coral heads sheltering many tropical fish. Most divers wait until the slack of an incoming tide to dive Portlock Point, as that minimizes danger from

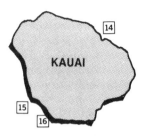

KAUAI

General Store 16
Hanalei Bay 14
Old Koloa Landing 16
Poipu Beach 15
Sheraton Caverns 16

OAHU

American fighter planes 4
Fantasy Reef 2
Hanauma Bay 1
Japanese Zeros 4
Kahe Point Beach Park 5
Lava Flows 3
Magic Island 3
Maili Cove 6
Makaha Beach Park 7
Makua Beach 8
Moku Manu Islands 12
Pohakunui Beach 5
Portlock Point 2
Punaluu Beach Park 11
Pupukea Cove 10
Rabbit Island 13
Three Tables 10
Waimea Bay 9

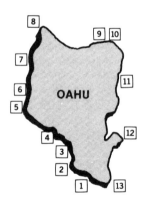

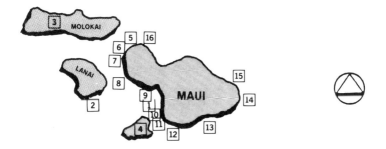

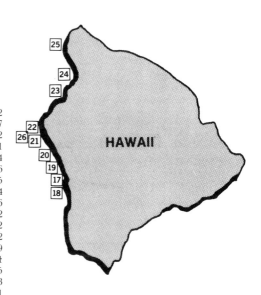

MAUI

Ahihi Bay 12
Black Rock 7
First Cathedral 2
Five Caves 11
Hana Bay 14
Honokohau Bay 16
Honolua Bay 5
Kahoolawe 4
Kapalua Beach 6
Knob Hill 2
La Perouse Bay 12
Lanai 2
McGregor Point 9
Mokuhooniki Rock 1
Mokule'ia Bay 5
Molokai 3
Molokini Shoal 1
Monolith Rock 2
Napili Bay 6
Nuu Bay 13
Olowalu 8
Second Cathedral 2
Sergeant Major Reef 2
Shark Fin Rock 2
The Grotto 4
Ulua Beach 10
Ulua Ridge 4
Wai'anapanapa State Park 15
Wailea Beach 11
Wash Rock 2

HAWAII

Anaeho'omalu Bay Beach Park 23
City of Refuge 17
Hapuna Beach State Park 24
Honokohua Bay 23
Kahalu'u Beach County Park 20
Kailua Kona 21
Kaiwi Point 26
Kauhako Bay 18
Kealakekua Bay 19
Mahukona Beach Harbor 25
Old Kona Airport State Park 22
Palemano Point 17
Pine Trees 26
Puako Beach Park 24
Pyramid Rock 26
Redhill 26
Sea Village 26

the "Molokai Express." This current, caused by the funneling of ocean water between Oahu and Molokai, usually runs anywhere from 2-5 knots, and, as the name indicates, it runs out to sea — towards Molokai. More than one diver has ventured too far out only to find themselves being wafted inexorably out to sea. To avoid being picked up by the Express, stay within 75 yards of shore.

Further up the coastline, towards Diamond Head, **Fantasy Reef** provides a beautiful spot for a boat dive. Patch reefs separated by sand channels draw big animals like turtles and eagle rays. Delicious menpachi, a reddish 1'-long squirrelfish, can be spotted schooling in caves. However, alongshore currents generally limit this dive to the more experienced.

The calmer water at **Lava Flows**, right off Waikiki, is another common destination of dive boats, and one that's easy enough for new divers. Currents don't present problems here and, since the Lava Flows are past the surf line, there's little surge to contend with. The maze-like passageways and channels between the coral-covered lava rock outcroppings can be explored at length, since depths don't go much beyond 40'.

Magic Island, about a mile to the west of Waikiki in Ala Moana Park, also lures divers. Complete amenities exist, including bathrooms and a lifeguard. A shore entry can be made over the slippery seawall and from there it's about a 150-yard swim out to the reef. Surge presents the only obstacle to diving here — if the surf is breaking more than 3', you can count on having to cope with some strong surge. On calmer days, though, Magic Island is a diver's delight. Finger reefs start on the lava rock as shallow as 20'. Lava tubes and caves poke out from the surge channels and often shelter regal slipper lobster, harlequin shrimp, and eels.

Night diving is popular at Magic Island, with opportunities for lobster hunting, photography, and shell watching. On a night dive you stand a good chance of seeing one of the many species of cowries that inhabit Hawaiian waters. A live tiger cowrie, out prowling, with its nubby, patterned mantle half covering its shell, is much more beautiful than specimens seen in collectors' boxes. A few night divers have even witnessed a cone attacking a cowrie, in a rather one-sided battle that the cone usually wins if it has caught the cowrie off guard. Besides the famous cones and cowries, Hawaii has a host of other shells, including helmets, tritons, spiders, conchs, volutes, miters, tuns, and harps.

The waters outside the entrance to Pearl Harbor furnish a living history lesson into the events of December 7, 1941. Both **Japanese Zeros** and **American fighter planes** in various stages of preservation can be found in depths of usually less than 100'. While a few planes are intact and recognizable, many have already metamorphosed into reefs as corals and sponges overtake them. Low visibility characterizes Pearl Harbor.

Kahe Point Beach Park, up from Barber's Point, has some of the most developed coral on Oahu. To reach the reefs, enter through the small cove to the east of the swimming beach. The bottom slopes very gradually out to a large reef. Even close in, visibility is good over the scattered coral heads and clean white sand.

Pohakunui Beach, just a mile to the west, offers a similar dive except that the reef lies much closer to shore. Pohakunui doesn't offer all the amenities of Kahe Point, like lifeguards and restrooms. Both dive sites have easy, safe, and calm waters, since the near shore area is protected from tradewinds by the Waianae Mountains. However, about 200 yards offshore the winds create a surface current running out to sea. It's easy to avoid this altogether by staying close to land, but if you do decide to go out past 200 yards, be sure and budget your air so you won't be forced to try and snorkel back against the current.

If you're a wreck diver, or interested in the development of artificial reefs, stop at **Maili Cove** to see a 165' minesweeper that was sunk by local divers in 1981. Sitting on the bottom 90' down, the ship has already been occupied by many fish. Moray eels have taken up residence, coral is beginning to grow, and divers have even seen turtles and rays checking out this new addition to the reefs in the area.

If you can't handle surf entries, forget about this site, since its enormous 30' winter surf qualifies it as the scene of a surfing competition. But, in calmer weather, experienced divers will find **Makaha Beach Park** great diving, especially around the caves and grottos of the offshore ledge. If the surf is high, be sure and time your entry and exit around the wave sets. The marine life around the grottos is fantastic. Often lionfish may be seen hiding out in the dark recesses of the caves. With their poisonous spines folded down they look much less impressive, but a careless grab might get you in trouble. Other tropicals include the omnipresent butterflyfish of every possible description, and schools of damselfish ranging from bright blue, to black and white, to green. Tiny blue spot puffers, if they weren't so common, would surely be among the most admired of tropicals. Makaha is also a good place to see sea turtles.

Makua Beach, just down from Kaena Point, is another fascinating dive. The shallow sandy bottom gives way to coral patches around 50 yards out. Like other sites along the leeward shore, though, the surface current starts up 200 yards out. Since at 400 yards offshore the depth is only about 70' and the coral and clarity just keep getting better, it's easy to forget the offshore surface current and just keep going out. Be sure and time your dive so you don't have to snorkel back.

OAHU — North Shore

The north shore of Oahu withstands some of the most gigantic surf anywhere, with breakers of over 40' recorded. But that's in the winter. In the summer, the north shore metamorphoses from a treacherous surf-ridden diver suicide zone into a calm, clear, easy, and fascinating diving area — safe enough even for beginners. So if you ever find yourself in Oahu in the summertime, count your blessings and head for the north shore.

Waimea Bay has a reputation as one of the most scenic beaches in Oahu — the kind you see on the glossy brochures at the travel agents', with a curving white sand beach surrounded by green-clad hills and eager swimmers frolicking in the clear aquamarine water. Well, it's all true, and it's as beautiful as the brochures promise. Around the basalt rocks on the left of the beach, tropicals can be seen in depths shallow enough for snorkeling. Rips sometimes develop further offshore.

Pupukea Cove is the stand-out dive on the north shore. It's also called Shark's Cove, due to the resemblance of a rock formation to a tiger shark. The site of the most recent lava flows on Oahu, Pupukea has an incredible underwater lavascape. The left side of the cove stairsteps down into ledges. Across the rock and sand bottom to the right, you come into a fairytale land of lava tubes, caves, and arches. As in much of this area, coral isn't widespread, due to the rough water of winter. Moray eels, yellow and black Moorish idols, and at least 45 other species are common, and even sea turtles and dolphins have been seen here. Surf action in the caves requires caution, as depth doesn't go below 30'. After you're through with all the underwater scenery, there are showers and a sandy beach to help you unwind. Like all north shore sites, it's only diveable in summer.

The next cove down from Pupukea also have a winding maze of caves. The rocky bottom at **Three Tables** slopes gently down into a wild eroded series of depressions and tunnels that harbor plentiful marine life. The best diving is all above 60'. Since there is little surf or surge in summer, this is another good spot for beginners. Easy entries and exits and great invertebrate life make these spots favorite night dives.

OAHU — Windward Shore

For most of the year, the windward, or west coast of Oahu faces into the tradewinds, resulting in rough surge and surf. Since this is also known as the rainy coast, with almost daily showers, many streams carry runoff into the ocean, with correspondingly lower water clarity. Consequently, this side of Oahu is seldom visited by sport divers. However, on those sporadic winter days when the Kona wind blows strong from the southeast, this side of the island is protected and calm and divers flock to it. They are attracted by great coral reefs, abundant fish, and shells. The best diving is offshore, requiring a boat.

One favorite spot lies just off the **Punaluu Beach Park**. The coral development is fantastic, and the reef creatures are thick. The honeycombed reef lies in depths from 50' to almost 100'. Daytime dives reveal lots of tropicals, including such rarities as the potter's angelfish and, on deeper dives, the long-nose hawkfish. These are just a few examples of the exotics found on the windward shore that make this region the center for Hawaiian fish exporting, which is carefully licensed and requires hand netting.

Currents can make night diving in this area difficult, but for the advanced diver the rewards can be spectacular. The crevices and caves provide many invertebrates with daytime hiding places. At night, the usual situation is reversed: most of the colorful fish hide away (except the big-eyed cardinal and squirrelfish) and invertebrates forsake their daytime cover to forage about. You can see mollusks,

especially hunters like miters and cones; lobster, including the gaudy little slipper lobster; nudibranches and their cousins the gorgeous many-hued flatworms; and some sea anemones that only feed at night. Also at night, many corals feed. A cave whose roof is only faintly orangish during a daytime visit will be intensified at night into a ceiling of orange flowers, as the polyps open hungrily. And you can't forget the sea urchins, which come out in force at night and make it necessary for divers to stay positively buoyant.

Kaneohe Bay, south of Punaluu, at one time contained one of the most extensive coral communities on Oahu. However, careless development around the bay resulted in heavy runoff and the coral suffocated under the sedimentation. Today, Kaneohe Bay is a worst-case example of how not to develop around fragile coral reefs. The underwater view has changed from a lovely coral garden into a hideous scene of silt and algae — the only reason to dive Kaneohe today would be for documentation of pollution.

The **Moku Manu Islands**, just off the peninsula from Kaneohe Bay, still offer some of the most fascinating diving on Oahu. The rough surf and rapid currents limit this dive to experienced divers only, but, on those rare occasions when the islands are diveable they're well worth it. Visibility can be outstanding, and depth doesn't go much below 80', giving you plenty of time to explore the craggy dropoffs and huge boulders. Fish abound in the many crevices.

Fish also thrive around **Rabbit Island**, just off Makapuu Beach Park. Like most of the rest of the west side dives, a boat is needed to reach the island, although it looks temptingly close. Good coral development on basaltic rock ledges starts at depths of 35'.

MAUI, AND NEARBY ISLANDS OF LANAI, MOLOKAI, AND KAHOOLAWE

Maui is a diver's paradise for at least two reasons: Lanai and Molokini Shoal offshore, and humpback whales. From November to April, the endangered whales congregate off the island of Maui, where the calves develop the skills needed to make transpacific journeys. The whales are a common sight from a boat, with the calves often practicing their buoyancy control just beneath the surface. While few divers see a humpback underwater, many more hear them. Actually, "feel" them is a better description, for you become aware of the calls not really through your ears but through your entire body, as the sound resonates through body cavities.

And if that's not reason enough to visit Maui, **Molokini Shoal** will be. Certainly, some of Maui's most exciting diving is found at this fingernail-moon of an island just off the southwest coast. Several charters daily run out to the shoal. The green crescent of land that protrudes above the water is actually the lip of a dormant volcano. Abundant corals have lined the inside of the U-shaped crater. The reef begins as shallow as 20', and depth inside the protected crater doesn't go below

90', making Molokini a good site for scuba or snorkeling. More experienced divers explore the incredible scenery of the outside walls of the crater, which plunge from 10' to below 300'.

Since Molokini has been a game preserve for some time, the aquatic life is fantastic and friendly. Almost all of Hawaii's famed tropicals can be seen here (including the rare boar fish, usually seen on the back wall), as well as tame colorful groupers, jack crevalle (ulua), eagle rays (often in military formation), white-tipped reef sharks, and even occasional spinner dolphins. One year, a whale shark hung around for awhile! Red-slate pencil urchins fill the shallows. Visibility at Molokini is usually well past 100', which, combined with the tame reef life and colorful coral, makes it a favorite spot for photographers.

Sometimes dive boats stop at **Mokuhooniki Rock**, near Molokini, for their more adventurous clientele. Surrounded by deep water, this is the spot for pelagics like sharks, rays, ulua, etc.

With some of the most professional and helpful charter boat operators anywhere, Maui has diving destinations for everyone, whether you want a calm easy snorkel, or to explore the fantastic island of **Lanai**. Known as the home of the most rugged and varied lava formations in Hawaii, Lanai provides diving characterized by majestic structures like huge arches and caverns. An entire congregation could "worship" at **Second Cathedral** and not feel crowded or claustrophobic, since the huge cavern has twin arches that offer easy exit. Depth is a pleasant 60'.

Monolith Rock, another favorite destination on Lanai, is a huge plateau 40' beneath the surface. Besides admiring the spectacular scenery of the plateau, whose offshore side falls to 110' deep, divers stay busy feeding and stroking a pet moray, watching garden eels do their sinuous little dances from their burrows, and admiring large black coral trees.

At **First Cathedral** the latticework in a hollow pinnacle draws divers; at **Knob Hill** it's a series of arches and ridges bedecked with tropicals. At least 20 other fantastic sites are found in this region of Lanai, including **Wash Rock**, **Sergeant Major Reef**, and **Shark Fin Rock**. Expect to see hordes of tropical fish, shallows filled with red-slate pencil urchins, octopus, hermit crabs, and maybe a manta or eagle ray.

Dive boats also visit **Molokai** and, occasionally, **Kahoolawe**. Since the latter is owned by the Navy, it's almost always off-limits, as well as having less natural protection. However, on the rare occasion that the weather and Navy both permit diving, some of the favorite sites are **The Grotto**, where a cave entrance opens up into the wall 35' down, and **Ulua Ridge**, where a huge reef snakes along the bottom.

If you're going back to Maui in hopes of visiting the submarine *Bluegill*, you can forget it, since it was dropped into the abyss after complaints were received of its danger to divers.

MAUI — West Shore

But there's good shore diving to be found off Maui, too, with generally shallow, lively reefs to explore. The majority of beach diving takes place along the sheltered west side. **Honolua Bay** at the northwest tip of the island is a state Marine Life Conservation District. Pretty, shallow reefs of 30' maximum are on each side of the bay. Tame tropicals abound, including lemon butterflyfish, convict tangs, and both gray and blue-spot puffers. Sometimes great clouds of tiny, electric-blue damselfish hover over the coral heads.

At **Mokule'ia Bay**, a beautiful reef on the left side drops to 45'. Entry is easy, and snorkelers enjoy the shallow right side of the bay. Summer is the best time to dive here; in winter you'll need to check the wave height. **Kapalua Beach** and **Napili Bay**, also north of Kaanapali, appeal mainly to snorkelers.

Black Rock, just out from the Sheraton in the midst of Kaanapali, is another favorite spot for visiting divers. According to the old Hawaiian culture, this rock was the spot where the souls of dead Hawaiians made their spirit leap into another world. Today you can leap to another world just below the water's surface, if you're snorkeling. Divers with gear prefer to enter from the beach to the south of the Sheridan. A large school of goatfish regularly hovers around the 35'-deep lava cliff, and eagle rays and moray eels are sometimes seen. Night diving is fun and easy here.

Just to the south of **Olowalu**, where the road meets the water, a large shallow coral reef laced with channels promises excellent snorkeling or diving. Beautiful coral development and many fish enliven the 30' depths. If the surf's high enough for bodysurfing, don't enter the water.

From the lighthouse at **McGregor Point**, and also from all the other Pali overlooks, you'll find prime humpback watching territory, as well as several sites for good diving. At the lighthouse road itself, you'll find access (watch the lava rock entries, though) to a large reef that seldom goes below 30'.

And after the dive, you can watch for humpbacks offshore while you relax. Even from land, humpbacks are fascinating to watch. Unlike the stately procession of grays off California, marked mainly by spouts and an occasional head, the humpbacks off Maui put on an acrobatic show. As an early whaler observed, humpbacks are as graceful as "a swallow on the wing", and much given to splendid leaps from the water, the known record being 40 breaches in succession! Their 15'-long flippers add to the displays and no doubt enhance their similarity to flying birds. Their amazing singing ability places them above all other cetaceans in this respect, as their elaborate songs are changed simultaneously, every year. Since males are the principal singers, the songs are thought to be territorial in nature. The males also have tremendous fights among themselves for the right to escort a female and her calf. Presumably, they want more than merely to provide escort service, but mating and birthing are still humpback mysteries.

Ulua Beach, just south of Kihei, has a great shallow reef for snorkeling that is also a favorite night dive. Showers are available at the beach. **Wailea Beach**, just to the south, is one of the best dives in the area, with a large reef that falls away to 50'. Access and entry are easy, the water is calm and protected, the gorgeous beach has showers, the scenery is beautiful underwater, and the fish life is fantastic!

At **Five Caves**, near the cemetery at Makena Landing, some of Maui's most interesting beach diving can be found. The offshore rocks fall away into a maze-like series of caves 45' deep that shelter more than their fair share of invertebrates. Cones, tuns, miters, and cowries all might be glimpsed at night, out stalking. By day, they might be seen tucked away into nooks around the caves. Slipper lobster and small red crabs and squirrelfish also hide away during daylight hours inside the caves. A white-tip reef shark has been known to reside here, and sea turtles often pass through. Use caution around the rocks if surge is present — high surf guarantees it will be.

Ahihi Bay, Maui's first marine preserve, is worth a visit if you're familiar with the area, since access down the rough dirt road is difficult. If the surf is down, clarity and diving will be excellent, with the healthy fish life of a protected reef.

Another marine preserve, and one that offers some of the most colorful coral on Maui, is **La Perouse Bay**. Although dive boats regularly run over to the bay, it's also accessible by road to those who don't mind hiking with gear over lava flows to some of the most beautiful black sand beaches imaginable. Since lava fingers separate the beaches, it's even possible to have a beach all to yourself! You'll find great snorkeling or scuba diving in the shallow, sheltered bay, with Maui's most varied assortment of corals. Brilliantly colored fish, like the tasty hinalei, with blue fins, yellow belly, and double rows of green rectangles on its red sides, compete for your attention with the corals in an environment that has gone color-mad.

MAUI — South and East Shores

Since this side of the island is far from the diving centers of Lahaina and Kihei, is rugged and without easy shore access, and receives the full brunt of the tradewinds, far fewer divers visit it. There is good diving, but only if the sea is flat and calm.

Nuu Bay has some of the most exciting fish life on Maui, with big jacks, occasional sharks, eagle rays, and manta rays, and a huge, colorful reef that drops to a sand bottom 120' down. The catch? Access, of course. This is along the mountainous drive to Hana, and I'm not going to attempt to give directions. If you're part explorer, check with local divers.

There's a good chance that you'll be able to dive at **Hana Bay**, but check locally first, since currents can make diving impossible on many days of the year. You can enter the shallow water over the rocks near the lighthouse. If you're making a first dive here, or are snorkeling, stay inside the wash rocks. A beautiful reef with good coral and fish life drops to 60' on the unprotected outside of the wash rocks.

Since **Wai'anapanapa State Park** doesn't have protection either, you can only dive it in very calm weather. Its beautiful cave, as well as showers and camping, make this a wonderful spot to visit even if you can't dive the 35'-deep reef with its craggy lava formations. If you can, be sure to see the archway on the right side of the beach. If the surf makes diving impossible, you can always snorkel in the freshwater pool within the caves, where a light will reveal long skinny silvery fish hiding in the crevices.

At the far northern end of the east side, close to Honolua Bay, is **Honokohau Bay**. While it isn't as easy and protected as Honolua, it does have a colorful and craggy reef to explore, with butterflyfish, damselfish, puffers, and almost every other tropical common to this island. Diving conditions are unpredictable, though, as you can only dive in very calm water.

HAWAII — The Big Island

Imagine you've committed a terrible crime which carries an automatic sentence of death — probably by having your head caved in with a club. There's only one way out, and that's to escape to an isolated promontory. You can either run a

ED ROBINSON, Tom Stack & Associates

A squadron of eagle rays is a common sight in Hawaiian waters.

gauntlet of enemy troops who guard the only opening in an immense lava wall, or you can swim several hundred yards across a bay you believe to be shark-infested. If somehow you make it, your crime is forgotten, whether it was breaking one of the many taboos (like letting your shadow fall on royal ground, if you're a commoner, or eating bananas, if you're female), or merely something political, like siding with the wrong king in a war. Regardless, you will be able to walk out under your enemies' noses, and they can't touch you.

If you chose to swim the bay, you made the right decision, since the waters aren't shark-infested. In fact, the **City of Refuge** offers some of the best shore diving on the island. This National Park, at Honaunau, just an hour's drive south of Kailua Kona, has carved lava steps giving easy entry into the water. City of Refuge has some of the most advanced coral growth on Hawaii, with the pale yellows, greens, and oranges of the coral animals forming a backdrop to the tropicals flitting about. You'll be surrounded by filefish, butterflyfish, parrotfish, and the curious goatfish (weke), who make a pitiful goat-like bleating when distressed.

Clarity around the City of Refuge usually exceeds 100'. If you spend enough time underwater in the area, you can also expect to see manta rays, eagle rays, and green sea turtles. Besides easy entry, a very protected and scenic locale, and a fascinating historical setting, the City of Refuge is equipped with a freshwater spigot.

Just two miles to the south is **Kauhako Bay**, where entry is more difficult due to offshore rocks and occasional heavy surge. The best diving is to the south, along rock ledges teeming with fish. Dolphins have even been spotted here.

North of the City of Refuge is **Palemano Point**, where the shoreline is rocky enough to require that gloves and kneepads be part of local divers' and snorkelers' gear. Since there's a 150' walk to the beach, snorkeling is more popular than scuba. The shallow reef is alive with sea urchins, longnose butterflyfish, and Moorish idols. Water clarity is excellent in this protected location.

Kealakekua Bay is home to Captain James Cook's monument and the place where he died in a fight with the natives of these islands he had discovered. Since the bay is a marine preserve, the fish are very tame and you can always be sure of a big crowd if you bring a few handouts. This is a great spot for snorkeling, with protected water, colorful coral, and an interesting pebble beach.

Another safe, easy dive that's a favorite with snorkelers is found at **Kahalu'u Beach County Park**. A reef offshore protects the shallows, where tame tropicals school around lava ridges spotted with hard coral clumps. Restrooms are available.

At **Kailua Kona**, snorkelers tolerate visibility of about 10' close to shore to look for coral, tropicals, and maybe even antique bottles to the right of the pier.

For more exciting diving, visit **Old Kona Airport State Park**, by boat if possible. If you're going from land, be wary of sea urchins and surge. Kneepads and gloves are advised for protection from the rocks. A channel on the north end of the beach winds out for 75' to deeper water, where a tank will come in handy. Lava

ledges and tropicals appeal to snorkelers within the bay. Further out, a resident white-tip reef shark will pose for a few photographs before it tires of the attention and vacates its cave with a massive swish of its tail.

Snorkelers, more than divers, enjoy **Honokohua Bay**, just north of Old Kona Airport, because of its 1/4-mile walk to water. Clarity isn't the best here, although it improves at the south end of the bay. Shells, fish, and a smattering of coral enliven the sand bottom.

Anaeho'omalu Bay Beach Park, to the north of Marker 77, is also favored mainly by snorkelers who enjoy the broad sand beach, shallow water, pretty tropicals, and restrooms.

More serious divers head to **Puako Beach Park**, past Marker 71. Easy entry over the boat ramp leads to interesting reefs with lava arches, moray eels, shells, and scenic settings for photographers. If the wind is strong, currents will develop.

At **Hapuna Beach State Park**, snorkeling is preferred due to the 350' hike to the beach. A small cove on the north end leads into shallow reefs. If the surf is high, surge will make snorkeling unpleasant.

Wind creates the main problems at **Mahukona Beach Harbor**. On calm days, though, divers find easy access through the landing to shallow water where artifacts such as anchors, chains, and bottles can be spotted, along with all the "ordinary" sights like butterflyfish and puffers. Besides restrooms, showers are also nearby.

At **Kapa'a Beach County Park**, near the northern tip of the island, there is much less shelter. Experienced divers do take the plunge if surf and wind are down. Clarity is very poor (5') close in due to the lack of protection, but improves as you go further offshore.

Undoubtedly, though, most diving off Hawaii takes place from boats just off the Kona coast. Most boat dives are very close to shore — only the rugged lava rock and lack of access make boats necessary. Divers prone to seasickness especially appreciate these short boat rides! Diving the Kona coast is distinguished by very calm waters; only a few days a year, usually in January, are too rough to dive. Add to that the fact that currents, surf, and surge (which can limit diving on the other islands), don't present many problems either, and you have great diving accessible even to beginners. And the diving is varied enough to keep the same people coming back again and again. Spectacular dropoffs, with depths of 100' or more only 100 yards offshore; fantastic marine life, including dolphins, sea turtles, manta rays, eagle rays, false killer whales, and a host of reef-dwellers; and surreal lava scenery make Kona diving unforgettable.

Divers visit **Pyramid Rock** to see the schools of the gorgeous pyramid butterflyfish. At other sites, like **Kaiwi Point** or the reefs just off from the **Redhill** cinder cone, the main attraction is the fantastic underwater topography. Since Hawaii is by far the youngest member of the island chain, the volcanic forces that created it are still powerful, as anyone who has watched the recent eruptions can attest. Pinnacles, caves, dropoffs, arches, and lava tubes are everywhere on the Kona coast. The variety is endless: one minute you'll be cruising over a pastoral-looking landscape of rolling reefs and black sand valleys, and the next you'll come up against the twisted parapets of a feudal lava castle. Near Redhill, one lava tube spirals on for almost 100'. There is something surreal about the craggy lava, the darkness inside broken only by shafts of light filtering through tiny cracks in the ceiling . . . and then you catch a movement from the corner of your eye, and twist around just in time to see a goldentail moray shrink back in its hole. Diving the Kona coast is totally unforgettable, and overwhelmingly Hawaiian.

Other favorite sites include **Pine Trees** and **Sea Village**. Night diving is popular for the phosphorescent night waters as much as for the enhanced invertebrate action. Add to that the mysterious sound of whale song, commonly heard off Hawaii in winter, and you have the setting for an unforgettable dive. On many of the boat dives you can include a reef and a ledge in the same dive, since the reefs usually lie at depths of 30-60' and the dropoffs start at 60' and go to 200'. The most interesting diving, though, is found in the top 100'. Below that, scientists believe spherical lava mounds called "pillow lava" form the base of the Big Island and probably continue for thousands of feet downward. The thought that you're actually diving on the slopes of the world's highest mountain (19,680' to sea level, and then another 13,796' to the top of Mauna Kea) makes diving the Big Island especially exciting and awesome.

KAUAI

Kauai's the oldest of the major Hawaiian Islands — more than ten times older than Hawaii. Kauai's the wettest, with more than 40' of rain a year. Waialeale Mountain is the wettest spot on earth. Naturally, Kauai's also the greenest island, with the lush tropical jungle that comes from all that rain.

Kauai's probably as famous with birders as it is with divers, since islanders steadfastly refused to import the mongoose, which hunted many of the native birds on the other islands to extinction. As a result, Kauai is the undisputed birdwatching capitol of the state. If you can break away from the schools of bright reef fish, flocks of equally bright honeycreepers and other exotics await you in the jungle. Darwin could have formed his theory of evolution just as easily using the bizarre Hawaiian honeycreepers as he did with the Galapagos finches.

Kauai has a special appeal for divers who want to really get away from it all, for this island doesn't suffer from the overdevelopment that plagues some of the more popular tourist hangouts. Add to that the lush, tropical forest appearance of Kauai, and the generally shallow reefs brimming with fish, and you have a very special destination. For one thing, Kauai is queen when it comes to shells. The north shore of the island is buffeted by high surf and tricky currents all winter, but in summer the gorgeous beaches of **Hanalei Bay** invite divers with their calm waters. The broken lava rock reef is riddled with holes that have collected dead

shells and other aquatic debris during the winter.

Another beautiful creature that Kauai seems to have the most of is sea turtles. Divers on Kauai regularly penetrate the dappled darkness of lava tubes, looking for the gentle giants, which sometimes rest in the tubes. In fact, it's not unusual to see several turtles on just one dive!

Along the south shore, many snorkelers and scuba divers visit the rocky ledges off **Poipu Beach**, which is easily accessible by beach or boat. An amazingly varied lava terrain, complete with caverns, lava tubes, arches, and reef drops sustains an incredible variety of life. The offshore reefs swarm with schools of surgeonfish, octopus, lobster, slipper lobster, parrotfish, mollusks, and tame moray eels and butterflyfish. Tuna, whale sharks, manta rays, and even humpbacks have been seen. A few spots always seem to hide whitetip reef sharks. Even black coral can be spotted on a nearby wreck. Like all the coral of Hawaii, it is protected by state law.

At the **Sheraton Caverns**, lava tubes and green turtles are the highlights. Thousands of lemon butterflyfish swarming around the caverns at the **General Store** compete with the remains of a 19th century steamer for your attention. And at **Old Koloa Landing**, which can be reached from shore, you'd better bring tidbits for the tame morays and tropical fish. Shallow depth of 25' makes this a popular second dive.

Some other wonderful sightings can be made in these waters. A very uncommon sight is a Hawaiian monk seal, one of the rarest animals in the world. Usually found on small atolls to the west, monk seals have been known to visit Kauai. A far more common sight is the spinner. These small, slender dolphins can be seen throughout the islands, usually doing what they're named for — spinning. Scientists still don't know why they leap clear of the water to revolve rapidly several times, but some theorize the spinners are trying to raise their body temperature after a deep dive.

Other boat dives sometimes visit the reefs offshore from the Na Pali coastline. The vertical ramparts of this rugged coast supposedly saw the landing of the first Hawaiians and, looking at the undulating green ledges, you can almost believe that time has stopped, and you're in the landing party, watching blue-footed boobies wheel and dive for fish to feed their nestlings.

Hawaii laws concerning diving: It is unlawful to spear any crustacean or octopus. Many marine sanctuaries exist, and spearguns are not allowed on most dive charters (this is a practice, not a law). Dive flag is required.

PACIFIC NORTHWEST

ALASKA   **OREGON**

The common stereotype of Northwest divers is of rugged machos who have to be crazy to challenge the Pacific Northwest. Diving in frigid waters amidst such monsters as giant octopus and killer whales, so the story goes, calls for Charles Atlas types.

Like most stereotypes, this one is based on a grain of truth and then stretched way out of proportion. The truth — Pacific Northwest waters are COLD! Temperatures range from a summer surface high of 65° to winter temperatures that can be below freezing in parts of Alaska. The average temperature below the thermocline in Washington is 45°. Thermal protection is required for all diving.

But as for the monsters, there's not much truth to the stereotype. Octopus, even big ones, are usually timid and unaggressive. While the idea of a creature with a 20' armspan loaded with suckers that together create a pull of 2000 lbs. is pretty scary, the fact remains that the vast majority of all octopus retreat quickly from human encounters. Some divers who've logged hundreds of Northwest dives claim to have encountered an aggressive one. That generally means that the creature advanced on them, flashing angry color warnings, slowly enough that the divers could take some great photos as they retreated.

By all rights, killer whales — or orcas, as they're increasingly called — should be among the most fearsome of sea creatures. Their size, their speed, their intelligence, and their incredible set of teeth should make them the most dangerous creature in the sea to man, especially since large mammals are their normal prey. But one of the greatest mysteries of the oceans is that they aren't. There has never been a substantiated attack on humans by orcas. They occupy the same niche in the sea that we do on land — that of the climax predator, who has no natural enemies to fear. And since their underwater sonar lets them know of a diver in the water long before he knows of them, the number of underwater sightings of orcas is slim indeed.

Actually, there is less danger from sea creatures in the inland waters of Washington, the most popular diving area in the Northwest, than there is on a coral reef or in a California kelp bed. Sharks are non-existent. The most dangerous sea creatures you'll encounter are sea urchins and jellyfish. The water teems with peculiar sea life, including big-eyed ratfish, gaudily painted red Irish lords, hideous but comical looking wolf eels, and an incredible host of beautiful and colorful anemones, sea stars, and nudibranches.

Waves and surge don't present any problems in the protected waters of inland Washington. However, tidal currents can be strong, making it necessary to follow a carefully planned dive between tidal exchanges.

The Pacific Northwest offers a great diversity of diving. Besides the straits and sounds of Washington, you'll find pristine mountain lakes, difficult but rewarding reefs along the rugged and scenic Oregon coast, and a virtual undersea wilderness of wrecks and wildlife in Alaska.

ALASKA

To many, this state's very name conjures up images of polar landscapes ringed in ice. Yet, near Ketchikan and Sitka, in southeast Alaska (referred to as "Alaska's banana belt") water temperatures in summer compare to those of central California: around 45°. And air temperatures, even in winter, rarely go below freezing, thanks to the warming effect of the Japanese current.

The stereotype of the last frontier is more fitting, though. While many Alaskans have discovered diving, they couldn't begin to make a dent in statistics like these: Alaska has 3 million sizable lakes and over 10,000 rivers and streams. Two-thirds of America's continental shelf lies off Alaska. Alaska has twice the shoreline of all the lower 48 states put together! So, despite all our images of vast snowy interiors, perhaps a more accurate picture would be of a practically unexplored maritime state.

To explore it, a diver needs to be adventurous and rugged. Since extreme tidal currents are the rule in Alaska, it's important to dive with experienced local divers, as their knowledge is very important to insure your safety. Polar regulators are often necessary at colder sites.

Ketchikan, the southernmost city, is also one of the main headquarters for Alaska diving. The wet, forested shores of **Revillagigedo Island** and the dozens of other nearby islands offer many fascinating dives. At the majority of sites, beaches slope down gently into staircasing cliffs that keep on descending far below human ability to follow. Some sites offer the ultimate in wall dives, with sharply dropping cliffs that fall off almost immediately to 600'. Visibility usually averages around 25' before the plankton bloom of late summer, which can lower clarity to nothing in the top 20' of water. Winter water clarity improves greatly, but the temperature falls to about 32°. Of course, thermal protection is required year-round. Strong tidal currents are frequent.

These cold waters sustain a wide assortment of marine life including clams, scallops, halibut, abalone, lingcod, wolf eel, king and Dungeness crabs, octopus, giant tube worms, moon snails, and nudibranches more bizarre and colorful than anything in the tropics. Alaskans especially enjoy diving in the late evening, without using any lights, taking advantage of the long days of summer.

Sitka Sound, right outside of Sitka, has a rocky reef ranging in depth from 10-100'. Marine life at this site is fantastic. Big kamtschatkana (also called pinto) abalone stick to the rocks around the kelp beds. Colorful creatures of every hue and shape, including sea fans, soft corals, and anemones, carpet the rocks. Boat dives are the best, but beach diving is possible. March to May is the best season, and the most colorful diving is above 30'.

Dungeness crabs, caught lurking under a thin layer of sand, seem miniature when compared to the gigantic king crab. These strange beasts reach a huge size; the record holder was 5' across the legs, weighing almost 25 pounds. Even today, although they are a commercially sought-after delicacy, specimens 3' across might still be seen.

Near Juneau, divers have spotted an even stranger sight — a "pod", or big ball, of young king crabs, two to three years old, that may number as many as 3000 individuals. They apparently gather together for protection. One congregation of pods stretched for over a quarter-mile. While male king crabs (the only ones you can take) are becoming rarer, the smaller but equally delicious snow, or tanner, crabs, still proliferate.

The huge, gentle humpback whale also can be spotted in the area. Approximately 70 to 100 of them gather in Glacier and adjacent bays in early summer. Unfortunately, their timing usually coincides with the plankton bloom, which must be a delicious pea soup to them. For divers, though, it means the best whale watching will take place from a boat.

The Juneau area is vast and wonderful for the underwater enthusiast. Dive stores are available; they run charters to the more distant sites, where wrecks compete with marine life for the diver's attention.

But there are also excellent beach dives. Both the **Shrine of St. Teresa** and **Sunshine Cove** offer easy entries into protected waters. Sunshine Cove, about 20 miles north of Juneau, is known for its scallops. In fact, certain spots around Juneau produce swimming scallops the size of small dinner plates. Naturally, the local divers keep the exact locations of these beds a coveted secret, but everybody has their weakness, and the persistent visitor has been known to be rewarded with a guided trip to the lairs of these giants.

In early spring, divers brave the mid-30° waters in search of king crabs, which enter shallow water then. If you think trying to catch lobster can be hilarious, wait until you chase one of these big fellows. If they're too much for you, you can always console yourself with tanner or Dungeness crabs.

Only a short run from Auke Bay is the wreck of the ***Princess Kathleen***. This ocean liner went down on Lena Point in 1952, and today sits, virtually intact, with the bow 50' below the surface on a low tide. Since tides can range from 10-15', they make a very significant difference when planning dives. The speed of the moving water at a tidal change can be an extreme hazard if divers don't compensate for it.

The coast of Alaska is home to at least 17 different species of whale — and seven of these are endangered.

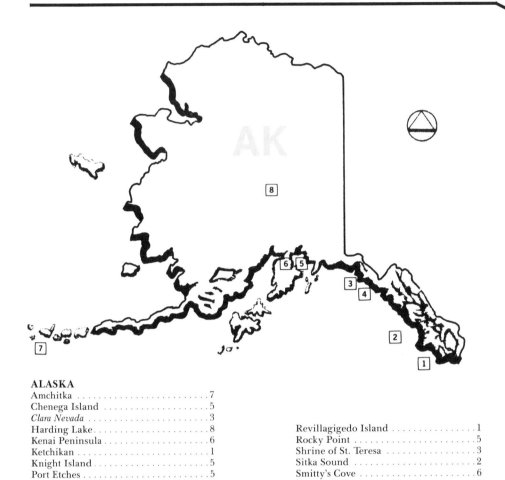

ALASKA

Amchitka 7
Chenega Island 5
Clara Nevada 3
Harding Lake. 8
Kenai Peninsula. 6
Ketchikan 1
Knight Island 5
Port Etches 5
Prince William Sound 5
Princess Kathleen 3
Princess Sophia. 3

Revillagigedo Island 1
Rocky Point 5
Shrine of St. Teresa 3
Sitka Sound 2
Smitty's Cove 6
State of California 4
Sunshine Cove 3
Whittier 6

Since the primary tidal current is in the top 20-40' of water, deeper dives are possible if one can successfully navigate the shallower depths.

A little to the north on Vanderbilt Reef lies the wreck of the **Princess Sophia**, which went down in 1918. Ghostly white *Metridium* anemones cover this wreck, and halibut, lingcod, and rockfish swirl around the anemones. Guaranteed to give you an eerie feeling, this is a deep dive with clarity of 15-40'.

Still further north up the Lynn Canal is the wreck of the **Clara Nevada**, which sank in 1898 on Elder Rock. Although it isn't as intact and awesome as some of the other wrecks, the broken and somewhat scattered remains are still the source of occasional treasures.

In the opposite direction from Juneau, divers visit the wreck of the **State of California** in Gambier Bay on Admiralty Island. Since this wreck is very deep,

and tide depth plays an critical factor in the safe execution of the dive, this is reserved for experienced divers. Sunk in 1913, the ship now lies at a 45° angle with the bow in about 80' of water.

The beautiful **Prince William Sound**, with mountains plunging right down to the water, is a wilderness wonderland for divers. Air is available in both Valdez (about $6.00 a tank) and Cordova (about $10.00 per tank). Many sites, such as **Chenega Island**, offer steep vertical dropoffs like the acclaimed walls of the Caribbean. Divers have enjoyed clarity of 50' in summer.

Teeming kelp beds in **Port Etches** and old cannery sites on **Knight Island** lure exploration-minded divers. Each spring there is a wild herring roe harvest, usually in the Tatitlik area. Divers simply cut the kelp from the bottom after it has become laden with the eggs.

Rocky Point, also in Prince William Sound, 17 miles out of Valdez, attracts spearfishers. Tidal currents of one knot or more limit the diving to the experienced, who find halibut and other bottom fish on sandy plateaus between the rock faces. Anemones and sea stars of every description, including some found only in Alaska, brighten the waters.

The **Kenai Peninsula** offers innumerable dives for the hardy. Homer and Seward are popular areas. **Whittier** is a favorite destination, since a train runs from Anchorage to Whittier that is equipped to take vehicles. Divers gather each spring at Whittier for a weekend of diving, fellowship and king crab catching. This King Crab Festival attracts divers from all over the state.

Nestled between the high surrounding mountains and the deep blue water of the fjord, Whittier is a spectacular destination. Diving is pretty spectacular, too, especially at the west end of town in **Smitty's Cove**. This was the site of a military harbor until an earthquake spilled much of the equipment into the drink. The wrecks of several barges, a crane, and even railroad cars invite underwater exploration. Some divers have recovered such prize artifacts as brass flamingos from the mainly rocky bottom, 90-100' down. Sea life is abundant, with halibut in the sandy stretches, and sea urchins, wolf eels, blennies, and nudibranches around the rocks.

At Turnagain Arm of Cook Inlet, diving is limited due to the tremendous tides that occur — only the Bay of Fundy in Nova Scotia has tides that surpass these. It's a good place to see that bizarre phenomenon called a bore tide, where a literal wall of water sometimes forms, caused by incoming tides that may rise more than 28' in only six hours.

If you're in the Aleutians, you might want to visit Izembek Lagoon, although you probably won't want to dive there. The largest eelgrass meadow in the world, Izembek is the nursery for Alaska's rich sea life. The lagoon is home to a million migrating waterfowl in October, including black brant and Canada geese. Bald eagles, peregrine falcons, and whistling swans live there year-round. At **Amchitka**, further out in the Aleutians, Steller's sea lions by the hundreds frolic with visiting divers, although perpetual and heavy wave action limits the number who visit.

INLAND

Fairbanks divers, who have compressed air available in their city, dive the abandoned gravel pits and lakes of the area. **Harding Lake** makes an interesting freshwater dive, although there isn't much aquatic life to view. It's safe to say that much of the inland diving in Alaska is done by gold dredge divers, and lucky ones have found at least a nugget or two.

Alaska laws concerning diving: No spearing is permitted in fresh water. Saltwater spearing is allowed in accordance with seasons, limits, and regulations for sport fishing. Diving flag is required in state parks.

OREGON

Anyone who has ever seen the wild and rugged rock coast of Oregon should know that it is not the ideal place to learn ocean diving. Besides being one of the most beautifully scenic coastlines in the world, Oregon also has the distinction of being the most wave-battered. Waves born 6000 miles away in Japan find nothing in the vast Pacific to buffer their intensity until they reach Oregon. For divers, this means good diving is non-existent over much of the coast, and available only on rare calm days at other sites. July, August, and September offer the calmest months. Tide tables are essential for Oregon diving.

But a few protected sites do exist, and **Port Orford**, 48 miles south of Coos Bay, is one of the best. This small, sheltered cove offers easy access off a jetty into the clearest waters of coastal Oregon — in summertime, visibility here has reached 50'. Since summer clarity in most areas varies, depending on the calmness of the day — from 0-15', with 10' the average — it's easy to understand why divers come from all over Oregon to Pt. Orford.

Like most Oregon sites, Pt. Orford has year-round water temperatures averaging 50°. While water clarity improves tremendously in winter, the unpredictable weather makes diving chancy. Currents and surge are as changeable as the weather.

The marine life found in these cold waters will amaze those who haven't experienced it. Almost everyone who dives regularly in Oregon does macro photography. As soon as you experience the incredible density of invertebrates covering every

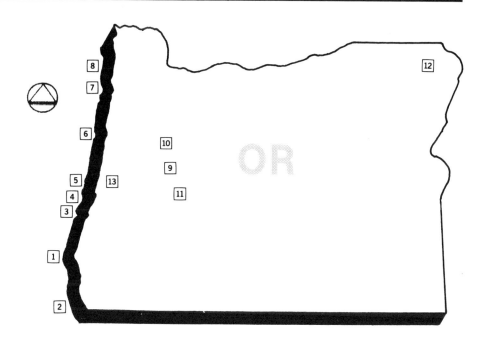

OREGON

3 Arch Rocks 7	Pirate's Cove 6
Baltimore 4	Port Orford 1
Blue Lake 10	Simpson's Reef 4
Brookings 2	Sunset Bay 3
Clear Lake 9	Umpqua 13
Coos Bay 4	USS Brush 4
Nehalem Bay 8	Wallowa Lake 12
Newport Reefs 6	Winchester Bay 5
O'Dell Lake 10	Yaquina Lighthouse 6

solid surface, you'll know why macro is so rewarding. Besides anemones and nudibranches, the Oregon coast is rich in scallops, abalone, lingcod, and sea urchins. At **Brookings**, south of Pt. Orford, rockfish and cabezone are abundant. Experienced divers enter through Harris Beach State Park. Strong surge generally prevents novice diving.

At **Sunset Bay**, south of Coos Bay, you'll find secluded, calmer waters, suitable for all levels of divers. Watch boat traffic and tidal exchanges. A rocky outcropping at the tip of a 40' deep sandy inlet, reached by boat or inflatable, supports lingcod, scallops, octopus, and black rockfish. No spearing is allowed. Several offshore reefs, like **Baltimore** and **Simpson's Reef**, can only be reached by boat. They are less suitable for novices, due to heavy surf.

Coos Bay, in the central part of Oregon's coast, is famous for its wreck diving, which includes the **USS Brush** in about 60' of water, and others further offshore. Don't expect an intact vessel, though: after the ocean off Oregon has been working on a vessel for a few years, it resembles a rock and steel weaving more than a boat! Divers are still reporting antique bottle finds from the wreck of a Prohibition-era rumrunner; its location may be pried from local dive stores.

The most noticeable reef inhabitants include black rockfish, cabezone, and lingcod. Most Oregon divers refrain from spearing the male ling in winter or early spring if he's obviously in the midst of his egg-guarding duties. After the much-larger female ling has laid the egg mass, she abandons it to the care of her mate, who refuses to budge from the spot. He guards the eggs aggressively from the perch and rockfish that hover nearby, hoping to catch him offguard so they can devour the eggs.

Beginning at the North Spit of Coos Bay is a wilderness of gigantic sand dunes that extends up the coast for almost 55 miles. Reaching heights of hundreds of feet, these are among the highest coastal sand dunes in the world. **Winchester Bay**, in the midst of the Oregon Dunes National Recreation Area, is an excellent spot for a jetty beach dive. The triangle jetty protects a small area from surge and wave action, so you'll have a good chance to explore. You'll also find good crabbing and photography, with sunflower and sea stars by the hundreds, and schooling rockfish.

The offshore reefs around Newport are generally accessible only by boat, due to the steep oceanside cliffs. One exception is the **Yaquina Lighthouse**, located on a rocky point a couple of miles north of Newport. Weather causes many more days to be off-limits than diveable — if the Pacific isn't dead calm, then the water will have the clarity of seafood gumbo, and surge and currents will be impossible.

Steep stairs lead down to a gravelly beach which drops off into a series of vertical rocky faces separated by craggy overhangs and dead-end passages. The rocky point itself presents a photogenic scene, with the classic old lighthouse surrounded by basking seals, sea lions, and seabirds. This is also a favorite spot to watch for the gray whales, which pass very close to shore on their migration south. Underwater, you might see scallops, crabs, clams, anemones, and nudibranches, but due to the numbers of hungry seals, anything edible is scarce. High tide is best for diving, low tide for tidepool watching.

Nearby, **Pirate's Cove**, on the outskirts of Depoe Bay, provides easy accessibility to a more protected area with great underwater color in the soft corals.

One of the unproven stories of orcas that have injured man still circulates ... a logger claimed he and his buddy were skidding logs down slopes and into the ocean off British Columbia when his buddy crashed a log down into a pod of orcas for laughs. Although the orcas left immediately, they returned later, as the two were rowing back to camp, and overturned their canoe. The logger who injured the orcas vanished immediately ...

The **Newport Reefs** themselves, starting about a quarter-mile offshore, are one of the most popular charter destinations in Oregon. Currents and surge here are less of a problem than at many spots, although the volatile ocean and weather still require experienced dive planning and cause the cancellation of many trips.

The reefs generally rise from 100' depths to within 40' of the surface. An incredible variety of sea life makes sightseeing here among the most exciting anywhere. Tame wolf eels emerge to be "petted" by the divemaster who has befriended them. Octopus of 5' or more can be seen, and pods of orcas have even been sighted underwater. More commonly, cabezone, lingcod, and greenlings are seen, along with bright green anemones.

Little diving activity occurs north of Newport as the coast becomes progressively more rugged and the weather even more dangerously changeable. Near Tillamook, **3 Arch Rocks** offers a magnificent setting, with abundant sealife around the massive rock structures. For bottle collectors and wreck researchers, the area around **Nehalem Bay** can be a bonanza. An eddy behind an island has created a "relic hole" where many prize antiques have been discovered.

INLAND

The perfect freshwater dive site would have easy access. It would be free from troublesome motor boats. It would have lots of fish life and aquatic plants. It would be located in a beautiful natural setting, and have interesting underwater topography. Above all, the water would be crystal clear and unbelievably clean. And, for the purist, it would be natural rather than man-made.

Oregon's **Clear Lake** has all of these assets, plus an underwater petrified forest, diving goldeneye ducks, and a family of otters. Located in the Cascade Mountains 75 miles east of Eugene, this beautiful lake was formed eons ago when a volcanic eruption dammed the headwaters of the MacKenzie River. Evidence of this fiery past is still easily seen in the black lava outcroppings and walls that jut out from the volcanic silt bottom. An ancient submerged forest of gigantic trees still remains standing for the diver to explore, and makes a good backdrop for photography.

But the most incredible thing about Clear Lake is the visibility — 100' or more on the surface. Many springs bubbling up from the bottom cause the clarity to decline with depth, as the force of the water roils the silt bottom. The springs also cause water temperatures of 38-42°, so be sure to wear at least a full quarter-inch wetsuit, or better yet, a drysuit. It helps make the cold worthwhile when you see all the big brook, cutthroat, and rainbow trout that flourish in the chilly water.

Beach entries are easy. No motorboats are allowed on the 161-acre lake. A small store on the shore rents rowboats. At this writing it sells no air, so bring a full tank or two from Eugene or Corvallis. Camping and a lodge and restaurant are nearby.

Watch your depths, and familiarize yourself with an altitude conversion table, since the 3800' elevation limits your bottom time. For a real thrill, try a night dive on a full moon — the light reflected from the white bottom makes lights unnecessary.

Other high mountain lakes in Oregon that you'll need to make altitude adjustments for include nearby **Blue Lake**. Although it's smaller than Clear Lake, it also offers great visibility. **O'Dell Lake**, to the south of Clear Lake, has caves with Indian artifacts at 60' depths, past a rock slide.

Wallowa Lake, in the Wallowa Mountains of northeast Oregon, was once the home of Chief Joseph and the Nez Perce, so you can imagine the potential for artifact hunters. This glacial lake in its beautiful setting of forested mountains is quite deep, going beyond the scuba range. The bottom is sand until you start encountering large boulders left behind by glaciers. Clarity always surpasses 50'.

Some of the best freshwater diving in the state is found in coastal rivers, among them the **Nestucca**, **Umpqua**, **Wilson**, **Kilchis**, and **Trask**. Summertime diving offers great clarity. During spawning, salmon of up to 50 lbs. make fantastic photos.

Oregon laws concerning diving: Only rough fish may be taken by spear in fresh water. In salt water, anglers' seasons, limits, and restrictions apply. Salmon, steelhead, grayling, whitefish, and other game fish may not be speared.

WASHINGTON

It surprises most people to learn that Washington state has over two and a half times the saltwater shoreline of California. But only 186 miles of that shoreline fronts the Pacific — the remaining 2,500 miles is all inland, surrounding the vast reaches of the Strait of Juan de Fuca, Puget Sound, and the San Juan Islands.

And it's the huge inland sea that attracts the vast majority of divers. Washington's Pacific Coast is a wild and woolly affair, containing the only remaining wilderness beach trail in the lower 48. One hiker who made an over 150-mile trek along the winding coastal trail reported that he did see a few spots that looked calm enough for scuba — except he'd need a helicopter to get his equipment down to the shore! However, the southern part of Washington's coast is accessible, and some hardy souls do find a measure of protection at **Westhaven State Park**, just inside Gray's Harbor.

But practically all visiting divers head for the calmer inland waters. Surf and surge are almost nonexistent; instead, divers must cope with the fierce currents that result from some of the most extreme tidal changes in the world. Washington

divers read tide tables like newspapers. Like most skills, though, dealing with currents takes practice. Good water reading and precise dive planning are required for many of the advanced dives. Fortunately, there are plenty of protected spots where divers new to the area can practice and acclimate themselves.

And it's more essential than ever to work with experienced local divers, since timing your dive to the tide table can make all the difference between a fun dive and a terrifying experience. Since diving is a very popular sport in Washington, dive stores are professional, up-to-the-minute on conditions, and glad to offer advice. Diving on slack tide is the practice in areas of heavy current, with precise timing to start the dive thirty minutes before slack tide begins.

As far as temperature, it's COLD! The average is 45°, summer and winter, below the thermocline. If you're a drysuit diver, so much the better; if not, you'll at least need a well-fitting 1/4" suit, and an extra vest will be worth the investment. Many prefer to dive in winter, when visibility increases dramatically, possibly up to 80'. In summer, though, water clarity is highly variable. Often in early summer the top 20-30' of water will be clouded from a plankton bloom, with clearer water under the thermocline.

PUGET SOUND — North End

One of the most popular diving areas in the Pacific Northwest is the wreck at **Edmonds City Underwater Park**. The habitat created by submerging this old steel drydock has attracted a great variety of marine life; and being an underwater preserve has maintained high populations of fish despite the popularity of the site. Rockfish swim leisurely around the anemone-covered ribs of the wreckage, but red Irish lords and cabezone prefer to lurk about the bottom. Depths are shallow, with a maximum of about 40', so there's plenty of bottom time for exploring. A long swim of 300' and boat traffic, including a ferry which docks close by, could create hazards for novices. A nice beach, bathrooms, and parking contribute to the popularity of this site.

Slightly to the south is **Edmonds Oil Docks**, where you can explore and photograph a large pier community that includes anemones and the pile perch that swim around them. You must check the tidal currents and prepare yourself for a long swim. Parking and a nice beach area are available.

A dive mainly for beginners is found just north of Seattle at **Richmond Beach County Park**. A long walk from the parking area leads you to an easy access over sand dunes. This isn't the place to experience the best of the Northwest, but the gradually sloping sandy bottom with scattered rocks will introduce you to sea pens, kelp, and anemones.

Much better diving can be found at several sites in Elliott Bay, right off Seattle. It's a rare city that offers good diving close to downtown (but then Seattle is a very beautiful and unusual city in many respects), yet Seattle has several excellent sites.

At **Duwamish Head**, you'll find plenty of parking, bathrooms, and a boat launch. There are three places to dive here. First, to your right when facing the beach, is the Old Seacrest Marina. Anyone interested in nautical history should head here first, as the water around the abandoned and demolished old marina hides many sunken boats and old bottles. (Duwamish Head was the site of the first settlement in Seattle.) Second, straight off the beach, are the pilings of an old ferry slip. In addition to further chances for artifacts, you have a diverse piling community to admire. Third, the rocks to the left of the boat ramp harbor octopus, invertebrates, and rockfish.

Alki Beach at 63rd Street is a dive suitable for beginners. The Boeing Seahorses decided to improve marine life here by planting old refrigerators, cars, etc. Rockfish hover around the piles of stuff. Parking, bathrooms, and picnic areas make this a convenient location.

The lighthouse at **Alki Point** is a more exciting dive. If you don't have a boat, you'll find the walk down the beach a long one. You'll understand why they call this "Octopus Ledges" when you see all the holes, some with octopus tenants. The depth doesn't fall below 45' close to shore. Dive at slack tide. As slight current exists even at slack, this is not a novice dive.

WASHINGTON

Abandoned Ferry Landing ... 6	Lake Chelan ... 23
Agate Pass ... 6	Lake Merwin ... 22
Alki Beach ... 4	Larabee State Park ... 20
Alki Pipeline ... 4	Lewis River ... 22
Alki Point ... 4	Lime Kiln ... 14
Bead Lake ... 25	Lover's Cove ... 15
Blake Island ... 6	Low Island ... 14
Blakely Rocks ... 5	Matia ... 17
Boulevard Park ... 20	Neah Bay ... 13
Center Reef ... 14	Octopus Hole ... 11
Columbia River ... 26	Old Fox Island Ferry Landing ... 9
Crescent Lake ... 21	Orcas Island ... 15
Danger Reef ... 14	Patos ... 17
Day Island ... 9	Peapod Rocks ... 15
Dead Man's Bay ... 14	Point Wilson ... 12
Deception Pass ... 18	Richmond Beach County Park ... 3
Diamond Knot ... 13	Rosario Beach ... 18
Duncan Rock ... 13	Salt Creek ... 13
Duwamish Head ... 4	Saltwater ... 7
Echo ... 17	San Juan County Park ... 14
Edmonds City Underwater Park ... 2	Spokane River ... 24
Edmonds Oil Docks ... 2	Stuart Island ... 17
Fort Ward ... 5	Sucia ... 17
Fort Worden ... 12	Tacoma Narrows Bridge ... 8
Fox Island ... 9	Tatoosh Island ... 13
Frost Island ... 16	Titlow Beach ... 8
Gibson Point ... 9	Tolmie State Park ... 10
Iceberg Point ... 16	Tongue Point ... 13
James Island ... 16	Union Wharf ... 12
Keystone ... 19	West Beach Reef ... 15
Kopachuck ... 8	Weathaven State Park ... 1

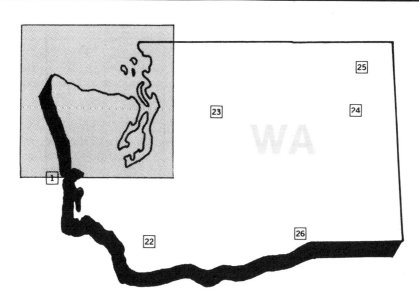

NORTHWEST DETAIL

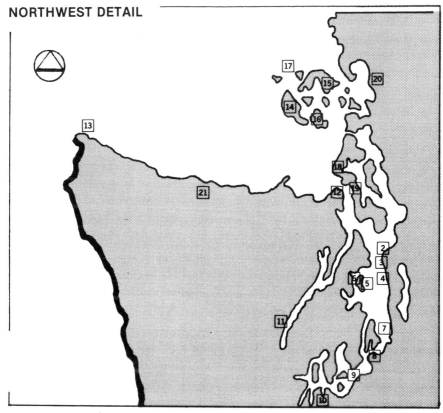

From the beach just past Alki Point you can see kelp growing at a 45° angle from the beach. To reach this forest around the **Alki Pipeline** (it carries rainwater off the streets to the bay) go up the beach a little, swim straight out, and then, using your compass, take a straight left. Rocks cover the pipeline and provide the foundation for one of the most gorgeous sites in Seattle. Night dives reveal ratfish with gleaming red eyes and octopus roaming hand over hand. In daytime, nudibranches, other beautiful invertebrates, and lingcod lure photographers. Not too well-known, this is one of the best dives in Seattle.

Bainbridge Island, an interesting ferry ride across the Sound from Seattle, hosts one of Washington state's underwater parks at **Fort Ward**. All the state underwater parks are complete reserves, and Ft. Ward is no exception. Marine life is nothing short of incredible, with beautiful red Irish lords that rely so heavily on their camouflage that you can touch them before they bolt. Black rockfish get big here, and so do cabezone. Painted greenlings and striped sea perch lend their colors to the interesting rock formations around Orchard Rocks at the edge of the park.

A lot of divers launch a boat at the fort and go around the point to **Blakely Rocks**. Considered by many the prettiest spot close in to Seattle, Blakely Rocks also has fascinating rock formations, with many shallow caves that harbor delicate pink anemones. Photographers in particular love this spot. Currents are the major hazard here, so dive the slack.

The **Abandoned Ferry Landing** at Harper's (right out of Port Orchard) is another reason divers cross the Sound by ferry. This is an ideal spot for beginners and tourists — no boat needed, no real current, with the major problem being some small boat traffic to look out for. Crabs, tube worms, purple sea stars, orange sunflower stars, white and orange nudibranches, and crystal nudibranches all make frequent appearances around the pilings. Antique bottle collectors find this a paradise.

The waters around **Blake Island** offshore are a protected underwater park. Since it requires a boat, the island isn't visited too often. Large lingcod, wolf eels, and cabezone can still be seen.

If you've had an advanced class or a specialty current diving class (available in one day of local training), you should visit **Agate Pass** off Bainbridge Island. Dive at slack only! Even world-traveler Ron Taylor was impressed with the color and life when he went down at the bridge pilings here. A shallow area of about 35' teems with giant sponges, giant anemones, giant fish — including lingcod, cabezone, and rock perch. It's hard to believe the quantity, the variety, the size, and the beauty of the marine life here.

Evidence of the pounding the sea gives to Oregon's coast can best be found at Tillamook Rock, where storm waves hurled a 135-lb. boulder over 100', where it crashed through the roof of the lighthouse keeper's home.

PUGET SOUND — South End

Another underwater park that's popular with both fish and divers is **Saltwater**, halfway between Seattle and Tacoma. It's fun to see all the life in this big sunken barge. And, there's little current — in fact, the main problem with Saltwater is the 850' swim out to the buoy. After you manage that, the rest is easy, with depths of only 50'.

The interior of the broken old barge seems to be a fish nursery school, with small sculpins and other bottom dwellers hugging the floor while schools of copper and black rockfish hover overhead. Octopus are everywhere! Picnic tables, parking, and an indoor pavilion make this a very popular site, but it's best when not too crowded. The very long swim makes it more suitable for intermediate divers.

Among local divers, the **Tacoma Narrows Bridge** is famous, although it's only diveable on a few days of the year when the tide slacks enough, and even then only by those very experienced with tidal current diving, Northwest style. Considerable advance planning is required. Anyone who has seen the eerie footage of the bridge "resonantly vibrating" itself, over a period of days in 1940, before it finally gathered momentum and collapsed, should realize that this is a very exciting site. The mangled remains of "Galloping Gertie" make a terrific habitat, with blocks of concrete the size of buildings providing homes for big octopus, big lingcod, and big wolf eels. Extreme currents in the 60' depths also produce fantastic growths of filter-feeders.

Titlow Beach, nearby, at the west edge of Tacoma, is more suitable for most divers. A short swim off the beach leads you to a piling community. This community is integrated — you'll find both orange and white anemones — but it's suffering from overcrowding, with not a bit of bare space left on the pilings. Dive on the slack, and the low current will make this safe enough for checkouts. Depth is 25' maximum.

Day Island, despite the name, is actually a peninsula which provides access by car to a beach dive. Limited parking and a fairly long snorkel out to the cliff complicate this dive. Add to that the depth — the cliffs begin in 60' and drop to 120' — and you have an advanced to intermediate dive. In September or October, when clarity improves past 75', this site is spectacular. "Canyon dive" might be more descriptive — for below 60', the bottom drops off into a canyon whose walls are flower gardens of anemones, chimney sponges, and basket stars. Shallower depths teem with marine life, including octopus, free-swimming scallops, and wolf eels.

Those new to the Northwest often assume that the ferocious looking wolf eel is a major problem to divers. Actually, about the only problem they present occurs when a careless diver, searching for an octopus, sticks his hand into a likely looking hole. Most divers always carry lights to shine back into crevices for this very reason. Even when his lair is being invaded, though, the wolf eel would rather run than bite. Recorded attacks are rare to nonexistent. Much more common has been the depletion of the wolf eel from its previous territory due to trophy hunters or aquarium collectors.

Fortunately, more and more divers are starting to appreciate the wolf eel, who can crunch crabs and sea urchins to bits with one big bite. The creatures are easily tamed to take food from a diver's hand. Unfortunately, they can't seem to distinguish one wetsuit from another, so taming only makes them more vulnerable to human predation. A very persistent researcher, Dr. Marliave of Vancouver, was the first to successfully rear baby wolf eels in captivity. Thanks to his dedication, there are enough captive-born wolf eels now to satisfy aquarium demands. In fact, he's been so successful that he's replanted eels (actually blennies) in areas where they've been wiped out. Once eliminated from a region, the wolf eels won't return without human help.

Fox Island, another Tacoma Narrows diving area, contains numerous sites. One of the favorite spots is at the bridge. Examining the bridge pilings and searching the rocks reveal many inhabitants. Sailfin sculpins and red Irish lords often shelter under the ledges of the rock outcroppings. Around the bridge abutments, schools of sea perch and rockfish swirl, and rose and purple sea stars pile atop each other on the rocks. This dive is safe for beginners with this caution: don't worry if you feel caught by current, as it dissipates right past the bridge. Swim at an angle out of it.

Although there are some access problems, the **Old Fox Island Ferry Landing** presents an interesting look at a piling community composed of many types of invertebrates, including barnacles as big as your hand, and sea stars 2' across. Keep your buoyancy slighty heavy so you don't float up into one of the many nets caught on the pilings.

Gibson Point, on the other end of Fox Island, has parking and a long downward walk to the beach. At low tide, the water level and the cliff are even with one another — this is one of the few places in Washington where you can make a giant stride entry on a beach dive! The cliff steps down past 100', with abundant opportunities for macro photography. Great diving characterizes this entire area, but you need to stay alert for boat traffic.

Across the Tacoma Narrows Bridge on Henderson Bay, the state has created another underwater park, called **Kopachuck**, which is a lot like Saltwater Park. It's a long swim over a sandy bottom out to an old wooden barge lying in 40-60' of water. On the way, schools of sand dollars speckle the sand, and if you're lucky, you might see a huge, flat, orange nudibranch crawling along. It looks totally unlike its delicate frilly cousin, the alabaster nudibranch, which you might also see along the bottom, looking for whatever it is that serves as lunch for nudibranches.

If you're not a nudibranch aficionado before you dive Washington, you will be after. Some of the most beautiful and varied sea slugs in the world inhabit these cold waters.

DON PETERSON

Formerly feared, the shy octopus is now recognized as one of the most intelligent invertebrates.

Another "beach" dive that requires a strong swimmer is **Tolmie State Park**, just north of Olympia at the southern tip of the Sound. I always knew Washington divers had the reputation of being hardy, but judging from the distances they swim out to their underwater parks, "hardy" is a mild description. A high winter tide makes this a swim of 550 yards! Needless to say, a paddleboard or inflatable boat comes in very handy.

Other than the distance, Tolmie presents few problems. Currents are negligible. Three old wooden barges lie between 40-60' deep. They offer great housing for the local sea life. The clean white sand around the barges looks landscaped, with orange burrowing anemones gently waving their tentacles, ranks of sea pens, moon snails, and geoduck clams up to 10" across. And that's just on the surrounding sand — inside, red Irish lords and sculpin park in darkness, and around the high wooden railing of the largest barge, rockfish form swirling clouds.

HOOD CANAL

For many people, the desire to see huge octopus brings them to the Pacific Northwest. While specimens weighing as much as 150 lbs. and stretching 28' across the armtips have been recorded, now resident divers consider a 35-pounder a big one.

At the **Octopus Hole**, just north of Hoodsport on the Hood Canal, the odds are very good that a patient and careful observer can find an octopus. Night dives offer the best opportunity, but even during the daytime you can spot their lairs if you look carefully for small holes and crannies under ledges that have bits of crab shell scattered in front. Don't expect an aggressive monster to come out and attack, for most octopus are among the shyest of creatures. "Octopus wrestling" generally means trying to hold onto a blob of jelly as it struggles frantically to escape, flashing a kaleidoscope of colors from scared gray to angry red.

The more you learn about octopus, the more fascinating they become. Their eerily human eyes betray their feelings as much as their color changes do. Even super-objective scientists lose it a little when discussing the octopus. It seems they can not only use tools (the young of blanket octopus collect the stinging tentacles of Portugese men-of-war and affix them to their arms, discarding the weapons once they've become large enough to kill prey without them), but can also display true intelligence in their ability to react spontaneously to situations. Mother octopus guard their eggs diligently for as long as eight weeks, never eating or leaving their lairs. They have been known to break the egg capsules and release the young octopus prematurely if danger threatens the eggs.

OLYMPIC PENINSULA

Port Townsend, at the east tip of the Olympic Peninsula, has a couple of interesting dives, one safe enough for checkouts, and one for the advanced only. **Union Wharf** offers easy access just off the ferry dock into some of the best treasure hunting waters of the area. Bottle collectors have a field day here, with finds of bottles from the late 1800's. Rumors of gold coin finds still circulate. And if your luck is bad at collecting relics, there's still beautiful scenery along the submerged pilings, as well as a good chance for a cabezone dinner. Boats present the only hazard here.

However, at **Fort Worden**, boats will be just one of your worries. The old historic fort projects right out into a narrow channel where tidal exchanges create rushing currents. Diving can only be done here exactly on slack, with perfectly calm weather, and on a very small tidal exchange. And only by very experienced divers. The reef, called **Point Wilson**, is rich as only a current-bathed spot can be.

The north shore of the Olympic Peninsula, bordering the Strait of Juan de Fuca, lures experienced divers for the wildest diving in the state. Since this is the major corridor for oceanic water to enter Puget Sound, marine life is best described as "teeming," and that's probably an understatement.

The angler fish of the abyssal depths has overcome the problem of locating a mate in the gloom by having the young male seize the female angler, usually on the side, with his jaws. He then degenerates into a parasite, sharing the female's bloodstream. As many as five degenerate males have been found clinging to one female. Scientists are studying the anglers' immunologic system to discover how the female keeps from rejecting the male.

Salt Creek, at Salt Creek County Park, offers fantastic diving, but due to high surf and surge, you can only dive in summertime when the weather is mild and fair. Incredible color and many fish make this dive and Tongue Point (at the opposite end of the park) favorites with photographers.

Off Tongue Point is found the wreck of the *Diamond Knot*, reached only by boat. Weather conditions permit trips to be organized only a few days of the year, and because of the depth and currents, they are open only to advanced divers. This freighter of about 350' sits, intact, with its topmost parts at 75' and the decks at 100-130'.

Up around this point is found some of the best diving in the entire state. Like all these exposed dive sites, it's only diveable on fair summer days, and like many rare treats in life, it's impossible to describe. When people discuss schools of fish at Neah Bay, they don't mean 50 to 60 fish, or 500 to 600 fish, they mean 5000 to 6000 fish. "Extremely colorful" doesn't do justice to the underwater scene here; saying lingcod are giant is an understatement.

Tatoosh Island, just off the bay, offers the same thrill, and the lee side is frequently visited when the weather's up and other nearby sites are out of the question. Clarity is regularly 50-100'. Salmon fishing is king around Neah Bay, so if you get enough people together, a fishing boat might take you out. Since there are no air facilities, bring many tanks.

If you're one of those divers who keeps a list of the best dives from around the globe, and you haven't been to Duncan Rock, your list is incomplete. This is a dive for those who have been everywhere, seen everything, and lost their ability to get excited unless they're dropping in on one of the most exciting underwater scenes in the world. I'm assuming you're experienced in challenging diving, not just calm-plop-over-the-side type diving, for Duncan Rock sits out in the ocean off the tip of the peninsula, and saying it's challenging is putting it mildly. It can only be visited in perfect weather. It is the ultimate dive in Washington. Anything — any ocean-going creature you can imagine that is found in the Pacific — can be seen at Duncan Rock. Clarity is usually 100' in diveable weather.

SAN JUAN ISLANDS

At high tide, there are 457 islands in this archipelago. At low tide, 768. And only 172 of them have names. As you can imagine, opportunities for diving and exploring are practically limitless. Since these are islands, and since there is much private land to complicate matters, a boat is necessary to reach many of the best sites. Charters are frequent out of Seattle or Anacortes. However, a ferry departs Anacortes five times a day, every day, with service to Lopez, Shaw, Orcas, and San Juan Islands, and you can find abundant opportunities for beach diving.

Probably the most popular site is at San Juan County Park on San Juan Island. A beautiful campground nestled in the trees slopes down into a shallow, sandy bay, covered with eelgrass. Kelp-lined rock rims the bay and drops off into a wild jumble of boulders and caves. Residents include scallops, both rock and swimming, abalone, big rockfish, and anemones and sea stars by the dozens. If you want still more, you can take a paddleboard out to little **Low Island** about a quarter-mile offshore. Better be familiar with the currents before you try it.

Another good site on San Juan Island is **Dead Man's Bay**, on the west side. A nice beach leads out into good diving, and camping is allowed. With a boat, you can visit **Lime Kiln**, nearby. Abandoned ruins mark the cliff near the lighthouse station. Diving near the cliff is gorgeous, with many lingcod in the area.

Going by boat also opens up two beautiful reefs off the northeast side of San Juan Island. **Danger Reef** (so-named because it presents a navigational hazard) is an excellent site to find abalone, as is the adjacent **Center Reef**. This rocky pinnacle, riddled with fractures and ledges, rises to within 30' of the surface. As expected, the hiding places offered are quickly exploited by wolf eels and octopus. Bull kelp covers the top of the reef, which drops to about 80'. Clarity is usually very good at these offshore sites.

On **Orcas Island**, good diving is everywhere, and much of it seems practically virgin. Most dives require a boat and diving experience. **Lover's Cove** has to be one of the most popular dives. Reached by boat out of West Beach, this shallow reef of only 10-15' drops off into infinity in short order. Bright blue sea stars amidst a field of red urchins and delicate pink Medusa anemones are just a few of the wonders you'll see here. For the deep freaks who feel unfulfilled at many sites in Puget Sound, this will be heaven. Current here can be wicked so plan accordingly and be prepared with a pickup boat.

And at **West Beach Reef** itself, the underwater scene is a never-to-be-forgotten spectacle. Although it's only about 180 yards off the shore, the current is so fast you can't reach the reef by swimming. Paddle boards or small boats are available to rent, and the intense life makes it worth it. Everything seems cleaner and more vivid on a current-swept reef.

Peapod Rocks, off the northeast corner of Orcas, is a state underwater park. These pinnacles and outcroppings offer some intriguing underwater formations as well as a fantastic variety of marine life. Since this is current diving, you have to know what you're doing! Beautiful underwater scenes make this location great for photographers.

Experienced local divers watch the waters here and throughout the Northwest for the red tide that occurs sporadically from July to September. A shimmering green fluorescence in the waves usually signals the outbreak of the organism even before any red coloration of the water. While it makes for great night views, the organism also causes the most severe shellfish poisoning known. Any shellfish collectors should follow the example of the coastal Indians, who abstained from clams and mussels from the beginning of surf phosphorescence in summer until fall. The other reason divers watch the red tide outbreak carefully is that the best visibility of the year usually occurs in autumn right after a red tide.

Frost Island is unique since it is both accessible from shore and safe for novices. The Anacortes Ferry will bring you to Lopez Island and Spencer Spit State Park. Frost Island is a walk across the spit and a 100 yard swim away. Dungeness crabs hide in the sand flats on the way out — look for two eyes sticking up. Schools of fish haunt the kelp that grows on the rocky wall of the island. Frost Island is a good place to see some strange creatures, including sea peaches and pipefish. Night diving is exciting here, with prawns coming up from the depths and orange sea pens glowing bright green when you touch them. If you like abalone, make it a point to visit Iceberg Point while you're on Lopez Island.

The diving is good on either point of the Bay at James Island, although you have to take a boat out of Spencer Spit to reach it. Some very unusual invertebrates, including cloud sponges only 50' deep, make it worth it. These strange, ghostly-looking clumps are common in deep water in the Straits of Georgia, but unusual this far south. They look ancient, and they may be, since some estimate a good-sized clump to be hundreds of years old. They make for a very eerie scene.

Adventurous explorers with boats available to them find fantastic diving at the little group of northern islands that includes Sucia, Patos, Matia, and Echo. At Stuart Island, diving the wall by the lighthouse at Turn Point is like diving down the face of a skyscraper. This is an advanced dive only, with fantastic opportunities for sighting marine mammals. Since this is near the migratory path of orcas, they're always seen from the boat, although sightings of orcas underwater are rare. But entire rolls of film have been shot underwater of the rare Dall porpoise, a black-and-white animal that looks like a miniature orca. Spring offers the best chance to see them.

WHIDBEY ISLAND AND BELLINGHAM AREA

Deception Pass has to be one of the most talked about dives in the country. Since it's incredibly dangerous, it's talked about more than it's actually dived, as there aren't that many people willing to immerse themselves in a maelstrom just for a thrill. Water comes rushing through the pass at 8-11 knots. Standing above and watching the swirling current makes one wonder how anybody could get in — but occasionally divers do on a long slack, and some live to tell about it. Walls that are ablaze with every color of anemone possible, and big lingcod, cabezone, and kelp greenlings are the main appeal.

*A hermit crab species from Hawaii (*Polydectes cupulifera*) habitually carries two small sea anemones, which it uses as weapons, and as slaves, to catch food. It is interesting that this active "carrying" of the anemones in the crab's front claws (instead of the passive carrying where anemones are planted on the shell) has caused it to be the only species that uses its second pair of legs to carry food to its mouth, since the first set are always busy holding the little anemones.*

For the wimp divers among us, **Rosario Beach** offers a nearby safe dive. Just walk down the sand into Urchin Rocks and you're in the midst of a pretty underwater forest. Kelp, red waving plumes of seaweed, and millions of little green urchins make a background against which red crabs and red Irish lords can be spotted. Since this is part of Deception Pass Underwater Park, everything's protected. Visibility isn't the best here, due to nearby river runoff — it improves at high slack tide. Camping, parking, showers, and bathrooms make it convenient. A long snorkel will take you out to a little island off the beach where clarity improves and the diving is great.

Keystone, near Fort Casey, is another underwater reserve on Whidbey Island that rates as one of the most fun dives in Washington. The fort sits like a sentinel right at the entrance to Puget Sound, and is interesting enough to walk up the hill and see.

But it's underwater at Keystone where the scene really gets interesting. There are two main areas to see. First, the jetty itself, which extends out 75 yards to a maximum depth of 65 feet. You enter right off the beach; no snorkeling is necessary. A giant carpet of white *Metridium* anemones covers the gradually sloping bottom. Sunlight reflects off this gorgeous scene, lighting up pink free-swimming scallops. Purple tube worms and bright sea stars compete with urchin hordes for space on the pilings. But for many, the best part is the kelp greenlings that beg you to break open an urchin for them. Tame enough to be stroked, these are beautiful fish, with a rippling long dorsal fin and the graceful, slinky manner of exotic dancers. Big copper rockfish, lingcod, wolf eels, and cabezone all lurk around the rocky base of the pilings.

The second dive of the day at Keystone is usually made at an old piling community to the left of the jetty. From shore, it looks so shallow you could wade out to it, but it slopes quickly down to 20-30' at the pilings. You can always find octopus here, if you know how. You have to move slowly, and peer into crevices with a light. Keystone is a great place to relax and spend an entire day, with parking, bathrooms, picnic tables, and a restaurant nearby that's open in summer. For tourists, there's camping available nearby at the fort.

Larabee State Park, eight miles south of Bellingham, is sometimes visited for its easy access, camping, and novice conditions. Smooth sand with very few rock outcroppings gives up crabs and bottom fish to divers. The only thing to watch out for is boats, so use your flag and swim along the bottom. **Boulevard Park**, right in Bellingham, also promises good crabbing. And since an old wharf is located here, artifact hunters search the area, often successfully, for antique bottles and other relics. Clarity in these sandy areas is much less than at more typical, rocky sites.

The fauna of the American West Coast is more similar to that of the Caribbean that it is to the fauna farther east in the Pacific. This implies that the open ocean has been more of a barrier to animal migration than Central America, which has been submerged for periods in the past.

INLAND

Practically every section of Washington offers some interesting freshwater diving. **Crescent Lake**, west of Port Angeles in the Olympic Peninsula, is a very clear, glacially carved lake where divers can explore underwater cliffs as well as an eelgrass covered sandy bottom.

Lake Merwin, just north of Vancouver in southwest Washington, plunges to 500' at the dam. Divers explore the lake's shallower sections, finding buildings, cars, wagons, cemeteries, and other relics left behind from the days when people still lived in the canyon. Night diving supplies the crayfish for campfire meals.

Underwater photographers in particular like the **Lewis River**, nearby, as 10-30-lb. salmon and steelhead make for exciting photos.

Lake Chelan winds for 55 miles through the forested slopes of the Chelan Mountains. On its way, it picks up its share of divers, who sightsee in the precipitous underwater landscape of bright blue, glacially fed waters, and maybe catch sight of a rainbow or koho salmon. Flooded homesteads and sunken boats entertain divers in the cool water, where summer surface temperature is 65°. Clarity averages 30'. Boating presents the major hazard.

Around Spokane, adventurous snorkelers head for the whitewater of the **Spokane River**, where fast-moving rapids promise quite a ride. For lake diving, most head north to the Panorama Country of northeast Washington, which has dozens of lakes ranging in size from one acre to 1162 acres. **Bead Lake**, deep in the Kaniksu National Forest, is one of the best, with 160' depths and clarity averaging 50' in early summer.

Other drift divers head for the **Columbia River** at Kennewick. Current speed varies according to the release from McNary Dam. A common practice is to catch eddies along the shoreline to return you upstream. Depth is 35' over a hard clay bottom, and temperature never rises much past 58°, so wetsuits at least are imperative. Clarity ranges from 7-25'. Heavy boat traffic requires a flag and cautious diving.

Washington laws concerning diving: No license is required for spearfishing. Only carp may be speared in fresh water. In salt water, all bag limits, size, season, and area restrictions for anglers apply to divers. Salmon, shellfish, and octopus may not be speared.

CALIFORNIA

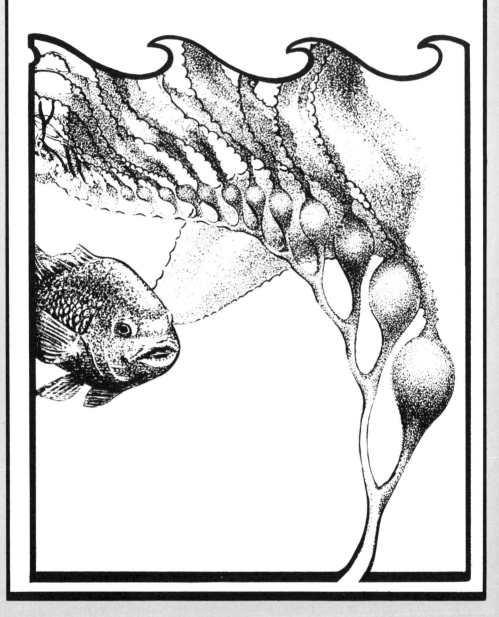

NORTHERN   CENTRAL   SOUTHERN

The rugged mountains, primeval redwoods and fantastic variety of scenery that the state of California contains hardly need elaboration, since they're famous worldwide. But the parallel universe that exists just offshore, underwater, defies description. Swaying 100' kelp plants that each support more inhabitants than the city of Los Angeles does, massive canyons that begin right offshore and plunge down into abyssal depths, toothy pinnacles that erupt from over 90' down to break the surface, a chain of offshore islands that includes the best Pacific kelp diving in the world, the chance to swim with an unmatched diversity of marine mammals ranging from the 5' sea otter to the mighty gray whale — all these reasons plus many more make California a diver's paradise.

But diving this paradise can be challenging. Despite its name, the Pacific can often be intimidating and potentially hazardous to those unfamiliar with its moods. While many easy sheltered spots do exist that are safe enough for fledgling divers, you can never forget that you're in a real ocean and subject to all its power.

Much of California's diving is done right from the beach, so there's a special set of conditions, like surf, rips, and surge (and, at some spots, cliff-climbing), that requires you to perfect a matching set of capabilities. Beach diving through even a moderate surf demands that you know your stuff — including the limits of your strength. As a general rule, you can assume that the further north you go in the state, the rougher the seas will be. While it should be obvious to everyone that each new locale brings a new set of conditions that must be checked out with local divers, there is some truth to that old saying that if you can dive Northern California, you can dive anywhere.

And millions of Americans do dive California. The state is the second most frequented destination in the continental U.S. for traveling divers — despite the fact that California's cold waters don't qualify for the snowbound diver's dream of slipping into bathtub-warm water. With a year-round temperature range of 45-65° in northern and central California, and 50-65° below the thermocline in the southern part of the state, this is definitely wetsuit country.

The cold water deters few Californians. Diving in America originated here, and estimates are that today about 40% of all U.S. divers live in California — at least 600,000. Yet even with all this intense pressure from humanity, the aquatic environment has held up remarkably well. Many areas still exist where you can experience the spine-tingling feeling of slipping into practically virgin territory. The California Department of Parks and Recreation has led the nation in establishing a series of underwater parks and reserves. State campgrounds exist near many of these sites. Don't expect to be able to pull in and find a spot, though. The state maintains a toll-free number for reservations — (800)622-0904.

For most divers in love with California's waters, kelp and the myriad of life — over 750 species — that it supports is the reason they stay wet. Whether it's giant, bull, elk, or feather boa, a kelp forest creates a scene as dramatic and inspiring as the redwoods do.

Underwater, on a sunny day, a kelp bed is awesome, spectacular, a lush jungle filled with darting fish and beautiful cathedral light flickering down through the swaying fronds. A diver can (and many do) easily devote a lifetime to watching the distinct layers of life that exist in a kelp bed. Schooling fish, shells, nudibranches, and predatory hunters each prefer their own distinct layer, while brilliantly colored encrusting sponges, anemones, sea stars, and other invertebrates carpet the bottom rocks around the holdfasts.

Probably the unanimous vote for most popular kelp resident would go to the abalone. In the United States, this tasty vegetarian mollusk inhabits only the West Coast. Since California has laws forbidding the exportation of the "sea sirloin" out of state, many visiting divers plan their trips around the hunt for abs, since out-of-state licenses are available for the April-November season.

North of Yankee Point, the creatures can only be taken while free diving. North of San Francisco, capable divers usually meet success; the odds are worse farther south. There are seven species, with varying requirements for minimum size and season so, if you're planning on doing any abalone collecting, be sure and familiarize yourself with the specific laws.

California has other tasty denizens, like clams and scallops and spiny lobster (southern only), as well as beautiful shells like tops and turbans and chestnut cowries. In fact, the main color of the underwater scene is found in the invertebrates and plants, from algae that glow luminescent blue, to streamers of long red algae leaves, to the famous purple hydrocoral found in only 15 other places in the world, to the hordes of encrusting sponges, tunicates, bryozoans, anemones, and red, orange, and pink sea stars.

The most conspicuous fish in the south is the garibaldi, as bright orange as a California poppy, whose plucky disposition, combined with its beauty, has earned it total protection, as well as the title of "official state marine fish." The fearless garibaldi are fun to watch, especially in spring and summer, as the feisty males will even attack you if you venture too near their carefully tended red-algae nests.

California has other brightly colored fish, too, like the rainbow perch and the sheephead, who changes color when it changes sex. Even brilliantly striped miniatures, like the several different species of gobies, can be spotted in southern California.

But the majority of California's fish aren't aquarium-style beauties — they're drab, but delicious. From the elongated lingcod, whose flesh may be green, depending on diet, but delicious nevertheless, to the white sea bass, a roving croaker that offers the ultimate in a spearfishing challenge, to the king of them all, the protected black sea bass, a territorial giant who may grow past 400 lbs. and live longer than 80 years — California offers the ultimate in fish excitement.

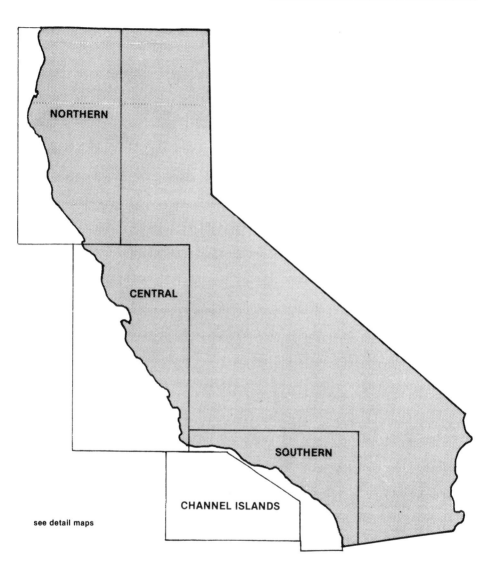

NORTHERN

CENTRAL

SOUTHERN

CHANNEL ISLANDS

see detail maps

For divers new to kelp, swimming amongst the stuff without getting entangled can take practice. As with most situations, panic is your major enemy. If you're proceeding into a thick kelp bed, swim near the bottom where corridors occur between plants. Plan your dive so you can surface at the edge of the kelp bed, rather than right in the midst of it. If you do have to surface in heavy kelp, always look up and reach up with your arms to separate the strands as you go. Don't hurry. Just relax and take your time, and the odds of getting seriously tangled are very slight.

If a kelp strand does catch on your tank valve, don't thrash about mindlessly (often a tempting thing to do). Just reach back, find the culprit stalk, and bend it between your fingers to break it — or better yet, use your knife. (Kelp's elasticity makes stretching and pulling at it useless.) Once you've practiced a little and gotten the hang of it, swimming around kelp becomes second nature. Entanglement is not a fear of the experienced kelp diver, so take your time, and accustom yourself gradually to the new experience, and soon you'll be as much at ease in the underwater forest as you are in its terrestrial equivalent, the redwoods.

NORTHERN CALIFORNIA

OREGON BORDER TO FORT BRAGG

The far northern coast of California is among the most rugged and desolate shores in the world. Huge cliffs plunge down into wave-battered boulders. Most of the coast lies exposed to the full force of the surf, and lee can be a hard thing to find. The other factor that influences diving in this region is the low visibility — good clarity means about 15', and bad means something like a chocolate shake.

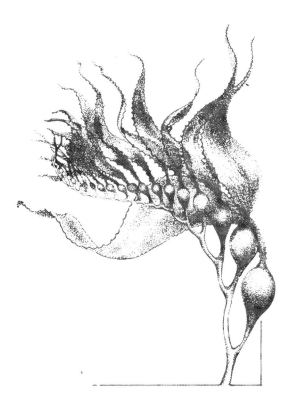

NORTHERN CALIFORNIA

Albion	12
Anchor Bay	15
Camel Beach	4
Cape Mendocino	6
Casper Point	10
Cleone Beach	9
Crescent City	1
Crescent City	15
Elk	13
Fisk Mill	16
Fort Ross State Historical Park	17
Gerstle Cove	16
Harbor Drive at Noyo	10
Heeser Drive	11
Humboldt Bay	5
Jetty	1
Little River Beach	4
McKerricher Park	9
Mendocino Headlands	11
Norlina	16
Patrick's Point State Park	4
Pebble Beach Drive	1
Point Arena Rock	14
Russian Gulch State Park	11
Salt Point State Park	16
Shelter Cove	7
Sonoma Coast State Beaches	18
St. George Reef	2
Stump Beach	16
Timber Cove	17
Trinidad Head and Bay	4
Van Damme State Park	12
Westport	8
Wilson's Creek	3

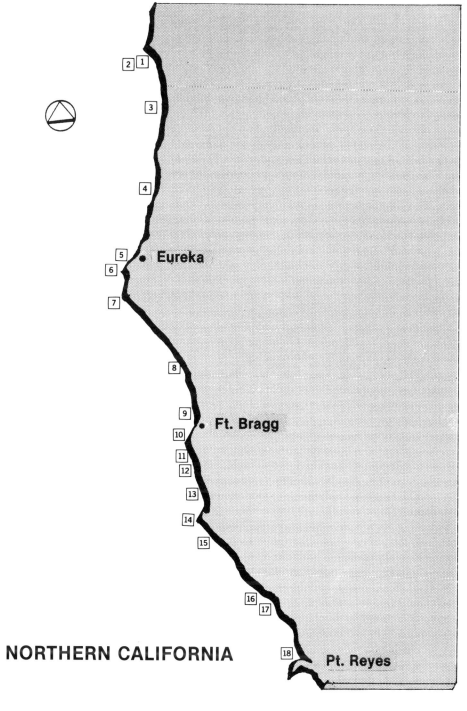

2 1

3

4

5 ● **Eureka**

6

7

8

9 ● **Ft. Bragg**

10

11

12

13

14

15

16

17

NORTHERN CALIFORNIA

18 **Pt. Reyes**

So it comes as no surprise that this section of the California coast isn't a diving mecca like other regions. With the exception of a few easy spots, much of the area requires the diver to be familiar with heavy currents, surge, and rough surf entries. If you can handle that, you'll find some interesting, uncrowded diving. The marine life is fantastic. All the invertebrate filter-feeders like anemones and encrusting sponges apparently find the cloudy waters a dream come true, for they reach a size and diversity here practically unparalleled in California waters. In fact, this region has more in common with Oregon than it does with southern California — frequently the maps of marine biologists label it "Oregonian Seascape." Of the southern California species, one that does manage to find its way up here occasionally is the red abalone — often reaching tremendous size.

Starting at **Crescent City**, the **jetty** at the north end of the harbor is a nice dive. You can find easy access off the rocky beach, just a short walk from the parking lot. This is a great spot for macro-photography, as the area is literally blanketed with anemones.

Pebble Beach Drive parallels the coast from the harbor north for a few miles. At several spots it offers easy beach access to some good diving. Free divers frequent this area looking for abalone, as scuba can't be used in abalone-taking north of Yankee Point in Monterey County. This far north, abalone are few and far between, but big enough to make a search well worth it. One diver told us that a 9-1/2-inch abalone was the smallest he'd ever taken — although he never found more than one on any dive.

The **St. George Reef** offshore from Crescent City offers some of the most exciting diving of this region. It's characterized by about a two-knot current, so you'd better plan a boat drift dive. To get to the reefs, which are 15 miles offshore, you'll need to make arrangements for a boat at the Crescent City harbor. This reef system, with some of the most predictably clear water around, is home to octopus, blue rockfish, black rockfish, and lingcod, as well as incredible numbers of anemones, including the gorgeous white *Metridiums*. The specialty here, though, is scallops — some spots are swathed in them.

Sixteen miles south of Crescent City in the Redwoods National Park is **Wilson's Creek**. Although the highway dips right down beside the ocean, the entry, over a very rocky beach, is still difficult. This site can also be murky due to runoffs from the redwoods.

The Atlantic palolo worm has an extraordinary mating ritual which has been observed on certain nights in July, usually under a third-quarter moon. These strange, light-hating burrow dwellers make the lower third of their bodies brightly colored and thin-walled, in preparation for spawning. One night they abandon their burrows to writhe and twist until their bodies break in two. The front end survives and returns to the burrow while the brightly colored posterior swims up to the surface to join in a huge swarm. At the first light of dawn, these worms are stimulated into more contractions which burst their thin-walled bodies and spill eggs or sperm (depending on the individual worm's sex) into the sea. These halves, now spent, either die or are eaten.

Twenty miles further south you find **Patrick's Point State Park**. This spot also has a difficult entry — about 200' down an almost vertical trail to a rocky beach. Needless to say, many divers bring boats up here from Eureka. There's a beautiful kelp forest at Patrick's Point made up mainly of bull kelp and all the associated wildlife, including sea lions and harbor seals.

Wildlife watchers and artifact divers both find **Trinidad Head and Bay** a powerful lure. This historic landmark still hides artifacts from the days of sailing ships 200 years ago. The varied bottom scene, which includes sandy stretches broken up by rock outcroppings, shelters abundant fish. Like most northern California sites, surf can make for a rough entry.

From Trinidad Head to **Little River Beach** (also called **Camel Beach**), the coast highway offers many sites for a rocky beach entry. Scallops, kelp greenlings, vermilion rockfish, blue rockfish, cabezone, and lingcod are but a few of the many reasons divers frequent this area. Bull kelp, which is more typical of this part of northern California than giant kelp, forms some pretty lush stands through here, so there's lots of associated life.

You can also dive at **Humboldt Bay**, in Eureka, in the mouth of the bay along the inland side of the jetties. Beginners to this site often assume that the ocean side would offer the best diving, and they consequently get roughed up by heavy surf in the shallow water. Even to dive the inside, you must be careful to enter the water between 20 minutes before and 40 minutes after slack high tide. This is important since the swirling mud of low tide and the 6- to 8-knot current between tides both preclude pleasant diving. The life underwater makes it worth some careful planning — in fact, the state is considering designating this area an underwater park. Attempts are being made to establish artificial reefs in this area.

From Eureka to Cape Mendocino the coast is largely inaccessible. For a few miles just south of **Cape Mendocino** the coast road parallels the beach, and there are some dive spots available. In general, though, this section of coastline, almost to Fort Bragg, has little diving activity because of access problems, high turbidity, and little protection. Also, extensive kelp beds are rare. **Shelter Cove** does have boat launching and some lee available. Several access sites around **Westport** (Westport Landing State Beach, Kibesillah Fishing Access) are occasionally visited by the diver familiar with rough water.

Traveling south, you come to **McKerricher Park. Cleone Beach** offers easy access across the blackish sand, with day use and camping facilities available. Many people visit to watch the herd of harbor seals that lives on the point off Cleone Beach, or to watch the gray whale migrations from December through March. Free divers work these waters for abalone. Some scuba is done here, although the surf can be rough and unpredictable. This is one of those Pacific coast spots where lulls of up to 20 minutes can occur between sets of big breakers. This can be dangerous to the diver who has entered the water during a calm spell, only to find a mountain of surf confronting him on his exit!

MENDOCINO COAST — Fort Bragg to Point Arena

This stretch of coastline offers some of the best diving in northern California. The fantastically sculptured and twisted rocky bottom of the Mendocino area provides a haven for kelp holdfasts, and dense stands of giant and bull kelp intermingle. These luxuriant forests, in turn, provide for abundant fish life, which is an interesting mixture of northern and more southerly species. Sea strawberries, a beautiful soft coral, cover much of the shallow subtidal zone with their pink bodies and white polyps. To top it off, the best visibility in northern California is found throughout here.

Just south of Fort Bragg, **Harbor Drive at Noyo** leads to an underwater scene complete with thick kelp, good fish populations, and some abalone. A diver's flag is needed, since boat traffic can be heavy. **Casper Point** offers easy access off a wide sandy beach into jagged rock walls carpeted with yellow finger sponges and bright strawberry anemones. With an inflatable boat, you can visit practically untouched areas offshore.

From **Casper Point** to **Albion**, most of the coast offers great diving. The jagged, rugged coast hides reefs, pinnacles, and unexplored islets. Many 19th-century lumber ships went down on these reefs, and their widely scattered remains can sometimes be found. This 15- to 20-mile stretch offers hundreds of hours of great diving. Below are a few of the highlights.

One very popular spot is **Russian Gulch State Park**, with camping and fresh-water showers near the beach. Most divers enter the water through the sheltered main cove and then spread out offshore or into adjacent coves. Inflatable boats can be carried by hand, or larger craft can be launched at Noyo. The sandy beach, rare for northern California, gives you the opportunity to look for starry flounder or Dover sole on your way out to the rocky ledges, which shelter abalone, rockfish, kelp greenling (also called sea trout), wolf eels, and others. While at the park, it's worth a hike up to see the Devil's Punchbowl, a collapsed sea tunnel about 100' across that's now lined with wildflowers. It's a good example of the blowholes that are common to the Mendocino coast.

The exposed bluff known as **Mendocino Headlands** has some of the greatest diving around during calm water, with clarity that can be 40' — check water conditions. Take **Heeser Drive** to the fishing access just north of Mendocino. The underwater cliffs, tunnels, arches, and twisted rock surfaces are covered with a gaudy carpet of invertebrates that make other areas seem pale. Kelp is mainly found in the top 60' of water, with shrublike palm and blade kelps forming an understory to the bull and giant kelp fronds. The bottom drops off to 300' in short order.

Van Damme State Park is such a protected spot that it's safe enough to conduct check-out classes in. This is another great place to take an inflatable boat or board to explore the varied life of the offshore islands. The beach dive is interesting, with patches of gravel, cobblestones, and large boulders dotting the sand. So many nutrients thrive in these waters that fishes usually confined to rocky reefs here wander over the sand. Abs are plentiful, and sometimes are found on boulder islands that seem much too small to support them. Above ground, the park offers freshwater showers and camping, as well as a fern valley, and a pygmy forest where trees reach maturity at 1' tall.

The large protected bay at **Albion** a few miles further south presents another great dive, complete with boat launch ramp. This bay covers an extensive area, and since fewer divers hunt these waters, abundant game still exists on the rocky outcrop to the north. Abs can be found without too much strain here, and so can lingcod, greenling, perch, and rockfish.

The town of **Elk** (population about 200) has an easy walk on state-owned land to the water. Sheer walls, boulders, and caves create a scenic underwater landscape, and calm coves nearby lure snorkelers.

Point Arena Rock at Manchester State Beach has recently been added to California's underwater park system, although wicked swells, strong currents, and sudden fog make it such a dangerous dive that the Underwater Society is attempting to have warning signs installed. A reef extends out 1-1/4 miles from the lighthouse to the big jagged landmark that is Port Arena Rock.

SONOMA COAST — Point Arena to San Francisco

Beautiful rocky scenery and good water clarity make this area a center for diving activity. Visibility declines southward as you go towards San Francisco. Clarity ranges from 0-40', averaging 20'. With abundant marine life, including frisky sea lions and some decent-sized abs, the diver can find plenty underwater to keep him busy.

Remains of the wreck *Crescent City* can be found in about 30' of water south of Fish Rock at **Anchor Bay**. Good fishing and ab hunting are found on the rocky ledges to the north of the bay, after an easy walk to the beach. Further south, **Horseshoe Cove**, in the Kruse Rhododendron State Reserve, has great diving within the sheltered cove itself. Adventurers can explore forever in the rocky reefs further out.

Salt Point State Park, about 40 miles south of Point Arena, has camping, fresh water, an access road with ramp, and stairs down the sheer sandstone bluff. **Gerstle Cove**, the protected main entry area, is rich in life, since it's a state underwater reserve and all marine flora and fauna are protected. Diving in the cove can be a mouth-watering experience, as huge red and pinto abalone abound.

The white goatfish of Hawaii, when eaten in summer months, can sometimes cause a hallucinogenic episode in which one of the symptoms may be a feeling that your feet are floating above your head.

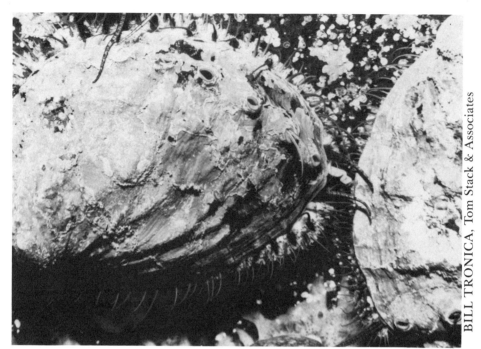

BILL TRONICA, Tom Stack & Associates

*Abalone, like these pintos (*Haliotis kamtschatkana*) can be hard to spot due to the encrusting organisms living on their shells.*

Adjacent coves such as **Stump Beach** and **Fisk Mill** are open to the taking of marine life, and they still have healthy populations of abalone. The huge slab of flat rock that characterizes much of the bottom around the park erupts into pinnacles, cliffs, and boulders. It is around these varied areas that bull kelp and especially large specimens of northern palm kelp flourish. The latter almost exceeds its designation as a shrub understory since here it reaches a height of 8'. Large octopus hide in the fissures among the boulders and peer out between big powderpuff *Metridiums* and orange *Tealia* anemones.

There is some evidence that the practice of dolphin-riding — young boys and girls riding undomesticated dolphins — was widespread in the ancient Mediterranean.

The **Norlina**, a huge freighter grounded by fog in 1926, lies scattered over the bottom south of Gerstle Cove. Below about 50', urchins form a living spiny carpet and seem to exclude any other life forms.

Another favorite dive site in this area is **Fort Ross State Historical Park**, located just south of Salt Point. If offers an access road for gear dropoff, and there is limited camping nearby. This fort was built by the Russians, who kept Aleuts in slave-labor camps here to export sea otter skins. It later became the headquarters for a 15,000-acre ranch and, to give you some idea of how rugged this country is, the fort served as the principal access to the region until well into the 1920's. Cabezone, lingcod, and perch swim around the remains of many old lumber and cargo ships that have been pummeled and scattered over the shallows.

Timber Cove, nearby, has a small boat launch that drops you into a protected cove inhabited by sea lions, rockfish, cabezone, lingcod, and red abs.

The **Sonoma Coast State Beaches**, stretching from Jenner almost to Bodega Bay, are actually a series of beaches and coves divided by rocky headlands. Diving access is provided as well as piped fresh water. The degree of protection offered varies considerably, and many spots have strong undertow, heavy surf, sudden groundswells, and murky water. Pinnacles and islets offshore and rocky outcrops around the beaches abound in perch, steelhead, salmon, and rockfishes. Sometimes, red abs can also be found hiding in rock fissures. Many artifacts and traces of shipwrecks can be found throughout the area. For current conditions, always check locally.

Immediately south of the Sonoma Coast beaches lies Bodega Head, which protects Bodega Bay. From here to the Golden Gate, diving activity drops off sharply. Reasons include very turbid water, rough seas, rugged terrain with limited accessibility, and few significant stands of kelp. However, one reason tends to eclipse all others — sharks. Although most recent attacks have been on surfers, they've been nasty enough to scare everyone off. The Department of Parks and Recreation reports that the Bodega, Tomales, and San Francisco Bays, along with the Farallon and Año Nuevo Islands and all waters in between, are suspected nursery areas for the great white shark.

Point Reyes National Seashore, although containing beautifully rugged headlands, isn't a frequented area, due to the rough water and limited accessibility. Elephant seals are sometimes observed hauling out here, which is close to their sanctuary on the Farallons. This wave-lashed series of five islands can't be visited without a permit, as they shelter more than 10,000 huge elephant seals, as well as seabirds like the weird-looking puffin and the common murre.

Crater Lake, Oregon, takes second place for clearest fresh water in the world, with vertical visibility of 131' reported. First place goes to a Japanese caldera where clarity is 136.5'.

CENTRAL CALIFORNIA

With underwater attractions like Monterey Bay and Point Lobos, it's easy to see why central California has such a great reputation with divers. Beautiful scenery, abundant game, and some well-protected accesses have made this one of the favorite regions for diving in the state.

SAN FRANCISCO TO DAVENPORT

About seven miles south of San Francisco at Point San Pedro lies **Shelter Cove**. Four miles further south at **Moss Beach** is another good dive spot, with extensive tidepools that non-divers can explore. Both offer fairly easy rock entries, although diving isn't advisable on a swell over 5-6'. These sites offer beautiful diving in summer, and occasional great diving in winter if there's a lull in storms. Lingcod, cabezone, and the bigger species of rockfish all tempt spearfishers.

Further south at **Half Moon Bay**, a beautifully rugged coastline aboveground is matched underwater by luxuriant kelp beds that shelter white croaker, greenling, abalone, lingcod in winter, and a large population of brilliantly colored sun and sea stars.

Princeton Jetty, a good spot for macro, is one of the few access points along this rugged stretch of coast. Visibility averages 10'. **Bolsa** and **Pigeon Point Lighthouse** are similar dives a few miles further south; around the lighthouse rocks, abs may be found by the diver who's willing to search.

Diving access is prohibited at the Año Nuevo Islands because it would interfere with the immense herds of pinnipeds — Steller sea lions, California sea lions, harbor seals, and elephant seals — that depend on these islands for breeding. The islands are also a suspected shark nursery, but a few divers brave the waters to the north and south of Año Nuevo.

Scott Creek and **Greyhound Rock** both entail a long walk or kick on a surf mat. Both have sandy main beaches with rocky areas that are offshore at Greyhound Rock and to the north at Scott Creek. Those willing to kick a board for some distance will find scattered offshore reefs and pinnacles, marked by kelp beds.

MONTEREY — Monterey and Carmel Bay to Point Lobos

Visibility almost doubles in this beautiful and famous region to an average of 20' with sometimes much greater clarity. Monterey Bay has extensive kelp beds, and is very calm and protected, especially in summer. Photography is very popular here, as is spearing for the abundant fish life. Great opportunities exist to frolic with the sea lions which will sometimes approach divers for a game of one-sided tag. Gray whales are almost always visible from the shore during migrations and a few lucky souls have watched the massive mammals swim by underwater.

The scene below the waves is extremely colorful with up to two or three layers of brilliant encrusting life piled up on a single rock. Iridescent blue algae seems to shimmer and glow, and waving fingers of anemones add to the surreal scene. You can usually park within 10-20 yards of the dive site and attain depths of 40-50' just 200 yards offshore. It's little wonder that people come from all over the world to dive here, especially when you add the amazing underwater topography — one of the world's largest submarine canyons erupts into jagged pinnacles.

In the **Santa Cruz** area at the northern tip of Monterey Bay, many people dive the **Natural Bridges Beach**. It's famous for halibut during summer, and offers an easy entry over a sandy beach. Campgrounds and picnic areas are nearby. In addition to the sandy beach dive, there's a rocky reef to the north with some kelp. Boat traffic can sometimes be heavy, so be sure to use a flag.

Harbor seals congregate at **Lighthouse Point** and at the Santa Cruz harbor. Many dive the pier for flounder and other flatfish. Others go to the 1-, 2-, or 3-mile reefs off the lighthouse, which are good areas for finding big fish. Lots of marine life, including occasional blue sharks, crabs, sand dollars, and olive rockfish, can be seen.

From Seacliff south, the bottom is mainly sand with very scattered reefs. At **Capitola**, many groups have cooperated to improve the diving by adding a large man-made reef, marked with a bright orange buoy and extending about 1/2-mile straight off the end of the Capitola pier. Placed on the shale bottom early in 1982, it already hosts strawberry anemones, barnacles, numerous sea stars, and schools of juvenile olive rockfish and blue rockfish.

From Capitola south, very scattered reefs and ledges project through the sand offshore. This area is heavily gill-netted in summer and also heavily beach-fished, with many salmon, perch, kingfish, flounder, and halibut taken.

Cannery Row in Monterey may be famous as the site for Steinbeck's novel, but for divers its fame lies in the great sites offshore. Chinese were the first to harvest the rich seafood resource here — near what is now the Hopkins Marine Station, the Chinese netted squid by torch light and dried them for export to Asia. Later, the canneries processed tons of sardines, closing down only when the silvery pilchards became too rare to justify the catch expense.

Divers enjoy the easy access provided by the **Monterey Breakwater** and **Macabee Beach** into the almost always calm waters off Cannery Row. However, Monterey has stringent laws regarding parking, dressing, and loading gear — read and follow closely the posted signs to avoid being cited.

Easy parking and a sandy beach entry make the rocky breakwater popular with novices and pros alike. The best spots are 150 yards out, where you can watch cormorants and seals swimming underwater. Visibility is usually about 30'. Some lucky night divers have watched squid breeding and laying eggs, and report that the animals are so fearless and singleminded that they can be handled. Many more divers have seen the eggcases which carpet the bottom with thousands of whitish teardrop-shaped sacs.

Other interesting sights often observed off Cannery Row, in the vicinity of the breakwater or the sunken **barge** nearby, include male cabezone fearlessly guarding their brood of up to 600,000 purplish eggs. This takes place from December to March.

In October and November, ocean sunfish (*Mola mola*) as big as 600 lbs. enter the bay, sometimes in large numbers. They are usually observed being cleaned by senoritas or sharpnose surfperch. Some divers have seen sea lions tossing the sunfish about like huge, clumsy balls. More have noticed dead sunfish littering the floor of the bay, apparently victims of these sea lion games.

Hopkins Reef, offshore from the Hopkins Marine Station, has no access through the station, but by boat or board it's just a short distance from Macabee Beach, and the lush kelp and varied marine life make it worth the effort.

The stairs at **Lover's Point** have for years led to great diving — but a law passed in 1984 forbids all diving in and/or from the cove from May 1 through September 30. Check with local dive stores, as the Central California Council of the Underwater Society is negotiating with the Pacific Grove City Council to reform this restrictive law.

CENTRAL CALIFORNIA

Avila Beach	34	Monterey Breakwater	26
Barge	26	Morro Bay	32
Barn Cove	28	Morro Rock	32
Bolsa	21	Moss Beach	19
Cannery Row	26	Natural Bridges Beach	23
Capitola	25	Otter Cove	26
Carmel Point	27	Partington Cove	29
Carmel River Mouth Beach	27	Pigeon Point Lighthouse	21
Carmel State Beach	27	Pinnacles	27
Carmel Trench	27	Pismo Beach	35
Chase Reef	26	Point Arguello	37
Copper Roof	27	Point Buchon	33
Devil's Jaws	37	Point Lobos	28
Diablo Canyon	33	Point Sal	36
Gosford	38	Point San Luis	34
Greyhound Rock	22	Princeton Jetty	20
Half Moon Bay	20	Rocky Point	28
Hopkins Reef	26	San Simeon	31
Hurricane Point	28	Santa Cruz	23
Jade Cove National Monument	30	Scott Creek	22
J. P. Burns State U/W Park	29	Shell Beach	35
Lighthouse Point	24	Shelter Cove	19
Lover's Point	26	Stillwater Cove	27
Macabee Beach	26	Whalers Cove	28
Monastery Beach	27	Yankee Point	28

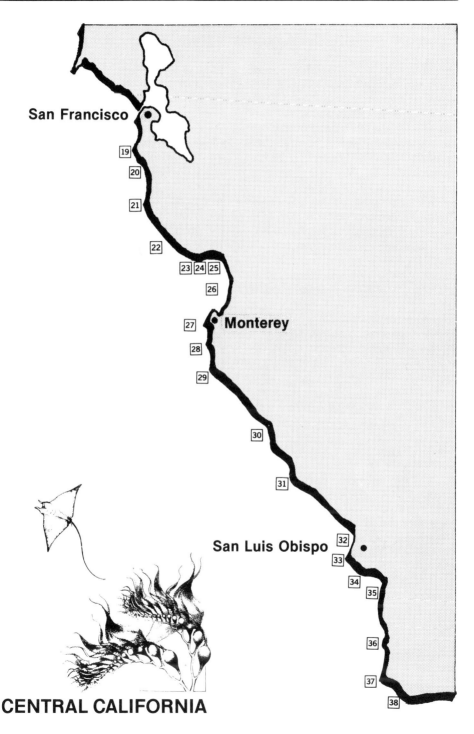

San Francisco

19
20
21
22
23 24 25
26
27 Monterey
28
29
30
31
32 San Luis Obispo
33
34
35
36
37
38

CENTRAL CALIFORNIA

A long shallow entry off a rocky beach at **Otter Cove** leads out to some beautiful kelp. **Chase Reef**, offshore, can be tricky to find, so check with local divers. By inflatable or surf mat it can be reached through Otter Cove. The good visibility, big fish, and generally calm 30-80' depths will make you glad you asked.

Out of the bay and around the tip of the peninsula, the diving picture changes dramatically. No longer are the waters calm and protected. Gone, too, are the easy beach accesses. From Point Pinos clear down to Pescadero Point, the coast is more exposed, with heavier swells and less predictable weather. Boats frequently charter the stretch from Point Cypress down to Stillwater Cove on calm days. Very heavy kelp forests, abundant fish, and lots of otters make these boat dives unforgettable. Visibility of 50' has been reported, and much of the area seems untouched.

Since they're hard to find, go with an experienced captain to the world-famous **Pinnacles**, which rise from the incredible depths of the Monterey Submarine Canyon. With totally different topography, each of the two pinnacles creates an indelible memory. The inner pinnacle is rugged, with sheer faces, ledges, crevices, and a typical slope of about 30°. The outer pinnacle stairsteps into a series of basically flat plateaus that reach to within 50' of the surface before being bisected by immense canyons plunging to 110'.

The visibility can be as much as 90', although 40' is more typical. A photographer's dream come true, the myriad pockets and crevices offer fantastic opportunities for macro work with every color of the rainbow running together like a water-color palette. Strawberry anemones, club anemones, gorgeous purple hydrocorals, and solitary orange stony corals compete with the more mobile chestnut cowries and nudibranches to dazzle the eye. Hordes of fish dart and school through the kelp atop the 50' plateau and help create an impression so memorable that many rank the Pinnacles as one of California's best dives.

Carmel Bay, while smaller than Monterey Bay, is at least as famous for its under-water beauty. With better clarity, but also rougher surf and more difficult entries, Carmel Bay attracts the experienced diver in search of some incredible kelp dives.

Stillwater Cove is often included on dive charters out of Monterey. There's a good chance that Stillwater may become accessible by land through the Beach & Tennis Club — check locally. The most protected cove in Carmel Bay, Stillwater offers the diver a chance to glide like a bird through forests of giant kelp.

A rocky entry off the south end of **Carmel State Beach** also leads into thick kelp after a long, shallow swim. Parking is a problem here and at **Carmel Point**, known locally as **Copper Roof**. Watch for signs describing new restrictions. The rocky ledges and boulders are covered with swaying masses of kelp, all moving languidly in the same direction, like participants in some hypnotic voodoo ritual. Visibility averages 40', and you'll appreciate every inch of it as you admire the abundant fish and, if you're lucky, a sinuous sea otter.

Carmel **River Mouth Beach** offers the diver such amenities as bathroom facilities, but, alas, parking is once again difficult. Entry off the sand at the north end of the beach is easy, thanks to the protective peninsula. Swim out and around to the kelp bed.

Monastery Beach, just off Highway 1 north of Point Lobos, is one of those rare exciting places where a submarine canyon close to shore drops off into endless space. The **Carmel Trench** of the Monterey Canyon drops off to below 1000' less than 1/8-mile offshore. The north end of the beach has a steep yard-high dropoff, which makes for some big surf and difficult entries and exits. The south end has a much more gradual slope into the water and is a little more protected from swell action, although surf can kick up pretty quickly here too, especially in the afternoon. After exiting through wicked swells that didn't seem quite so bad when you entered, you'll know the meaning of the phrase "Monastery crawl." Rocky points on either end of the beach and a large pinnacle at the north end lure divers with pretty kelp, lots of invertebrate color, and schooling fish. Gumboot chitons, up to 1' in size, cling to rocks, looking remarkably like the soles from old shoes.

About 1/2-mile around the point lies what has been called "the greatest meeting of land and water in the world" — **Pt. Lobos**. The first underwater reserve in the nation, Pt. Lobos has been protected since 1960 and offers the diver the rare chance of seeing the ecology of a beautiful underwater seascape in a wholly natural state. Immortalized by masters such as Ansel Adams, Brett Weston, and other members of the f.64 Club, the primitive-looking headlands clad in Monterey cypress are home to large flocks of cormorants, pelicans, gulls, and other water birds, while the waters around the point shelter Stellar's and California sea lions and large families of sea otters.

To dive **Whalers Cove**, you'd better be in line by 6:00 AM, since only 30 divers per day are permitted, and all spaces are filled by 7:00 AM. All the waiting and rigmarole are well worth it. The further out you swim, the more beautiful it gets, as you enter a fantastic world of swaying kelp, huge tame fish, beautiful stained-glass colors, and playful sea otters.

Point Lobos is one of the few places in the world where divers have a good chance of seeing otters underwater. The animals have lost some of their wariness and will sometimes accept food (squid being their favorite), but be aware that this could be mis-interpreted as harassment, since federal law protects them, as a threatened species, from harassment.

Sea otters belong to that elite handful of tool-using animals, and watching them crack urchins open with a stone on their chest as they loll in the waves is entertaining. Hunted almost to extinction for their incredible fur, which is the densest and most luxuriant of any mammal, and which commanded as much as $1700 a pelt as they became rare, they have recovered somewhat under protection and now number about 2,000 animals.

CALIFORNIA

BIG SUR

The hauntingly beautiful coastline of Big Sur hardly needs description, for it is famous worldwide. The lonely feeling this steep and rugged area inspires is especially true for divers, as access is almost nonexistent for miles and miles. For the experienced diver who craves adventurous dives in almost virgin waters, the Big Sur coastline can be heaven. Charters to this area usually depart from Monterey. Clarity is good because so much of the bottom is solid rock; there are pinnacles, islets, and cliffs galore, with a usually steep shoreline dropoff. To top it off, giant kelp beds form vast underwater jungles and support abundant fish populations.

South of Point Lobos, around **Yankee Point**, the heavy kelp continues, with one bed running from 30' clear out to 100'. A few hardy souls manage to hike in from Highway 1 across the state property — but it's at least 1/2-mile of rugged going with full scuba gear to a difficult rocky beach access.

Much of this area is visited so infrequently that common names aren't well known. **Hurricane Point**, **Rocky Point**, and **Barn Cove** are some of the better-known sites. Large schools of fish and lots of game still exist due to the scarcity of hunters. This region can't really be dived except on very calm days with swells of only 2-3'. So, if you find yourself here on a beautiful mild day and have the opportunity to go out with a dive boat, consider yourself one of the chosen.

About the only other convenient access in Big Sur country is found at **Julia Pfeiffer Burns State Underwater Park**. This is really back in the hinterlands, so a well-planned dive trip, with air and equipment from Monterey, is essential. By prior arrangement with the park personnel, you can drive your vehicle down the steep unpaved road to unload your dive gear.

The setting is spectacular, with waterfalls plunging over granite cliffs directly into the ocean. Giant kelp forms tremendous stands and the rocks of the inter-tidal region are covered with pretty palm kelps. Sea lions, otters, and a magnificent array of colorful creatures — nudibranches, sea and bat stars, and top shells — call the canyons, caves, bluffs, and underwater tunnels home. All diving groups must check in with the park office, and diving is limited to the **Partington Cove** area at the northern end of the park. Since the coastline is exposed and the bottom drops off sharply (typical of the entire Big Sur coast), this isn't the place to learn beach entries.

About 20 miles south of J.P. Burns is a highway sign marking the **Jade Cove National Monument**, which is one of only two sites in the USA where gem-quality jade may be found. Actually there are two coves; the southern one is marked and, while it has a smaller quantity of jade, the quality is better. The northern cove is just the opposite.

This is a very difficult dive starting with the entry, 200' straight down a torturous trail. Rough surf and surge makes just picking up pieces of jade along the beach and in the intertidal zone seem suddenly appealing, once you finally make it down the cliff! For those who do hazard an entry, the most effective method of finding jade is simply to find a likely spot amongst the numerous ledges, wedge yourself in, and start digging.

Through this procedure, jade can almost always be found, ranging in size from thumbnail to fist. One expert claims to bring home almost 60 lbs. from every trip. The jade comes in all colors — to distinguish it from the prevalent serpentine, scratch the pieces with a sharp metal object. The soft serpentine will show white where it's been scratched, while the harder jade will just show a black line of metal deposit. Depths are usually less than 30' and visibility usually is about 5-8'.

A few hardy souls also venture to spots around **San Simeon** or other points further south. Since the diving is difficult and the area remote from any services, these dives are limited to long-time explorers of the California coast.

MORRO BAY TO POINT CONCEPTION

The gigantic granite dome of **Morro Rock** protects sandy Morro Bay from the ravages of the open sea. Diving along the rock is fascinating because of the dense accumulation of invertebrates. Urn sponges, powderpuff and giant green anemones carpet the rock. Beautiful red-leaved algae sways out from the many crevices and ridges in the rock face. Pinnacles dot the offshore reaches near the main rock and offer good fishing for both rockfishes and the ugly but delicious bottom-dwelling cabezone.

In the sandy flat stretches within **Morro Bay**, divers look for halibut amongst the eelgrass. Diving over an eelgrass meadow can be fascinating. These super-productive "wheat fields of the sea," besides serving as potential human food, also nourish and shelter countless lives, including waterfowl, hermit crabs, clams, flatfish, crabs, and even such unlikely creatures as octopus and perch. Dock pilings within the bay support an interesting collection of life, with such northern species as powderpuff (*Metridium senile*) anemones sharing space with the southern species which begin to show up here. Visibility within the bay can be limited and divers need to beware of the discharge canal from the Pacific Gas and Electric plant. The warm-water discharge does attract many fish, who apparently enjoy a warm bath as much as we do.

Shell Beach south of Morro Bay is known for its lobsters; it also is fairly protected due to **Point San Luis (Avila Beach)**. The Avila Beach area is mostly sandy bottom. By boat north towards **Diablo Canyon**, very interesting rocky bottom occurs. Lots of cliffs, dropoffs, and rising rocks as well as generally good clarity attract divers.

South, towards the islets of **Point Buchon**, fringing kelp beds support abalone, as well as lingcod and cabezone. Seals are frequently seen and sheephead begin to become more frequent. Gorgeous nudibranches are easily observed all along this section of coast, with more species variety due to the intermixing of northern and southern forms.

Pismo Beach, famous for its big clams, is a sandy-bottomed area that also supports halibut, flounder, and other flatfish, as well as sand dollar colonies. Check locally before doing any clam digging, as California has put aside reserves. License and other requirements must be met.

From **Point Sal** to **Point Arguello** there is no public beach access because Vandenburg Air Force Base covers the whole region. By boat, usually from Gaviota State Park to the south, divers can find some excellent and uncrowded — but very rough — diving. Pt. Sal has a dangerous undertow to discourage collection of its lobsters and abalone. **Devil's Jaws** draws many wreck enthusiasts to its rough waters and 15-70' depths to see the 13 Navy ships that went down there in 1913.

From Pt. Arguello south, a very large kelp forest extends towards Pt. Conception. Also on government property, this rocky point is reached by boat. Many big fish still inhabit the area due to the difficult access. Large sheephead, white sea bass, and snapper can be found. The wreck of the ***Gosford*** lies in a fairly protected location just east of Pt. Conception, in about 40' of water.

*Giant kelp (*Macrocystis pyrifera*) is one of the fastest growing plants in the world, capable of growing more than a foot a day. Reaching 200 feet or more in length, giant kelp provides the backbone for one of the world's most productive ecosystems.*

DON PETERSON

SOUTHERN CALIFORNIA

In northern and central California, often your biggest problem is finding beach access. Southern California, on the other hand, has plenty of beaches that allow access to kelp-covered reefs. Your main problem will probably be finding a parking space once you get there. Many popular state-maintained sites have great amenities, including showers and lifeguards. Watch for the flags posted on the beach alerting you to water conditions.

Gently sloping sandy beaches that lead out to shallow, rocky reefs alive with waving kelp and darting fish characterize much of the area. Don't enter surf unless you're sure you can cope with coming out of it after your dive, when you're likely to be exhausted. It's a good idea to watch the water for awhile before you enter, to familiarize yourself with the waves and to spot any murky, swirling rips so that you can avoid them. Sharp thermoclines often exist in summer — while it may be 70° on the surface, 30' down it can be as much as 20° colder.

Since the curve of the coast from L.A. to San Diego is one of the most heavily populated shorelines in the world, don't expect game to be as abundant as it is in less crowded regions. Sport and commercial fishing, as well as spearing, have depleted certain populations. However, spots do exist (usually reached by boat, or after suffering on a torturously steep trail) where you can get a taste of practically virgin California diving. Even in the most popular areas, there are enough fascinating rocky reefs, beautiful kelp forests, neon *Corynactis* anemones, and spectacular fish like the garibaldi, to make your dive memorable.

Many of southern California's kelp beds were already suffering from pollution before the infamous winter storms of 1983 ripped hundreds of plants from their holdfasts. "EL Nino" added another blow by warming water temperatures past the tolerance level of kelp. Barracuda and other southerly species were found further north than they'd ever been seen before. But for the kelp beds, the warm water was disastrous. Replanting programs have been undertaken to try and restore the beds to their former splendour.

SANTA BARBARA AREA — Tajiquas to Point Mugu

Twenty-five miles north of Santa Barbara, **Tajiquas Beach** promises fine diving away from all the crowds found at the more popular beach parks. The beach is well protected, like most in the Santa Barbara area, since the coastline faces south and receives few of the large swells so common above Point Conception or below Ventura. An interesting result of this sheltering is that kelp gets a foothold in the stable sand. It's odd to see kelp forests growing out of sand, but apparently some of these plants have been in the same spot for years, since some of the holdfasts are gigantic — as much as 4' across. Since sea urchins prefer rock bottoms, they offer little threat to these sandy forests.

64

SOUTHERN CALIFORNIA

1000 Stairs 5
Aliso Beach 17
Alligator Head 22
Arroyo Burro State Park 5
Avalon 11
Barn 19
Bathtub Rock .21
Bird Rock .15, 24
Boomer Beach 23
Carpinteria Beach State Park 6
Casa Cove 23
Christmas Tree Cove 12
Coal Oil Point .4
Coral Beach 9
Crescent Bay 15
Crystal Cove 14
Dana Point 17
Dead Man's Reef 15
Devil's Slides .22
Diver's Cove 15
Doheny State Underwater Park 18
El Capitan State Beach 2
Escondido Beach 9
Goldfish Point 22
Haggerty's 11
Hendry's 4
Horse Pastures 14
La Jolla Canyon 22
La Jolla Cove .22
Las Tunas State Beach 10
Leo Carrillo Park 7
Main Beach 15
Malaga Cove .11
Malibu Beach .9
Margate 11
Mesa Lane 5
Mohawk Reef 5
Moss Street 16

Naples Reef 3
New Hope Rock 25
Paradise Cove 9
Pendleton artificial reef 19
Picnic Beach .15
Point Dume 8
Point Fermin Park 13
Point Loma 25
Point Mugu State Park 7
Point Vincente County Park 12
Refugio State Beach Park 1
Rocky Beach 15
Royal Palms State Beach 13
S-37 submarine 26
Salt Creek 17
San Elijo State Park 20
Scotchman's Cove 14
Scripps Canyon 22
Shaw's Cove 15
Tajiquas Beach .1
Tide County Park 20
Torrey Pines State Beach 21
Westward Beach 8
White's Point .13
Woods Cove 16
WWII Corsair fighter plane 14
Zuma Beach 8

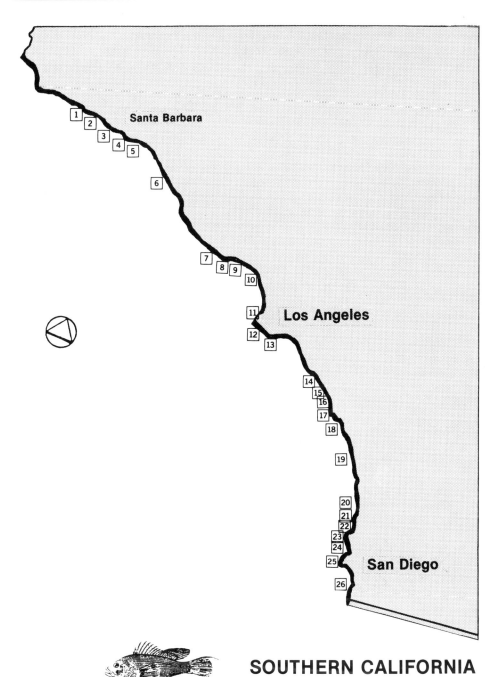

Santa Barbara

Los Angeles

San Diego

SOUTHERN CALIFORNIA

At Tajiquas, you'll find an interesting variety: rocky-bottom kelp in close, and sandy-bottom kelp out beyond the surf line. Summer is the best time to look for halibut hidden amongst the holdfasts. Depths go to 50'. Visibility in this area is extremely variable, depending on currents, runoff, upwellings, etc. Generally it is better than at other spots around Santa Barbara. The easy access, interesting scenery, and safe conditions make Tajiquas popular, even with class checkouts.

Large areas of the coast are inaccessible due to steep cliffs and private property as you head south. You can dive at **El Capitan State Beach**, although large crowds, many surfers, and occasionally dirty water cause many divers to seek out smaller beaches accessible off a dirt road between El Capitan and Refugio.

Refugio State Beach Park does have better diving than El Capitan. The water's cleaner, and the bottom is more interesting, with a rocky outcrop to the east of the sandy beach extending out to meet up with offshore reefs in about 50' depths.

For twice the clarity, take a boat to **Naples Reef**, about one mile offshore from Elwood Pier. The state is considering adding this beautiful reef to its underwater park system. Naples consists of a 1/2-mile-long reef, with the reef top at 25', dropping via sheer walls and ledges to a maximum depth of 55'. Massive kelp usually flourishes on the reef, along with pink abs, scallops, lobster, and prolific fish life, including such game fish as white sea bass in summer. Strong currents usually require a boat tender.

Coal Oil Point, accessible through Isla Vista, is interesting but messy due to the natural oil seepage, strong enough to form an oil film on the surface. Decent visibility and a flat rock bottom that stairsteps into ledges draw area divers, who are adept at keeping out of the oil by diving in the morning, staying out of the kelp, and various other techniques.

Hendry's is a more popular site, with clean water, easy access, and facilities. A 300' swim over a shallow sand bottom leads out to a kelp bed. Watch for guitarfish and halibut on the way out.

Mohawk Reef is the name given to a large area off Santa Barbara. The boulders and caves of the reef can be reached through several beach access points, since the reef is just offshore. Taking a boat is the only easy access, though.

The best beach access is to walk south towards Mesa Lane from **Arroyo Burro State Park**. You can dive right off the snack bar at Arroyo Burro, where a sandy bottom will eventually lead to rocky ledges 50 yards to the southeast.

An incredibly steep dirt path at **Mesa Lane** leads to car-size boulders in only 10' of water. The main part of the reef lies at 30', with the kelp ending on the outer edge about 40' down.

The sea hare, besides being hermaphroditic, often mates in daisy chains, with each one being male to the one in front and female to the one behind.

Another killer climb is known locally as the **1000 Stairs** (also called Santa Cruz Boulevard). While you don't have the uneasy feeling of imminent death that Mesa Lane provides, 1000 Stairs requires at least the legs of a marathon runner. Water clarity is poorer here, generally only 5-10'. Rocky ledges covered with *Corynactis* and kelp are home to lobster, scallops, calico bass, and opaleye, while the sandy channels that snake between the ridges shelter halibut. Near the light-house to the west, a shallow reef projects out to connect with the Mohawk system.

Below the Santa Barbara area, a long sand beach extends practically to Ventura, broken only by a few good diving spots. **Carpinteria Beach State Park** has a reef about 100 yards off the western edge that supports a huge kelp bed. At **Point Mugu State Park**, you can find kelp beds and finger reefs 1/4-mile out. Both these sites offer good enough diving to be under consideration for inclusion into the state's underwater park system.

LOS ANGELES AREA — Leo Carrillo to Las Tunas

Leo Carrillo Park is one of the favorite spots for diving in North Los Angeles, with both extensive kelp and such amenities as hot showers. The more than a mile of shoreline offered by this park is separated into two beaches by the rocks of Sequit Point. Many divers enter right off the point if they're familiar with rock entries. In summer, the up-coast beach is more protected from southern swells. In winter's west swells, the down-coast beach offers the best protection.

An extensive kelp bed parallels the shore, starting as close as 50 yards out. Depths on the inside of the kelp range from 15-35'. Water clarity in prolonged droughts reaches a high of 35', but 15' is more usual. Halibut, a few lobsters and abalone, opaleye, grass rockfish, cabezone, kelp bass, and lingcod are some of the creatures you might see.

For a look at the diverse life found in a productive sandy beach, try **Zuma Beach** and adjacent **Westward Beach**. In summer, you can swim out over extensive sand dollar beds only 45 yards offshore in about 25' depths. In winter, the sand dollars move out to deeper water as much as 100 yards offshore to avoid the rough surf. Crabs and shells, such as the moon and the Belcher's murex, as well as sea pansies and a few beautiful tube anemones, all inhabit the region of the sand dollar bed. Further out, just inside the kelp, breathing tubes sticking out of the sand signal the alert diver to a pismo clam bed. Surfperch are the most common fish. Watch for the murky rips that are common here, and check with the lifeguard about the current conditions, as an alongshore current sometimes picks up, heading southeast.

For the experienced diver who wants a little more excitement, or for the photog-rapher who wants brilliant colors and better clarity, you can find it just around the bend. **Point Dume** is the place, if you're experienced in swift currents of as much as 4-5 knots, and a rapid dropoff to extreme depths. A 500'-deep canyon, marked by a bell buoy, plunges down only 1/4-mile out from shore.

To reach Point Dume, walk over the rocks from the southern end of Westward Beach to Pirate's Cove, the next small sandy beach downcoast. A 300' swim will take you out to the exposed rocks and surrounding patch reefs. However, renting a boat at Paradise Cove, two miles downcoast, is recommended, since you really need a tender to dive Point Dume safely.

The reefs are only about 40' deep but, since current sweeps this area, clarity is at least 10' better than at adjacent sandy beaches. Color is provided by the giant invertebrates found here, which relish the nutrient-bearing current. Strawberry and club anemones, bright sea stars, and brilliant corals cause the walls to glow. At least four or five incredibly different nudibranches can often be seen on just one dive. For excitement, the deep canyon so close offshore sometimes funnels huge sea creatures into viewing distance. Orcas, gray whales, blue sharks, and torpedo rays have all been spotted here.

A very popular spot just down the coast is **Paradise Cove**. Despite poor visibility caused by Point Dume's blockage of cleansing currents, divers enjoy thick kelp-covered finger reefs and an easy entry. Boat traffic, fishing off the pier, and crowded conditions are the main hazards. At 400 yards out, past the kelp, it's 60' deep.

Escondido Beach and **Coral Beach** also offer easy access into kelp beds; Coral Beach is more crowded.

For clearer water, many divers head to **Malibu Beach**. In the winter, especially, visibility at Malibu can be good. The beach drops off sharply to 25' and then gradually slopes out, covered with cobblestones, eelgrass and featherboa kelp. At 50' depths, 1/3-mile offshore, you can find a small reef. Even further out, by boat, you can find an artificial reef of quarry rock and concrete shelters. Boats present the major hazard, so use a flag.

Las Tunas State Beach, also called Burned-out House by longtime California divers, is another sandy beach with scattered rocks, that slopes gently out to a reef 1/4-mile offshore in 60' of water. Fish life becomes more abundant just outside the kelp, and clarity improves to as much as 35'.

PALOS VERDES

Some of the best diving in this part of California is done by boat off the craggy Palos Verdes Peninsula. Boats can reach the more isolated reefs where access by land is non-existent and where clarity improves with the increasing distance from shore. However, for those prepared to hike down cliff trails, Palos Verdes does have several access points.

Malaga Cove has one of the easiest accesses, with a paved path down to the pebbly beach. Entry isn't too difficult, despite the shallow rocks, because Malaga is sheltered from most swells. The intriguing bottom varies from eelgrass-covered sand to rock uplifts, becoming more and more boulder-strewn as you go further west in the cove. Thick kelp begins about 1/8-mile out and continues for some distance over the gradually sloping bottom; maximum depths in the kelp are only about 30'. Marine life is plentiful, with angel sharks sleeping in sandy hollows under the big rocks, lobster, octopus, occasional yellowtail, and enormous schools of blue rockfish, especially in summer.

A more difficult cliff trail leads down to **Haggerty's**, which has about the best conditions for photographers in Palos Verdes. Clarity here sometimes surpasses 35'. The ledges and boulders of the reefs are thickly furred with brilliant encrusting sponges and pink coralline algae. Spider crabs, chestnut cowries, a few jewel-like ringed top shells, and psychedelic-orange garibaldi are all willing to pose for photos. Depths are shallow enough for plenty of bottom time and, while Haggerty's isn't as protected as Malaga, it's still a fairly easy dive.

Margate, on the other hand, requires a difficult entry over a rocky beach prone to big swells, and that's only after you've negotiated the arduous cliff trail! Experienced divers find these difficulties worth it because Margate is a popular marine traffic zone. Schools of baitfish lure barracuda. Yellowtail and white sea bass are commonly seen in summer; black-barred leopard sharks cruise the bottom all year.

About 1/2-mile out in 70' of water is the wreck of the *Avalon*, a former passenger ferry to Catalina. Evidence of a misguided salvaging effort lies next to it in the form of a salvage crane, which apparently failed in its task of raising the 265' ship. Lobster and fish of many kinds inhabit the wreck.

A steep switchback trail worthy of a Nepalese trek is the only way down to **Christmas Tree Cove**, and there are no Sherpas here to carry your gear for you. The hike is definitely the most hazardous part of this dive. After you enter the ocean from a sandy beach, you drop down almost immediately into 30' depths. The water usually provides at least 15' of visibility. A swim over a cobblestone- and boulder-strewn bottom leads you out to a reef whose bottom drops into sand at depths of 50'. White-chinned female sheephead with pink backs poke about amongst the sea urchins and small abs on the rocks. Rusty-brown sea fans bend easily against your backwash, and schools of small rockfish hover over the reeftop.

Point Vincente County Park has a wide, but steep path down to the water, as well as facilities like restrooms. Shallower water will take you into depths of only about 25' at 1/4-mile out, but the rock formations and scattered reefs contain many fish including opaleye, calico bass, morays, and different species of perch.

Royal Palms State Beach, suitable for all divers, is a similar dive except that you can drive right to the beach. Featherboa kelp adorns the sloping rock bottom, 45' deep 200 yards offshore. A divers' agreement exists in this area to not spear the sheephead, in hopes they'll take care of the overabundant urchins.

Volunteers map hydrogen sulfide vents at **White's Point**, off Weston Avenue. Good protection, plenty of parking, and varied life makes this a popular dive. **Pt. Fermin Park**, part of the L.A. County Marine Refuge, is also a good dive, and its historic lighthouse marks the southern tip of the Palos Verdes Peninsula.

ORANGE COUNTY — Newport Beach to Dana Point

It's possible to dive Corona del Mar but, because of the tremendous crowds (including waterskiers), Horse Pastures and Scotchman's Cove just to the south offer much safer and more enjoyable diving.

After driving through the gently rolling hills of the Newport area, it's quite a surprise to see all the weirdly shaped crags and pinnacles underwater at **Horse Pastures**. Strong surf occasionally makes entry impossible but in normal conditions, this spot doesn't require advanced divers. Reefs coated by every imaginable hue begin just past the surfline and continue sporadically as far out as 1000'. At 1/4-mile out, depths are still less than 65'. Crags, overhangs, and pinnacles create lots of micro-environments.

This is an excellent area for photography, especially further out where the clarity improves. Garibaldi are everywhere; in spring and summer they're easily observed tending their red-algae nests on the rock. In fall, their blue-streaked young swarm over the reef in clouds. Other fish abound, including opaleye, calico bass, and sheephead, although large specimens aren't common. Featherboa and giant kelp grow on the inner reefs, while the outer rocks have a dense turf cover that includes pink and rust sea fans and pink rosebud bryozoans.

Scotchman's Cove, just down the coast, is another diver's delight. It has recently been incorporated into the state park system under the name of **Crystal Cove**. Large rocks break the surface in the surfline and continue underwater in ledges and reefs as far out as you want to go. A massive kelp bed 75 yards out conceals some of the best reefs, which lie beyond the kelp, ranging in depths from 10-50'. Rock scallops, fan corals, large red *Tealia* anemones, white sea bass, finger sponges, calico bass, lobster, abalone (protected from Palos Verdes to Dana Point), sheephead, bat rays, halibut, sand bass, spider crabs, bonito — these are just a few of the more memorable inhabitants. In the early 1960's, a 481-lb. black sea bass and a 70-lb. white sea bass were both taken from Scotchman's Cove. Since a 400-lb. black is about 80 years old, you just don't see a fish that big very frequently.

About 1/2-mile out from the south end of Abalone Point, the remains of a **WWII Corsair fighter plane** litter the sand. For many years the intact plane provided thrilling diving until someone apparently caught an anchor on it and, trying to retrieve it, yanked the plane apart. Clarity averages 15-20' at Scotchman's, but can be much higher in fall or during dry spells.

If you're hardy, you can swim out to **Dead Man's Reef**, 1/4-mile offshore from **Crescent Bay**, the first cove in the Laguna Beach area, but watch for boats. The reef top begins at 20' depths and continues down to about 70'. A sandy bottom sheltering halibut and large sand dollar beds is broken by intermittent finger reefs that eventually connect with Dead Man's Reef.

Fifty-seven stairs lead down to **Shaw's Cove**, one of the most protected and fun dives in the area. High cliffs and outlying reefs combine to protect the cove from heavy surf or wind. Rock ledges on the north end of the cove become twisted reefs underwater, marked by nearly vertical walls, large crevices, and caves. Up to four divers at a time can explore one tunnel that stretches back into the rock for almost 15'. (Don't enter in high surf.)

Clear water, averaging about 15-25' in summer, and abundant colorful life make Shaw's Cove a favorite of photographers. About 50 yards out, at a depth of 50', the reefs abruptly end in a pocked, cave-riddled descent into sand. Octopus, morays, and lobster hide out in the fissures. Lacy fernlike bryozoans, coralline algae, beautifully colored sponges, and anemones cover the rock surfaces. Small fish, including halfmoons and opaleye, have become almost tame.

Diver's Cove was the site of a big championship spearfishing meet in 1951 — now it's the start of a marine sanctuary that extends to Main Beach, and a favorite checkout site. Reefs on each side of the cove extend out past 300 yards, where depths are about 50'. Big canyons cleave the northwest reef and provide interesting diving. A wide variety of marine life, including some southern species like grouper that occasionally wander up, inhabits the cove. **Picnic Beach** and **Rocky Beach** offer similar dives, with visibility ranging from 10-30'.

Off **Main Beach**, to the seaward, **Bird Rock** and nearby reefs hold lobster and sometimes draw gamefish. Featherboa kelp predominates. Often a group of kelp rockfish cling to different fronds, hanging motionless like ornaments on a tree.

The crescent-shaped beach at **Woods Cove** reduces winter surf, but the south swells of summer can make entries challenging. On the south end, small finger reefs lead to a huge reef 100 yards out, at a depth of 30', with tunnels large enough to swim into. A turf-smothered airplane engine is a real challenge to discover out in the middle of the cove. Water clarity averages 10-15'.

Moss Street offers better protection. A 60-step stairway on the cliff descends to the sandy cove. Ledges and fissures in the reefs about 75 yards offshore hide lobster, rock oysters, scallops, and abalone. Clarity can be as much as 10' more in winter than in summer, when it averages about 20-25'.

A sandy entry at **Aliso Beach** leads to reefs on the northwest and southeast. Finding the most abundant sea life requires a 400' swim to the southeast. These reefs contain many interesting fish, including the bright rainbow perch, with their horizontal red and blue stripes and vertical orange bars.

Zoologists estimate that the copepod is the most abundant animal in the world.

If it's game fish you're looking for, then **Salt Creek** is about the best place around. Average clarity declines to only 8', due to runoffs from the creek, but fish apparently like the murkiness. Sheephead, yellowtail and black sea bass, calico bass, and white sea bass all frequent the small reefs about 1/3-mile offshore. Large kelp beds parallel the shoreline about 350' out, and the best diving is between 50-70'. Low visibility and heavy boat traffic make this a spot for the more experienced diver.

Dana Point extends out into the Pacific for 1/4-mile. At the west end of the Dana Point Harbor, you can enter over a small sandy beach and search the rocks for lobster, abalone, and scallops. Offshore, the San Juan Rocks are tempting, but beware of heavy boat traffic. Another convenient access to the water off Dana Point is from **Doheny State Underwater Park**, which has less boat traffic and more developed facilities, including showers.

SAN DIEGO COUNTY — Northern Part

The northern half of San Diego County sees fewer divers than the famous La Jolla region to the south. Northern San Diego diving is characterized by lower water clarity (averaging 15') and usually a long swim through the surf to the reefs well offshore.

As always, difficult conditions are themselves a lure to many divers, since they guarantee fewer visitors and therefore more game. Lobsters of up to 18 lbs. have been captured in the Carlsbad area. Naturally, divers get a little close-mouthed when it comes to specifics about a good lobster reef, but **Carlsbad State Beach** (known locally as **Tamarack**) and the **Encino Power Plant** are some of the favorite dive spots.

Fall offers the best time for diving, as low surf makes the 200-yard swim out to the kelp easier. Thick featherboa and giant kelp harbor lots of life, including sheephead and kelp bass, as well as the aforementioned lobster populations. Maximum depths are only about 35'.

If you want to avoid the swim, you can always launch from Oceanside and head three miles south. More often, though, divers with boats head about seven miles north to the reefs off Camp Pendleton that are inaccessible by land. If you're tired of all the dives where you never see a fish over 8" long, then this is the area for you. Some big fish life has been preserved because of the remoteness. Thick kelp at the **Barn** and huge holes at the **Pendleton artificial reef** both provide shelter for large specimens of sand and kelp bass, sheephead, and opaleye. Others that dwell amongst the rocks include abs, gorgonians, chestnut cowries, and anemones. These dives call for experienced participants, as open sea conditions prevail, and currents sometimes pick up to 1-1/2 knots.

Many reef fish, such as snapper or grunt, change from bright shades of red, blue, and yellow to mottled gray when night falls. This camouflage enables them to hunt at night.

At **San Elijo State Park**, the reefs begin only 35 yards offshore in depths of less than 30'. Eelgrass and palm kelp wave gently in the shallows. As soon as you hit the reefs garibaldi surround you. You can explore many kelp-covered ridges scattered about for almost 1/2-mile out, and never go deeper than 60'.

At **Tide County Park**, just to the south, a similar seascape exists, with deeper ledges and undercuts on the reefs supporting more invertebrates, making for better photos. Red abs in the day and lobster at night are the specialties. No facilities exist at this small beach.

By the time you move downcoast to the **Torrey Pines State Beach**, you've entered the San Diego-La Jolla Marine Life Refuge, where only migratory fish may be hunted. **Bathtub Rock** is about 1/4-mile offshore in 35' depths. Some big grouper and calico bass may be seen around the ledges of the rock.

SAN DIEGO COUNTY — Southern Part

Many think of San Diego as the birthplace of American diving since the Bottom Scratchers, the San Diego dive club — the first in the nation — formed in 1933. Whether you're interested in the history of diving or not, San Diego will appeal to you. **La Jolla Cove**, referred to by locals as simply "The Cove," is the best place to start sampling diving, San Diego style. The beach is well protected from the south swells of summer, making access easy for all divers. In winter, though, big surf sometimes hits the beach, creating rips and dangerous entries and exits.

Clarity here ranges from 5-100', averaging 20-30'. Big rock formations interrupt the sandy bottom that gently slides down to a depth of 35' about 200 yards offshore. **Alligator Head**, on the west end of the cove, falls down in rocky cliffs and deeply undercut ledges. Photography is great around the kelp-covered convoluted rock surfaces. Fish life is abundant and protected, with tame morays, garibaldi, silvery mackerel, large rockfish, and schools of yellowtail.

Between La Jolla Cove and the marine canyons to the north are several other sites, like **Goldfish Point** and **Devil's Slides**. Because of rips, sharp dropoffs, and surf, however, these spots do present difficult entries and exits. Most divers enter at La Jolla Cove and swim around to Goldfish Point's undersea caves and reefs of featherboa with rock wrasses, sheephead, and kelp bass.

For real excitement, you can dive the marine canyon that bisects La Jolla Bay. Part of the San Diego-La Jolla Underwater Preserve, up to 300 divers a weekend visit. The northeastern branch, called **Scripps Canyon**, is an unfathomably steep and narrow gorge that begins 200 yards offshore. Since in several areas the canyon drops off precipitously to over 300', this isn't the place to first experience deep diving. Nor is it the spot to learn how much weight you need. Scripps Canyon is for the experienced diver to enjoy and explore.

A maze of small gorges and valleys intersects the main canyon. At 110' down, one gorge is so narrow that you can touch each wall with your outstretched hands. In places, huge slabs from the wall have broken off, forming ledges piled with boulders. These little outposts of life at 110-150' make a startling contrast to the barren walls. Rose-colored gorgonians and their attendant nudibranches find sanctuary in these talus piles, as do lingcod and sand bass. Occasionally, torpedo rays and angel sharks wander in.

The other branch, **La Jolla Canyon**, is much more easily reached from shore and, since it's less precipitous, offers a safer dive. A sterile sand flat leads out to a series of mudstone ledges that rapidly stairstep down for several hundred feet, with each step becoming progressively steeper and longer.

About 4000 to 7000 years ago, the shores of this canyon were campsites for coastal Indians, and divers have recovered many artifacts of their presence. Daytime diving reveals little life, but at night your lights scare up small octopus, sarcastic fringeheads, and heart urchins. Occasionally, species characteristic of great depth, like thresher sharks, stray into the bottom of the scuba zone here. During squid spawning, the bottom is ankle-deep in white egg cases. Sea lions, bat rays, guitarfish, angel, horn, and blue sharks, black, and white sea bass come to feast.

From La Jolla south to Point Loma there are at least 15 spots, mostly on pocket beaches, that entice divers. **Boomer Beach** is one of the favorites, although the best way to reach Boomer is to enter the La Jolla Cove and kick a paddleboard around Alligator Head to the outer reefs at Boomer. Shore entries are for the experienced only, since big surf and dangerous rips and currents make beach diving hazardous.

On the broken rock patches of the outer reefs, a population of grouper thrives. San Diego divers for years refrained from spearing the highly territorial fish after they'd been nearly wiped out from intense spearfishing pressure. Today, grouper are a protected species in California. Colorful invertebrates like sea stars and nudibranches abound on the reefs, which reach a maximum depth of 90'.

At **Casa Cove**, shallow depths of no more than 35' and anemone-hugged walls combine to make a photographer's paradise. However, a sharp dropoff close to chest level can make exits very difficult if the surf's up. A beautiful environment of eelgrass with sandy channels is just to the south.

High tide is the best time to dive **Bird Rock**, because then many of the sharp rocks close to shore are underwater. This shallow, rocky eelgrass meadow is famous for abalone, which still exist in as little as 5' of water. Halibut also abound in the sand channels. Rips and surf over the shallow reef can make for hazardous diving.

Sea cucumbers shed their stomach and intestines to confuse and repel predators; or they spin sticky white threads from the anus which swell about them. Besides sticky white threads, the anus also contains the respiratory gills and several small animals who call it home.

Finally, many divers head out in boats to the incredibly dense kelp forests off **Point Loma**. The reef starts at 25' on the inside, dropping to a depth of over 100' outside the kelp. Interesting rock formations spring up everywhere, including a sea cliff that parallels the shore, topping out at 65'.

At **New Hope Rock**, vertical ledges covered with gorgonian fan corals in pinks and rusts suddenly lead to rock arches furred with *Corynactis* anemones and bright sponges. Visibility often exceeds 50', and is usually at least 25'. Fish life is fantastic, with occasional big black sea bass to admire. Yellowtail, white sea bass, lingcod, morays, sheephead, and the lovable garibaldi are also frequently seen. The world's record sheephead — 36-1/2 lbs. — was speared here. Photographers find the color-packed reefs of Point Loma a dream.

Just north of Tijuana Slough, a vintage **S-37 submarine** lies in only 20-40' of water just past the surf line. This particular sub, already obsolete by the start of WWII, had the distinction of being the first U.S. sub to sink an enemy destroyer in the Pacific. Diving the S-37 today is hampered by big surf. Lobster and torpedo rays now inhabit the historic vessel.

DON PETERSON

California sea lions are the tame "seals" most often seen in marine shows.

THE CHANNEL ISLANDS

Ask any California diver to name ten favorite dive sites, and chances are that right at the top of the list will be a reef, cliff, or cave on one of the Channel Islands. Once you've become hooked on kelp diving (and nowhere has better kelp diving than the Channel Islands), then other dives just don't measure up. Even gorgeous coral reefs seem flat; where are the layers of life, the 60' of watery jungle with fish cruising above you, below you, and around you? And where are the sea mammals, the sea lions and harbor seals that pull at your fins, peer in your mask, and beg as shamelessly as a dog for your catch?

As for temperature, well, yes, pulling on a clammy wetsuit for the second time is difficult. But it builds character. Like the surge and currents and rough surf, it weeds out the weak. It separates out the pansies from the adventurous, and it helps thin the crowds in Eden.

Not that the Channel Islands have always been considered Eden. Their scruffy chaparral has been neglected or abused for much of California's history. Only recently has their incredible undersea magnificence become well known.

And what magnificence it is! These eight small islands, with the largest only 21 miles long, comprise one of the world's most productive and unique marine habitats. Cold water sweeping down from the north mixes with the warmer counter-current coming up the southern coast. Nutrient-rich upwellings from deep in the sea add their note to this temperature hybrid by establishing a rich plankton basis for a food web so diverse and luxuriant that it supports over 213 species of finfish and 150 of shellfish.

Kelp takes off in this environment. Rocketing up at more than a foot a day, *Macrocystis* here forms the most massive beds in the world. The diversity and abundance of marine mammals are unequaled, with sightings of 27 species of whales and dolphins, six species of seals and sea lions, and the sea otter, all within the waters of the Channel Islands. One whale species in particular, the California gray whale, is frequently observed, as its entire population passes through the area twice yearly on migration. Most of California's seabirds have become totally dependent on the islands for nesting, as increased development has forced them off the mainland.

Small wonder, then, that in 1980 the Channel Islands Marine Sanctuary, consisting of the northern four islands — Anacapa, Santa Cruz, Santa Rosa, and San Miguel — plus Santa Barbara, was formed to protect this priceless national treasure. All waters within a six-mile radius of each island are included. However, except at certain localized reserves, the taking of marine life is allowed, subject to the laws of the California Department of Fish and Game.

One regulation divers should note is the rule forbidding the removal of any artifacts, either on land or submerged. This is designed to preserve any relics of the many Indian archaeological sites that still exist on today's seabed.

Previous discoveries from such sites have included the remains of a now-extinct giant mouse, and a dwarf woolly mammoth that stood only 6' high. The mammoth bones, in particular, astonished scientific circles, for their gnawed condition indicated the presence of human hunters on the islands as far back as 30,000 years ago.

At its peak, the Indian population may have numbered 20,000 scattered over the islands. But the Canaliños, with their sturdy canoes, thatched huts, domestic dogs, and stick weapons, were no match for the Spanish discoverers. Those who didn't succumb to the transplanted Aleuts (imported labor to reap the sea otter bounty) were done in by the culture shock brought on by missionary "rescuers" who evacuated them to the mainland.

With the exception of a few ranchers or castaways, most of the islands have remained, basically, a wilderness over the years. To today's diver, the Channel Islands offer an opportunity for exploration of some practically virgin territory. Abalone, lobster, and other choice species that are scarce on the mainland can still be found around the more remote islands. The topography of the underwater scene is nothing short of incredible, with pinnacles, arches, and caves galore. With the best visibilities on the west coast, there's little doubt that the Channel Islands offer California's best diving.

Catalina, the populated one, is probably the best place for newcomers to start. It and San Clemente have the best protection and the clearest waters, with clarity that can exceed 75-100'. These two islands also host more typically southern marine communities.

Cold-water species mix with warm around the northern Channel Islands, and visibilities there are usually in the 40-50' range. With less protection and rougher water, the northern islands aren't visited as frequently, and so still shelter more game species. Numerous dive boats, including some state-of-the-art vessels with all the amenities, visit the islands. Local dive shops can supply details if you're interested in a cold-water Eden.

ANACAPA

Anacapa Island is distinctive for several reasons. First, it's the only one of California's offshore islands to have escaped the patriotic and religious naming frenzy of the Spaniards. "Anacapa" comes from a corruption of a Canaliño Indian word meaning "ever-changing", and if you ever approach the island on a foggy morning you'll know why they called it that. Second, it's one of the few breeding grounds of the endangered brown pelican left in the entire USA. Third, and of most interest to divers, Anacapa rises out of the ocean only 11 miles offshore from Oxnard, making it a favorite destination for dive boats. In fact, its popularity is so great that reservations are a good idea in summer.

CALIFORNIA

Actually, Anacapa is a series of three mountaintops linked together by sand bars that are exposed at low tide. With imposing cliffs and a peak of 930' on the largest link in the chain, Anacapa is a spectacular sight both above and below the water. Since certain areas around the island have been set aside as either invertebrate refuges or total reserves, be sure and familiarize yourself with the regulations before collecting anything.

CALIFORNIA CHANNEL ISLANDS

Arch Rock 5, 32
Arch Rocks 6
Bat Ray Cove 3
Beacon Reef 18
Bee Rock 13
Begg Rock 35
Bird Rock 27
Blue Cavern Point 26
Casino Point U/W Park 22
Castle Rock 44
Cat Rock 2
Cathedral Cove 5
Cathedral Rock 40
China Point 45
Cluster Point 14
Cortes Bank 48
Descanso Cove 22
Dutch Harbor 37
Eagle Rock 28
East End 37
East Fish Camp 4
East Point 17
Eel Point 46
Emerald Cove 27
Equator 4
Farnsworth Bank 31
Fishhook 39
Frazier Cove 9
Frenchy's Cove 1
Golden Horn 15
Goldfish Bowl 1
Gull Island 8
Hen Rock Reef 23
Indian Rock 27
Ironbound Cove 29
Isthmus Reef 27

Italian Gardens 23
John C. Butler 43
Johnson's Lee 16
Little Farnsworth 24
Little Flower 41
Long Point Light 23
Morse Point 8
Mosquito Cove 41
Nine Fathom Reef 44
Ning Po 30
Painted Cave 6
Potato Patch 12
Pothole 32
Prisoner's Harbor 10
Pyramid Cove 39
Pyramid Head High Spot 40
Richardson's Rock 20
Ripper's Cove 25
Sandy Point 15
Scorpion Anchorage 7
Seal Cove 46
Seven Fathom Reef 38
Ship Rock 27
Smuggler's Cove 11
Sutil Island 34
Talcott Shoals 19
The Pinnacle 24
Three Mile Reef 36
USS Gregory 47
Valiant 22
Wagon Tracks 42
Whale Rock 29
Wilson's Rock 20
Winfield Scott 3
Wyckoff Ledge 21

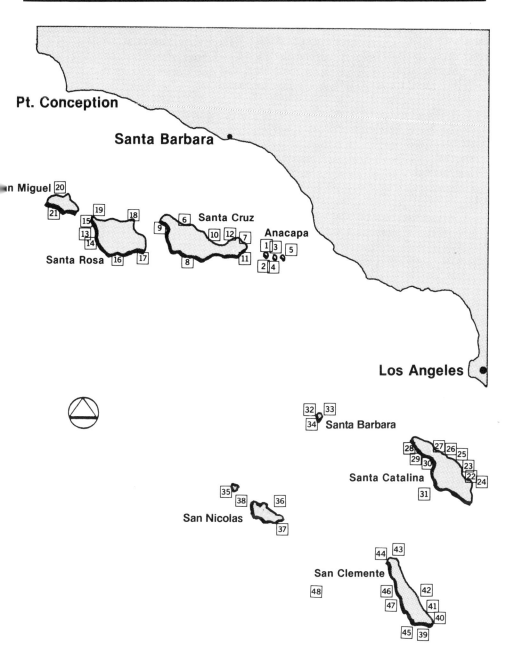

Pt. Conception

Santa Barbara

n Miguel 20

21

19
15   18
13
14
Santa Rosa   16   17

9   6   **Santa Cruz**
10   12   7
8   11

Anacapa
1 3   5
2 4

Los Angeles

32   33
34 **Santa Barbara**

28   27 26
29 30   25
23
22   24
Santa Catalina
31

35
38   36
San Nicolas
37

44   43
San Clemente
48   46   42
47   41
40
45   39

CHANNEL ISLANDS

Frenchy's Cove, on the lee side of the west island, commemorates a modern-day hermit, Frenchy DeDreau. He lived here in a hut, dining off the bounty of the sea, until the 1950's. Today boats anchor in his cove, picnickers feast on his sandy beach, and divers enjoy the sights of his underwater mini-kingdom. Shallow and protected, Frenchy's Cove is a great place for snorkeling or diving in calm, clear water. Deeper water to the west of the cove hides massive kelp beds that harbor much life, including big sheephead, abs, and scallops.

Another popular spot on the lee side of the west island is **Goldfish Bowl**. A pot-holed sandy bottom with rock outcroppings supports a good-sized kelp bed. Garibaldi and morays both hang out around the rocks, while giant kelpfish hide among the fronds of kelp, changing their colors to suit their background. Schools of blue rockfish sometimes swirl by. The observant diver might spot a red-striped convict fish peering from its hole among the bottom rocks. These little six-inchers rely on their camouflage getup to protect them, except during the mating season when the plucky male will challenge anything that threatens his eggs. Depths within the bowl are seldom below 30'.

A favorite spot with dive boats on the weather side of the west island is **Cat Rock**. The rock provides some protection from swells, and on a calm day visibility can be very good. A reef runs for several hundred feet out from the island, gradually sloping to about 70'. Good kelp beds and abundant life, both fish and invertebrate, make for good diving and excellent macro photography.

The lee side of the middle island offers **Bat Ray Cove** and numerous small caves to the west. Lobsters and green morays hide out during the daylight hours within these sanctuaries; they won't cause you any problems, but surge might. Halibut abound on the sandy bottom.

A small cove to the east contains the remains of the *Winfield Scott*, lying in about 25' of water. This wooden sidewheel steamer ran aground in 1853 with 450 passengers and $800,000 in gold aboard. The gold, passengers, and baggage were all removed before the ship went down. The rats, however, were left to fend for themselves, which they did, and their descendants have caused serious ecological damage to the island. Today the *Winfield Scott* is a testimony to the force of the ocean, as all that remains are the giant old paddlewheel, some brass spikes, copper nails, and bits of copper sheeting. As at all wrecks within the Channel Islands' Marine Sanctuary, artifacts are protected.

East Fish Camp, just across the island on the weather side, has good kelp diving as well as the remains of the *Equator* scattered over the bottom at 30' depth. Swells and currents outside the cove can present hazards.

The cliffs along the lee side of the east island drop straight down to 20-30' and then slope down gradually, to only 80' at about 200 yards out. Great macro opportunities attract divers, especially to the **Lighthouse** reef and the **Arch Rock** area. However, strong currents make this area for the experienced only, and then you need a tender in the boat for pickups.

Strong currents also run along the weather side of the east island. The 50' depths within **Cathedral Cove** are dotted with pinnacles. An eroded cliff opens into a big yawning mouth of a sea cave that you can enter by skiff if the surge is low and the weather's calm. Sea lions sometimes jump off their waterside perches in annoyance at your intrusion into their territory. If the surf is low enough, you can explore back into several mineral-colored chambers.

SANTA CRUZ

Santa Cruz, at 21 miles long, is not only the biggest of the Channel Islands, but also one of the most diverse in life, both above and below the surface. The cold waters of the California Current which flow down from the north mix with the warmer California Counter-Current which hugs the shoreline from the south. This produces a unique underwater melange of northern and southern species. Lingcod swim amidst garibaldi; *Metridiums* and seafans share the same undersea wall.

Above-ground, Santa Cruz is much more hospitable-looking than some of the other islands, with beautiful rolling meadows and groves of such rare trees as the Santa Cruz pine, ironwood, and island oaks, none of which are found on the mainland. Freshwater streams course through the valleys, and formerly supported one of the largest cattle ranches in the west. The coastline of almost 60 miles veers between jagged cliffs pocked with untold numbers of grottos, and isolated sandy beaches.

Underwater you'll see plenty of fascinating species to add to your memory bank. With some of the richest kelp beds anywhere, Santa Cruz has a truly fantastic array of marine life. Bright yellow 8"-long lemon nudibranches whose egg mass resembles a curly flower; brilliantly blue-spotted giant sea stars 2' across; blue and yellow striped seaperch hovering over red algae — these sights plus the hundreds of others you can see in the kelp beds of Santa Cruz will convince even the skeptic that the long boat ride and full wetsuit are worth it. Along the lee side from Willows Anchorage to Smugglers Cove are many scenic dives.

Painted Cave, near Profile Point, has to be included in the list of the most beautiful caverns anywhere. In calm weather you can pull a 65' boat into the mouth of this cave. The massive hole extends back over 500' into the recesses of the island. Abstract designs in rusty reds, greens, and golds cover the ceiling, created by untold centuries of iron and copper oxides in the dripping water.

Scorpion Anchorage reef drops down to around 70' and divers race to get to the beach side early in the lobster season. Sandy bottom supports halibut and sand dollars, while scallops, calico bass, and abs can be found around the rocks of the reef. On the western edge, a cave is usually inhabited by a swell shark. Since it's a fairly deep cave, be careful how far in you go.

Gull Island has the most dependable calm water on the island, with clarity often past 50'. A long reef extends seaward and also back towards Santa Cruz, ranging in depths from about 10-70'. Colorful marine life includes beautiful tiny gobies with scarlet and blue stripes and bug eyes, as well as less mobile creatures like the delicate *Tealia* anemones with their waving, malevolent arms. Sea lions and harbor seals frequent this area.

Morse Point is another favorite spot. Here rocks break the surface and create a large shallow reef that extends out for almost 1/4-mile. Since the top is very shallow and the sides fall away to only about 50', snorkeling is good in calm water. Big lobsters and abs seek protected spots in the reef.

Frazier Cove, on the western tip, is rarely safe to visit. On the few calm days it is diveable, lobsters and black abs are thick in the heavy kelp and scenic rock formations.

The number of dive sites around Santa Cruz is limited only by your imagination and time schedule. Other interesting places around this gigantic kelp aquarium include **Prisoner's Harbor** (named after the unlucky Mexican convicts purposefully marooned there); **Smuggler's Cove** (in honor of Prohibition); **Potato Patch** (beautiful but with treacherous currents and surge); and **Arch Rocks** (great topography of arches and cliffs).

SANTA ROSA

Santa Rosa sometimes gets overshadowed by Santa Cruz, its larger neighbor just to the east. Santa Rosa is almost as big as Santa Cruz, has almost as many unique species, and almost the same topography.

But one thing Santa Rosa has that Santa Cruz doesn't is **Bee Rock**. This huge outcropping pokes above the shallow reefy area that extends all along the west side of the island. High wind and swells can rule out Bee Rock, which sits in 60' of water. Cracks and crevices start small and then develop into full-sized ravines, big enough to practice skydiving in. The shapes and colors of life that decorate the rock like Christmas tree ornaments would take years to classify. Purple nudibranches, blue and yellow algae bushes, encrusting sponges from scarlet to yellow, dome-shaped blue bryozoans, and anemones of almost every hue are a few of the standouts.

Like **Cluster Point** and **Sandy Point** and all the rest of the west side, Bee Rock is exposed to the weather and conditions are often rough with lots of surge. The iron remains of the *Golden Horn* are scattered in 20' depths near Sandy Pt. but surge generally precludes diving.

Calmer waters are found around South Point, from **Johnson's Lee** to **East Point**. Both sites have water clarity that usually approaches 40', and shallow water with huge kelp beds. Fish abound, from surf perch and rockfish to halibut and black sea bass. East Pt. is also well-known for big lobster.

One interesting fish that an observant diver might notice in the open water region of the kelp bed is the senorita. This little yellow and black cigar of a fish seems, like the garibaldi, designed to be noticeable. And that's the case, since the senorita advertises its services as a cleaner fish — one who eats parasites off other fish — and in turn is thought to receive some immunity from predation. The senorita is one of the very few examples known in temperate waters of the "cleaner relationship" so common in the tropics. Sometimes a crowd develops around the senorita as fish of different species wait their turn. Even the *Mola mola*, who especially seems to need cleaner services, is drawn from its normal open ocean haunts to seek the attentions of the senorita.

Beacon Reef, just off Carrington Point on the northeast tip of the island, is a good spot for both shallow and deep diving. The pinnacled top of the reef is only about 10' down, while, just to the north a short distance, depths are past 90'. The beautiful reef helps contribute to Santa Rosa's reputation as a great place for game, with lots of lobster. Current through the Santa Cruz Channel can result in poor clarity.

Talcott Shoals is an immense area of almost 20 square miles. An experienced skipper is a must, since some areas are only 10' deep and very surgy, while others stairstep down into a series of ledges that go below 100'. The shoals are famous among experienced West Coast divers for white sea bass, lingcod, halibut, and big lobster.

SAN MIGUEL

The outermost of the offshore islands, San Miguel lies directly in the path of the savage winds that sweep down the California coast and veer out to sea at Pt. Conception. Lacking the shelter of its neighbor islands, which are more or less protected by the curving shoreline, San Miguel takes it square in the face.

And a weathered, craggy face it is. Rising to 830' at its highest, San Miguel presents the lowest profile of all the Channel Islands. Overgrazing by sheep caused the demise of the heavy vegetation reported by discoverers. Erosion and shifting sand dunes followed, although now recovery by native vegetation is underway.

San Miguel's main claim to fame rests with its pinnipeds. Apparently they like stormy weather, for nowhere else in the world will you find five breeding species side-by-side, with transients of a sixth species. Over 10,000 breeding animals crowd into the Pt. Bennett beach alone! California sea lions; their northern relatives, the larger Steller's sea lion; huge elephant seals; playful harbor seals; and the northern fur seal all fight for breeding territory, while the critically endangered Guadalupe fur seal drops in occasionally.

In a rather revealing tale of man's capacity for rapacity, the Guadalupe fur seal was believed extinct after the slaughters of the 19th century. However, two Mexican fishermen discovered a small remnant herd on Guadalupe Island in 1928. After capturing two bulls for the San Diego Zoo, the fishermen had a barroom brawl over just what to do about their discovery. One of them decided to return to the island, where he slaughtered, as far as the world knew, the last individuals of the species. Luckily, a few seals, which by then were pretty cautious, hid out in the deep caves and slowly increased their numbers until, in 1954, a breeding colony was again rediscovered on Guadalupe Island. With protection there is a good chance the seals will again regain their former abundance.

The main thing divers have to fear from pinnipeds underwater is laughing too hard, although they have been known to dislodge masks, and steal catches. They apparently consider the wetsuited diver a clumsy, uncoordinated unfortunate who can easily be made the brunt of all sorts of fun games. Harbor seals and sea lions love to play tug of war with your fins, and they also seem to enjoy indulging in a game of tag in which you are always "it." It's a little unnerving to have a seal hurtle directly at your mask with the speed of a freight train, only to veer aside at the last possible moment.

Since the boat ride is about five hours and the weather is unpredictable, San Miguel remains in a relatively untouched state. **Wilson's Rock**, to the north of the island, has great dropoff diving, with steep sides that plunge almost 180' straight down to the ocean floor. Razor-sharp ridges support a teeming jungle of invertebrates. The water is so deep and, often, so clear, that it's easy to feel like a huge bird flying down an exotic landscape that goes on forever into the deep blue.

Along with the delicate fern-like bryozoans, bright anemones, and game fish, torpedo rays are occasionally seen. An ignorant spearfisherman who tried to spear one could literally be in for the shock of his life, as a big animal is theoretically capable of delivering up to 2500 watts. Since that is sufficient to cause death, and since electric rays are one of the few aggressive rays in the ocean, wise divers back off quickly when they see one. Fortunately, speed isn't their strong suit (with weapons like that, who needs to be quick?), neoprene insulates, they rarely use full power, and they are easily avoided.

Richardson's Rock, nearby, is also an invertebrate heaven. Giant green anemones up to 1' across find homes on the wall, along with the smaller strawberry and club anemones. Black-and-yellow-rockfish and sheephead abound; occasionally black sea bass or blue sharks are seen.

Wyckoff Ledge drops from its plateau at 20' to more than 120' in short order. The top of the ledge is ridged and cut with ledges and gullies, harboring exotic shells as well as big ocean-swimming fish like white sea bass. The deep, cold water of San Miguel supports some of the most abundant marine life in the Channel Islands.

The largest eye in nature is found in some species of squid — one eye measured 16 inches in diameter.

SANTA CATALINA ISLAND

Today many of the more than 500,000 people a year that visit Catalina Island go to discover incredible underwater sights. Kelp beds so amazingly dense they have to be seen to be believed; wrecks like the *Valiant*, which is supposed to conceal more than $250,000 worth of jeweled treasure; bizarre creatures like the horn and angel sharks that park on the white sand around kelp; cliffs, ledges, and caves galore; the fabled Farnsworth Bank, where advanced divers can find themselves wandering through a purple hydrocoral extravaganza — whatever your underwater interest, Catalina has something for you.

Many dive boats make regular runs to Catalina out of San Pedro or Long Beach. Facilities do exist on the island for air, rentals, and even guide service. **Big Fisherman Cove** boasts a U.S.C. Marine Science Center complete with a multi-person recompression chamber. Divers should respect any undersea experiment they come across. While most are within Big Fisherman Cove, at times certain activities like kelp-banding occur in spots all around the island.

Most Catalina diving is done on the frontside, facing the mainland, as this area is protected from all but the rare Santa Ana winds of winter. Water clarity around Catalina can hit as much as 120' in winter, but summer plankton blooms can lower it to 50'-70'.

The most famous dive site on the island is undoubtedly **Casino Point Underwater Park**. After an easy entry off a concrete apron, you are in 60' of water within only 20 yards. Kelp beds, underwater cliffs, and seven wrecks from 40-70' long make this a very popular spot. Roped off for divers, Casino Pt. has an air compressor nearby in summer.

Just a few hundred yards away in **Descanso Cove** lies the wreck of the *Valiant*. The Avalon harbormaster must issue a permit for this dive, as heavy boat traffic, especially in summer, will sometimes make it impossible. The 163'-long *Valiant* was the ultimate in luxury yachts of her day. Although the vessel reportedly burned for days before sinking in 1932, many interesting artifacts of the high life enjoyed aboard her during the Roaring Twenties have been found. These include brass coins stamped "good for one drink" on one side, and "MV Valiant" on the other.

Today the steel hull remains mostly intact, sheltering various critters like lobsters and eels as well as a rumored $250,000 worth of jewelry that was never recovered.

Hen Rock Reef, one mile south of the Long Point Lighthouse, provides excellent, and relatively untouched, diving in 45-75' of water. Lobster, octopus, scallops, seafans, sargo, sheephead, and various flatfishes are common. The nearshore rocks, only 10-35' deep, also provide beautiful dives, with many crevices and even a tunnel through the southeast corner of Hen Rock.

Little Farnsworth, also called **The Pinnacle**, is a dive site so special that local divers refrain from taking anything from it. Laws don't protect it — only the divers' sense of wonder does. Huge steep-sided boulders covered with seafans, anemones, sponges, and red algae suddenly rise out of a flat sand bottom 85-135' deep. The tops of the rocks are in 65-70' of water. Around the rocks, angel sharks lie in the sand, with blacksmith, mackerel, sheephead, and sea lions swimming about. Deeper water fish such as yellowtail, white sea bass, barracuda, bonita, and sunfish sometimes rove in. Since boat traffic and current can be heavy, it's best to tie up and dive down the anchor line. Part of the attraction of this site is its mystery — it's not correctly marked on any charts. It's about one mile southeast of Avalon and 100 yards offshore.

Another special location for Catalina diving, not normally used by charter boats, is the **Long Point Light** and the protected cove just south of it. A great deal of underwater filming for tv and movies has been done here, including *Sea Hunt*, *Orca*, and *Jaws II*. A sheer cliff drops in places as much as 100'. With much of the same life as Little Farnsworth, Long Point is known for its especially bold moray eels.

The small cove offers such protection that it's an excellent night diving spot. An underwater tunnel winds completely through Long Point, opening into a room that was discovered by accident on a night dive! In addition to the usual Catalina marine life, this is a good place to see bat rays, horn sharks, and swell sharks.

Another lee side location that attracts divers is **Italian Gardens**, just northwest of Long Point. Cobblestones give way to a silty bottom, with 160' depths possible only 100 yards offshore. Rocks and ledges provide good substrate for kelp holdfasts. This area is subject to surface chop in the late afternoon.

Ripper's Cove is susceptible to murky water due to the silt bottom, but when the clarity is good, it offers excellent sightseeing and photography. Rocky, kelp-covered headlands surround the cove on both sides. Lobster, kelp bass, sheephead, sculpins, and rockfish abound.

But the majority of diving on Catalina takes place from boats between Blue Cavern Point and Emerald Bay. Secret passages of more than 150' in length that suddenly lead out into the cathedral light of a kelp bed give **Blue Cavern Pt.** its name. Schools of blacksmith dart and glide through the kelp, all changing direction simultaneously, as if governed by a single mind. Currents and surge in the caverns can be strong, so exercise caution.

Isthmus Reef near the Marine Science Center at Big Fisherman Cove is a very popular dive. The south side of the reef becomes a vertical wall that drops from 40-120'. Heavy kelp covers the reef and supports a varied population of kelp bass, blacksmith, and some of the smaller rockfishes. Most large game fish like white sea bass are scarce, as are abalone, lobster, and others subjected to intense hunting pressure. Garibaldi, on the other hand, are common and friendly, and the brilliantly orange and blue-speckled young add a wonderful color accent to the reefs in late fall. Bright orange kelp snails in their dull shells also add color and prove once again that some mollusks are more beautiful inside than out.

Further offshore, **Bird Rock** rises from a sandy channel. Vertical faces covered with fan corals and colorful algae front the outer side. Depths go to as much as 190' before the rock meets a sandy bottom. The western wall descends more gradually, through a series of canyons and broken rock piles. Marine life abounds here and at Ship Rock, nearby, and includes torpedo rays, white sea bass in summer, octopus, morays, lobster (early in the season), and even a few abs.

Jagged, toothy-looking **Ship Rock** contains more than its fair share of life. Flat, 5'-long angel sharks hide out during the daylight hours under the talus pileup of the northwest side. Their equally harmless relatives, the ancient, curly-mouthed horn sharks, can also be seen by the dozens, parked on the bottom, side-by-side with bat stars and red sea cucumbers. Sea lions thrive around the naked white rock, and frequently frolic with divers. Beautiful amphitheaters on the west side at depths of 90' or more make spectacular settings for photographs. Kelp thrives in varying densities on different sides of the rock, with some areas suitable for natural light photos. Sheephead, kelp bass, blacksmith, and other typical inhabitants of kelp abound. Surge, some occasional tricky currents, and extreme depths require careful diving.

Indian Rock at **Emerald Cove** offers a more serene setting. Calm water attracts snorkelers as well as scuba divers. Rocky ledges and shelves stairstep out from the rock to 170'. Giant kelp predominates to 60' depths. Below that depth, the very weird-looking elk kelp grows in small stands, often on sandy bottoms. This plant has a single unbranching stalk, up to 80' long, that supports one big "balloon" — a gas-filled buoyancy device from which sprout two huge, leathery blades. Very aptly named!

And if elk kelp alone isn't strange enough for you, there's also a dwarf elk kelp found nowhere else in the world but Catalina and San Clemente Islands. This deep-dweller can survive in sandy bottoms down to 200'. Only the stalk is dwarf — about 6' long instead of 80'. The spectacle of massive antlers of 30' flowing gracefully from the absurdly short stalk is not an easily forgotten sight to one interested in plants.

The windward side of Catalina sees fewer divers, since swells and surge combine to lower clarity to an average of 30'. Nevertheless, **Eagle Rock** and **Whale Rock** both attract some divers, if weather permits. Depths go to at least 100' at both spots. Lots of game fish, black coral, and sea fans are the outstanding reasons to dive these areas.

At **Ironbound Cove**, less experienced divers can also get wet, since it's pretty well protected from the swells, and depths are about 60' maximum. Visibility is less, but if you see the squid spawning anytime from January to April, and the feeding frenzy it causes in many species of fish, you won't mind the low clarity.

You can look for pieces of the **Ning Po** lying in the muddy bottom of Catalina Harbor, in less than 20' of water, if you're so inclined. This 18th-century Chinese junk started out as a pirate vessel and ended up a dynamited Hollywood prop.

And finally, the most easily reached, spectacular, and exotic dive spot in California — as well as one of the most dangerous and challenging to dive — lies only 1-1/2 miles off Ben Weston Point. **Farnsworth Bank** is a rocky area of canyons, plateaus, pinnacles,gradual slopes, and steep cliffs. Since it is open ocean with strong currents and extreme depths, caution must be exercised. For the experienced diver following a careful dive plan, however, this will be an incredible journey into a fantasyland. At 50' a pinnacle juts up to meet the descending diver. The south edge of the pinnacle falls off into infinite blue space almost immediately, but the other sides offer a more moderate slope down into sand gullies and ridges before they, too, slide down into the unknown. Other, deeper pinnacles and ridges also protrude up from the depths.

The bank supports a vast array of life, including large schools of jack mackerel and anchovies, halibut, lingcod, white sea bass, and yellowtail. But by far the most spectacular resident is the purple hydrocoral, which attains such a size and color here that the area has been set aside by the California Department of Fish and Game as a hydrocoral preserve. Every diver who ever soars down a rock cliff covered with the gorgeous and rare purple bonsais should utter thanks that this scenic wonder was preserved from the thoughtless few who were destroying decades of growth with the snap of a finger.

Among the other marine life divers have the opportunity to see around Catalina Island are nudibranches, sea hares, blue-banded gobies, guitarfish, leopard sharks, thornback rays, harbor seals, pilot whales, and gray whales.

SANTA BARBARA

Santa Barbara, 38 miles out of San Pedro Harbor, has been under the jurisdiction of the National Park Service since 1938, when President Roosevelt set it and Anacapa aside as the Channel Islands National Monument. At only 1-1/4 miles in length, Santa Barbara is the smallest of the Channel Islands, and therefore the most susceptible to abuse.

After decades of mistreatment, including the importation of rabbits, ants, sheep, and goats, as well as widespread burnoffs, Santa Barbara was a natural disaster. Two species of plants and at least five species of birds had been wiped out. The once widespread sea otters had been eliminated and breeding pinnipeds had almost deserted the island. The ubiquitous imported ice plant had choked out the fragile native wildflowers, and even the huge stands of tree-like yellow *Coreopsis* had been devastated by the hordes of hungry rabbits.

Now part of the Channel Islands Marine Sanctuary, Santa Barbara is recovering. Decades of work by devoted naturalists have paid off. Once again from far out at sea you can admire the *Coreopsis* blooming high atop the ocean cliffs Non-native species are gradually being eliminated so the indigenous wildlife can recover.

Today a visitor stands a good chance of meeting sea lions or harbor seals underwater. Elephant seals sometimes are seen lolling in the surf and gray whales pass very closeby on their annual migration in December and January, making the island a favorite spot for whale-watchers.

Underwater, the scene hasn't changed as drastically over the years. Lush kelp growth, rugged coves, innumerable sea caves, and sprawling reefs harbor one of the most productive ecosystems anywhere.

A favorite spot located just off the northern tip of the island is **Arch Rock**. This spectacular sea monument rises from 60' depths to within 5' of the surface. A large school of surf perch interspersed with a few blacksmith regularly guards the arch, and often sea lions drop by. The light flooding through the 100'-wide opening creates a surreal, spectral effect that is broken only when a group of divers decide to ride the surge,like a roller coaster, back and forth through the arch.

To the northwest of the Arch, the **Pothole** country begins. A gently sloping plateau of bull kelp and eelgrass extends out for at least 150 yards, with craters up to 8' deep pocking the rock. Lobster, abs, and scallops find refuge in the holes together with many sea urchins. On the outer edge, the plateau gives way to some house-sized boulders and pinnacles, marked by beautiful red swaying fans and abundant fish life. The water clarity in this area of solid rock structures is excellent, and combined with the landscape, has set the stage for many good photographs.

Under the **lighthouse** on the northeastern tip of Santa Barbara, you come across a reef marked by many large caves and ravines. Since maximum depth is about 60', this area is susceptible to heavy swells with corresponding lower visibility. On a calm day, the clarity can be as much as 50'. The many schooling fish and big predators like white sea bass that sometimes rove in make this an exciting dive. Horn sharks sometimes sleep in ledges at the base of the ravines and green and pink abalone can be found by the sharp-eyed.

The plateau around **Sutil Island**, just off the southwest corner of Santa Barbara, supports a thick kelp bed and many exotic shells, garibaldi, anemones, and rockfish. Swells can hamper diving in this area.

SAN NICOLAS

As you approach by boat after the long trip from the mainland, it's hard to believe that anyone could survive alone on the barren and rugged island of San Nicolas . Yet an Indian woman, who hung back to look for her son, was marooned there when mission priests evacuated the remnant population of Canaliños in 1835. For almost 20 years, she lived alone on the island, subsisting on the mineral spring water and abundant sea life. Ironically, she died a few weeks after her "rescue" to the mainland.

Today, adventurous divers seek out this most remote and isolated of all the Channel Islands, which is owned by the U.S. Navy. With a fantastic assortment of undersea life, and some spectacular underwater landscapes (of which Begg Rock is the most famous) San Nicolas makes for exciting diving — if the weather permits. Swept by ungodly winds and far enough out to sea for unpredictable weather, diving San Nicolas can be a chancy proposition.

Your odds are especially bad if you're aiming to dive **Begg Rock**, located eight miles northwest of the island. Some estimate that only one of every four charter attempts makes it. Usually those routed by fierce weather end up on the lee side of Santa Barbara. Since lobsters and abalone aren't found at Begg Rock, and ground swell can make macro photography difficult, the appeal of this dive is mainly to explore the wild scenery.

The unprepossessing rock itself gives you little idea of what's in store; only about 15' of excrement-covered stone protrudes above the waves. Below water, though, it's a different story. A series of three pinnacles (only one breaks the water), Begg Rock looms up from 240' down. The best diving is in a plateau that gently slopes down into a 140' valley before abruptly climbing to a 60' razorback ridge. Only deep freaks dive the outer edge of the ridge as the vertical, almost barren wall drops straight down to 240'.

The inner valley, though, teems with life. *Corynactis* anemones give way to white *Metridiums* below 100'. Extremely rare this far south, the *Metridiums* at Begg Rock are especially big, and so sensitive to water movements they'll even wave enticingly at divers. Chestnut cowries, wing rosy murexes, scallops, and brittle stars all compete for space with the smaller white anemones that carpet the walls. Beautiful vermilion rockfish add their color to this scene, as do big pink female sheephead, who seem past due for their metamorphosis into males. If you hit a calm day, water clarity will be 125' to 150'.

Closer to the island, **Three Mile Reef**, **Dutch Harbor**, and **East End** offer great diving and abundant sealife, including electric rays and blue sharks. At Three Mile Reef canyons dropping steeply for 90' cleave the hard volcanic rock of the reef. Soaring through narrow deep canyons is ordinarily reserved for birds, but here scuba gives you the same weightless feeling. Beautiful turf, exotic shells, octopus, and morays all make for great photos.

Seven Fathom Reef is also known for cutbacks and ledges in its volcanic rock upholstered with invertebrates, including scallops. **The Boiler** is known for red abalone and lobster. In addition to lots of kelp and great clarity, this area has gained a reputation as a prime place to see large black sea bass. Extreme depth, currents, and surge limit San Nicolas Island to the experienced diver.

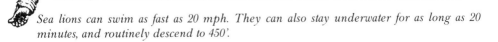

Sea lions can swim as fast as 20 mph. They can also stay underwater for as long as 20 minutes, and routinely descend to 450'.

SAN CLEMENTE

The southernmost of the offshore islands, San Clemente is also considered the most distinctive by scientists. Unlike the northern Channel Islands, which were once part of the mainland, San Clemente was thrust up from the depths in a volcanic explosion. Today you can explore the many undersea crevices and caves that mark its slopes, and sometimes shelter sea lions or harbor seals. Magnificent high cliffs facing the sea are home to species of fox and bat found nowhere else, as well as more common species such as eagles, ravens, pelicans, and albatross. Springtime adds a special note of beauty to the island, as wildflowers, some nine or more feet high, carpet the slopes.

For many people the surprise is that San Clemente still exists in any recognizable form after the tons of explosives that the Navy has dropped on it in practice drills. Divers should exercise caution and studiously avoid any military relics, like live shells, that they come across underwater.

And, unfortunately, all the *terra firma* is off-limits: no one may set foot on the island except military personnel. The harbor facility at Wilson's Cove on the north end of the island is for military use only, except in emergencies.

Luckily for the diver, though, the Navy has no objections to civilians enjoying the waters around San Clemente. Many dive boats out of southern California regularly make the trip. The 65 miles from San Diego, a common point of departure, are usually covered during the night, leaving you with almost a full day of diving before the anchors are pulled up and you start back for the mainland in late afternoon. With wonderfully calm water and the best water clarity in California, diving San Clemente is among California's (to many people, the world's) best diving.

Pyramid Cove is a common first stop. This sheltered natural cove at the extreme southern end of the island gradually slopes down into a huge forest of kelp. The clear, indigo-blue water and jumbled boulders make for good snorkeling or diving.

Pyramid Head High Spot, just 1/2-mile south of the point, is known for pinnacles that rise from the seafloor over 100' down to within 60' of the surface. The spectacular **Cathedral Rock**, a huge stone arch near the main pinnacle, is one of the reasons San Clemente is tops with photographers. Other reasons include yellowtail, schooling jack mackerel, barracuda, and black sea bass — any of which you might see along the east side. Sheltered by the high plateau of the island, the lee side presents the diver with calm water in all but the rare winter Santa Ana winds. Practically anywhere you can drop anchor on the east side offers good diving down the cliff face that drops to below 150' within only 50' of shore.

About one mile up from Pyramid Head, a curving outcropping of rocks, known variously as **Fishhook** or **Little Flower**, breaks the surface. With clarity that is often 100', these pinnacles make great backdrops for photography. For once, plant life steals the show. Iridescent blue algae and blue-tinted sargassum weed make a beautiful contrast to the yellow-orange of palm kelp. Giant kelp intermingles.

As you drop down the cliff face, the kelp continues. Looking up through the shifting light patterns of swaying kelp creates a feeling similar to gazing through the stained glass windows of Europe's famous cathedrals. Sandy ledges jut out from the cliff face and catch bits of coral or newly vacated shells. Caves and crevices extend back into the rock, and your lights reveal lobsters and morays hiding out among the branching corals. Schools of blacksmith dart and glide through the leaves, and sheephead sometimes swim right up to investigate you. Magenta nudibranches, adding their bit of color, slowly cruise along, as serene and confident as ocean liners. Elk kelp and the bizarre dwarf elk kelp can be seen on deep sandy bottoms around the east side.

Other good spots along this side include **Mosquito Cove** and **Wagon Tracks**. While the sea cliff seems to end in a sandy bottom at about 150', charts show enormous depth right offshore. Probably the cliffs continue plunging down far below the scuba range. All that endless space right below you gives diving here an especially awe-inspiring feeling.

The northwest end of the island shelters the ***John C. Butler***. Lying at about 100', the stern section of this former destroyer escort provides a haven for marine life. In the few years that have passed since the Navy blew the vessel in half during target practice (the bow lies somewhere out in the deep) the sea has claimed the wreck. Every square inch of metal is packed with life, from the pinks and oranges of anemones to red sea fans to blue and yellow encrusting animals. Fish swarm about the depth charges and baby lobster hide in the darkness of the cabins. The beautiful blue water makes the gaudy marine life seem especially color-saturated. Couple that with the clarity, which can exceed 110', and you have one of the most photogenic wrecks in California.

Castle Rock is an interesting rocky crater off the northwest tip of the island. Thought to be volcanic in origin, the crater is inhabited by purple hydrocoral as well as abalone and lobster. Depths don't fall much past 40'. Currents can get pretty strong on the outside, towards **Nine Fathom Reef**, almost one mile further out. Calico and kelp bass and an occasional white sea bass draw divers to the reef, about 60' deep. Purple hydrocoral also provides a lure. It's a real eye-dazzler when seen growing amidst big green anemones.

Since the west side has no shelter, it's only diveable on very calm days. Consequently, it sees far fewer people and so still shelters more game. Very thick kelp and a more gradually sloping bottom — 60' deep at 200 yards out — make the west side an entirely different diving experience.

China Point does offer some protection. Abalone and big lobsters hang out here, and around **Eel Point**. Thick kelp also shelters opaleye, calico bass, garibaldi, and giant kelpfish. An occasional huge black sea bass is reported; in fact, this is one of the few spots where you still stand a decent chance of meeting one of the huge beasts.

Pieces of the superstructure and engine from the **USS *Gregory*** lie in less than 20' of water between Mail Point and Lost Point. Since weather and surge usually make diving impossible, many artifacts can still be found on the rare calm days that the wreck is diveable. Like many sites in the Channel Islands and the southern part of California, the kelp bed in this area was almost destroyed by the storms of 1983 and the later warming of the water due to El Niño.

At **Seal Cove**, you might get to dive with some of the local residents, if they're in the mood. Unbelievably graceful underwater, they're as playful and curious as dogs, and quite a few divers have enjoyed watching them frolic in the dense kelp of the cove. More than a few have also had their catch swiped. Outside the cove, the bottom drops off and purple hydrocoral grows, especially in deeper waters where currents bathe it in planktonic food.

CORTES BANK

An immense area, actually the shallowest part of an oceanic ridge extending from San Miguel to San Clemente, protrudes from the ocean floor more than 100 miles west of San Diego. Depth over this region, known as **Cortes Bank**, ranges from 40' to beyond 120'. Huge rolling swells — often 20' high — strong currents, and terrific surge limit diving, understandably, to only the very experienced.

Rugged rocky spurs connected by gullies are covered with pinkish specimens of purple hydrocoral, but kelp and garibaldi are noticeable by their absence. Lobster apparently migrate in and out of the bank, since some years twitching antennae are everywhere, and other years they can't be found. Spiny dogfish and other sharks are very common, as are huge, tame sheephead (Mexican hookah divers used to work the area for abs and befriended them). Big black sea bass, *Mola mola*, and orcas have been seen. Sea lions swim out to take advantage of the thick schools of fish. **Tanner Bank**, 111 miles from San Diego, offers similar diving.

If you see a big lobster with a notched tail, don't disturb it. Lobstermen notch the tails of known "eggers" — extremely fertile females. Since the number of eggs a female releases can vary from 5000 to 100,000, depending on her size, lobstermen preserve the best breeders by marking and releasing them.

INLAND DIVING

It's not hard to understand why comparatively little freshwater diving goes on in the state of California. Combine the vertical orientation of the state with the fact that the vast majority of the population lives within only two or three hours of the coast, and you can see why inland diving gets overshadowed. Still, some great opportunities do exist for freshwater fanciers.

In northern California, **Lake Tahoe** is the most famous dive site. The high altitude and distance from recompression chambers require cautious diving. Use a capillary-action depth gauge, instead of the oil-type, since altitude diving requires very accurate depth readings as well as different repetitive tables.

D.L. Bliss State Park, near **Emerald Bay**, is one of the best areas, and is frequently used for checkouts. A white sand beach slopes down to 40', where a sand-covered wall drops off to 300'. About 200 yards south of the swimming area, the beach gives way to boulders, which lead out to the wall. You can see crayfish and occasional trout wandering around the boulders in the clear water — often past 100'. Since a thermocline exists, don't let the summer surface water temperature of 73° fool you — you'll need thermal protection.

Lake Shasta, near Redding, also draws some divers, although clarity varies greatly, depending on season and site. At **Lake Oroville**, water clarity ranges from 0-30'. A consistently clear area is on the middle fork, just below Feather Falls. Here a gravel and granite boulder-strewn bottom provides the opportunity to see many of California's interesting freshwater fish, including lavender suckers.

Many small lakes and streams in the foothills of the Sierras attract divers. The **Yuba River** with its clear, fast water and gravel bottom is the scene of a regular crayfish hunt. However, the higher the elevation, the greater is your chance of running into gold divers, who use hookah gear and dredging pumps to sort through the bottom gravel. Besides altering clarity for the worse, gold divers can also be quite zealous about protecting their claim.

In southern California, divers visit lakes around Los Angeles and San Diego. **Lake Perris** is one of the favorites. A state underwater park, Lake Perris is visited by more than 1000 divers annually, many on checkout dives. A specially designed habitat of concrete pipes can be difficult to locate if visibility is poor. Camping and day use facilities are available.

California laws concerning diving: Spearing is permitted for freshwater rough fish only in certain areas, with many species of sucker protected. Spearing for all fin fish in marine waters is subject to anglers' seasons and limits. Trout, salmon, striped bass, broadbill, black (giant) sea bass, garibaldi, and gulf and broomtail grouper are protected from spearing.

THE WEST

ARIZONA   COLORADO   IDAHO   MONTAN

When it comes to diving, the West is stll one of the last frontiers. An exciting feeling of exploration goes along with the thrill of the dive at many sites, especially at high altitude. Although the West is the most arid part of the United States, some surprisingly good diving can be found, often in beautiful mountain lakes or rushing trout streams. Geothermal springs, unique to this area, also add an interesting attraction. Cold water, high altitude, and remoteness from diving facilities are all problems the visiting diver will have to adjust to. Full 1/4" wetsuits are required for diving at almost every site, and the short summers of mountain country limit the diving season to only two or three months at the highest sites.

High altitude presents special problems that every diver needs to be aware of. Certain commonly practiced diving techniques, like diving to 50' or 60' without consulting charts, or ascending at the same rate as your small exhaust bubbles, can be dangerous at high altitude. ALWAYS PLAY IT ON THE SAFE SIDE IN ALTITUDE DIVING. USE ALTITUDE TABLES FOR EVERY DIVE, NO MATTER HOW SHALLOW. Ascent rates must be slower, dives must be shallower, and bottom time is much more limited. When you consider that most high altitude diving is in a remote location, far from any decompression chambers or knowledgeable hyberbaric physicians, you'll realize the extra degree of caution every altitude diver needs to use.

Local divers can be a big help in supplying tips and advice on altitude diving in their region. They can also be a source of altitude dive tables, and booklets designed to acquaint you with the special requirements of diving at high elevation. Since altitude dives are usually compounded by being cold water dives, use the next greatest depth when figuring no-decompression limits. Don't mix elevations in the same day. Remember that you may enter a repetitive group just by traveling to the dive site! And always check locally for exact elevations.

ARIZONA

Three-quarters of the surveys we received from Arizona reported on Mexico's Sea of Cortez, which Arizona's divers think of as their own backyard, since it's only about four hours' drive from the Phoenix area.

Having such an incredible dive site as the Sea of Cortez close by has put diving within the arid state itself to shame. The murky man-made reservoirs of Arizona fill quickly with silt and sediment with resulting low visibility. Compare that to the clear waters, rocky ledges, and fantastic marine life of the Sea of Cortez, and you'll understand why there isn't too much diving within Arizona's borders.

NEVADA   NEW MEXICO   UTAH   WYOMING

The best sites are **Lake Powell**, on the extreme northern border with Utah, and **Lake Mead**, in the northwest tip near Las Vegas, Nevada. Both of these lakes have interesting diving, with cave-pocked cliffs plunging to great depths and visibilities that average 25' in places. Since Lake Mead is mostly within Nevada, and Lake Powell (Glen Canyon Recreation Area) is mostly in Utah, extensive descriptions of these lakes can be found in our chapters on those states.

Ashhurst Lake in the Flagstaff area receives a few divers but many more fishermen, so watch out for boat traffic. **Lake Mary,** nearby, goes dry for part of the year. When it's wet, visibility ranges to 10' at best. Near Phoenix, **Saguaro Lake** is used for checkout dives, particularly for advanced classes that need murky water experience. Silt bottoms provide few interesting sights.

Arizona dive shops provide a great jumping-off place for trips to the Sea of Cortez, since they arrange trips there frequently and know the area well, often visiting such little-known and fascinating spots as Tortuga Island. Tortuga's beautifully colored cliffs and clear water supports an abundant marine life including jacks, turtles, large groupers, morays, manta rays, and diving birds.

Arizona laws concerning diving: Carp, buffalo, mullet, and suckers (except humpback suckers) may be taken by spear.

COLORADO

On August 9, 1981, Ralph Weeks and Thomas Christian set a world record (broken in 1984) in high altitude scuba at an unnamed Colorado lake where the elevation was 13,420' above sea level. The lake, near Breckenridge, averaged 20' deep. To reach it, the divers had to lug their equipment for three miles, gaining almost 2500' on the hike.

That says alot about diving in Colorado. If you're not used to high altitudes, you'll have enough of a problem just maintaining your normal energy level, without compounding it by breathing compressed air at depth.

If you are used to exertion at high altitude, and have a set of altitude tables handy, then Colorado has quite a few lakes and reservoirs that you can dive, including four reservoirs that have seasons for game fish spearing. Most Colorado diving, especially in the reservoirs, is characterized by low visibility.

In the Denver area there are several popular reservoirs that, typically, have set aside a certain area for diving. **Carter** (at 6000') is the favorite for diving close to Denver. **Jefferson**, near the town of the same name, is a little further out and a lot higher. Since mud bottoms characterize these reservoirs, clarity seldom exceeds

10-15'. Water temperatures in summer approach 60°. Both reservoirs are heavily used by boaters and skiers, making careful observation of diving regulations necessary. For instance, at Carter, you're limited to Dam 1, and then only after you've displayed your C-card at the marina.

For a dive that offers a little more privacy and much less commercialization, try **Tarryall Reservoir**, 20 miles southwest of Jefferson by dirt road. You'll see fewer people and more fish — mainly trout and northern pike — at this beautiful lake that offers great mountain scenery and clearer waters (up to 20'). Since this is a very high lake, with an unknown depth, most divers stay within the top 20'.

Horsetooth Reservoir, near Fort Collins, allows year-round spearing for game fish, but water clarity is usually terrible. You can find much better clarity in **Redfeather**, or one of the other natural lakes high in the mountains near Ft. Collins. June, July, and August are the only months these lakes are diveable, and fish are abundant (but protected). Depths average 30' and bottoms are silty.

Another lake that's also off the beaten path is **Pearl Lake**, 25 miles northwest of Steamboat Springs. Water clarity here is very good for Colorado (up to 25'), and an active trout, bluegill, and crayfish population keeps the dive interesting. Pearl Lake's elevation is approximately 8000'. The bottom slopes down gently to a small ledge before ending in mud and clay at 25' depth.

Also along the western slope of the Rockies, but much farther to the south, is **Blue Mesa Reservoir** in the Curecanti National Recreation Area. This is the largest lake in Colorado, with over 95 miles of shoreline. Since it's at an elevation of 8000', you'll need to use altitude-adjusted tables, and watch your depth, for this lake offers the opportunity to go deep. Night diving is one of the favorite activities here, with the possibility of swimming amidst thousands of sleep-dazed trout. Clarity is very poor in spring, especially so in years of heavy snowfall, and reaches 15' in midsummer.

Across the Rockies, in southeastern Colorado, is another favorite lake dive in the state, **Pueblo Reservoir.** Located five miles west of Pueblo in southern Colorado, this large reservoir (elevation 4900') has a maximum depth of about 90'. Clarity ranges from nothing to a high of 25', depending on how much boat traffic exists, and how much water they're withholding from the lake. Surface temperatures reach 70° in summer, and spearing is legal here for game fish during a restricted season.

One of the most beautiful lakes in Colorado is **San Isabel,** located high in the rugged mountains southwest of Pueblo. This natural lake is surrounded by National Forest, with camping available. You won't have to worry about the boat traffic so common to other Colorado lakes, since no motorized boating is allowed to destroy the tranquility of San Isabel. Easy beach entry leads you into the relatively clear waters, where visibility sometimes reaches 30', and the maximum depth is 65'.

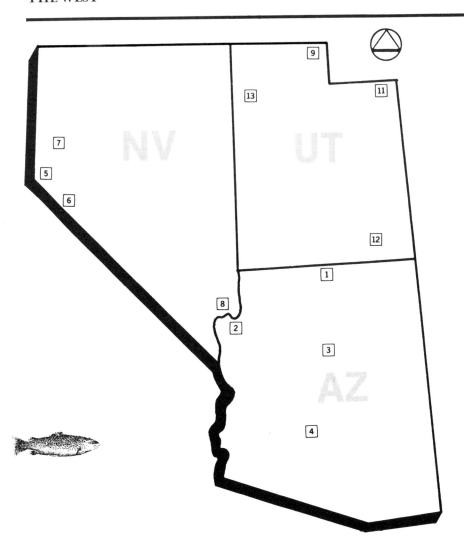

ARIZONA

Ashhurst Lake 3
Lake Mary 3
Lake Mead 2
Lake Powell 1
Saguaro Lake 4

UTAH

Bear Lake 9
Blue Lake 13
Cisco Beach 9
Fish Lake 10
Flaming Gorge .11
Glen Canyon Dam 12
Logan River 9
Tony Grove Lake 9

NEVADA

Boulder Beach 8
Donner Lake 6
Gold Lake 6
Kingman Wash .8
Lake Mead National Recreation Area . . .8
Lake Tahoe 5
Pyramid Lake 7
Ringbolt Rapids 8
Sand Harbor 5
Willow Beach 8

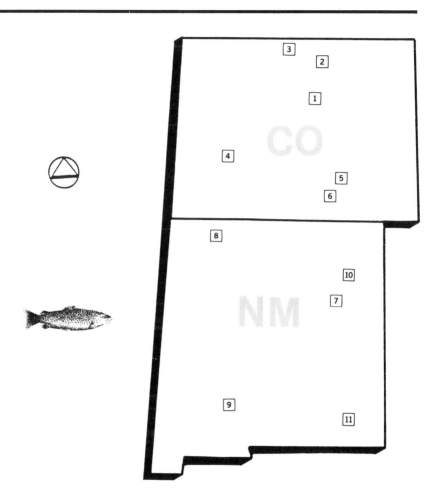

NEW MEXICO

Avalon 11
Blue Hole. 7
Caballo 9
Cochiti 11
Conchas 10
Elephant Butte. 9
Jackson 8
Lea 11
McMillan 11
Navajo Lake 8
Santa Rosa Lake 7
Sumner. 7
Twin Lakes 7
Ute 10

COLORADO

Blue Mesa Reservoir 4
Carter 1
Horsetooth Reservoir 2
Jefferson 1
Pearl Lake 3
Pueblo Reservoir 5
Redfeather 2
San Isabel 6
Tarryall Reservoir 1

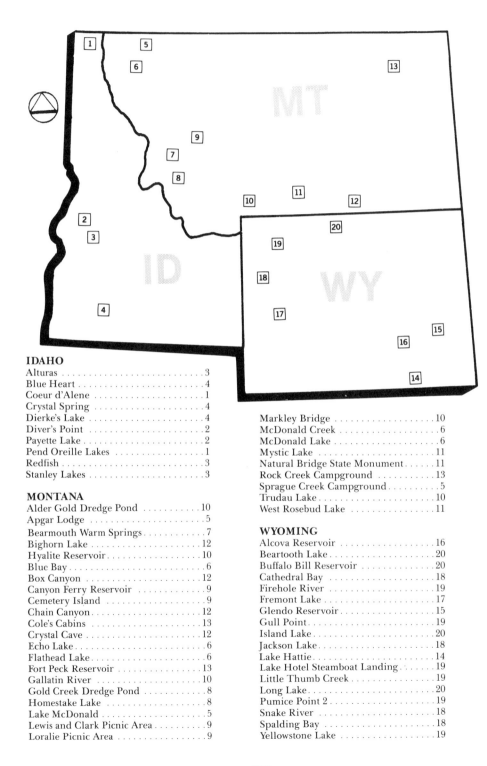

IDAHO
Alturas 3
Blue Heart 4
Coeur d'Alene 1
Crystal Spring 4
Dierke's Lake 4
Diver's Point 2
Payette Lake 2
Pend Oreille Lakes 1
Redfish 3
Stanley Lakes 3

MONTANA
Alder Gold Dredge Pond 10
Apgar Lodge 5
Bearmouth Warm Springs 7
Bighorn Lake .12
Hyalite Reservoir 10
Blue Bay 6
Box Canyon 12
Canyon Ferry Reservoir 9
Cemetery Island 9
Chain Canyon 12
Cole's Cabins 13
Crystal Cave .12
Echo Lake 6
Flathead Lake .6
Fort Peck Reservoir 13
Gallatin River 10
Gold Creek Dredge Pond 8
Homestake Lake 8
Lake McDonald 5
Lewis and Clark Picnic Area 9
Loralie Picnic Area 9

Markley Bridge 10
McDonald Creek 6
McDonald Lake 6
Mystic Lake .11
Natural Bridge State Monument 11
Rock Creek Campground 13
Sprague Creek Campground 5
Trudau Lake .10
West Rosebud Lake 11

WYOMING
Alcova Reservoir 16
Beartooth Lake 20
Buffalo Bill Reservoir 20
Cathedral Bay 18
Firehole River 19
Fremont Lake 17
Glendo Reservoir 15
Gull Point 19
Island Lake 20
Jackson Lake .18
Lake Hattie 14
Lake Hotel Steamboat Landing 19
Little Thumb Creek 19
Long Lake 20
Pumice Point 2 19
Snake River 18
Spalding Bay .18
Yellowstone Lake 19

Colorado laws concerning diving: Spearing is allowed for rough fish, except for rare and protected species. Game fish may be speared from July 16th to May 14th in Granby Reservoir, from July 16th to March 14th in Pueblo and Rifle Gap Reservoirs, and year-round in Horsetooth. Diver's flag is required.

IDAHO

Some of the finest diving in the West is found in the beautiful clear mountain lakes and trout-filled springs of Idaho. In fact, the state contains so many natural alpine lakes that the residents greatly prefer them for diving to the man-made reservoirs, which are mainly used for irrigation, and where visibility and water levels vary. All diving in Idaho is altitude diving, so be sure to refresh your memory on altitude tables. Maximum summer water temperatures are 65°, so bring a 1/4" wetsuit. Diving season in the higher mountain lakes generally runs from July to September.

The panhandle country of northern Idaho surrounds two famous resort lakes. **Coeur d'Alene** and **Pend Oreille Lakes** are vast (22 and 43 miles long, respectively) bodies of water, tucked into grooves between the mountains. The evergreens pour down the slopes and stop abruptly at the water's edge. With miles of shoreline, including many deserted inlets and coves, the lakes are home to kokanee salmon, bass, and trout. Both lakes attract divers from the Spokane area, approximately 35 miles away in Washington, which is the closest place to find air and rentals. Small resort towns nestle into the valleys beside each lake, and offer just enough civilized life to counterbalance the miles of surrounding forest. Visibilities at these lakes are outstanding. At Pend Oreille, which is the deepest freshwater lake west of the Mississippi, visibility often is better than 50'. However, the lakes were dusted by Mount Saint Helens so a layer of fine ash on the bottom can destroy clarity.

Payette Lake, near McCall, in the center of the state, is one of the most popular lakes for diving due to its fantastic bottom contours. At **Diver's Point**, a huge rock lies like a beached whale. On one side, the rock face gradually slopes down while the other side drops off steeply to below 100'. The varying bottom of this lake surprises you every time you get in. You can descend between two sheer cliff faces to 80', and swim out towards the middle of the lake, only to run into a rock wall that rises to about 35' and levels out into a plateau before it drops back down again. Much interesting exploration can be done in the lake, which usually has a stable visibility of about 20-30'. Since this rugged country gets more snowfall than any other inhabited region of Idaho, spring comes late to Payette Lake.

For the really adventurous, there's a series of high mountain lakes in the Sawtooth recreational area in the middle of the state. These beautiful small lakes nestled among wooded slopes that rise into high gigantic crags, many above 10,000', can be reached fairly easily by road through the town of Stanley. The views have been made famous by Sun Valley, just 40 miles to the south. **Alturas, Redfish**, and **Stanley Lakes** are the most accessible. Fewer people and a lot more trout invite adventurous divers to join the backpackers and fishermen who've already discovered these mountain gems. Visibility in summer is usually 40-60'. Depths taper to plateaus along some shorelines before plummeting to unmeasured distances. Schools of trout and squawfish make these lakes great for photography, and camping is available in the thousands of acres of primitive mountain wilderness surrounding the lakes. The average summer water temperature is 58°, and the dive season doesn't really start until July.

Just three miles east of Twin Falls is another popular spot, **Dierke's Lake**. Shallow depths (about 35') and lots of aquatic plants and several sunken boats support an incredible population of bluegills, bass, trout, and crappie. With visibility of about 15', this is the spot for a relaxed dive of fishwatching and close-up fish portraits. The city of Twin Falls manages a park on the shore, which is closed on Mondays. A lot of Idaho divers get their early spring and late fall diving in Dierke's Lake.

The Thousand Springs area, just west of Twin Falls on the Snake River, is so named because an underground aquifer bursts forth from the canyon walls. **Blue Heart** is one of the most popular dives in the state, with a constant year-round temperature of 58°. Since the shallow, two-acre pool only drops to 15', scuba isn't essential, but it's nice to spend all your time on an eye-level with the rainbow and golden trout that thrive in the crystal clear water. A dive platform makes things easy; boat traffic presents the only problem.

Crystal Spring is another fantastic nearby dive. This area raises about 80% of all the commercial trout eaten in the U.S. You'll believe the majority come from this spring-fed pond (a little smaller and not quite as clear as Blue Heart — only 100' clarity!) when you see the swarms of rainbows, which average five pounds. Depth ranges from 15-20'. The good news is there's no boat traffic in Crystal Spring; the bad news is it takes a 1/4-mile hike to reach it.

Many wonder about diving in the Snake River itself. Unless you like maximum visibilities of about 6" and terrible currents, we can't recommend the portion of the river that is within Idaho. However, a portion of the Snake that runs through Grand Teton National Park is reportedly a fantastic current dive — see the section on Wyoming for details. And **Brownlee** and some of the other reservoirs vary tremendously. You have to hit it just right to get any visibility at all. If you do go on a good day, you'll probably see lots of huge crayfish.

Idaho laws concerning diving: Spearing is allowed for rough fish only, during the open season on game fish. No spearing of game fish is permitted.

MONTANA

The Montana state bureaucracy was amused to receive our inquiry about diving in Montana. Most states responded to our request on information about suitable diving areas and state laws concerning diving with lots of glossy pictures and travel-agent style brochures. Not Montana. They sent our request to the state historical librarian, who seemed both incredulous that anyone would be ignorant enough to ask, and irritated that he had to be the one to answer. (Obviously not an outdoor type.) "Since Montana waters are frozen solid for the better half of the year, interest in diving is not what it would be in Florida." He then suggested that we contact the search and rescue diving units of the various sheriffs' offices, who were responsible for "most of the diving done here."

Since we assumed no one would be interested in pulling dead bodies out of Montana waters on their vacation, we didn't contact the sheriffs' offices. However, we did come across a much more reliable source — *Dive Sites in and around Montana*, by the Montana Dive Council. Not only do people dive in Montana, they dive in some very interesting and adventurous places, ranging from clear Lake McDonald in the beautiful Glacier National Park, to rushing trout streams, to hot-spring ponds that sustain tropical fish year-round.

WEST OF THE CONTINENTAL DIVIDE

But **Lake McDonald** in Glacier National Park of northwest Montana is usually mentioned first when people are talking about Montana dive sites. As in all park diving, you need to notify the ranger first; Apgar Visitor Center is the place to do it. Roughly ten miles into the park, you'll see easy highway access to the lake just past the **Sprague Creek Campground**. The rock and sand bottom drops off steeply about 10' out from the shoreline, then levels off at 65'. A few plants dot the white sand bottom, and rumor has it that still-standing trees are submerged somewhere in this vicinity. Clarity is 40' or better.

The **Apgar Lodge** area is another favorite dive site on Lake McDonald. Like all other Montana sites, the water is cold: from 55° to 60°. But the clarity is outstanding, with 50' of visibility, and there's much to see. Within the lake, an equipment cache of shovels, axes, stoves, etc. gives you a feel for the mining history of the region.

If you're more interested in natural history, then take a tour of **McDonald Creek** by zooming out of Lake McDonald and down the creek. Current divers will find a fascinating dive (flight would be more accurate) down the 10-15'-deep channel. In late September and October, thousands of salmon spawn in the creek, attracting eagles and even grizzly bears, and so the creek is closed during this period. However, late summer trips usually give you a chance to zoom up on one of the advance salmon schools, hanging motionless in the current, only to watch them flash downstream before you. Lures can be found in the rocks under the Camas Creek Bridge, .15 of a mile downstream. This is the takeout, so don't continue past this first bridge. Other than the current speed, occasional snags will be the only hazard.

Other dive sites in northwest Montana include **Echo Lake**, just east of Kalispell, where northern pike, pumpkinseed, and yellow perch swim through the vegetation-choked bottom. Clarity in this 15'-deep fishbowl reaches 20' at best. Just to the southeast of Kalispell is **Flathead Lake**; one of the best shore sites is found at **Blue Bay.** Newcomers to western diving are often surprised by the small tropical-looking fish common at this site and others — they're salmon fry! A very sloping bottom leads gradually out to a shelf that drops at a 45° angle. The best diving is about 35' deep, where clarity averages 15'. Boat diving will open up other interesting dives in Flathead, like Bird Island.

A boat will also come in handy if you want to dive **McDonald Lake**, near Ronan, in the Mission Mts. (Don't confuse this with Lake McDonald at Glacier Park — this small lake is located in the Flathead Reservation between Kalispell and Missoula.) Since this is Indian land, you'll need to get a land-use permit from a sporting goods store in Ronan or any of the larger towns. An incredibly precipitous bottom is the highlight of this dive, which includes plunging cliffs, jumbled boulders, shelves, canyons, and rockslides. Jim and Mary Chester of the Montana Dive Council report: "An incredible dive! Try flying off the cliffs, climbing a standing submerged tree, or swimming under perched boulders. Trout everywhere. When clarity is good, (it ranges from 15-35') perhaps the best dive site in Montana." Use a boat to dive off the cliffs one mile up on the south side, and be prepared for water that ranges from 45° on the bottom to 58° on the surface.

Two very different dive sites just off I-90 are a potent lure for travellers between Missoula and Butte. **Bearmouth Warm Springs** is about 1-1/2 miles west of the Bearmouth exit. A small waterfall on the right is visible from the highway, and a dirt road offers adjacent parking. Here you'll find warm, clear water (71° in July), colorful fish, and an air-filled cave. Travertine cliffs surround the white sand and bright moss of the pool. Since depth is approximately 10', snorkeling is common.

The other dive in this area, **Gold Creek Dredge Pond**, just three miles south of Gold Creek, is found by looking for the wreckage of a dredge in the field to the left. And, as might be expected, this dive is primarily for those interested in artifacts and in exploring machinery underwater. Clarity averages 10' and depth goes to 27'.

Artifact hunters will also be interested in **Homestake Lake**, lying just off I-90, near Butte, exactly on the Continental Divide. This small pond, formerly an ice pond for the Northern Pacific Railroad, is 15' deep, with almost no visibility and thick algae in late summer, but that won't deter bottle hunters.

The young of a species of octopus, observed near Honolulu, fasten bits of Portugese man-o-war to their arms. They use them to help capture prey until they are full-grown, and able to capture food on their own.

EAST OF THE CONTINENTAL DIVIDE

Canyon Ferry Reservoir, near Helena, is an immense impoundment of the Missouri River that offers some decent shore dives, such as **Lewis and Clark Picnic Area**, and **Loralie Picnic Area.** Clarity attains a high of 15' in spring and fall at these sites; the sandy bottom is broken by occasional rocks, and it slopes gradually at each site before dropping off further out. If a boat is available, **Cemetery Island** is the preferred site. Some areas, particularly the southwest end, are known for more vertical rock faces. Wind and boat traffic can make life difficult; talk to local divers for tips. Crayfish and schools of perch are common.

The Bozeman area is the center for some very interesting dives. **Markley Bridge** is a private bridge across the **Gallatin River** near Big Sky. A U-shaped hole in the riverbed, 10' deep, is covered with rocks and cobblestones. Large trout hide in the shade of the bridge, and lures collect on the rocks near shore. Clarity approaches 10'. Due to the speed of the current, this is one of the few holes that is diveable.

The **Blackmore Creek arm of the Hyalite Reservoir,** just south of Bozeman, is an interesting dive as much for the underwater scenery as for the fish life. Near the mouth of the creek a large, angular basalt block lies over some caves and a submerged creek bed that is 60-75' deep, depending on the amount of water in the reservoir. You can find an old bridge, still intact, by following the creek bed. You might also get a chance to see the rare and ripply-finned Arctic grayling.

At the **Alder Gold Dredge Pond**, the highlights are large brown trout and the possibility of finding mining artifacts among the remains of what was the world's largest gold dredge. Get permission from the KOA campground on the southeast edge of Alder to dive this flat and shallow pond.

But the favorite dive in this area of the state is undoubtedly **Trudau Lake**, near Alder. Talk to local divers about this one, as it is on private property, and the owners have excellent relations with local divers, who want to keep it that way. This is a steep-sided sink, with walls of the light limestone called travertine. Springs bubble up from the 15'-deep bottom. Swordtails and mollies have joined the native longnose dace, and thrive in the warm water (60° in December, 70° in June) and lush vegetation. In summer, access is easy, but in winter, divers ski cross-country for up to three miles through the snow for the chance to loll in the crystal water of this natural hot tub.

Anyone this far south in Montana shouldn't miss some of the exciting diving in Yellowstone Park. For details, see the chapter on Wyoming.

Another nearby (in Montana terms) site is **Mystic Lake**, which probably offers some of the most beautiful scenery in the world, since you have to hike three miles up an incredibly steep trail to reach this extremely high lake. (The reporter for this site suggests you get a horse to pack your gear.) The view alone is worth it, and the dive makes it doubly so. The rocky bottom slopes gently to 42', and the entire lake has great scenery and clarity of 30'.

West Rosebud Lake, on the same mountain road south of Fishtail, offers an easier access, with a walk of only 30'. Entry is off the northwest shore, depth is no more than 26', clarity averages 15', water temperatures are cold (rarely above 50°), and this is a good place to learn the differences between rainbow, brown, and brook trout, since they are all residents, along with whitefish.

Anyone traveling east of Bozeman on I-90 should make an effort to visit **Natural Bridge State Monument**, to the south, off Big Timber. A 1/4-mile hike on a steep trail will lead you to the spectacular scene of a 120' waterfall plunging into a hole of about 18' that has been cut by the force of the waterfall. Many trout lurk amidst the huge boulders, and clarity is good (20-30') considering the force of the water. Don't dive this pool in high water, or you'll be swept away.

Further east, in the Bighorn Canyon National Recreation Area, divers enjoy several steep canyon sites on **Bighorn Lake.** One site, near the Ok-A-Beh boat ramp, is known as **Crystal Cave.** About 200 yards along the cliff left of the boat ramp are two large caves, 60' down. Neither goes back more than 20', and one contains small crystals. Clarity averages 20', and water temperature was recorded at 60° in October.

To dive **Chain Canyon**, check ahead with the Park Service Visitor Center in Lovell, Wyoming, to make sure the gate on the dirt road from Barry's Landing to the canyon is open. In places the canyon is narrow enough to touch both walls. The vertical walls drop to 120', so watch your depth, and block the canyon mouth with a dive flag to lower the risk from boat traffic.

Box Canyon is accessible only by boat from Ok-A-Beh, but its sheer rock walls, large carp, crappie, and ling all make it worth the trip. Clarity in spring and fall can attain 60'! Use caution around caves in the walls, don't go too deep, and obtain permission first from the ranger at the Ok-A-Beh boat ramp.

Way up in northeast Montana, near Glasgow, you can dive **Fort Peck Reservoir** at either **Cole's Cabins** or the **Rock Creek Campground.** Both sites are easily accessible by foot. The attractions are fossils, geodes, freshwater mussels, and legal spearing for game fish; the drawbacks are almost no clarity, strong winds, and the rapid onset of bad storms, even in summer.

Montana laws concerning diving: Spearing is permitted for rough fish only, and only in certain areas. Check locally.

NEVADA

If the only diving in Nevada were found at Lake Tahoe, the state would contain some of the best freshwater diving in the country. As it is, Nevada has several other interesting dives in the mountains around Reno, as well as in the gigantic Lake Mead playground near Las Vegas.

But **Lake Tahoe** is undoubtedly the best. This incredible place, the "Gem of the Sierra," is world famous for its beautiful setting 6,200' up in the forested mountains, and, more importantly for divers, for its pristine waters whose clarity often surpasses 60-80'. **Sand Harbor** is probably the best place to dive the Nevada side of Tahoe (for sites on the California side see the chapter on California inland diving), since there you can experience a variety of shallow diving (20-30') over the clean, boulder-strewn sand. And further out, past the crayfish, driftwood, and jumbled boulders, you come to a vertical wall that drops off to about 900'.

Since Tahoe has 75 miles of shoreline, there's plenty of room to explore for those who want to get away from the crowds and commercialization. Lots of boulder-rimmed inlets still exist where you can have the deep blue water mainly to yourself. Tahoe offers an astonishing variety of diving, from easy little coves perfect for snorkeling over the bright sand, to immense vertical cliffs that plummet to below 1,200'. Since elevation is 6,200' and those walls do seem to entice you ever deeper, it is imperative that you refresh your memory on high altitude dive tables and watch your dive time and depths carefully. Reno dive shops will be glad to inform you. The best season for diving Tahoe is August, September, and October. Water temperatures on the surface in these months range from 56-60°, with only about 52° at 30' down. Winter temperatures generally are about 39°. Early summer visibilities can drop to around 30' if it's been a wet winter with lots of snow and rain runoff.

Another favorite of Reno divers is **Donner Lake.** While its clarity is only fair (about 15-20'), Donner has a lot of driftwood and freshwater clams to be found on its silt bottom that slopes down to around 250'. **Gold Lake**, another high altitude (6,200') lake about 70 miles from Reno, is a very interesting dive. Meadows of bright green water grass and other vining aquatic plants, together with freshwater sponges, make Gold Lake seem almost oceanic. Clarity averages 15'.

Only the hardcore ichthyologist or artifact hunter will want to visit **Pyramid Lake**, in the middle of the Paiute Reservation, since its visibilities are very poor and surface winds can cause some bad currents. However, for these specialists, a chance of sighting the cui-ui, a prehistoric fish found only in this lake, or finding an artifact from the Indian culture that prospered here for thousands of years, makes the rough conditions worthwhile.

Manatees, thought to be the origin of the mermaid legend, are the gentlest parents in nature, cuddling and nursing their calves incessantly for the first two years of life.

The huge **Lake Mead National Recreation Area**, near Las Vegas, has become a mecca for western divers. Staffed by helpful and extremely knowledgable park rangers, who have prepared a brochure listing dive sites and air sources, the area offers a wide variety of diving experiences. Actually, two lakes are included: the huge, 450'-deep Lake Mead itself, with over 550 miles of shoreline, and Lake Mojave, (often simply called the Colorado River in its upper stretches) which pours from the base of Hoover Dam and offers some excellent current diving in its upper 15 miles.

Even within Lake Mead, there are a great variety of sites, ranging from wide gravel-strewn beaches to awesome canyon wall dives reached only by boat. Big stripers, crappie, and catfish frequent the shallow rocky ledges. **Boulder Beach** and **Kingman Wash** are both easy access shore dives with good fish life and good clarity, which ranges from a winter high of 60' or more to a summer average of 25'. Don't let the summer surface temperatures of 90° fool you; thermoclines do exist and will make a wetsuit jacket come in handy for dives deeper than 30'. Since the air temperature in summer reaches 120°, a common problem is overheating, so get in and out of your suit in a hurry.

For dives in Lake Mojave below the dam, a wetsuit is indispensable, since water gushes out of the bottom of Hoover with a usual temperature of 52°. Rapids runners will find **Willow Beach** a moving experience, especially when the dam is dumping. Gliding through the tree-lined river channel in the current of 8-10 mph is guaranteed to be exciting. A boat wreck and much fish life in the generally clear water (30-50') gives you lots to do in the slow spells. Besides the usuals like carp, bass, and trout, you might see some real rarities like the endangered (and legally protected) Colorado squawfish or the aptly named humpback sucker.

An especially narrow canyon four miles below Hoover contains a section known as **Ringbolt Rapids**, after the bolts in the canyon walls that were used to winch paddlewheelers upriver. This is for the really adventurous only, or others who enjoy what one ranger referred to as "diving in a washing machine."

Rumors have circulated for years about mysterious springs deep in Death Valley that are supposedly bottomless. Devil's Hole, within the Death Valley National Monument, is the probable origin of these stories. In the past, divers explored this huge flooded cave. Due to a number of deaths, as well as the discovery that this is the only habitat on earth for the Devil's Hole pupfish, diving is now outlawed at Devil's Hole.

Nevada laws concerning diving: Spearing is allowed only for rough fish; no spearing in Lake Tahoe or certain other lakes. There are many rare protected species of sucker, chub, and dace, particularly in the Colorado River system.

NEW MEXICO

Besides the bizarre and breathtaking Blue Hole, New Mexico has other attractions for divers, like eleven lakes where it's legal to spear game fish.

But it's **Blue Hole** in Santa Rosa that takes the prize for best dive in New Mexico. This spring-fed grotto has a diameter of about 60' which then bells out to approximately 120' diameter at 40' down. Maximum depth is reached at 80', with a grate covering the cavernous mouth. Spring water at a temperature of 64° pours into the rock grotto at a rate of about 5000 gallons per minute. Divers from all over flock here to enjoy the beautiful setting. On a weekday, you can see the bottom while you're suiting up, but on weekends the clarity is much worse, because too many divers have flippered around the silt. About 15 golden carp share the site with divers. A city permit, good for an entire year, is required at a cost of $5.00. Besides stairs on the south side, the city has also built a platform for easy entry on the east edge. Showers, bathrooms, camping, and all the luxuries of the town of Santa Rosa are available to traveling divers. The origin of Blue Hole is still a mystery, but some theorize that it may share an underground connection with Carlsbad Caverns, almost 250 miles away. As many as 100 divers may crowd into Blue Hole on summer weekends. Overhanging rocks and the altitude (Santa Rosa is about 4300') present the only problems.

If it's too crowded for you, ask locally about diving conditions at nearby **Santa Rosa Lake**. It's only about 15 miles from Blue Hole, and since it's only been filled for a few years, it hasn't yet been thoroughly explored. **Twin Lakes**, also near Santa Rosa, are rumored to be opening for scuba, after being closed for many years.

Navajo Lake, near Farmington, is one of the most popular lake dives in New Mexico. Located in the northwest corner of the state, Navajo Lake is still yielding artifacts of its namesakes. To even more divers it yields spearing catchs of bass, catfish, crappie, perch, northern pike, and kokanee salmon. Some eroded rock formations and shallow caves provide scenic interest, and at least one wreck can be explored. Depths go below 360'. Visibility occasionally attains 30', especially in winter. Temperatures at the surface are 75° in the summer and 33° in the winter.

Other lakes where spearing is permitted for game fish include: **Jackson**, also in northwestern New Mexico and, for over 20 years, the host to a January 1st ice dive; **Elephant Butte** and **Caballo**, near Las Cruces; **Conchas** and **Ute**, near Tucumcari; **Sumner**, west of Clovis; and **Cochiti, Avalon, McMillan**, and **Lea**, in the southern part of the state. Lea is one of the Bottomless Lakes in the southeast corner of the state, so-called because the early pioneers couldn't gauge the depths. Today, you still can't touch bottom using scuba, but you can enjoy the rock sheer dropoffs. Like most New Mexico lakes, visibility is usually limited, averaging 15' in summer, and thermoclines do exist, making thermal protection necessary.

According to some marine biologists, the animal life of a kelp bed is as diverse as that of a rain forest.

New Mexico laws concerning diving: Spearing is legal for rough fish in all waters, for game fish in eleven lakes specified in text. License and bag limits same as anglers. Dive flag is required. Solo diving is prohibited; buddy team must have qualified surface tender.

UTAH

The diverse state of Utah has just as much variety when it comes to diving, ranging from a geothermal oasis in the desert to a high mountain lake filled with albino trout to the Bonneville cisco, a small fish native only to one lake in northeastern Utah.

Bear Lake is the home of the rare Bonneville cisco. This natural lake of 114 square miles is a favorite spot for divers. **Cisco Beach** on the east side offers the best access into the most interesting part of the lake. About 50 yards offshore, a dropoff angles down to 210'. Since the elevation is about 6000', diving below 60' is not recommended. Fish abound, including large mackinaw (lake trout) of over 40 pounds. Those interested enough to brave January temperatures can easily spot the Bonneville cisco as swarms of the small smeltlike fish rise to spawn. Ice divers find Bear Lake ideal, both for all the interesting fish life and because visibility under the ice improves to about 40'. In summer the visibility drops to 10-20' due to algae blooms and calcium precipitate, but the temperature increases to 68°.

Another favorite spot in this section of extreme northeastern Utah is **Tony Grove Lake.** Located up the beautiful Logan Canyon with its 3,500-year-old junipers, Tony Grove sits at an altitude of approximately 8000'. Since the lake's maximum depth is about 45', you won't be tempted to go too deep. Visibility in the cold water is good, usually about 35', and the water has that alpine sparkle to it that makes it seem much clearer. The thing that sets this lake apart from all the other pretty mountain lakes in Utah is that Tony Grove has a sizeable population of albino trout. You stand a good chance of seeing a pinkish or white fish on every dive. Apparently the population has become so inbred in the lake that the albinism gene is common. The albino trout don't seem to be handicapped by their strange lack of coloration. Freshwater sponges flourish here too. Night dives are popular in the **Logan River** for those who like the feel of flying.

Another of Utah's small, high lakes is **Fish Lake**, located in the center of the state just south of Richfield. This one deserves special mention because it's one of only two places in Utah where it's legal to spear game fish. And it's aptly named. Fish thrive, especially rainbow. Visibility sometimes reaches 45'. However, like nearly all other high elevation lakes in the Rockies, the water is cold — you need a 1/4" wetsuit, and you can't usually get in until the end of July.

Two man-made reservoirs draw many divers. One, **Flaming Gorge**, located in northeastern Utah north of Vernal, is set in a spectacular canyon of vivid red and orange-brown rock. The water appears intensely blue in contrast to the bright

earthy-colored canyon walls. Visibility averages 10-15' and depths far exceed scuba range. Boats can present a hazard, so stick with your diver's flag. A large population of fish usually provides some underwater entertainment.

The other impoundment is Lake Powell, created by the **Glen Canyon Dam** on the Colorado. Environmentalists vigorously opposed the building of this dam. Since its construction, scuba divers alone can see the beautiful canyon that's now submerged. This is one of the world's biggest lakes — its 1800 miles of shoreline exceed that of the West Coast of the U.S. — and it is shared with Arizona. Besides the cold water and high altitude hazards which are common throughout the West, divers also need to watch out for the main current of the Colorado River. Check with local ranger stations for current information. The only air available at Lake Powell is found at Wahweap Marina. It's in the Bullfrog area that the greatest concentration of underwater Indian ruins are found. Even though they've been submerged, they are still rigorously protected by the National Park Service, which administers the Glen Canyon area. Numerous caves in the red rock walls also present an underwater attraction to divers, but they are unsafe for those not trained in cave diving. Fantastic scenery of eroded red cliffs and spectacular overhangs creates good photographs. Also, many large mackinaw and other fish, including largemouth bass, might be glimpsed in Lake Powell. Below the thermocline at 25', temperatures are 65°. Clarity ranges from 20-30'.

Finally, we come to what is one of the most unique dives in the West. **Blue Lake**, south of Wendover in extreme western Utah, almost on the Nevada border, is a true oasis in the desert. This geothermal lake maintains a constant surface temperature of 68-72°. In the inlets, the temperature can be in excess of 90°. Swimming over the bottom at 50' depth, you can see the water bubbling out of the sand in hot spots reminiscent of Yellowstone. Visibility is highly dependent on how many divers are present; on a typically crowded weekend in winter, it may be 15-20', while on a summer weekday it will improve to about 40'. Winter is the favorite season, naturally. Getting out to the lake can be more difficult in early spring when the flats around are marshy, but in wintertime the frozen ground makes for an easy trip. Besides lolling in the unexpected warmth of a natural hot tub, you can watch bass and bluegill and sunfish, who seem to enjoy the warmth too. Boats are no problem, since Blue Lake isn't navigable.

Many people express interest in diving the Great Salt Lake. Apparently they've never tried to submerge themselves here — because of the high salt content, it's very difficult to get down! And even if you could weight yourself enough, the salinity would be hell on your gear.

Utah laws concerning diving: With a spearfishing permit, the waters of Deer Creek Reservoir and Fish Lake are open to the taking of two trout per day by spear. Season is June 1st through September 15th. Rough fish may be speared anywhere angling is legal. Diver's flag is required.

WYOMING

Wyoming is really the Wild West when it comes to diving. Beautiful small mountain lakes at extremely high elevations, big reservoirs, and the fantastic opportunities of the Yellowstone country are the highlights. Since diving will invariably be cold water at high altitude, refresh your memory on the altitude tables.

Near Laramie are several interesting lakes, of which **Lake Hattie**, just 15 minutes west of Laramie, is representative. Since its elevation (like most of Wyoming's diving lakes) is 7000-8000', altitude tables are essential. In the deepest section, the small alpine lake reaches 60', but the average depth is 30'. Visibility, best in July after the water turnover and before the plankton bloom of August, can reach 60'. Crayfish, trout, and friendly perch abound.

Glendo Reservoir, east of Casper, has several nice access points through coves. A silty bottom means clarity won't be as good as it is at the natural lakes. **Alcova Reservoir**, west of Casper, is another popular dive area, with camping nearby.

Fremont Lake, four miles north of Pinedale in west-central Wyoming, is the second largest natural lake in the state. Fremont Lake is 12 miles long and a half a mile wide. It's a popular site for swimmers and fishermen, with abundant mackinaw and rainbow trout. Water clarity can be excellent unless there is too much traffic in the lake. Since Fremont is deep, and at a high elevation of at least 8000', you need to watch your altitude tables carefully.

The **Snake River** in Grand Teton National Park is "a must for all water people" according to Neal Langerman's article in the Underwater Society's "Underwater Reporter." He reports that you can take a slow drift from Jackson Lake Dam to the Cattleman's Bridge in about two hours, and you will "see more trout than you ever believed existed." Other than cold, this dive presents no hazards. **Jackson Lake** itself is good diving, with clarity of up to 40' due to the rock bottom. **Cathedral Bay** and **Spalding Bay** are the most popular areas.

And, if you're willing to brave the tourist hordes, you'll find some fascinating (but cold) diving in Yellowstone National Park. **Yellowstone Lake** is the largest lake in North America above 7000', and its clarity is usually good, at least 20'. Since its maximum depth is more than 250', diving areas must be chosen carefully. The **Little Thumb Creek** area, just north of West Thumb, has an easy entry off a spit of land just past the creek. Thick vegetation, including floating balloon-like *Nostoc* algae, covers the gradually sloping bottom, until at about 300' out, a steep slope drops off, marked with many small caves, pinnacles, and thermal springs. Sometimes huge schools of trout are attracted to this area, where the primary danger is the possibility of going too deep. Boats, and the cold water (40° on the bottom) also require cautious diving. Notification of the ranger at Grant Village is also necessary — Jim and Mary Chester, who filed the report on this dive, suggest you inform them you are going, and show your C-card, rather than asking their permission.

Other areas of Yellowstone Lake suitable for diving include **Gull Point**, where fishing lures are abundant on a gravelly bottom (notify Lake Ranger District); **Lake Hotel Steamboat Landing**, where the remnants of the pier on a shallow bottom provide interesting but protected artifacts (same ranger district); and **Pumice Point 2,** where easy access at the picnic area leads out into a slightly hilly, silty bottom, interrupted by very warm little bubbling geysers! The aquatic life at this site consists of freshwater sponges, floating algae balls, and little worms struggling against the current at the point. Clarity averages 30', and depth doesn't exceed 35'. Notify the ranger at Grant Village of your dive.

For a really exciting dive, try the "Swimming Hole" of the **Firehole River.** It's about two miles from the start of the Firehole Loop, and you'll recognize the site by the man-made rock wall, the bearproof garbage cans, and by the still, wide appearance of the river, caused by a downstream obstruction. Here the river is forced between sheer cliffs, where it has cut a 30' hole. Enter over the cliffs on the downstream side, then climb out over the cliffs on the upstream side. The current will send you flying over the gravelly bottom, where you might sweep past caves, cutthroat trout, or even items dropped by swimmers. The rapid current and overhanging cliffs present possible hazards, so don't try this dive unless you're experienced with current diving. The water temperature can reach 70° in summer, and clarity varies wildly. Inform the Madison Junction Ranger of your dive plans.

There are many other high lake dives for the adventurous in northwestern Wyoming, including **Long Lake, Buffalo Bill Reservoir**, and **Island Lake.** Drive about 30 miles southwest of Red Lodge on Beartooth Highway to reach Island Lake, where camping and improvements are available. The lake drops to 48', but the best diving is around the island at 30', where huge boulders and rocky outcroppings promise a beautiful dive. Clarity is best in fall, reaching 30'. Extreme altitude and cold must be reckoned with.

Beartooth Lake, at the top of Beartooth Pass, also presents altitude hazards, as well as the hazards of boaters and fishermen. A Forest Service Campground has restrooms and drinking water. Many lures and friendly fish can be spotted in the shallow, plant-filled area, which drops off about 100 yards out to a depth of 85'. Clarity ranges from 15' in summer to 40' in fall, and the temperature on the bottom is 40° in July!

Wyoming laws concerning diving: Spearing for fish is legal only in certain areas from June 1st to August 31st. Dive flag is required.

THE GULF STATES

BRUNDAGE

ALABAMA   LOUISIANA

To many people, fish are the reason for diving. Whether you want to catch your dinner, or take a great grouper portrait, or just experience the excitement of swimming in their midst, it's hard to beat fish life for providing underwater interest.

And for concentration of fish — big fish — few places in the U.S. can match the oil rigs of the Gulf Coast. While diving amidst steel, cable, and geometric man-made structures may not thrill you, diving into a school of inquisitive 50-lb. amberjacks should.

For the scenic purist, there're the Flower Gardens, the Gulf of Mexico's little-visited tropical coral reef. Like many other Gulf sites, this is for the advanced diver, with open ocean conditions, occasional tricky currents, and extreme depths. Unpredictable weather makes it necessary to plan offshore trips ahead, leaving some extra time in case the notorious Gulf weather interferes. The reward is an unforgettable visit to the most unique coral reef anywhere.

Anytime, though, is a good time for freshwater diving in Texas or Alabama. Indian and Civil War relics, fish-watching on sheer underwater cliffs, and beautiful aquarium plants all lure divers into the inland waters.

ALABAMA

Alabama is the only state in the U.S. whose fresh water offers more to the diver than its salt water does. To those who think of Alabama as nothing more than cotton fields, the state will offer some surprises, like deep, reasonably clear reservoirs and quarries, and fast rivers where even today Civil War relics can be found.

Some of the best diving in Alabama has to be in the northern section, near Muscle Shoals. Dams on the Tennessee River have created two lakes, where water temperatures are 85° to 90° in summer, and 45° in winter. **Pickwick** has the best conditions for diving. Since this lake always has a current, at least on the upstream end (near the Wilson Dam it can reach six knots), it has less silt buildup than Wilson Lake, and clarity averages 10-15' over the gravel bottom. The middle of the lake offers the best diving, with a depth of 30', and many huge gar, carp, and drum to look for.

Wilson Lake, while less clear, has a locomotive engine and a series of abandoned locks to lure divers. Since commercial barges run on each lake, as well as smaller boats, divers must use caution. Indians appreciated this region long before divers did, and you can still pick up Indian artifacts of all descriptions. The famous

MISSISSIPPI   **TEXAS**

Civil War battle of Shiloh was fought near the banks of the Tennessee River, and artifacts recovered in the river and these lakes include swords, guns, and buckles.

For the drift diver, the 4-6 knot current of the **Tennessee River** promises an exciting ride. Civil War shipwrecks and artifacts, as well as underwater Indian mounds, give you reason to keep your eyes peeled as you drift along. Night diving will turn up many catfish.

Other good spots for inland diving include **Smith Lake**, about 40 miles northwest of Birmingham, and **Martin Lake**, northeast of Montgomery. Both are man-made reservoirs with interesting rocky bottoms and clean waters. Camping is available in both areas. Smith Lake, in particular, has good water clarity that usually averages 20' year-round. Photographers and sightseers find lots of aquatic life, including red-ear bream, striped and largemouth bass, and colorful painted turtles.

Near Tuscaloosa is one of the finest examples of the freshwater quarries that dot the state. **Blue Water Park** has diving platforms, submerged trees, and a boat wreck. Relics from mining days, including air shafts and concrete cylinders, provide underwater interest. Aquarium plants sprout up from the shallower stretches near the beach, and in deeper water (maximum 165') brim and catfish hang out. The 20-40' water clarity is among the best in Alabama.

The **Black Warrior River**, also south of Tuscaloosa, attracts hard-core wreck divers who covet the brass structures still found on the paddlewheel wrecks in the area. Low visibility of 5-10', currents, and many entanglements make this a dive for the advanced.

Even Alabama divers don't pay too much attention to their 55 miles of Gulf coastline. For one thing, it doesn't take too much wind to stir the shallow water into a sandy, unappetizing broth. For another, even on calm days there isn't much down there to see — especially when you consider that the interesting waters of Panama City are literally in the backyard.

There are five **Liberty Ships** just a short distance offshore. These vintage vessels were dismantled so that only shallow saucer-like hulls were lowered into the water. Lying at a depth of 60', the Liberty reef provides good refuge for fish. Snappers, amberjacks, Warsaw grouper, barracuda, and open-water wanderers like king mackerel cruise the area. Other good spots for fish include the **dry docks** south of Sand Island, although swift current here can make for tricky diving.

Sperm whales have been found, dead, tangled in cable at 3,720'. They are thought to be able to dive even deeper, due to stories like this: In 1969, a pair of whales was spotted diving in an area off the coast of South Africa that is known to be deeper than 6,500' for a 30-mile radius. When the whales surfaced — one 53 minutes later, the other an hour and 52 minutes later — they were captured and killed. In the stomach of one, there were two sharks known to be bottom dwellers.

Alabama laws concerning diving: spearing is legal for non-game fish only, with permit. Dive flag is required.

LOUISIANA

When you discuss diving in Louisiana, you're talking about just one thing — oil rig diving. The famous rigs of **Grand Isle**, only about 8-10 miles from the coast, and other rigs further out in deep water all support an unbelievable assortment of life. Encrusted with corals and anemones, sheltering urchins, shells, and lobsters, and providing a home for damselfish, wrasses, tangs, angelfish, fairy basslets, blennies, hinds, spadefish, and triggerfish, oil rigs offer exciting diving for photographers and sightseers as well as spearers.

Depths range from 60' at Grand Isle to more than 200' at the platforms further offshore. Visibility varies from 30' close in to 100' or more well offshore. At most closer sites, there's a murky layer for the top 25' or so, caused by mixing of the nutrient-laden fresh water with the surface waters of the Gulf. Although the summer water temperature is warm, divers usually wear wetsuits or jeans and a long-sleeved shirt to protect themselves from the barnacles. Oil rig diving has been compared to being in a space station, listening to the hum and throb of the immense machinery around you.

While winter weather is the least predictable, it is also the best time to catch glimpses of the real giants. Even during the summer months, though, the fish life around the oil platforms is amazingly dense. The famous NOGI awards of the Underwater Society of America originated here as awards given to the winner of the New Orleans Grand Isle spearing tournament. Today the oil platforms still offer some fantastic opportunities for spearing. The most popular prey includes red snapper, grouper, and amberjack. Cobia (also called ling or lemonfish) are valued for their fine flesh and fighting spirit. Jewfish, once sought after as trophies, now are hunted mainly with cameras, since the big ones tend to be unappetizing, stringy — they often are more than 70 yrs. old — and afflicted with parasitic worms. Few other aquatic adventures can match coming across one of these giants.

A murky layer varying widely in depth usually covers the bottom just offshore from Louisiana. Because of this, there is no wreck diving or other coastal diving to speak of. The state even turned down the federal government's offer of Liberty Ships, apparently because they realized that all the topsoil washing down the Mississippi would soon bury them anyway.

Unless you like diving in mossy bayous, freshwater Louisiana probably isn't for you. **Lake Claiborne, Corney Lake**, and **Lake Bistineau** offer the best inland diving. All have depths of less than 40' and water clarity, at best, of about 10'.

Louisiana laws concerning diving: It is legal for any skin diver operating for sport in any salt or fresh water to take commercial fish or saltwater game fish when submerged in the water and using standard spearing equipment. License and creel limits are the same as for anglers.

MISSISSIPPI

Mississippi is the forgotten state on the Gulf Coast. The rigs of Texas and Louisiana are famous and often visited. Yet Mississippi also has at least 40 offshore **oil rigs** and, because they aren't visited as often, the diving is probably better. Located 35-40 miles offshore from Pascagoula, the best diving rigs have maximum depths of over 250'. Visibility at these rigs can be almost 200' on exceptional days. On not so exceptional days, it can be less than 50'. The fish life, though, is more predictable; it's usually fantastic. Huge schools of red snapper and lemonfish, gigantic jewfish, grouper, barracudas and 50-60-lb. amberjacks routinely put in their appearances. Diving in the midst of this intense, crowded aquarium is exhilarating and habit-forming.

There are other offshore diving spots, too, like **Liberty Ships**. Placed in two locations off Horn Island, these artificial reefs draw their share of marine life. One set of ships was sunk in about 45' of water only three miles off the island, and the other group lies at a depth of 60' about twelve miles out.

For another close-in dive, try the wreck of the ***Walker.*** Deliberately placed in 65' of water, this wreck and the adjacent barge ***Marguerite*** are only about six miles south of Pascagoula Pass. While visibility is variable, this site makes an easy spot to see some Gulf fish like grouper, snapper, amberjack, and tropicals. Other offshore wrecks are available to those who have a depth recorder and Loran C.

Inland diving in Mississippi is limited, as most lakes are so muddy that you can't see your hand in front of your face. However, two spring-fed lakes do exist which

"To the dolphin alone, beyond all others, nature has given what the best philosophers seek; friendship for no advantage. Though it has no need of man, yet it is the friend to all men and has often given them great aid."
— *Plutarch*
On the Cleverness of Animals

offer reasonably good diving in early spring before the plankton blooms. **Davis Lake**, off the Natchez Trace Parkway near Tupelo, and **Lake Bogue Homa**, just west of Laurel, both receive some diving attention as the clearest public lakes in the state.

Mississippi laws concerning diving: No spearing of game fish in fresh water. Dive flag is required.

TEXAS

Everything's big in Texas — including the variety of diving. Rugged hill country lakes with dramatic underwater dropoffs, crystal clear spring-fed rivers, offshore oil platforms with some of the most dense concentrations of fish anywhere, and even a tropical coral reef — the huge state of Texas has it all.

Distances between good dive sites can also be big. "Miles and miles of Texas" (as Bob Wills would say) separate dive sites. Offshore diving (and all good ocean diving is well offshore) requires pre-arrangements, and even then the variable Gulf weather may blow away the best-laid plans.

GULF OF MEXICO

In an interesting twist, human activity in the northern Gulf has greatly increased the fish concentrations by providing what nature did not. Vast expanses of flat sand give fish nowhere to hide from roving predators, and the continually shifting sand doesn't support many bottom dwellers.

In a totally unintended side effect of the search for oil, some of the most productive artificial reefs anywhere were created. The miles of steel pilings, girders, cables, support beams, and assorted trash around **oil rigs** lure fish from the surrounding desert-like expanses like moths to a candle. Tiny tropicals like blennies and gobies, giant loners like jewfish and rays, and huge schools of snapper and spadefish all seek the protection of the rig platforms, which can cover as much as an acre in size and stretch higher than the Empire State Building. Practically every inch of cold steel vanishes under the layers of encrusted marine life. Sponges, soft and hard corals, anemones, sea fans, and the ever-present barnacles all compete for space on the rigs.

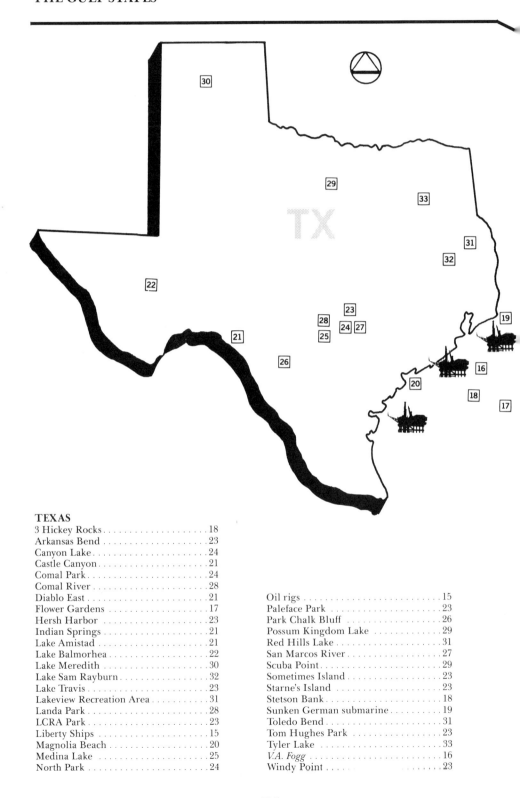

TEXAS

3 Hickey Rocks .18
Arkansas Bend 23
Canyon Lake 24
Castle Canyon .21
Comal Park 24
Comal River 28
Diablo East 21
Flower Gardens 17
Hersh Harbor .23
Indian Springs .21
Lake Amistad 21
Lake Balmorhea 22
Lake Meredith .30
Lake Sam Rayburn 32
Lake Travis 23
Lakeview Recreation Area 31
Landa Park 28
LCRA Park 23
Liberty Ships 15
Magnolia Beach 20
Medina Lake 25
North Park 24

Oil rigs 15
Paleface Park .23
Park Chalk Bluff 26
Possum Kingdom Lake 29
Red Hills Lake 31
San Marcos River 27
Scuba Point 29
Sometimes Island 23
Starne's Island 23
Stetson Bank .18
Sunken German submarine 19
Toledo Bend .31
Tom Hughes Park 23
Tyler Lake 33
V.A. Fogg 16
Windy Point 23

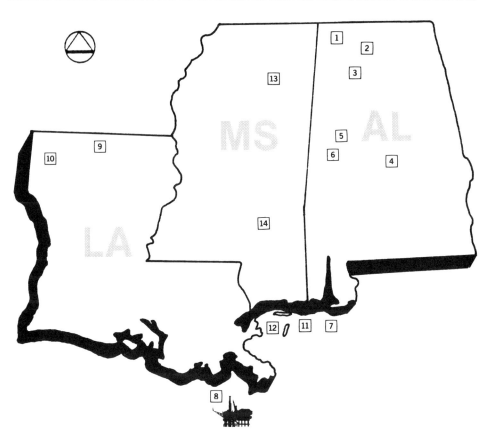

ALABAMA
Black Warrior River 6
Blue Water Park 5
Dry docks 7
Liberty Ships .7
Martin Lake 4
Pickwick 1
Smith Lake 3
Tennessee River 2
Wilson Lake .1

LOUISIANA
Corney Lake .9
Grand Isle 8
Lake Claiborne 10

MISSISSIPPI
Davis Lake .13
Lake Bogue Homa 14
Liberty Ships 12
Marguerite 12
Oil rigs 11
Walker 12

It's a bit of a mindblower to see delicate little butterflyfish cautiously emerge from hiding amidst piles of scrap iron and twisted cable to make their way to the girders to feed. Yet, if you can revamp your ideas of what underwater scenery should be, oil rigs can be as interesting as any natural reef.

Oil rig diving is advanced diving. Top currents or surge can throw you right into steel crossbeams with uncomfortable results. To avoid the crossbeam that on many surface rigs is only a few feet beneath the surface, experienced rig divers immediately descend before advancing towards the rig platform.

Weather is a special problem for visiting divers. It takes little wind to blow the shallow Gulf into a mess, and water clarity can plunge from 150' to nothing in a day's time. Summer months present the most consistently good weather. Depths around the Texas rigs generally don't exceed more than 120'. The dozens of offshore platforms are best reached from Beaumont, Galveston, Freeport, and Corpus Christi. Since one rig varies very little from another, we won't list them all individually. Dive shops in these areas can guide you to the current favorites. Individual shops vary widely in charter services. Since many areas are well offshore (often 40 to 50 miles) and require larger boats, it's a good idea to plan in advance.

Liberty Ships also provide a mecca for fish, although their depth — top of the vessels at 80' — limits the diving to the more experienced. These WWII supply vessels have fulfilled their peacetime missions admirably and serve as a magnet for local fish populations. Jacks and triggerfish swim around the tops of the wrecks. Don't be too surprised to round a corner and see a 300-pound jewfish staring at you. These highly territorial fish often swim up to a diver as if to challenge this new invader. Others who frequent the Liberty reefs include big barracuda and delicious red snapper.

The wreck of the **V.A. Fogg**, about 50 miles out from Galveston, takes first place for best wreck in Texas. This 600' freighter went down with all hands in 1972. Today, the massive hulk sits on the bottom in 120' of water with upper parts of the wreck at 65'. In calm weather, visibility around the *Fogg* might exceed 100', but 50' is a more predictable average. The abundant marine life attracts both spearfishermen and photographers. Tricky currents and jagged edges around the big holes blown in the sides of the wreck make this a dive for the experienced. In addition to grouper, amberjack, spadefish, and tropicals, a lucky diver might spot an ocean sunfish or sea turtle drawn in from open ocean.

For real open ocean diving, though, take a trip to the **Flower Gardens,** the northern Gulf's extraordinary coral reef. It's hard to imagine, but 110 miles off Galveston a tropical coral reef exists, complete with massive brain, star, and finger corals. For years fishermen and geologists have been aware of the reefs, called the East and West Flower Garden Banks. However, everyone assumed the reefs were

In a single huge Florida loggerhead sponge, Dr. A.S. Pearse counted 17,128 animals.

simply dead relics of ancient coral communities until, in the early 1960's, a scientist/diver electrified the scientific world by announcing that the Flower Gardens were living and growing true stony coral reefs. Isolated by hundreds of miles of open ocean, and further north than any reef-building corals are supposed to be, the Flower Gardens represent a unique and irreplaceable natural resource.

Being 110 miles out to sea has understandably limited the number of visiting divers, but any divers interested in seeing a coral reef different from anything else in the Caribbean or Florida owe it to themselves to visit the Flower Gardens. Charters have improved dramatically in recent years, with the addition of large and modern boats that make the trip much more comfortable. Charters in summer make the 24-hour round trip every weekend.

Diving that far from any reference point requires some careful planning and cautious diving. For those who do brave it, though, the Flower Gardens are unforgettable. Clarity can exceed 100', and usually averages at least 60'. Once you descend past the heavy surface current, you'll usually find only minor bottom current. At 60' down, massive coral heads begin. Massive isn't an overstatement, either; some of the largest coral heads anywhere are to be found at the Flower Gardens. The huge heads, as much as 10' across and 20' high, form many sheltering nooks and crannies for fish. Small patches of white sand dot the areas between the eroded toadstool shapes of the coral heads. You don't see many sea fans, sponges or branching corals in sport diving range, although sea fans have been seen at depths below 200' using submersibles. This has led to theories that breakable corals can't survive here in the middle of "Hurricane Alley." The devastating Hurricane Alicia of 1983, which swept directly past the Flower Gardens, bore this theory out, as only a few heads were upturned, and damage was generally unsubstantial.

Rare cone and turban shells, as well as 140 species of fish, including cardinal soldierfish, marbled grouper, longnose and spotfin butterflies, rock beauties, Spanish hogfish, parrotfish, angelfish, gobies, filefish — all those exotics you used to think were strictly tropical — are living happily in the waters around the Flower Gardens. Until quite recently, the fish were totally unafraid of divers, and even big grouper would swim up and peer into your mask. Although this has changed a little, the fish are still fairly tame. Few divers hunt fish or mollusks here since the Gardens are such a rare and fragile environment.

Besides these altruistic considerations, other more compelling reasons exist for not eating the fish. For years, the area served as a dumping ground for oil and chemical industries, and high traces of chemical and metal contamination have been found in some of the Flower Garden's fish. Homebody species like grouper are especially susceptible to this poisoning.

You'd think abuses like this wouldn't be permitted on such a small-scale ecosystem as the Flower Garden Banks. Unfortunately, this coral outpost faces threats greater than cold temperatures or hurricanes. Since they are located on what geologists call a salt dome, and salt domes often cover oil reserves, the Flower Gardens are in a prime area for oil exploration. The best way to permanently insure that the struggling corals of the Flower Gardens will be allowed to continue alive would be to declare this relatively small area a national marine sanctuary, similar to Looe Key or the Channel Islands. However, the National Oceanic and Atmospheric Administration, which alone can give the Gardens this designation, sat on the petition for almost ten years before rejecting the Flower Gardens as a possible sanctuary in the summer of 1982. Shortly thereafter, Interior Secretary James Watt offered a lease to oil companies on the two blocks containing the East and West Flower Garden Banks. It appeared that the fate of the Flower Gardens was to be decided by oil industry lobbyists and the Reagan Administration instead of fishermen, divers, scientists, and all the rest of us who have a stake in the survival of the Flower Gardens, the Gulf's unlikely outpost of coral. Luckily, in 1984 the coral reef was granted a reprieve. Exxon, which had bid on the area, was confronted with public outcry, culminating in a dramatic last-minute telephone plea by Governor Mark White of Texas, and so dropped the lease. Only continued effort on behalf of one of the northern-most coral reefs in the world will make this reprieve permanent.

A few other reef outcroppings like **Stetson Bank** and 3 **Hickey Rocks** also exist out in the Gulf, although none contains the extensive coral development of the Flower Gardens. Stetson Bank, so named because a sonar depth tracing of the area resembles the famous hat, is about 70 miles out of Freeport, towards the Flower Gardens. Also perched on a salt dome, this area of rocky plateaus and ridges, covered in fire coral and encrusting sponges, as well as some superficial star coral growth, supports an unbelievable fish population. Species common to the Caribbean like filefish, angel and damselfish, surgeonfish, scorpionfish, and parrotfish intermingle with morays, slipper lobster, cowries, and even banded coral shrimp! The top of the plateau lies in 50-60' of water, and clarity, like all Gulf sites, is dependent on the weather. If you get a priceless day of glassy seas, you might see 100' visibility — but on a more average day, 40' is the norm.

Other spots in the Gulf of some interest to divers include a **sunken German submarine**, located near Beaumont in 60' of murky water, and the wreck of a **Civil War gunboat**, almost indistinguishable due to heavy marine growth, 30 miles off Galveston.

For a shore dive, visit **Magnolia Beach** in Matagorda Bay, near Port Lavaca. Although clarity is usually pretty bad, once in a while it's clear enough to see an old steam locomotive tossed into the brine by a hurricane in 1928. Dive clubs in the area have also reported seeing schools of barracuda, up to 150 strong, inspecting the 35' depths.

Finally, one last fact draws divers to the Gulf. Except for the Florida Keys, possibly no other region in the U.S. has seen so many treasure ships meet their doom as had the Texas coast. The infamous Jean Lafitte, who headquartered his pirates on Galveston and Padre Islands, supposedly left behind much treasure in the Spanish ships he scuttled. And some believe that somewhere around north Padre,

the last vessel of Cortez' 1553 fleet still remains to be located. Known to be burdened with stolen Aztec gold, this wreck still lures treasure hunters after more than 400 years.

INLAND — Southwest

Out in the west Texas hills, nestled among the yucca and sagebrush, lies an endless, incredibly blue lake, fed by deep springs, and offering some of the finest diving in the Southwest. Indian relics and many species of fish can be found among the eroded limestone parapets and underwater cliffs and caves. This beautiful reservoir, **Lake Amistad**, was made by damming the Rio Grande.

Distance doesn't mean much in west Texas. Even though Amistad is in the middle of nowhere — San Antonio, the closest big city, is three hours away — it is rapidly becoming one of the most popular dives in Texas and a lure for divers all over the Southwest. The United States shares the 67,000 acres of water with Mexico; a chain of buoys mark the line. The National Park Service, which controls the U.S. side, holds its divers' workshops every year at a large cove called **Diablo East**. Some of the best diving in the lake is found around here, with underwater ledges, caves, and a sunken platform and boat to explore. As at all National Park sites, divers should register at a ranger station before diving, and receive the latest word on sites and conditions. A boat is advisable to really explore the hundreds of dives available on this huge lake.

Another favorite spot, **Indian Springs**, on the Devil's River arm, maintains a constant 73° temperature even in winter. Spearfishers particularly like this spot as fish congregate in the warm water. Tilapia, also called African perch, are one of the favorite targets. These tough fighters grow to about six pounds and, reportedly, make good eating. The fish are so plentiful that the Park Service encourages tilapia spearing.

Flooded haciendas, windmills, bridges, orchards, and cemeteries also bring out the explorer in you, as they're scattered all over the lake. The roof has been removed from a hacienda that sits at 30' depth in **Castle Canyon**, making it a site safe enough for beginners. Visibility in the indigo blue water can reach 40' or more, depending on the area. It's better around the springs and rock cliffs, and worse in the coves, where it might average 25'. Since the lake has only been in existence since 1969, silt hasn't yet had time to build up, and the fish life is still in the "boom" stage that follows creation of a new lake.

Above the water, eagles nest in the magnificent red-stained limestone cliffs. Spectacular Indian cave paintings can be seen by boating up the Diablo River arm, and especially, the western end of Pecos Canyon — there are an estimated 300

Some scientists estimate that nine out of every ten living creatures reside in the oceans.

archaeological sites on the U.S. side alone. To top it off, toll-free entry to Mexico is just across the dam. Boats, marinas, and dive services are available, as is camping. With all these conveniences in such a remote and unexplored region, it's not surprising that some call Amistad the ocean of the Southwest.

Lake Balmorhea, between Fort Stockton and El Paso, also has very clear spring-fed waters, although depths in this small lake reach only about 30'. The beautiful location in the foothills of the Davis Mountains and the crystal waters draw many divers.

INLAND — Central

The hill country of central Texas has some of the finest lakes for diving in the state. **Lake Travis**, the best of a series of lakes on the Colorado River, winds for over 65 miles through rugged hills before ending at Mansfield Dam just 15 miles west of Austin. One of the most popular dive sites on the lake happens to be near the dam at the **LCRA (Lower Colorado River Authority) Park**. The best diving is just off the point, on the dam side. Water clarity is usually pretty good, ranging from 10-35'. Summer water temperature hits 85°, but below the thermocline it drops dramatically, and your wetsuit will feel good. Tame perch and bass can sometimes be lured with food from their hideouts among the ledges that under-cut the steep cliff.

Other good dive sites are found along the steep wall (formerly the outside bend of the River channel) that stretches from just north of the Oasis Cantina del Lago (a restaurant on Comanche Trail with a great lake view) to past Marshall Ford Marina. A boat makes this entire region accessible, if you know how to anchor to keep a wind shift from driving you into the wall.

A shore dive is available at **Tom Hughes Park**, if you don't mind carrying your gear down a fairly steep trail past quite a few naked sun worshipers. Follow the road past the Marshall Ford Marina until it deadends into a parking lot; a short, but steep trail will lead you to the cove. Although clarity isn't great within the cove, it improves dramatically once you begin following the ledge to your right. Huge boulders the size of houses perch on a gradual slope that drops into a steep cliff, formerly the river channel, at 50'.

Windy Point, another popular spot, juts out into the lake across from the dam and is easily accessible to divers via Comanche Trail. A day-use fee of a few dollars is required for each car entering the Park. Shallow diving at Windy Point isn't spectacular, as the underwater scene is less dramatic here, and clarity is dependent on wind strength. But on deep dives, there are dropoffs to explore, as well as large pecan trees, still standing, with their highest branches at 90'. The ease of access makes this a good spot for night dives.

Access to a boat opens up some of the best diving on the lake. **Starne's Island** (sometimes called Rattlesnake), has dramatic scenes of mammoth boulders and plunging walls, formed by Sandy Creek, which entered the Colorado here. Night diving scares up big catfish.

At **Sometimes Island**, a buoy marks the spot of the former gravel screening plant, often visited by local charters. A beautiful wall drops right off the edge of a foundation at approximately 65' in normal water conditions. For shallower dives, you can explore two rows of massive concrete stanchions (formerly part of the trestle system used to bring up gravel), and admire a wooden ladder, preserved since 1933. Extensive caverns can also be found off Sometimes Island.

Although the underwater scenery isn't as majestic, divers do occasionally visit the upstream part of the Lake. **Hersh Harbor** and **Arkansas Bend** each have underwater cliffs. At **Paleface Park**, stolen cars add a bit to the scene. Clarity at this end of the lake generally is half as much as by the dam.

Canyon Lake, about 70 miles southwest of Austin near the German community of New Braunfels, also has a good reputation with divers. Water clarity averages 15-20'. Much of Canyon Lake slopes gradually down into the former river bed at about 110'. At **North Park**, near the dam, the bottom drops off more rapidly, with standing trees and big carp to look for. Camping is available here and at **Comal Park**, another diver hangout. Spearing for carp, buffalo, gar, and other rough fish can be exciting, as 20-30 lb. fish are common.

Another interesting hill country lake, **Medina Lake**, west of San Antonio, has rocky ledges that drop off to around 120'. Tunnels, caves, a man-made reef, and the wrecks of several cars and boats draw divers. Many fish, including 2'-long catfish, have been fed so regularly that, like dogs, they beg for handouts.

If you find yourself near Uvalde, also west of San Antonio, stop at **Park Chalk Bluff**. This oasis on the Nueces River, just north of town, draws fishermen, campers, and local people wanting to get wet, but no one will be able to really appreciate the year-round cold, clear water without using snorkel or scuba. Arrowheads and many friendly fish to watch will lure you underwater; above, there's a high bluff to admire.

But undoubtedly, the most famous river dive in Texas is the **San Marcos River**, at the town of San Marcos. With several species of plants and fish found nowhere else (Texas wild rice, San Marcos gambusia, fountain darter and San Marcos salamander) and some of the most productive Indian sites anywhere, this small, clear river is unique enough to have been the subject of an award-winning documentary featured on public television. Drifting along with the easy current, using either scuba or snorkel, in this spring-fed river of year-round 72° temperature, is exciting and relaxing at the same time. Beautiful aquarium plants like *Elodea* cover the rock bottom; common species like bass, crayfish, and turtles mingle with exotics like African cichlids and Amazon mollies.

Major archaeology digs have occurred along the San Marcos, and recovered Indian artifacts fill several exhibits around town. A team of underwater archaeologists have recently discovered artifacts from every civilization dating back to the Clovis Indians of more than 13,000 years ago. No diving is permitted in Spring

Lake inside the city of San Marcos, so entry is usually made just below the small dam. No spearing is allowed in the river.

Comal River, another cool, clear, spring-fed river, gives the diver a good three miles of drifting from its headspring at **Landa Park** before it joins the turbid Guadalupe. With depths averaging 8-10' and visibility of about 35', snorkeling is as much fun as scuba unless you're planning on doing underwater photography in the deeper holes. Divers find winter as good a time to explore as summer; maybe even a better time, since the visibility improves to 50' and you have the place all to yourself. Sunlight reflects off the white slab stones that cover the bottom, while plants create a huge natural aquarium for thousands of fish, crayfish, and turtles. In times of drought, the river may be too low to float, so check locally.

Jacob's Well, near Wimberly, is worth mentioning for its historical importance and mystical beauty, although it has been closed for several years due to drownings. At one time it attracted cave divers from all over the U.S. to its crystal waters and solid rock shaft. However, after several inexperienced divers had killed themselves in the cave, and local divers had risked their lives once too often on rescues, it was closed. Since it is the most challenging cave dive within hundreds of miles, and has been celebrated as the title and subject of a novel by Stephen Harrigan, it still lures divers, even though they face charges of criminal trespassing.

It's been said time and time again, but it bears repeating: cave diving is dangerous if you're not a certified cave diver. It doesn't matter if you've made a million open-water dives, diving in a cave is another matter entirely, and the only way it can be done safely is by divers trained and equipped especially for this rigorous environment. See the article on training for cave diving in this book.

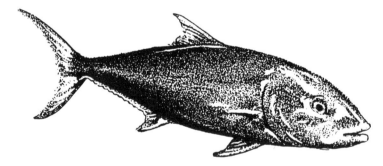

INLAND — North Central

Possum Kingdom Lake, on the Brazos River about 75 miles west of Fort Worth, attracts local divers, as well as taking top honors for the funniest name. **Scuba Point** is a favorite access area. Silty bottom gives way in many areas to piles of jumbled boulders that shelter catfish, perch, bass, and carp. Winter and fall visibility is best (up to 20'), although temperatures may drop to 48°. A state park along the southeast shore offers camping.

Panhandle divers head to **Lake Meredith**, 40 miles north of Amarillo. Maximum depth is 89'. Clarity varies from nothing to 30'.

INLAND — East

Two reservoirs located in the pine forests of east Texas draw their share of local divers despite poor clarity, shallow depths, and dangerous boat traffic. **Toledo Bend** and **Lake Sam Rayburn** are vast lakes which together cover an enormous area. Toledo Bend in particular is famous among anglers for bass production. Night diving along the edges of moss beds is the best way to get a shot of a monster bass. **Lakeview Recreation Area** at Toledo Bend is the best access. Visibility is in the 5-15' range. Depths slope out gradually over a sandy bottom to about 25' maximum. **Red Hills Lake**, a 17-acre spring-fed lake near Hemphill, beside Toledo Bend, offers a similar experience, but there's no boat traffic to worry about. Great campsites are in the surrounding National Forest.

Tyler Lake, about 90 miles east of Dallas and just south of the town of Tyler, also offers the photographer some good opportunities. Red-ear bream and 2-lb. goldfish abound, making good photographic models. Fall, winter, and spring visibilities are around 20', but plankton blooms can limit summer diving. Underwater habitats such as a sunken airplane and platform are planned to help focus fish populations in this 35'-deep lake.

Thermoclines aren't the problem in east Texas lakes that they are in the deeper lakes of the hill country. However, boat traffic in most of Texas' lakes requires use of a dive flag and cautious surfacing. About the only other hazards divers need to be aware of are monofilament and trot lines, which can reach out and snag you before you know it. A good dive knife can handle any problems they create.

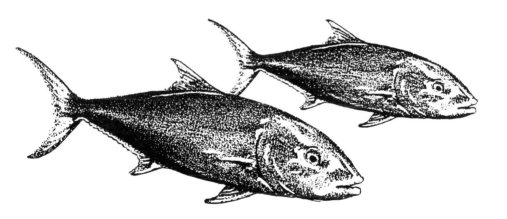

Texas laws concerning diving: Saltwater fish species may be taken by spear, except for red drum and spotted sea trout. In fresh water, only rough species may be speared.

THE
MIDWEST

ARKANSAS   IOWA   KANSAS   MISSOURI

Flying from New York to California once, I sat next to a native New Yorker, who inquired where I was from. When I replied "southern Missouri," he responded "must be awfully boring to grow up on the plains."

With that he revealed more than his ignorance of geography. He expressed a belief, common to some residents of the coasts, that the Midwest is one interminable plain, something to be driven through as quickly as possible or, preferably, flown over. And the idea of diving in the Midwest arouses nothing but ridicule from the most jaded of divers.

But those of us familiar with this region know better. Big lakes, quarries, crystalline springs, fast clear rivers — all these and more exist for diving. Cruising down beautiful tree-lined rivers of cold, clear water, and watching hundreds of interesting fish swimming through graceful aquatic plants is an experience that can be on a level with almost any ocean dive.

Shallow summer dives in the Midwest don't absolutely require thermal protection. But if you're planning on going below the thermocline, which varies from place to place but averages 35' in depth, then you'll at least need a wetsuit jacket. Many divers have found deep dives in inland lakes to be much more difficult and conducive of nitrogen narcosis than deep ocean dives. Cold, darkness, and a lack of distinct features to orient towards makes going deep much less rewarding than staying in the lighter, fishier surface waters.

Boat traffic presents the other major hazard of Midwestern diving. Use of the diver's flag is essential. For some, it's also tempting to enter caves and tunnels found in quarries or reservoirs. This is much more dangerous than entering spring caves, since flooding has rendered their openings — often shale — highly unstable and filled with silt.

ARKANSAS

In just a few short years, Arkansas has had a more dramatic image change than just about any other state in the Union — from a hilly backwoods to one of the fastest growing states around. The rest of the country has finally noticed the spectacular, but still down-home, beauty of Arkansas.

The same thing has happened to diving in Arkansas, too, with the result being that divers from at least six states regularly dive the state. A chain of beautiful, clear lakes set in the scenic Ozark Mountains, with legal spearing for some game fish and plenty of opportunities to get off the beaten path and explore, have made Arkansas a mecca for Midwestern divers.

NEBRASKA OKLAHOMA SOUTH DAKOTA

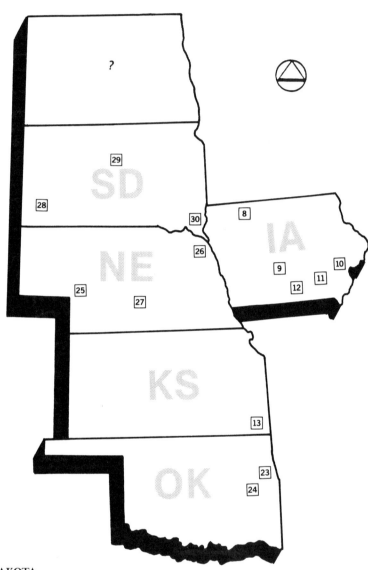

SOUTH DAKOTA

Alexandria Quarry 30
Lake Oahe 29
Pactola Reservoir 28
Tailwaters of Oahe Dam 29

NEBRASKA

Crystal Cove Lake 26
Lake McConaughy 25
North Platte River 25
Sand pits 27

KANSAS

Blue Hole 13
Strip mines 13

IOWA

Big Creek Lake 9
Big Spirit Lake 8
Brown's Bay 8
Cedar Valley Quarries 10
Gull Point 8
Lake Rathbun 12
Lake Yenrouge 11
Terrace Park 8
West Okoboji 8

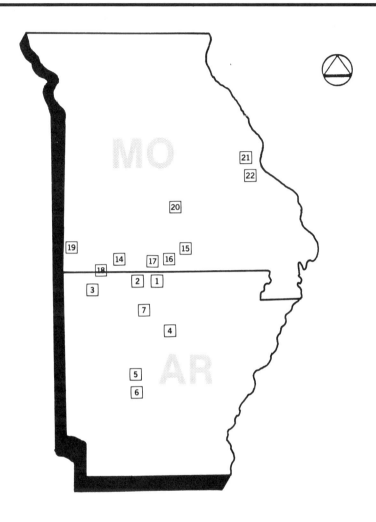

OKLAHOMA

Fort Gibson Lake 23
Lake Eufaula 24
Lake Tenkiller 23
Strayhorn Landing 23

ARKANSAS

Beaver Lake 3
Buffalo River 7
Bull Shoals Lake 2
Dam Site Area 1 3
Greer's Ferry Lake 4
Lake DeGray 6
Lake Ouachita 5
Mondel City 3
Norfork Lake 1
Robinson Point Island 1

MISSOURI

Black Water Quarry 21
Bonne Terre Mine 22
Bull Creek 14
Casey's Hole 14
Current 15
Eleven Point River 16
Enchanted Forest 18
Jack's Fork River 15
Norfork Lake 17
North Fork River 17
Oronogo Circle Mine 19
Roubideaux Springs 20
Swan Creek 14
Table Rock 18

Arkansas shares **Norfork Lake** with Missouri, although the best diving is on the Arkansas side, out of Gamaliel. You can night dive at **Robinson Point Island**, where the beam from your light mesmerizes bass and crappie, and even an ordinary boulder outcropping looks special. On day dives in the summer, you won't need a wetsuit if you stay above 35', since the surface temperature reaches a high of 85°. Water clarity is especially good around Robinson Island. On a good day, you can see the surface from 40' down. If you tire of exploring the bluffs and flat rocks of Robinson Island, there are numerous coves where you can try to imagine who lived in the old stone homesteads before this was all flooded.

Bull Shoals Lake, just west of Norfork Lake, also straddles the Missouri-Arkansas line. Since most of the lake is in Arkansas, and since Arkansas permits some game fish spearing (Missouri doesn't), most of the diving takes place on the Arkansas side. Like most of these Ozark impoundments, an extremely varied bottom terrain keeps diving interesting, and the rocky walls help water clarity. In winter, clarity can be 40', but the temperature also drops to about 40°, so much more diving takes place in summer, when clarity ranges from 10-30' and water temperatures on the surface reach 80°. Below the thermoclines, though, water temperature will drop to 60°. Night diving for crawdads, spearing 50-lb. catfish or 15-lb. walleye, searching for old homesteads, and simply enjoying the underwater scenery are favorite pastimes. Many caves lead back into the bluffs, but are too dangerous to enter. Air, camping, and other facilities are available.

Another favorite dive in northern Arkansas is **Beaver Lake**, just north of Springdale. Beaver's one of the prettiest man-made lakes in the Ozarks, and it also has some of the clearest water — usually at least 20' visibility. At the **Dam Site Area 1**, bluffs shelve down gradually to 180', and twisted, craggy cedars jut out of the rock. Most divers stay in the upper 70' to avoid the narcosis that comes more easily in dark, cold water, where there's little to orient you.

Determined artifact divers have located the site of an old country crossroads at **Mondel City**. Marked by a few house structures and a junkyard, this four-corners can be an interesting trip into the submerged past. Surface support is needed because of the combination of junkpiles, a mud bottom at 65', and boat traffic in the area. Searchers have been rewarded with antique bottles, coins, and Civil War relics.

At **Greer's Ferry Lake**, about an hour north of Little Rock near Heber Springs, you can free-fall down rock walls for more than 100', or look for bass, walleye, trout, catfish, gar, or even one of the schools of hybrid bass that was created from a mix of landlocked striped bass and white bass. Beautiful scenery, camping, clarity of 15-20', and charters every summer weekend add to the popularity of Greer's Ferry.

Some barnacles are so particular about their host they will attach to only one species; for example, the turtle barnacle is found only on loggerheads. Other barnacles are not only species-specific but also locale-specific: thus the humpback whale supports a particular barnacle that attaches to nothing in the world save the throat and belly of a humpback.

At **Lake Ouachita**, just out of the famous Hot Springs area, you can spear 40-lb. catfish, as well as certain other species, with the favorite diving areas being around the small islands, which provide a refuge for both fish and divers from the many boats. Almost all the diving takes place above 40', where the fish are most active. Rock ledges drop down into bottoms draped in coontail moss, as it's known locally. **Lake DeGray**, to the south, is famous for its huge catfish and thick schools of crappie. It's a good place to look for the uncommon freshwater jellyfish.

Since Arkansas is a rugged state with many remote sections, there's plenty of room to explore. Arkansas has many beautiful rivers that offer great snorkeling or shallow diving, but you have to watch out for both canoeists and rapids. You can snorkel down the famous **Buffalo River** in late fall or early spring, usually on a weekday if you don't want to be overwhelmed by canoe traffic. For adventurous divers in wetsuits, nothing can beat a bright fall day with the beautiful Buffalo all to yourself.

Arkansas laws concerning diving: Spearing for both rough and game fish is legal in Lakes Beaver, Norfork, Bull Shoals, Greer's Ferry, Ouachita, Blue Mountain, Catherine, Conway, DeGray, Erling, Greeson, Hamilton, Harris Brake, Millwood, Nimrod, and Table Rock, with the exception that black bass aren't to be taken by spear in Beaver, Bull Shoals, Norfork, or Table Rock. Season is June 15th to March 15th, daylight hours. Only one-half of the angler's limits may be taken by spear. License and dive flag required.

IOWA

A lot of people are surprised to learn that western Iowa has its own Great Lakes Region, made up of a series of natural lakes. **West Okoboji**, probably the favorite for divers, is spring-fed from subterranean outlets located below the 140' maximum depths. At **Gull Point** and **Terrace Park**, the favorite activity is hunting for historic bottles and Indian artifacts. One of the more interesting finds was a stone battle ax, possibly over 1,400 years old, that was just retrieved in 1980.

At **Brown's Bay**, a 20' wooden tower rises up from the 35' depths; fish orient around the structure and are tame enough to photograph. Photographers must be careful not to stir up the silt of the bottom, since many areas around the lake are shallow. Clarity runs from 5-20' here and at **Big Spirit Lake**.

At Big Spirit Lake, you won't find as many Indian artifacts since many tribes believed the lake was evil and avoided it. However, you might spot the wreckage of an 0-47 observation plane or a Model-T ice truck. Since the Great Lakes Region is one of Iowa's favorite vacationlands, campgrounds are plentiful, as is boat traffic on the lakes.

Divers from the Des Moines area head to **Big Creek Lake**, which wasn't created until the 1970's. The lake flooded a five-mile-long valley to an average depth of 55'. Walls lead down into the former creek bed, where divers can find sailboats and at least 150 ice houses that went down in an early thaw. Tiger muskie, walleye, bluegill, bass, and carp are commonly seen. Clarity averages 10-15'.

From the late 1800's until a torrential rain around 1910, heavy mining took place at the **Cedar Valley Quarries**, just north of West Liberty. River flooding caused the filling of the quarries overnight. Today much of the mining equipment sits on the bottom just as it was left by workers intending to return. Flat rock stairsteps down to the 65'-deep bottom at most of these quarries. Clarity averages 15'.

Lake Yenrouge, just north of Sigourney, is located in a county park that has camping, picnic areas, and a beach leading into the 25'-deep water. In spring, divers watch bass, bluegill, and catfish. Crappie sometimes attack their reflections in divers' faceplates. Near Ottumwa, you can dive **Lake Rathbun**, "Iowa's Ocean," but be prepared for poor visibility due to mud and coal shale bottoms that stain the water.

Iowa laws concerning diving: Spearing is permitted for rough fish only; certain areas prohibited. Dive flag is required.

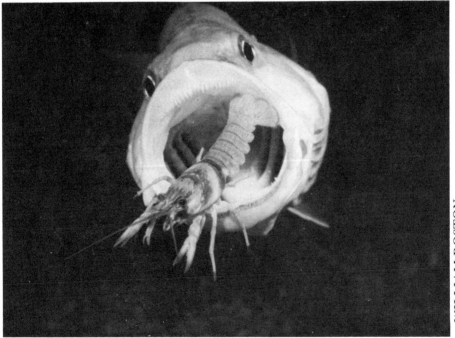

WILLIAM ROSTON

The common crayfish is a popular food with many freshwater fish, including this bass in Swan Creek, Missouri.

KANSAS

Kansas has a lot more wheat than it does water. Aside from some low-clarity lake dives, diving in Kansas is pretty well confined to the southeast corner of the state near the Missouri border. **Strip mines** in the Pittsburg area, generally less than 35' deep, can be visited by divers. Loose shale rock presents dangers.

The **Blue Hole**, near Galena, was a former quarry mine. Water clarity of up to 70' in the spring makes this dive unusual. You can swim right down the former road into the quarry, where a small-gauge railroad trestle with rails and assorted mining equipment keep things interesting. Don't enter the pits, shafts, and tunnels that lead into the mine itself, whether you're an experienced cave diver or not. They are composed of loose shale which has become extremely dangerous after years of immersion. Cave-ins are frequent and unpredictable.

Kansas laws concerning diving: Spearing is permitted for rough fish only; prohibited areas exist. Dive flag is required.

MISSOURI

Missouri takes top honors when it comes to variety of diving within a landlocked state. Clear springs, immense flooded underground mines, large reservoirs, quarries, and fast cool rivers that provide great snorkeling rides are the state's highlights.

All of the best rivers for diving are in the hilly Ozarks region in the southern part of the state, where at least 14 species of fish exist that are found nowhere else in the world. Spring is the best time to explore these rivers, when they're usually running at their fullest. Many of the unique fish are darters and shiners, which put on colors only during spawning displays. Check with local divers if you're unfamiliar with river levels — you want fast water, not flood stage.

Spring is the only time when you can run down little streams like **Bull Creek**, north of Branson, known as one of the clearest rivers in the state. From above, you can't see anything but dappled light and shadow playing over the gravel bottom. As soon as your mask is in the water, though, it's a different story. Schools of bleeding red shiners hover over the rocky riffles, all facing the same direction as they engage in a "spawning aggregation." If you take your time and investigate around the rocks, you might see a colorful little darter. It's a pity that the famed snail darter of Tennessee doesn't resemble its Ozark cousins, or the Army Corps of Engineers might not have been so eager to drown them out. Red dots, alternating blue and orange bars, and blue-green and red banded wavy fins apparently help the male saddle darter attract a mate. Since these fish are only 2-3" long, you have to look closely. However, they apparently don't consider anything as monumental as a diver a threat, since they carry on their normal activities oblivious to your presence.

When you tire of fish-watching and decide to continue back down the creek, the best posture is with arms extended, in the "flying Superman" pose, so that you can push off the boulders and direct your course. You might come to a longnose gar impertinently holding his ground, despite your barreling down on him at top speed. Now, a gar doesn't measure up to a sea turtle or a manta or a blue shark for excitement, but something about hurtling towards a toothy 3' gar who's adamantly refusing to budge, in a section of rapids that's only 1-1/2' deep, and so narrow that the trees touch overhead — well, it's intimate. Too intimate. But you zoom right over him, grazing his dorsal, and then the creek spits you out into a pool, where you cruise over to admire some waterlilies, only to catch a glimpse of a big smallmouth darting back into the dim recesses under a tangled treeroot. When you direct your eyes downward, you see rows of longear sunfish guarding their little nests, refusing to budge unless you edge them out. As soon as you do, hordes of minnows dart in to feast on the eggs, so you guiltily move on down the stream.

Casey's Hole, on **Swan Creek**, near Forsyth, is a good spot to visit if you haven't the time or inclination to snorkel the whole creek, but still want a taste of what creek life is all about. The 15'-deep pool contains many species of fish and, in summer, swimmers as well. They stir up the water and reduce clarity, but Casey's Hole is still the best place around for concentrations of fish. Several good-sized smallmouth live near the boulders, and schools of redhorse, big drum, and gar mill around constantly. Night diving is excellent here and in the deeper pools near the Swan's junction with Bull Shoals Lake.

Several other crystal clear rivers in southern Missouri make fantastic canoe and snorkel trips. This region is second only to Florida in concentration of springs. However, there are important differences. Many of Missouri's springs are single outlets, gushing from caverns with such force that entering them is impossible. In addition, the steep rugged terrain and remoteness from any services make scuba diving less popular than snorkeling. For the free diver, though, few things are more enticing than floating in the gin-clear outflow above a rippling spring.

The most famous of these fast spring-fed rivers is the **Current**, originating near Montauk State Park. This easy river is floatable year-round, due to the many springs that line its banks. Among the most memorable of these springs and sinkholes are Sinkin Creek tributary, where you can snorkel under a huge natural bridge big enough to canoe through; Welch Cave Stream, where you can enjoy an eerie snorkel run with lights, looking for aquatic albinos; and Blue Spring, Missouri's ninth largest. Its azure depths have been explored past 100', but it is now off-limits to scuba, although snorkeling is allowed.

Jack's Fork River, which is a tributary of the Current, is also a National Scenic Riverway. Its wild beauty is appreciated by many canoeists. Racing through a deep rock gorge, the upper Jack's Fork is floatable only in spring. Several springs and a spectacular cave pool provide fascinating exploring.

The **Eleven Point River**, originating near Thomasville, is nearly doubled in size by the influx from Greer's Spring, the second largest in the state. However, with a rapid flow of over 300' per second and a drop of 62' down a steep hillside, Greer's Spring can only be admired from solid ground. Many other wild springs along the river, which flows through the Irish Wilderness, can be explored with scuba or snorkel. The entire river basin makes great diving since in many places solid rock slabs and exotic aquarium vegetation line the bottom.

On the **North Fork River**, near Twin Bridges, you stand a good chance of zooming up on a busy beaver family underwater — anyway, I have, twice. If you're spending much time in any of these rivers, a wetsuit jacket will be much appreciated, since the clear spring water is also cold. Oz Hawksley's book, *Missouri Ozark Waterways*, has much useful information about access sites.

The southern part of the state also contains the best reservoirs for diving. **Table Rock, Bull Shoals**, and **Norfork Lake** are the top three. Both Table Rock and Bull Shoals are impoundments of the White River, and both are enormous reservoirs with maximum depths below scuba range and thousands of miles of rocky, forested shorelines.

Since Bull Shoals and Norfork Lake are mainly in Arkansas, see the section on that state for coverage of these reservoirs. Some divers in Missouri visit the headwaters of Norfork Lake, where the beautiful North Fork River meets the backed-up lake, as fish seem to love this junction. Night diving is interesting here.

But almost all of Table Rock Lake is in Missouri, and divers come from miles around to explore its blue water. One favorite area is known as the **Enchanted Forest** because of the moss-draped standing trees. The rocky ledges along the dam, just west of Branson, provide many divers with good fish stories, and sunken cabin cruisers scattered throughout the lake provide interesting exploration. Since the shoreline is varied, with gradually sloping beach entries in some areas, and abrupt dropoffs to below 200' in others, both beach and boat dives are available. Bass, catfish, and walleye abound, as well as bright sunfish. Water clarity is best in April and May, with some divers swearing they could see the surface from 40'. More typical clarity is 10-20'. Water temperature in spring is as low as 50°, and in summer, above the thermocline, as high as 86°. Air and camping is available at the lake.

In the southwest corner of the state near Joplin, divers visit the abandoned lead mines that used to be a big industry in this region. **Oronogo Circle Mine**, north of Webb City, is the favorite. The mine is terraced down to about 270' deep. Mining tunnels lead off from the main body of the mine — these are highly unstable, and much too dangerous for anyone to enter.

One dive that experienced cave divers do enjoy is **Roubideaux Springs**, just off I-44 in Waynesville. A dirt road parallels Roubideaux Creek, and you can park adjacent to the spring. The spring bubbles up at the base of the cliff and forms a pretty pool where water clarity is usually at least 50'. Once you're in the water, you can make out a small opening, 4' in diameter, under a ledge. This leads into a water-filled cavern that measures 40'x70', with a depth of only 45'. Sunlight trickles into the room from the opening and little silt exists to cloud the water. For those who aren't cave divers, it's fun just to explore the cavern, staying in sight of the opening. For the cave diver, though, permanent lines lead off into branches and caverns that can be explored if you've had the training and are properly prepared with octopus rigs, double lights, etc. (see cave diving article in Florida section). Otherwise, you can explore Roubideaux Creek, which has clear water, trout, crayfish, and aquarium plants decorating its rocky bottom.

Two different spots keep divers active in the St. Louis area. **Black Water Quarry**, just off Highway 70, has all the facilities, including air, showers, and snacks. You can enter the quarry from a small beach. Depths don't exceed 60', and clarity ranges from 10' to as much as 40' under the ice in winter. Sometimes you can spot one of the paddlefish that were stocked in the quarry. They're apparently surviving, and the sight of one of these 5'-long fish plowing through the water, mouth agape, is mind-boggling. Shallow caverns and deeper caves tunnel back into the rock. Since these aren't natural formations, they're highly unstable and subject to cave-ins. No diving is permitted in the caves or tunnels.

You can dive in the "world's largest man-made caverns" at **Bonne Terre Mine**,

RICK FREHSEE

The diving dock at Bonne Terre Mine as viewed from the balcony above.

The old Number 1 ore elevator is just one of many artifacts to explore in Bonne Terre Mine.

one hour from St. Louis. For a fee, dive guides will conduct you along dive trails that have been laid out through the flooded mine, past mining artifacts and huge man-made pillars. Dives are made in groups of six, with two divemasters, one in front and one in rear, to make sure no one strays off into the unmarked tunnels. Divemasters light up the miners' shacks, trails, stairways, and columns. One side tour takes you into a cavern with an air pocket, 60' down. The abandoned equipment and rock tunnels seem incredibly surreal, especially if you come out into the snow of a winter day. Cold weather diving is very popular here, since water temperature remains at a year-round 58°, with air temperature just a few degrees higher. The cobalt-blue water sustains no life, and there is very little silt on the flat rock bottom, so clarity is fantastic — at least 100'. Maximum depth in the regions that the tours visit is 80'.

Missouri laws concerning diving: spearing is allowed for rough fish only; dive flag is required.

NEBRASKA

Nebraska is almost a one-lake state when it comes to diving. **Lake McConaughy**, twelve miles north of Ogallala in western Nebraska, has the best diving in the state. Over 100 miles of white sand beaches surround the 30,000-acre impoundment on the Platte River. The lake still has a rustic air, with almost no famous resort chains, but instead small cabins and campgrounds tucked among the cottonwoods. Since the creation of Lake McConaughy immersed the site of an Ogallala Sioux village, many artifacts can be found just by walking the beaches.

Underwater, the favorite activity is spearfishing, and the favorite spot is near the dam, where maximum depth reaches 140'. A surface water temperature of well above 80° in summer may fool you — a sharp thermocline exists, and if you're planning on staying down for more than about 30 seconds, a wetsuit is necessary. Clarity at the lake is the best in Nebraska, varying from less than 5' to well over 25'. The lake has given up many record fish, both to hook and line and to spear. Over the July 4th weekend in 1982, a 19-1/2 lb. striped bass broke the old record for a striper caught by a spear. In just one weekend during a recent championship tournament, the scene was reminiscent of the early days of scuba, with 3-1/2 tons of rough and game fish speared.

Big surf near the outlet and high winds during unpredictable storms pose the major hazards. Boat traffic necessitates use of a dive flag. At the **North Platte River**, below the dam, you can enjoy a drift dive, watching crayfish and the abundant fish life found in the river.

In the eastern part of the state, **Crystal Cove Lake** near Sioux City, Iowa, covers about 30 acres, and, since no power boats are permitted, divers enjoy the calm waters. A bizarre, irregular bottom of hardened, boulder-size sand formations in every possible shape provide underwater interest. Clarity can be as much as 20', and fish thrive here, including bass, bluegill, catfish, gar, carp, bullheads, northern pike, and muskies. Aquatic plants grow on the 65'-deep bottom. Cold water means a full wetsuit will be necessary if going below the thermocline at 35'. No night diving is allowed.

Stretching all along I-80 from North Platte to Grande Island is a series of small lakes known locally as **sand pits**. These were created during highway construction. In spring and fall, clarity of 10-15' allows divers to explore their waters. During summer, algae blooms inhibit diving activity. Maximum depths are usually less than 40'.

Nebraska laws concerning diving: Spearing is legal for rough fish year-round, and for game fish from July 1st to December 31st in certain lakes including McConaughy, Ogallala, Minatare, Box Butte, Lewis and Clark, Harlan County, Enders, Swanson, Red Willow, Medicine Creek, Sutherland, Maloney, Jeffrey Canyon, Johnson, Sherman, Elwood, and Merritt. Dive flag is required.

NORTH DAKOTA

If you know anything at all about diving in North Dakota, you're ahead of me.

OKLAHOMA

The greatest concentration of man-made lakes in the world is found in the "Green Country" of eastern Oklahoma. **Lake Tenkiller**, 65 miles southeast of Tulsa, stands out from the rest as the one most suitable for diving. Building foundations, standing trees, brush piles swarming with crappie, bluffs undercut with small caves, and the wrecks of cars and boats make diving Tenkiller intriguing. At **Strayhorn Landing**, on the west side of the lake, a 20-passenger school bus sits on the bottom in 40' of water. Nearby, you can explore swingsets and various boats and cars all on the bottom. Numerous islands around the lake offer camping hideaways for those with a boat. Depths go to 165', and clarity averages 20' in summer, when surface temperatures reach 90°.

Lake Eufaula, near the town of the same name, sees some diving activity, especially spearfishing tournaments, although water clarity is unpredictable, due to the clay soils.

If you're caught in Oklahoma without any money, you can always try mussel shell collecting. Some divers make over $150 a day, although most use hookah gear instead of tanks. The favorite area is in the shallow streams feeding **Fort Gibson Lake**, 30 miles north of Tenkiller.

Oklahoma laws concerning diving: Spearing is permitted for rough fish only; dive flag is required.

The phytoplankton of the earth's oceans produce most of the oxygen in our atmosphere.

SOUTH DAKOTA

South Dakota contains two main areas that interest divers. One is the famous vacation attraction of the Black Hills. Several lakes and reservoirs nestled in these pine-covered 7000'-high mountains make for good diving. The most accessible to visiting divers, and one that offers a lot of underwater interest, is **Pactola Reservoir**. For a good orientation to the history and ecology of the area, stop at the Forest Service Visitor Center located at the reservoir. Maximum depths in the dark blue lake reach about 160'; rock ledges and boulders cover the sides for much of the way down. Pactola has good clarity for a Midwestern lake, averaging about 20'. The remains of an old camp at 15' depth make a good subject for photos, as do the abundant fish and still-standing trees. Since the surface temperature at Pactola doesn't go above 72°, and the thermocline drops it at least 10-15° colder, a full wetsuit is recommended.

A chain of four gigantic lakes was created from the Missouri River. **Lake Oahe**, the uppermost of the four, and the one closest to services in Pierre, has by far the best diving. This 250-mile-long lake offers innumerable spots to dive, with some of the favorites being the sites of a tugboat, an old calvary fort (which still surrenders valuable artifacts such as old bottles and military equipment), and the site of an Arikara Indian village.

Since the Arikara were pushed from the area by the Sioux before the 18th century, artifacts like arrowheads, bone tools, and stone grinders found from this site have special historical importance. Although the maximum depth in Oahe is past 200', you can find good snorkeling off several of the beaches, where gentle slopes and extensive flats can be found. For deeper diving, many areas of rocky walls exist. Game fish such as walleye, bass, kokanee salmon, and perch may be speared during season, which usually starts July 1st.

Easy shore access will lead you to the **tailwaters of Oahe Dam**, where you can plan an exciting drift dive in current of up to five knots if they're letting the water out. If not, you can poke around more leisurely, looking for artifacts. Many buffalo skulls in varying degrees of preservation have been recovered. Fish abound in the gravel-bottom river, and since maximum depth is only about 30', you'll have plenty of time for observation. Besides the more common inhabitants like burbot (the only freshwater cod), 3'-long shovelnose sturgeon, crawdads, catfish, and walleyes, you might see the huge and archaic paddlefish. Clarity ranges from 15' up. From January to April is a good time to dive the tailwaters, since the moving water prevents ice buildup and attracts fish. Sometimes gar and other rough fish gather by the hundreds to hang in the current in a stupor. Great photos can be taken, since the fish are practically oblivious to your presence. No diving within 100 yards of the powerhouse.

In eastern South Dakota, **Alexandria Quarry**, near the town of the same name, is operated exclusively for divers by King Neptune's Scuba, just across the state line in Sioux City, Iowa. Permission must be granted from them to dive the quarry, which has varied rock face walls. The spring-fed quarry attains its best clarity in winter — as much as 80' — with summer's 30' being typical. Maximum depths are 85'.

South Dakota laws concerning diving: Year-round spearing for rough fish is allowed, except in South Dakota-Minnesota boundary waters, where the rough fish season is from April 28th to November 30th. Spearing for game fish is legal in Lakes Francis Case, Sharpe, Oahe, and Lewis and Clark, and in Belle Fourche and Angostura Reservoirs; seasons and precise locations vary. Dive flag is required.

MERLIN HILMOE

Schooling gar present a surreal scene in the tailwaters of the Oahe Dam.

GREAT LAKES STATES

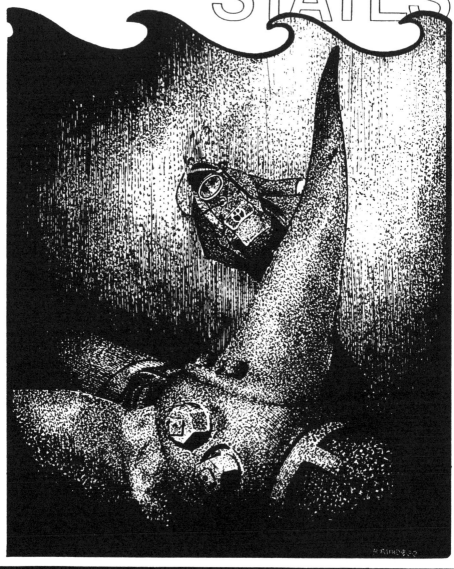

ILLINOIS   **INDIANA**   **MICHIGAN**

Diving in the Great Lakes is practically synonymous with wreck diving. Nowhere else in the world is there such a concentration of wrecks available to the diver. Since fresh water preserves wood to a remarkable degree, nowhere else will you find as many sunken vessels from the previous century in a basically intact condition.

Spend enough time wreck diving in the Great Lakes, and you can learn the entire history of the enormous shipping industry of the area. In the late 1800's, as many as 1700 steamboats and 1500 sailing ships navigated the immense and often dangerous inland seas, usually without any instrumentation to speak of. For some captains, even a compass was an unnecessary amenity, as they navigated by pointing the hour hand of their watch at the sun and then guessing that south was somewhere between that point and the "12" on the dial. Such haphazard navigation, coupled with ferocious and unpredictable storms, often caused doom for these vessels. Hundreds of exciting wrecks litter the floor of each lake, ranging from upright wooden sailing ships from the 19th century to colossal modern steel freighters.

To explore these wrecks, remember that penetrating sunken vessels is an exacting sport similar to cave diving, since free ascent to the surface is often impossible. Specialized equipment beyond that needed for ordinary scuba is essential. Training for wreck diving is available at many dive stores.

Beautiful terrain of boulder-strewn shores and sheer cliffs line the lakes at the most scenic locales. Favorite spots for traveling divers include Wisconsin's rocky Door Peninsula which separates Green Bay from Lake Michigan, and Minnesota's North Shore on Lake Superior where sheer cliffs plummet hundreds of feet to the water and where the wreck-diver's paradise of Isle Royale lies 22 miles offshore.

In addition, the Great Lakes states have multitudes of smaller lakes and quarries that offer exciting diving, with fish life that ranges from barracuda-like muskie to prehistoric sturgeon and paddlefish. Like the Great Lakes themselves, these waters are COLD. Lake Superior, the wildest and coldest lake, has a year-round temperature of 34-39° below the thermocline! Special considerations have to be made to deal with extreme temperatures like these. Regulator freeze-up can be a problem, so diving with two regulators is the practice. Drysuits are preferable, although hardy divers do submerge (briefly!) in full weight, farmer-john style wetsuits, with vest and hood.

ILLINOIS

Besides its 70 miles of shoreline on Lake Michigan, Illinois also has abundant strip mines for diving in the Carbondale and Peoria areas, as well as the diving center of Pearl Lake near Beloit.

Although many traveling divers don't realize it, Illinois' Lake Michigan shore is a substantial attraction for many divers, despite its proximity to Chicago. Chicago has gone to great lengths — even reversing the Chicago River to flow away from the lake — to keep Lake Michigan clean. Still, clarity can be low enough to be measured in inches instead of feet. The closest diving site off the Chicago area is the **4-mile crib**, east of Burnham Harbor. Rumor is that certain advanced divers explore the interior of an abandoned pumping station, accessible only after a swim through a submerged intake pipe.

For dives more suitable to the average diver, there are a couple of interesting wrecks close to Chicago which have given up an amazing variety of souvenirs. Both the wooden steamer *Iowa* and the steel steamer *Flora M. Hill* were victims of ice. The *Iowa* was trapped by pack ice in 1915, and although tugboats were unable to reach the vessel, 71 passengers and crew walked to safety across the ice. Since the 202'-long vessel was cut in two by the ice and later dynamited as a shipping hazard, there isn't much intact wreckage to be seen, but divers still head out to the site, two miles off the Chicago light, to look for magnetos and other souvenirs from its cargo of automobile parts.

The 130' long *Hill* carried a cargo of brass beds and running lamps for early automobiles when the ice trapped her in 1912. The crew of 28 walked to safety across the ice. Although the *Hill*, like the *Iowa*, was later dynamited, you can still see the boiler, props, and rudder in the midst of piles of metal plates that were the hull. Since 1976, when the *Flora M. Hill* was found, the solid brass lamps have shown up in the homes of many divers, and more are still to be found.

Pearl Lake is also found in northern Illinois, near the town of Beloit. This 30-acre flooded quarry offers swimming on the south shore and diving on the north, where activities range from fish-feeding to exploring the remains of boats, trucks, a school bus, and a twin-engine Beechcraft airplane. The sandy bottom has an average depth of 35-40' and a maximum depth of 75'. Clarity is very good by Illinois standards, often attaining 35'. As in all Illinois sites, a wetsuit is necessary, since the water can range from 70° on the surface to less than 50° below the thermocline.

South of Peoria, in Fulton County, several **strip mines** attract divers. Abundant aquatic life, as well as submerged trees, gives you plenty to look at underwater. Most of these strip mines slope steeply to a slightly rounded bottom 30-50' deep. Summer clarity ranges from 15-25', and spring might produce visibility of more than 35'. Miles of monofilament present the major hazard.

The Carbondale region in southern Illinois has its share of **strip mines**, too. Bass, bluegill, carp, catfish, turtles, snakes, frogs, and crappie are among the most notable inhabitants. In addition, submerged cars, usually with shady pasts, create interesting habitats for exploration.

Illinois laws concerning diving: Carp, buffalo, suckers, gar, and bowfin may be taken by underwater spearfishing, with license.

INDIANA

With less than 50 miles of Lake Michigan shoreline, Indiana barely qualifies as a Great Lakes state. Little diving is done along Indiana's Lake Michigan shoreline, since its highly industrialized and heavily populated cities of East Chicago, Gary, and Michigan City do little for water quality.

Off the water tower at the western end of the Indiana Dunes National Park, divers visit the remains of the *J.D. Marshall*, 600 yards offshore and 32' deep. This 154'-long wooden steamer capsized in 1911, and floated upside-down for almost a month, strewing tools and equipment over the bottom until the boiler finally fell out and caused the steamer to sink. Now the boiler and the large propeller rest near the upside-down hull, and provide good photographs if clarity permits. Many tools can also be found in the sand.

Some diving also takes place in Michigan City's **Washington Park**, where you can dive off a pier heavily used by anglers into shallow water with a sand and rock bottom. Clarity varies but is never more than 10'. Usually, heavy boat traffic reduces visibility as well as safety — use a flag. Perch, lake trout, and salmon can be spotted underwater by the diligent. On solid ground, you can visit the old lighthouse museum, the zoo, and the rest of the lakefront park.

But the center for diving activity in north Indiana is **Frances Park**, four miles west of Logansport. Divers come from Fort Wayne, Indianapolis, and South Bend to this small town on Highway 24 north of Kokomo. The quarry at Frances Park averages 25' deep, with visibility of 5-20' in summer, depending on how many divers have stirred up the water. The quarry has been developed especially for divers, with railroad-tie fish habitats, train wheels, and a gravel shaker underwater. Hundreds of bluegill, big bass, and channel cats provide good photos, but the real standout at Frances Park is the paddlefish, also called the spoonbill cat.

To call them "prehistoric" is like calling Palancar a "nice little reef." Spoonbills were plugging along in the rivers of the Mississippi Basin before dinosaurs had even begun to evolve, when today's coal deposits were still cycad and tree fern forests. When you see a spoonbill come weaving out of the gloom towards you, with its gallon bucket of a mouth agape as it filters plankton from the water, you are looking at the most ancient of all North American large animals. Unfortunately, you are also looking at a creature whose kind is in rapid demise. Paddlefish may have survived Ice Ages and world wars, but it's unlikely they'll survive the Army Corps of Engineers, who have systematically dammed the paddlefish away from their spawning grounds on shallow gravelly rivers.

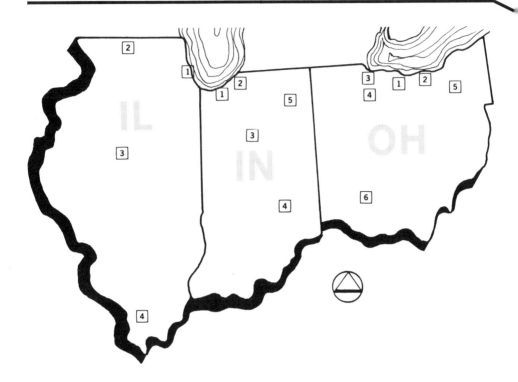

ILLINOIS
4-mile crib 1
Flora M. Hill 1
Iowa 1
Pearl Lake 2
Strip mines 3,4

INDIANA
Blue Springs 4
Fawn 5
Frances Park 3
J.D. Marshall 1
Lake Cicott 3
Pigeon 5
Shriner Lake 5
Tippecanoe 5
Washington Park 2

OHIO
Adventure 1
America 1
F.H. Prince 1
Nelson Ledges Quarry Park 5
North Carolina 2
Portage Quarry 3
Salisbury Quarry 3
Sportsman Lake 6
White Star Park 4

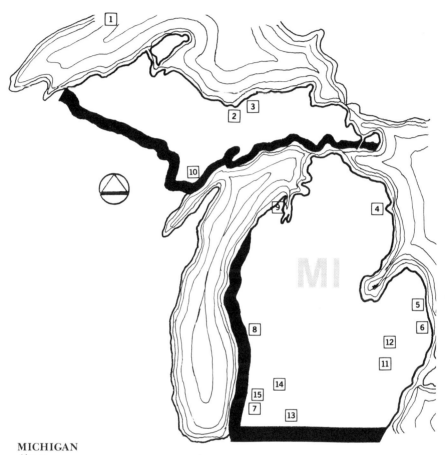

MICHIGAN

Algoma	1
America	1
Ben Hur	6
Boardman River	9
C.R. Price	5
Chester A. Congdon	1
Coulborn	6
Cumberland	1
Dreadnaught	2
Emperor	1
Francis Morozan	9
George M. Cox	1
Granada	2
Grecian	4
Gull Lake	14
Hartzell	9
Havana	7
Henry Chisholm	1
Henry Cort	8
Herman Hettler	2
Isle Royale	1
Johnson	4

Kiowa	3
M.E. Trembel	6
Manhattan	2
Menominee	10
Monahamphet	4
Monarch	1
Monrovia	4
Montana	4
Nordmeer	4
Oscar T. Flint	4
Otter Lake	12
Paw Paw Lake	15
Rock jetties	9
Smith Moore	2
St. Clair River	6
Stoney Lake	11
Superior	3
Union Lake	13
Walter Frost	9
Whitney Bridge	8

THE GREAT LAKES

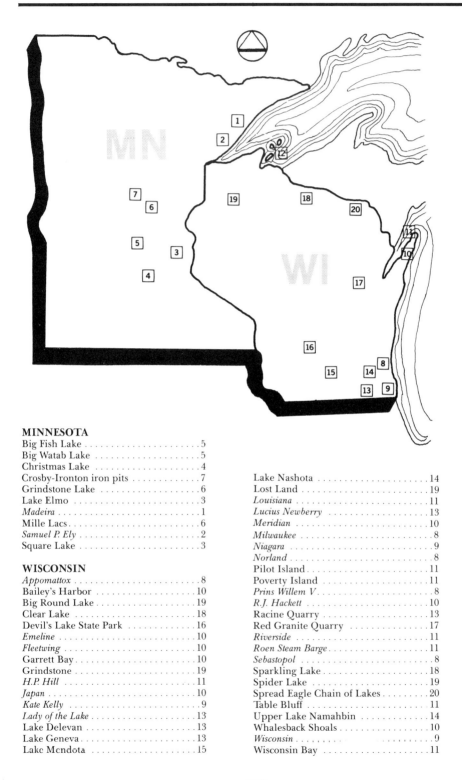

MINNESOTA

Big Fish Lake 5
Big Watab Lake 5
Christmas Lake 4
Crosby-Ironton iron pits 7
Grindstone Lake 6
Lake Elmo 3
Madeira 1
Mille Lacs. 6
Samuel P. Ely 2
Square Lake 3

WISCONSIN

Appomattox 8
Bailey's Harbor 10
Big Round Lake 19
Clear Lake 18
Devil's Lake State Park 16
Emeline 10
Fleetwing 10
Garrett Bay. 10
Grindstone 19
H.P. Hill 11
Japan 10
Kate Kelly 9
Lady of the Lake 13
Lake Delevan 13
Lake Geneva. 13
Lake Mendota 15

Lake Nashota 14
Lost Land 19
Louisiana 11
Lucius Newberry 13
Meridian 10
Milwaukee 8
Niagara 9
Norland 8
Pilot Island. 11
Poverty Island 11
Prins Willem V 8
R.J. Hackett 10
Racine Quarry 13
Red Granite Quarry 17
Riverside 11
Roen Steam Barge. 11
Sebastopol 8
Sparkling Lake 18
Spider Lake 19
Spread Eagle Chain of Lakes 20
Table Bluff 11
Upper Lake Namahbin 14
Whalesback Shoals 10
Wisconsin 9
Wisconsin Bay 11

Today, paddlefish are almost entirely restricted to implantation in quarries and reservoirs from captive-bred stocks. Their only relative is found in the Yangtze in China. Frances Park is one of the best places to see the bizarre fish, since the individuals at the Frances Park quarry are big — almost six-foot. Since they continually grow and are very long-lived — at least 30 years and, likely, more — there's a chance that these paddlefish at Frances Park may become 300-lb. giants like those reportedly netted in the 1800's. Lie still near the cliffs at the back of the quarry in fall or spring for the best chance at sighting a paddlefish.

Besides paddlefish-watching, at Frances Park you can go camping, ride horses, play miniature golf, or go on the waterslides. The kids can swim on the sandy beach entrance to the quarry, without bothering the divers too much, since the majority of the quarry is ringed by steeply sloping rock walls. Summer water temperatures of 80° make wetsuits unnecessary in the shallow quarry.

Lake Cicott, just west of Logansport, is the place to head if you want a dive that's a little deeper. Here the bottom drops off into mud at about 55'. A full wetsuit is needed year-round, since below the thermocline the spring-fed lake's temperature drops to 50°. Rumor has it that Lake Cicott is connected to a Canadian body of water by an underground river! At least, that's the story they tell to explain the periodic rises and falls in the lake level. Spearing can be done by permission only. Clarity is usually less than 10'.

South of Indianapolis, at Waldron (near Shelbyville) is **Blue Springs**, a favorite dive for people from as far away as Ohio. An abandoned stone quarry with about 15 acres of water has numerous underwater attractions, including a large cabin cruiser, a van, fossil collecting, and some large bass and sunfish. The main attraction, though, is the good water clarity, which is in the 20-30' range for most of the year. Access is easy, with a diving platform for each of the three areas of the quarry. Average depth is 50', with one area dropping off to 65'. Fee-operated, the quarry has no air available, but it can be purchased in Franklin.

Hundreds of lakes of glacial origin dot northeastern Indiana. Most aren't exactly scuba delights because of murky water and shallow depths. **Tippecanoe**, at 125', is the deepest. **Shriner Lake** is the favorite for diving, since it offers easy access and entry, and limited boat traffic. Ten feet from the shore, the bottom drops to 30', then gradually slides to a maximum of about 65'. Turtles, bluegill, and bass all thrive in the weedy water, where clarity averages 10'.

Also in northeastern Indiana, you will find two wide, fast, shallow rivers, the **Fawn** and the **Pigeon**. Check with local divers before you attempt to ride down these rivers.

Indiana laws concerning diving: You must have written permission to dive in any state-controlled lakes. Spearing is allowed for rough fish only.

MICHIGAN

With more than 3000 miles of shoreline on four of the Great Lakes, Michigan has more waterfront than the Atlantic coast between Maine and Florida. Its shoreline, on some of the largest freshwater lakes on the face of the globe, also contains some of the world's best wreck diving. Lake Superior bounds the north face of the Upper Peninsula, and its fury has created an amazing concentration of shipwrecks in the pristine water around the wilderness of Isle Royale. The Alger County region, centered at Munising, has such a fantastic record of Lake Superior's shipping disasters that a special preserve has been created to save them. Michigan's east coast is the only Lake Huron shoreline in the USA, with an area — also a preserve — of tremendous wreck diving potential located at Thunder Bay, near Alpena. And you can't forget Lake Michigan's east shoreline (the longest freshwater coast in the world), or any of the innumerable fine diving lakes scattered throughout the state.

LAKE SUPERIOR — ISLE ROYALE

Without a doubt, **Isle Royale** has attained the greatest fame of any Michigan site. No other known locale in the world has such an incredible concentration of accessible wreck sites. Isle Royale, situated in the middle of the commercial shipping lanes, surrounded by dangerous passages through shallow rock reefs, and subject to Superior's infamous gales and temperatures, has enticed many proud vessels to their doom.

Today Isle Royale is a National Park, and all divers are required to register with a ranger station before diving. If the words "National Park" make you groan and think of hordes of pudgy tourists in Bermudas burning up their Instamatics on a black bear that's creating a traffic jam, then read on. Isle Royale is a wilderness park, with no roads, no cars, and no permanent dwellings — just trees and wildlife. In winter, there's only incredible frozen solitude, a solid ice sheath ringing the island, and the howlings of the wolves as they track down enfeebled moose.

Summer, though, is a different story. Backpackers and day campers come by the hundreds from Minnesota ferries for a taste of wilderness adventure on the biggest freshwater island in this hemisphere. Dive boats swarm around the spot of green that is Isle Royale, lost out in the vastness of all that blue. At least a dozen major wrecks encircle the island, and countless other ones still haven't been fully explored. Each presents a totally unique and dramatic sight that gives you an unparalleled feeling of time travel. Water clarity is remarkable for freshwater, often averaging 60' or better.

The frigid water of Superior has maintained these wrecks to an astonishing degree, and the park service is assuring their preservation by a tough policy on artifact removal that includes imprisonment and fines up to $10,000. Be prepared for near-freezing water temperature, even in summer, as it seldom rises above 39°.

The *America*, in Washington Harbor, is one of the favorite wrecks. Sliced open by the rock reef in heavy fog in 1928, the *America* stayed afloat long enough for the passengers and crew to escape unharmed. Finally, the 183' steel steamer slid to its ultimate port, with the bow just 3' below the waves, and the rest of the vessel lying at a maximum depth of 80'. The midship and stern are still intact, and lower parts of the deck are littered with mounds of wreckage that have been knotted into a congealed mass by the yearly ravages of ice.

If you're properly equipped and experienced, you can penetrate the *America*, drifting down the stairs and entering the surrealistic dining room, where all the chairs and tables have tumbled like matchsticks. At night, everything seems dreamlike, including the bright brass fittings of the engine room or the grand piano in the ballroom.

The *George M. Cox* went aground in 1933 near the Rock of Ages lighthouse on the western tip of the island. Only the stern of the 259' steel passenger liner submerged, so all the passengers survived. There were hopes of salvaging the vessel until Lake Superior sent a raging gale that pushed the *Cox* off its precarious perch. Pieces of wreckage have been scattered over the reef, starting in 40' of water. Portholes and deck hatches are still in place, and you can follow the driveshaft right down the reef to the massive prop, 100' deep.

Less than 1/4 mile from the *Cox*, the wreckage of the **Cumberland** and the **Henry Chisholm** have been intermingled into one powerful testament to Superior's storms. The *Cumberland*, a wooden side paddlewheeler, sank in a surprise August storm in 1877, after only six years of service. Large sections of wooden hull and the remains of a sidewheel lie from 40' to 80' deep. The *Henry Chisholm* sank in the same spot two decades later. This 256'-long wooden freighter is remembered mainly by its 20'-high intact steam engine. The driveshaft, prop, and other wreckage continues down the slope of the reef, past 140'.

On the opposite end of the island lie the remains of the "Big Three," consisting of the **Emperor**, the **Chester A. Congdon**, and the **Monarch**. The mighty steamer

Emperor didn't manage to evade the dreaded Canoe Rocks, and twelve people perished when the 525' vessel went down in 1947. It takes several dives just to comprehend the immensity of this intact giant. The bow took the brunt of the impact, but the stern is in almost supernaturally good shape, with its mast still standing and huge winches for the massive anchor that still appear operable. The stern mast is first encountered at 60', and maximum depth at the stern end is 175', so this is an excellent place to extend your bottom time with a device such as Orca's Edge.

The *Congdon*, a 532' ore carrier, attempted to stand out a gale in 1918, positioned on what's now Congdon Shoal. Instead, the ship snapped in two. The bow drifted down, intact, to rest on one side of the Shoal, while the huge stern slid down the other side, where it lies at depths from 20' to past 180'. Most dive the bow side, as the spectacle of the neatly severed bow, complete with pilot house at 110', is not easily forgotten.

The *Monarch* was small in comparison. The 240' schooner had the ill fortune to encounter a blinding snowstorm on its final voyage in 1906. After it smashed into the cliff at Blake's Point, on the north end of the island, a daring transfer of passengers saved all lives but one. Today you can learn much about the everyday life of a ship as you can drift down a trail of scattered debris, ranging from a 155'-long piece of hull, to china, a bathtub, and brass fixtures — from 20' to past 90'. The Park Service has installed underwater signs marking points of interest, like the heavy construction necessary for wooden vessels operating in long navigational seasons. The *Monarch* is the only interpretively marked shipwreck in the States.

Just off Mott Island on the eastern side of Isle Royale is the wreckage of the **Algoma**. The *Algoma* was one of the most tragic of the Isle Royale wrecks. Forty-five people, including children, died when the *Algoma* sank in 1885. Wreckage from the 262' vessel has been widely scattered and broken up. The bow lies out in the depths somewhere, still undiscovered, while bits and pieces of stern have been strewn randomly from a depth of 10' to past 150'.

Further south on the east coast lie the remains of the steamer **Glenlyon**. This wreck isn't visited as often, since it's in an isolated position on an exposed reef, open to all bad weather. Caught in the midst of a heavy gale with zero visibility in 1924, the *Glenlyon* plowed right onto a reef. The crew survived and was rescued the following day, although two panicked sailors who took off in a lifeboat were blown clear down to the Apostle Islands. After the rescue, the insurance salvors decided to wait until spring to float the ship but, after enduring one winter, the *Glenlyon* was totally destroyed.

The 328' vessel today is scattered over the reef to a depth of 80'. It's rather sobering to come across pieces of bow, still intact but flattened as if crushed by a steamroller. The winch, anchor chain, driveshaft, prop, engine, and anchors are all still easily visible. A cabin remains basically intact and penetrable, still with the original tongue-in-groove ceiling, portholes, and door fittings. Since most of the wreckage is in about 30' of water, there are good possibilities for photography.

Although the *Kamloops* is too deep for sport diving, it deserves mention since for many years it reigned as the "queen of Superior's mystery fleet." Finally she was located by Captain Roy Oberg, out of Grand Portage, Minnesota, and in 1977 was seen by divers for the first time since her mysterious sinking 50 years before. She lies on her starboard side at depths of 175-265'. The reasons behind the sinking will forever be a mystery. A bottle containing the sad message "I am the last one alive, freezing and starving to death on Isle Royale, signed Alice B" was the only previous clue of what happened to the crew.

LAKE SUPERIOR — MUNISING AREA

The Munising area includes everything from Au Train Point east to Au Sable Point. It has been declared a state bottomlands preserve to protect its historically and recreationally important shipwrecks — 21 known sites, and at least 10 undiscovered ones. Besides containing some of the oldest intact wrecks around, this Lake Superior shoreline also offers the colorful rock cliffs and giant dunes of the Pictured Rocks National Lakeshore.

One of the most famous of the wrecks has long been thought to be the schooner **Dreadnaught** — but recently it was proven to be the **Granada**. Regardless of the identity crisis, the *DreadnaughtGranada* makes a fine dive. You can see the vessel before you descend, since clarity ranges from 30-60'. The 115' wooden schooner is basically intact, although the masts and deckhouses have long since been scoured away by ice, as the deck is only 15' deep. You can tour the outside of the old ship, swimming around the boxy hull and the rudder, and still have time to enter the crew's quarters where now only burbot crowd around the old stove. Well protected, and with a maximum depth of only 35', the *DreadnaughtGranada* offers one of the finest dives for novices, yet is still thrilling enough for the most jaded.

On the other hand, the **Smith Moore**, one of the area's most popular dives, should only be undertaken by the experienced. The 223' wooden freighter was sideswiped in a hit-and-run in 1889 and began inhaling water at a tremendous rate. A passing steamer rescued the crew and towed the *Smith Moore*, only to see her go down 300' outside the harbor. Since she was carrying iron and silver ore, the *Smith Moore* dropped to the bottom like a stone, to sit perfectly upright at 130'. Almost 100 years have gone by and left her untouched. The weather, ice, and waves that so abuse shallower ships haven't fazed this one. You can swim along the ornately carved deck rails and admire the name, still clearly visible just above the rudder. You can peer into a cabin to see all the accouterments still in their original places: bunks on the walls and stoppers in the sinks. Only the bow gives evidence of the reason why this beautiful ship sits on the bottom, instead of in a museum. Since this is a deep dive, below the thermocline in icy darkness, its dreamlike quality is best left to the more experienced.

Nearby, the remains of the **Herman Hettler** and the **Manhattan**, both wooden steamers, have been strewn over a vast area of lake bottom. All sorts of debris, including boilers, bits and pieces of machinery, a bathtub, and decking are strewn over the sand bottom at a depth of 40'.

It's hard to imagine the terrible scene as you gaze at the cliffs of Spray Falls but, in 1856, 18 survivors huddled out the night in a small indentation in the cliff. Thirty-four of their fellow passengers perished after their vessel, the **Superior**, lost her rudder in a storm and crashed into the rocks. Less than 15' of water covers the remains, which are broadcast over a sand and rock bottom. The tubed boiler and ship's stack are always visible; other items like gold coins, plates, rivets, and buttons are sometimes uncovered by shifting sand. The bright rocks and bubbling water make diving near the plunging falls intriguing.

Further east, the 225' steel freighter **Kiowa** foundered in a blizzard in 1929. The captain and a few crewmen deserted the ship in the only lifeboat, leaving the rest to fend for themselves. In a rare case of poetic justice, the lifeboat capsized in the gigantic seas, but the crippled vessel drifted onto a reef, where all the crew were rescued. It's a bit intimidating to see what Lake Superior can do to a steel freighter. The bow has been totally shorn off and upended, while the rest of the *Kiowa* has become a twisted mass of steel rubble. Some divers report that the *Kiowa* is a nursery for immature sturgeon schools and other juvenile fish. According to oldtimers, the *Kiowa* was carrying flax when she went under. The local fish all loved this addition to their diet, but it made the catches in the area taste like paint thinner — and fit only for faraway markets like Chicago! Depths at the *Kiowa* range from 30-50'.

LAKE HURON — Thunder Bay

Everyone has heard about Canada's Tobermory area on Lake Huron, but not everyone realizes that the U.S. also has an area of tremendous wreck diving potential along our Lake Huron shore. The Thunder Bay area, just off Alpena, has over 75 verified shipwrecks, ranging from 1880's schooners to huge modern steel freighters. At least 20 of these wrecks are known — the rest still wait to be discovered. This makes Thunder Bay a paradise for the wreck diver/researcher who wants to experience first-hand the intense rush of discovering and penetrating a virgin wreck.

But Thunder Bay also has attractions for the weekend diver who wants nothing more than an interesting dive. It's a good idea to check with local dive stores before planning anything, since this area has fewer tourist services. Also, clarity in Thunder Bay can vary from 1-50' on a daily basis. Luckily, clear water can usually be predicted if an offshore wind has been blowing for several days. While Huron isn't as cold as Superior, summer water temperatures can go as low as 40-45°, so be prepared. Generally, from June to August average water temperature is 60°.

If each of the five million eggs discharged by the common oyster at each spawning matured, within four generations there would be a mass of oysters eight times the size of our planet.

Cliffs on Lake Superior's rugged coastline.

One of the favorite dives is the wreck of the **Nordmeer**, which lies six miles north of Thunder Bay Island. You can see 30' of the pilot house protruding from the water as you approach this steel freighter, which ran aground with no lives lost in 1966. On clear days, the pilothouse can be seen from as far as five miles away. This ocean-going German vessel of 580' now rests on a flat rock and sand bottom at a depth of 50'. Clarity of 30-50' and the immensity of this intact wreck make this an exciting dive. Since you can easily penetrate the engine room and holds, the *Nordmeer* is a good place to learn wreck diving skills.

A very different wreck that is located just off Thunder Bay Island is the **Monahamphet**. Lots of wood from this old vessel has been scattered over the bottom, just 500 yards offshore, at a depth of 25'. Much machinery, including boilers and the cast-iron prop, can easily be seen.

For those who really want a good look at early engines, the **Montana** is a must. The wooden remains of this steamer have been torn up, but the big engine still offers an interesting look into engine design of the late 1880's. The wreckage rises from 75' to within 40' of the surface.

Another interesting dive takes you down to survey the 200'-long **Johnson**. Formerly a schooner, this wooden ship was cut down into a barge, and in that metamorphosis she shall remain, since she lies 45' down, intact, with the rudder turned hard left.

Other good dives around Thunder Bay include the **Oscar T. Flint**, which caught fire and sank rapidly, due to her cargo of stone. Debris is everywhere in the 35' depths around the 250'-long, partially intact frame.

The **Grecian** was a WWII Liberty Ship that had done her service time and was being towed for scrap. Instead, she ended up on the sandy, mucky bottom almost 12 miles out of Alpena, with a buoy to mark her location. It's 80' down to the deck, and 110' down to the base of the 296'-long steel steamer. The intact deck is littered with equipment, and experienced wreck divers explore three levels within the stern.

An even deeper wreck is the **Monrovia**, undertaken usually by more advanced divers, due to the depth and darkness. It's a spectacular sight to see the big steel freighter looming up at you after you've descended 100' to the top deck. The *Monrovia* is located 26 miles straight out of Alpena.

Besides wrecks, divers in the Alpena area enjoy a sinkhole with steep limestone walls and depth of 70'. Check locally for details.

LAKE HURON — Port Huron Area

The lower end of Lake Huron also contains some interesting dives, like the boat dive out to the wreck of the **C.R. Price**. This lake freighter turned bottom-up and sank in 1913, and now lies on a gravel bottom (silt buildup occurs in fall) at a maximum depth of 70'. The hull of the 500' freighter has broken open in spots,

and the superstructure is scattered around the bottom near the stern end. The prop is still attached. Clarity is extremely variable — up to 40'.

Sturgeons, which release as many as 5 million eggs at a time, don't mature until they are 15 to 20 years old.

MERLIN HILMOE

But the most famous dives in the Port Huron area are the dives on the **St. Clair River**. This river is the straw that funnels Lake Huron into Lake Erie — and, as you'd expect, the currents can get ferocious. The current speed picks up from six knots to twelve, so you can either drift the river, or visit one of the many shipwrecks. If you're going to dive a wreck, the practice is to plant your flag on shore at point of entry, and follow the cables that a local dive store has been instrumental in placing. Because of the speed of the current and the frequency of boat traffic, including large freighters, novices should practice elsewhere. Visiting divers should check with local divers who are experienced in river and traffic conditions.

Among the favorite wreck dives are the wooden schooner *M.E. Trembel*, which sank in 1890, and the *Ben Hur*, which sank just downstream while attempting salvage. Since these vessels were considered a navigational hazard, they were dynamited, and their remains are widely scattered. Dangerous crosscurrents make these for the experienced only. To gain river experience, try a dive at the "unloader" nearby, where currents aren't as severe.

The **Coulborn** also is a wreck-picker's delight, with old bottles, sections of chain, and just about anything else you could think of scattered over the 30'-deep, stony bottom. Cabled, and with a line running downstream to an ancient steam crane (and from there to shore), this is still a dive for the experienced, due to the terrific wash from freighters that can tear your mask from your face.

For drift divers, the technique is to pick up a sturdy stick from the bottom so you can poke it into the clay substrate and momentarily hold still. Entry is near the Blue Water Bridge, and exit should be made before the sewage treatment plant interferes with water quality. An incredible assortment of debris and artifacts presents itself to you once you've descended the gradual slope to the rock and clay channel, where the maximum depth is 90'. Pottery, bottles, Indian artifacts (the Canadian side of the St. Clair is a reservation), and items of every description dating back to the French and Indian wars have been found. Combine that with abundant fish life, including schools of pike and sturgeon, and clarity that can be as much as 20', and you have a very exciting dive for the adventurous, experienced diver who knows how to handle currents and large boat traffic.

LAKE MICHIGAN

Although Lake Michigan's shoreline is the longest freshwater coast in the world, its frontage on the state of Michigan doesn't draw the traveling diver like Lakes Superior and Huron do. This is largely due to the lower visibility, which seldom passes 15' in summer. However, in spring clarity can be more than 40', and many interesting dives can be made off the Michigan coast, especially for relic and bottle collectors. One of the finest finds anywhere was the recovery by a sport diver near Petoskey of an old Indian trading rifle from the early 1700's.

The southernmost good diving on Lake Michigan is located in the St. Joseph area, where the wreck of the **Havana** lies on a sand bottom at 55' depth just six miles north of the pier. Near Muskegon, divers visit the **Henry Cort**, a whaleback that lies in 30' of water off the pier. One of the best dives in the area is **Whitney Bridge**, which once spanned the Muskegon River, but now lies 60' down in the backwaters of Hardy Dam.

One of the greatest concentrations of shipwrecks found anywhere in the Great Lakes lies in the Manitou Passage, the dangerous straits between the Manitou Islands and the Sleeping Bear Dunes National Lakeshore on the Michigan mainland. This wreck diving paradise, located near Traverse City, appeals to both wreck researchers as well as casual wreck divers. Wrecks lie at depths ranging from far below scuba range to just a few feet below the surface. Vessels sunk in the area include everything from small sailboats to barges and old wooden schooners.

According to the 1952 computer analysis of the Shark Attack File, over nine men are attacked by shark for every one woman attacked. This statistic holds true for data from beach attacks also, where men and women are generally found in equal proportions. Since sharks do not ordinarily eat their victims, it is theorized that attacks may be a territorial response to chemical messages given off more strongly by males.

Since this area has been proclaimed an underwater park by the state, the wreckage is protected, and the Northwest Michigan Maritime Museum in Frankfort leads diving charter trips.

Although the rocky reefs around the Manitou Islands and frequent terrible storms are responsible for most of the disasters, that old scourge of shipping — piracy apparently caused many of the shipwrecks, especially around Frankfort. In the early 1900's, a favorite method was to build fires on the dunes and use a reflector to fool captains into thinking they'd passed the lighthouse. Once wrecked, the ships would be looted. This was successful for years, until the pirate was finally caught murdering a crew.

One of the favorite sites is the *Francis Morozan*, a freighter which ran aground just south of South Manitou Island. Since much of the ship is above water, this offers a good chance for snorkelers or scuba divers to investigate a shallow, submerged hull.

The *Walter Frost*, several hundred yards away, also ran up on the rocky reef off South Manitou. Lost during a winter storm in 1903, the wooden steamer has a remarkably preserved hull and engine at easy sport diving depth. Wreckage litters the lake bottom around the wreck.

The site of the *Hartzell* is just offshore from Frankfort. This schooner was partially salvaged and pieces of the ship are on display in the Frankfort Museum. According to historians in the area, the lone woman on board ship was the only victim, as she was left lashed to the mast while the men aboard all escaped.

Check with the Frankfort Museum for more information about shipwrecks in the area. A search is well under way for the *Westmoreland*, which went down in the area in 1854, rumored to be carrying a gold payroll worth about $3 million today!

For a look at the abundant and varied fish life of northern Lake Michigan, try diving **rock jetties** in the area. For bottle and artifact collecting, the old shipping docks and the **Boardman River** offer the best possibilities. Visibility averages 15' and summer temperatures are from 55-65°.

Menominee, located on the southern tip of the Upper Peninsula, gives divers access to the many practically untouched wrecks of Green Bay, ranging from schooners to old steamers. Clarity around the sunken vessels averages 10'. In winter, many crystalline quarries lure those with ice-diving certifications to the surreal world under the ice, where visibility can reach 100'.

INLAND

Stoney Lake, 40 miles north of Detroit at Oxford, is becoming one of the most popular lakes in the state. The sandy beach drops off to 20' and then slopes down to a gravel bottom, with a maximum depth of 65' in the middle of the lake. An underwater habitat where you can communicate on the bottom, a 27' sailboat, and a floating car-tire reef all keep Stoney Lake interesting. Bass, bluegill, white suckers, rock bass, and crappie make good photo subjects. Clarity averages 10-20' in summer, and over 50' in winter under the ice. Summer temperatures are from 54-75°.

About 40 miles further north is **Otter Lake**. It's more secluded and much less frequented by divers. You can enter through the park on the south side of the lake and explore down the gentle slope to 30', where the lake begins to drop off more steeply. Since this was a favorite site of loggers, many artifacts of their industry,including logs, can be seen underwater. Clarity often surpasses 20' in summer, but lights will be necessary on deeper dives.

Union Lake, in the town of the same name almost on the border of Indiana, attracts divers from both states. Public access is found at the northwest corner of the lake through a boat ramp. A Model A truck chassis and two submerged knolls that project to within 6' of the surface before dropping away to 65' can both be found in the vicinity of the boat ramp. Night diving on these knolls is the best way to see them, when your lights make the water plants mysterious and even a bluegill seems exotic. Summer clarity is under 10', and summer temperatures range from 40-70°.

Northeast of Kalamazoo is **Gull Lake**, which has an air station at the site. Depth goes to 120', and the bottom is mostly vegetation-covered sand. Winter and early spring provide the best clarity. At Coloma, just north of St. Joseph, **Paw Paw Lake** attracts the antique hunter. Many good bottles have been found in this shallow lake, less than 30' deep, where clarity usually hovers between 5-8'.

Michigan laws concerning diving: Underwater spearing with conventional hand-propelled spear is lawful during regular spearing seasons for rough fish. Rubber, spring, and Hawaiian sling-propelled spears may be used only in certain designated waters. Dive flag is required. Marine preserves exist, primarily for historical preservation of shipwrecks.

MINNESOTA

Minnesota's diving is fascinating, due to its combination of 15,000 lakes plus over 150 miles of shoreline on the largest and most pristine of the Great Lakes. The North Shore, as Minnesotans call their Lake Superior shoreline, is a wild and rugged place that can still arouse the spirit of the pioneering voyageurs in you. From the most southerly tip — Duluth — to Grand Portage, almost at the Canadian border, the North Shore is the gateway to some of the best diving in the Great Lakes region. Plan on cold waters if you're diving Lake Superior — from 35-50° in summer.

Minnesota divers think of Isle Royale as their own, since the island lies only 22 miles from Grand Portage. Actually, though, Isle Royale belongs to Michigan, even though almost everyone diving the island leaves by charter from the Minnesota mainland. See the section on Michigan for descriptions of the fantastic wreck diving available around this wilderness island.

The most famous wreck on the North Shore is undoubtedly the barge *Madeira*, at Split Rock lighthouse about 60 miles north of Duluth. Spectacular granite cliffs, waterfalls, and endless evergreen forests make the drive up from Duluth one of the most beautiful in the country. Agates can be found all along the shore. When you reach Split Rock, the scenery will make you pause in your hurry to get suited up. The lighthouse perches right on the edge of a 178'-high precipice. Check in before entering from shore. You enter the water through a half-moon beach just northeast of the lighthouse. On one horn, the towering cliff of Split Rock looms up, and on the other horn is Gold Rock, also more than 150' high. It was on Gold Rock that the *Madeira* ran aground in the infamous Black Friday storm of November 28, 1905. The steel-hulled, three-masted barge of 436' was only five years old when it went down. One of the sailors climbed the mast, jumped to the cliff, and secured a line, by which 17 crew members were able to save themselves. Only one sailor drowned.

A 300' swim brings you to the cliff, where pieces of the wreck begin appearing in only 15' of water. At 40', you see the bow section and, further out, a salvage chain hanging from the cliff marks the location of the stern, which lies in 80' of water. Going deeper, you find the wheelhouse and masts, still easily visible in the clear water, where you can usually see at least 50'. The intact bow and stern, lying on sand amidst granite boulders, present an unforgettable picture in the clear water and beautiful surroundings. Cold water (from 34° in spring to 50° in summer) and the possibility of storms present the major dangers. Don't dive in northeastern winds.

Further south, at Two Harbors, the wreck of the *Samuel P. Ely* also has a devoted following among all levels of wreck divers. On October 29, 1896, a steamer was towing the *Ely*, a three-masted schooner, to protection behind a breakwall when the tow line somehow broke. The *Ely*, adrift in the worst gale in over a decade, was impaled on the breakwater and quickly began to break apart. A courageous rescue by tug saved the eleven-man crew.

The wreck is most easily reached by boat across the bay at Two Harbors. Red paint marks the point of entry at the southwest breakwall. The remains of the *Ely* lie in only 30' of water on a solid clay and rock bottom. Although the bow and stern have broken off, the wreck is still intact enough to permit exploration. Shallow depth and a protected situation make the *Ely* a good dive for beginners. Water clarity varies from 15' to more than 50'.

Although at least 25 wrecks are charted right in the Duluth area, diving them is reserved for experts familiar with shipping schedules, since Duluth is the world's largest inland port.

However, anyone can enjoy diving the mulitudes of clear lakes scattered around the state. Northeast of the Minneapolis/St. Paul area, near Stillwater, **Lake Elmo** stairsteps down to about 190'. You must obtain permission at the site to dive Lake Elmo, which contains many old bottles and other artifacts.

At nearby **Square Lake**, depth averages 35'. You enter the water through a public beach. Square Lake is famous for its concentrations of tame fish. Crappie, bass, perch, and northern pike are everywhere. If you hover quietly near the water lilies and other aquatic plants around the edge of the lake, you might see the lightning-fast rush of a pike as it spurts after a perch. Crayfish and freshwater snails inhabit the sandy bottom. Clarity averages 20' in summer, and water temperature reaches 65°. Camping is available.

Christmas Lake, west of Minneapolis, is a favorite spot for ice diving in winter. While the very thought of this makes many otherwise rugged divers shudder, ice diving can provide the same feeling of supernatural tranquility and isolation in a world where time has stopped that you get cross-country skiing in a deserted wilderness. However, it's a sport that shouldn't be taken lightly. Double wetsuits — or, better yet, a drysuit — safety harnesses, ropes, and special training are all mandatory. Even chopping through the Minnesota ice that can be more than a foot thick requires some practice. Since the only way out is through the hole you came in, safety lines and tenders are necessary.

If all diving is entering another world, then ice diving is entering an especially foreign one. The water is unbelievably clear. All life seems to have disappeared, and you're alone with your bubbles, which gleam silver as they bounce against the opaque ceiling. The feeling of being the only human alive in a world where time has stopped and reality is meaningless is broken only when you emerge, into air that is at least 10° colder than the water was.

Divers from all over southern Minnesota take the St. Cloud exit off I-94 to enjoy **Big Fish Lake**, where maximum depth is 65'. The remains of many boats lure divers, including duck boats, row boats and even a 30' ferry used more than a century ago. In addition, numerous 19th century artifacts can be found, with a recent find of a wagon wheel half-buried in sand at 20'. Many walleye, northern,

sunfish, crappie, dogfish, and carp swim in the lake, with carp providing an attraction to those who want to sharpen their spearing skills, as they're in season in summer. Because of the easy accessibility and convenient services in St. Cloud, this is a good spot for night diving.

Big Watab Lake, nearby, is known for its deep, almost vertical dropoffs that begin near the shoreline, drop to 50', level off, and then drop down again. Water clarity is much better than at sandy-bottom lakes (like Big Fish Lake), ranging from 20-100'. Everything from clay pigeons to sailboats lies at the base of the dropoffs. Of the two lakes, Big Watab is better for ice diving. Both have public access and boat launching facilities.

To the north, near Brainerd, divers enjoy **Mille Lacs** and **Grindstone Lake**, as well as the **Crosby-Ironton iron pits**. Mille Lacs is more than 16 miles in diameter and filled with fish life. Bluegill, walleye, and pumpkinseed sunfish make good subjects for fish-watching or photos. Freshwater clams and crayfish are the subjects of good picnics after the dive. Grindstone is under special regulations that forbid any spearing.

The Crosby-Ironton mining pits are special dives for several reasons, not the least of which is the year-round visibility of 40' or more! Scattered throughout the region, most of the pits have public access, and some have public baths. Shade trees above the water invite swimming and picnicking; below the water, huge standing trees make great backdrops for largemouth bass and northern pike portraits. Abandoned mining artifacts are prevalent. Depths vary at each pit, but often exceed 200'.

Minnesota laws concerning diving: Residents only may take rough fish by spear from May 1st to February 15th. Dive flag is required.

OHIO

"Lake Erie is dead." For years newspapers and magazines headlined the fact. But Erie wasn't really dead, only wounded, and the powerful organization of Ohio divers was instrumental in toughening the laws against water pollution, while working at the same time to reform the state's restrictive diving laws. Since Erie is the murkiest and the shallowest (average depth of 32') of the Great Lakes, and given to unpredictable storms as well, it's smart to charter a boat to explore the following wrecks. Water temperature ranges from 50° in May to 78° in late August. Boat traffic can be very heavy; use caution, and your flag.

The steamer *Adventure*, though, doesn't require a boat. You can ferry to Kelleys Island and then drive to the north shore, where red-painted boulders with arrows point out to the wreck. The rounded rock bottom gives way to sand. A few of the glacial grooves that are so prominent on the island are visible underwater, as well. The clarity in the 10-15'-deep water is usually only about 5'. The hull has been demolished by storms, but scattered artifacts may be seen.

For clearer water (ranging from 8-10', and best in spring) and a more intact wreck, many divers charter a boat out to the wreck of the *F.H. Prince*, located 1/2-mile off the east shore of Kelleys Island. While on fire, the freighter ran aground, and was later scavenged by islanders. Since the deepest part of the wreck lies on a flat rock bottom at 18', snorkeling is sufficient to see bushels of ship's spikes, pottery, engine parts, and some territorial bass that don't want you invading their wreck.

The steamer *America*, off the northeastern corner of Pelee Island, is scattered over a rock and sand bottom. Portholes, nails, coins, and brass spikes randomly dot the bottom, while the boiler protrudes almost to the surface.

The tug *North Carolina* is probably the most exciting dive in Lake Erie, as she has only been underwater since 1968. The 80' tug rests on the bottom, almost upright and almost intact, about 1/2 mile offshore from Mentor-on-the-Lake.

INLAND

Since the state has restrictive policies on diving in state-owned lakes, and many of them aren't that great for diving anyway, most Ohio divers head to quarries. Hundreds exist, and some of the most popular are commercially fee-operated. Since many are regularly open only in summer, check with local dive stores if you're thinking of an off-season trip.

Salisbury Quarry, near Toledo, is one of the favorites. As many as 400 divers submerge in the 70-acre quarry on a big summer weekend. Like many of Ohio's quarries, Salisbury is owned and operated for fee diving, with air fills, restrooms, and snacks on the premises. The majority of the quarry is less than 45' deep, but one trench drops down to 65' and is usually lined with carp. You can look for a Corvair, boats, railroad tracks, a gym set, a school bus, limestone cliffs, and bass and sunfish in the quarry, where clarity ranges from 10-30'. Depth averages 25'.

Portage Quarry and **White Star Park** also keep divers in western Ohio wet. Portage Quarry, five miles south of dive services in Bowling Green, has 23 acres of water that averages 50' deep but sinks to 70' at its maximum depth. Divers prowl around a huge scale for weighing tons of stone and also explore various other mining artifacts, along with cars and a cabin cruiser. Many sunfish and bass share the water with humans. Clarity averages 10-20' and is best in summer. A sandy beach, camping, and volleyball can also be enjoyed for the price of admission.

Bowling Green also provides the closest air and services for visitors to White Star Park, in Gibsonburg. This abandoned stone quarry covers about 15 acres and drops to 75' maximum, with most of the quarry averaging 50' deep. Stone mounds,

trees, and a concrete building divided into two sections by a tunnel cover the bottom of the quarry. (Entering the building requires proper equipment and training.) Many catfish, goldfish, sunfish, and an occasional pike inhabit the quarry, where clarity ranges from 25-50' and more. This is fee-operated.

Eastern Ohio divers, as well as visitors from other states, take the plunge in **Nelson Ledges Quarry Park**, 40 miles south of Cleveland. Located in Amish country, and adjacent to Nelson Ledges State Park, the quarry is a favorite weekend "R & R" site, with a sandy beach and primitive camping available. Maximum depth is 40', and a dropoff of 5-15' runs along the middle of the quarry. Divers without wetsuits stay on the shallow side, while those with thermal protection go below the thermocline "off the wall." Fish populations are healthy, with good numbers of crappie, largemouth bass, and bluegill. The latter provide excellent photo opportunities in spring when they're busy guarding their bowl-shaped nests. Finding the location of a few boats that are frequently moved by search and recovery classes has become a favorite pastime. Clarity ranges from 5-30', and the closest dive support is 15 miles away in Warren.

In southern Ohio, **Sportsman Lake** (also a limestone quarry) has 20 acres of rocky bottom. This is a favorite site for photography, particularly of nesting bluegill and bass in the spring. Located halfway between Columbus and Cincinnati, Sportsman Lake is open only on weekends in summer, and for a fee.

Ohio laws concerning diving: You must use diver's flag, dive with buddy, and use pressure gauge, b.c., etc. No diving in many Ohio lakes. Of those open for diving, notification of park office must be made.

WISCONSIN

In Chippewa, Wisconsin means "gathering of the waters" — not a bad description for a state blessed with countless clear lakes, ranging from mighty Lake Michigan to wilderness ponds that have never yet seen a diver. Besides the natural beauty, man has added an attraction. The shipwrecks of Lake Michigan and Lake Superior's Apostle Islands act as powerful magnets for adventurous divers interested in time travel. At famous Door County, good water clarity combines with a century's worth of sunken vessels to provide sensational diving. Along the Milwaukee-Kenosha lakeshore, many easily accessible wrecks offer trips into the past, as well as souvenirs.

The Romans kept moray eels, whose flesh they highly esteemed, in special reservoirs where they were fed dead slaves.

LAKE MICHIGAN — Milwaukee Area

One of the most dramatic of shipwrecks is the **Prins Willem V**, less than three miles out of the Milwaukee harbor. This 258'-long Danish vessel met its doom in 1954, when the captain changed course for a tug but failed to notice that the tug was pulling an oil barge on an 800'-long cable. It's hard to think of anything that brings the tumult of a rapidly sinking ship to life more vividly than peering at the 8' gash that the cable opened in the side of this immense, intact wreck. You can read the name on the stern, and you can explore the superstructure, doors, portholes, and cargo hatches. The *Willem* lists to one side, sitting on a hard sand bottom 75' deep. On a calm day, currents are negligible and clarity can be 20'.

The other two standout wrecks of the Milwaukee area both went down in the same week in October, 1929. Fierce gales of more than 40 mph prevented most prudent captains from putting out, but Captain "Storming" McKay, who had a reputation for staying on schedule despite the weather, left anyway, in command of the car ferry *Milwaukee*. Exactly what caused the vessel to sink will never be known, as he and the 58 others aboard all died.

The mystery of this disaster creates a rather eerie feeling as you explore the remains of the 338'-long car ferry, which now rest 3-1/2 miles offshore, seven miles northeast of the Milwaukee light. The ferry sank so rapidly that an intense air pressure was created by the rush of incoming water — an air pressure strong enough to blow the pilot house off. It now lies about 200 yards west of the wreck. The rest of the vessel is fairly intact, and sitting upright. The main deck is at 90', with the maximum depth 135'. You can peer through the tangled mass of steel into the hold, where several automobiles and railroad cars loaded with goods still park. Since the wreck wasn't located until 1972, some brass artifacts can still be spotted. Currents can be strong here, making the twisted steel especially dangerous. Since in addition to great depth and strong currents, you also have to deal with clarity that seldom exceeds 5', this wreck is for very experienced divers.

On October 29, 1929, a day when most people were stunned by the stock market crash, the people in Kenosha were stunned by another crash, closer to home. The automobile and boxed cargo of the 209'-long steamer **Wisconsin** shifted in a heavy gale and caused the vessel to take on water at an ever-increasing rate. Boats from nearby Kenosha saved all passengers and most of the crew, but the captain and eight of the crewmen stayed aboard to wait for tow, believing the ship would continue to float. However, the *Wisconsin* slipped beneath Lake Michigan, thwarting any rescue attempts, and drowning the sailors who were reluctant to abandon their ship.

It takes an experienced diver to visit the *Wisconsin*, since she sits on the rocky bottom 130' deep, seven miles southeast of the Kenosha light. The superstructure has been washed away, and experienced wreck divers can penetrate through the cargo hull where they'll see several cars, among them a Hudson and an Essex, still parked, as if in an underwater showroom. The name *"General Robert M. O'Reilly"* can be seen painted on the hull — a reminder of the *Wisconsin's* service during WWII as a hospital ship. On a good day, clarity averages 10'. Since swift currents and high winds can spring up (in addition to depth of 90' minimum) this

wreck is for experienced divers.

Many other wrecks exist around the Milwaukee area, including the steamer **Norland**, three miles offshore and eleven miles southeast of the Milwaukee light, which foundered in a 1922 storm with no loss of life. The boiler and stern of the 120'-long *Norland* have dug into the clay bottom 55' down. Clarity is poor.

Another site that still has enough scattered wreckage to make for interesting exploration is the passenger steamer **Niagara**, which now lies on a sand and rock bottom, about 50' deep, just south of the city of Belgium. Charred timbers give evidence to the fire aboard ship that took more than 60 lives.

The **Kate Kelly** is a favorite dive located two miles north of Wind Point lighthouse, north of Racine. This 126'-long, two-masted schooner went down with the loss of all hands in an 1895 gale that blew 65 mph. Rediscovered in 1981, the *Kate Kelly* carried railroad ties, although divers today are more interested in the windlass, still in place, and the deadeyes and pulleys. Clarity over the 54' deep sand bottom can be quite decent.

While the **Appomattox** and the **Sebastopol** may not be the most exciting wrecks in the world, they're worth mentioning since they both can be reached by swimming or by taking a small boat off the beach near Milwaukee. The *Appomattox* has been scattered over a wide area, less than 200 yards offshore, in 20' depths. Large pieces of wreckage, including the boilers and bilges, can be found, and Lake Michigan still gives up interesting small relics to those divers willing to search.

The *Sebastopol* offers novices an easy wreck experience. This sidewheeler beached when only a year old, taking four crewmen down with it. Piles of cargo sit amidst the ship's ribs, sometimes covered by shifting sand. Clarity averages 15-20' in this protected spot, only about 13' deep.

LAKE MICHIGAN — Door County

If you think of freshwater wreck diving as a gloomy, rather eerie affair, then you haven't been to Door County. White sand, 15-50' visibility, and dozens of wrecks in waters shallower than 40' make Door County wreck diving often bright enough for natural-light photos. When you combine that with beautiful northwoods, more state parks, and more miles of shoreline than any other county in the USA, then you have one of the finest freshwater diving areas in the nation. Water temperatures average 50° in spring and late fall, and up to 70° in August.

Bailey's Harbor, a large protected bay on the eastern side of the peninsula, is a great introduction to Door County. At least eleven ships have gone down in the harbor, of which the schooner **Emeline** is the most intact, sitting upright near the north end of the harbor since 1896. Over the years the vessel has dug into the sandy bottom so that now the hull is almost covered with sand. Since it's only about 15' deep, the upper deck has been scoured away by ice. The sand bottom reflects light well, making the *Emeline* a good scene for natural-light photos on sunny days.

You can also reach the **Fleetwing** easily from shore, 100 yards out from an old boat-launching ramp in **Garrett Bay**. This ease of access, coupled with the interesting wreckage, has led to the *Fleetwing* being christened "The Most Dived Upon Wreck in Lake Michigan." The *Fleetwing* was carrying a cargo of lumber when she ran hard aground on the rocks in 1888. The wooden ribs arch towards the surface and white elm staves can sometimes still be located, along with other bits of cargo, pieces of the mast, and large sections of the bilge. All of the wreckage lies above 25', and clarity averages 20'. Local divers can guide you to the wreck of the schooner **Japan**, also in Garrett Bay.

At the very tip of the peninsula, there are good shore dives just offshore from On the Rocks divers' lodge. You can get permission from their dive shop to enter **Wisconsin Bay**, where a 40'-long fishing tug and submerged dock, coupled with good shelter and clarity of up to 25', are the attractions. Rock bass, smallmouth, crayfish, and perch hang out around the shelter, while salmon and northern sometimes put in appearances.

If the wind and currents aren't up, you can get permission to cliff dive down **Table Bluff**, just off the Main Lodge. An avalanche of huge boulders cascades down to 100' depth 150 yards from shore. Bright green stalks and patches on the boulders are a kind of freshwater sponge. You'll also see lawyer fish, sometimes called burbot or eel pout.

The islands off the tip of the Door peninsula contain some of the best wrecks. The narrow passage between Table Bluff and Plum Island was referred to by early French voyagers as "Porte des Morts" — Death's Doorway. From this the entire peninsula got its name. Apparently the early sailors took it for granted that an icy death was a risk inherent in their way of life.

Luckily for the sailors of the **Louisiana**, their ship stranded near enough to a civilized shore so that they were all saved. However, other sailors who were also out during the Big Blow of 1913 weren't so lucky. The gale lasted for four horrible days without ceasing and, by the time it was over, 20 vessels had slid beneath the waves and 248 sailors had died. The captain of the *Louisiana* wisely decided to seek shelter when the rough seas threatened to capsize his ship but, even in Washington Harbor, with both anchors down, the 70 mph wind blew the vessel up on the rocks, where it caught fire and sank.

You can dive the *Louisiana* from charter dive boat or from the shore, after you've ferried out to Washington Island. If you try to shore dive, be advised that it's a 1/4 mile swim off Schoolhouse Beach. The water of Washington Harbor is famous for its calmness, with visibility averaging 20'. The *Louisiana* extends out from the shoreline to 20' depths. Even though the 267'-long vessel burned to the water's edge before sinking, it still presents an impressive sight, with huge wooden beams and twisted iron bars covering the bottom. The *Louisiana* sank atop the remains of

MERLIN HILMOE

Lawyer fish, also called burbot or eelpout, is a type of cod

the steamer **H.P. Hill**, and the two ships have merged into one mass of wreckage. Some great photos have been taken around the *Louisiana*, especially since multitudes of fish are tame enough to provide good foreground subjects for the wreck. If the fish become too persistent, it's because they're used to having divers find tiny crayfish under the rocks for them. The bass usually outwit the northern pike and perch to be first to feast.

A charter run out to the sunken vessels around **Pilot Island** usually takes only 30 minutes from the Gills Rock area. Since the northwestern tip of the island, where most of the wreckage is, also gets swept by some strong currents through the Death's Door passage, this area requires a more experienced diver. You can just about learn the history of Great Lakes shipping disasters from studying the piles of wreckage strewn about the bottom. At least ten different wrecks have been identified here. Most are wooden schooners from before 1900. No one wreck really stands out at the northwest tip, since decades of ice, wind, and currents have turned even the proudest vessel into piles of decking and bilge pieces. One spot in particular must have been especially dreaded, since three different ships have gone down there. From an underwater perspective, it looks a little like a junkyard, with wreckage piled in tiers. To see the most, stay above 35'.

One thousand yards out, in the open water of the Porte des Morts passage, the schooner *Riverside* has managed to stay more or less intact for almost 100 years. In 1887 the *Riverside* was carrying a cargo of stoves when she foundered and went down in the passage. As you swim down, your first sight is the upside-down vessel with the stern hugging the bottom at 45'. You'll need a light to investigate under the capsized hull. The schooner seems to hang precariously on the edge of an extremely rough slope that levels off somewhat at about 65'. Since currents can be treacherous in the passage, and this is a deeper dive than most, only experienced divers should take the charter out. The reward might be water clarity approaching 50'.

If you're really adventurous, you can take a three-hour trip on a dive boat to the wrecks off the south side of **Poverty Island**. There, two ore carriers have gone to the bottom, and rest at different depths on a steep slope of huge boulders. The shallower wreck has become entombed in its cargo of ore, with only pieces of rigging, cable, and winches protruding from the hull. The deeper wreck lies at 45-65' depths, and is one of the largest and most intact wrecks around Door County. The decking has twisted and broken loose in places to reveal the thick-walled bilges. Heavy cables, apparently part of a salvage attempt, lead up to the shallower victim. The thermocline hovers around the middle of the deeper wreck, and drops the water temperature to a chilling 44°. Sometimes you can see the surface from 50' down — but since silt has encased the remains, it only takes a few careless flippers to raise tremendous clouds and destroy the clarity. No-decompression tables are essential.

The most recent and difficult wreck in the area is the ***Roen Steam Barge***, which is less than three miles south of Poverty Island. The top of the wreck lies at 75' and the base sits on the bottom 105' deep. The completely intact wreck is tilted upside-down, but since a crane and boom support the hull, divers can gain access to the main deck. Tools, cable, and debris litter the area. A small tug lies nearby, but requires a separate dive. Since the water temperature goes to 40°, the depth is extreme, and currents are possible, this is for experienced wreck divers who know the extra equipment needed (scuba unit for hanging off at 10', etc.). Penetration is not recommended for anyone.

At least two sights on the Green Bay side of the peninsula draw divers. **Whalesback Shoals**, about six miles northwest of Garrett Bay, rises from 100' depths on all sides to within 5' of the surface. In 1905 the Shoals snared the ***R.J. Hackett***, a 211'-long steamer with some historical significance, since she was the first steam-powered vessel designed to carry bulk cargo, which previously had been exclusively the province of sailing vessels. You don't even need scuba to enjoy the *Hackett* if the clarity is good (it ranges from 5-40'), since the depth is only 20'. Tons of machinery, including the engine, flywheel, shafting, and propellers, have been embedded in the sand. The boiler size is astonishing — a buddy team can enter it

together! The *Hackett* serves as a nursery for lake perch. In early summer, burbots, or lawyer fish, tempt the spearfisherman, since they infest the wreck like fleas on a dog. Boat traffic and some current require caution.

The **Meridian**, off the southern end of Little Sister Island Reef in Green Bay, takes an hour to reach by dive boat. It's an easy dive, in water under 45' deep, and without treacherous currents. Time has skeletonized the schooner. The deck sags down into the ribs, which still arch up after all these years. Bass and perch dart around the ribs. You might encounter the thermocline, cleaving the water temperature into two distinct entities, as much as 60° at the top of the wreck, and down to 45° along the *Meridian's* backbone.

INLAND LAKES

Of the thousands of Wisconsin lakes suitable for diving, none is more famous than **Lake Geneva**, in the southeastern hill country. The 26 miles of shoreline fronting the lake have always been a favored residence since the days when Indian villages nestled around the bays. In the late 1800's, sidewheelers ferried passengers and mail across the lake, and some of these ornate Victorian vessels inevitably made their final trip straight down, to end up admired only by scuba divers. The **Lady of the Lake** ended up near Buttons Bay, where the hull provides a haven for yellow perch and walleye. The **Lucius Newberry** caught fire at dockside in 1891; rather than let the flames spread, they cut her loose without even salvaging any of the ornate brass fixtures, velvet drapes, oil paintings, or fine china and crystal. The sidewheeler drifted until fire met water. In 1981 divers located the site where the *Newberry* went down. Over 4000 lbs. of artifacts, including brass and silver fixtures, engine tools, a 418-lb. anchor, and the melted remnants of a huge Mexican bell, were recovered to be placed in a museum. The boiler, sections of the bow, paddlewheel hubs, and driveshaft can still be explored underwater.

Divers have also boned up on the sites of old resort hotels and mansions to help locate an incredibly varied selection of relics. Lake Geneva is one of the best lakes in the country for bottle collecting; just out from a resort that had piled its garbage on the ice each winter, divers found over $10,000 worth of antique bottles. Clarity at Lake Geneva in summer averages 10-15'. Since the lake is extremely popular with boaters, too, diving is subject to certain regulations. You must register with the Water Safety Patrol, dive only from a boat, and use a flag. Depths drop to 135', but most relics have been found above 80' levels.

Lake Delevan, Geneva's nearby sister, only drops to 65' maximum and, consequently, has a lot more algae growth with less clarity — seldom above 2-4'. Bottle collectors put up with it, especially in spring or fall when visibility improves somewhat.

Racine Quarry, also in southeastern Wisconsin, drops to 60' with a trench extending down to 90'. Located in a county park with showers and concessions, the quarry attracts divers from northern Illinois. Water temperature rises to 80° in summer, and you can photograph perch and bluegill. Clarity ranges from 10-30'.

Two lakes near Delafield, just west of Milwaukee, provide good hunting for bottle collectors. **Upper Lake Namahbin**, although weedy, was the scene of many bottle dumps. You'll also find good collecting in the lower part of **Lake Nashota**, nearby, where visibility can be 20' or more.

Madison surrounds **Lake Mendota**. A flat sand bottom averages 60' deep. Big perch hide out in beds of water plants. But the real attraction here is bottle collecting, with antique bottles found from the middle 1880's. Clarity is best in winter, when it can surpass 50'. Summer presents heavy boat traffic and makes cautious diving with a flag necessary. Summer clarity averages 10'.

In the rolling country northwest of Madison, near the famous Dells, is **Devil's Lake State Park**. Although the lake isn't deep, averaging only 35', water quality is high. Visibility in summer is often 30', but hits a low of 5'. You can take some good portraits of bass, crappie, and bluegill. Crayfish lurk in the rocks along the shoreline and clams leave tracks of their wanderings in the sand. Camping, showers, and concessions are all available, there are miles of hiking trails through the dense woods around the lake, and services are just across the highway.

Red Granite Quarry, near the town of the same name west of Oshkosh, is one of the deepest dives in the state. The former granite quarry drops straight down to 130' on most sides, but the north face steps down in shelves. One area is more than 200' deep. Machinery provides some interest, but the granite walls are the main attraction, with mottled shades of pastel and bright patches of green sponge. Clarity surpasses 25' in summer; under the ice in winter, it's often past 50'. Few entrance points and extreme depths rule this out as a novice training site.

Although far northern Wisconsin is remote, more and more divers are discovering the beautiful lakes that until now have been exclusively used by fishermen. **Sparkling Lake** and **Clear Lake**, in the watery region around Minocqua, are two of the best. Pure, clear water harbors an incredible variety of life. Probably the most spectacular resident is the muskie. These slender five-footers have the same shape, the same toothy face, and the same incredible speed as the barracuda. Lying quietly near a bed of lily pads might give you the opportunity to try to freeze on film the rush of a muskie after a smaller fish. Whether you get the picture or not, you'll get a rush just watching the muskie. Since spearing is illegal in many northern counties, the fish are generally quite tame and can be easily approached. Night dives reveal a tactile quality to fishwatching as yellow perch, rock bass, largemouths, and pike all seem to be in a twilight zone and can often be approached and touched before they startle. At Clear Lake, public campgrounds are available, as is air, in Minocqua.

In northwestern Wisconsin, around Hayward, there are many great dive sites in lakes like **Grindstone**, **Lost Land**, **Spider Lake**, and **Big Round Lake**. The latter is typical. Big Round Lake covers 3300 acres and drops to 80' at its deepest. Clarity varies from 15-35', with 20' average. A hard sand, gravel, and boulder-

strewn bottom has very little weed cover and very many fish. Usually fish need the cover of aquatic vegetation, but at Big Round Lake they have man-made log cribs instead. Generally these cribs have been set in water of 10-20' depth, right on the edge of the drop to deeper water. Big schools of walleye fry, 3-lb. perch, crawdads by the dozen, and many, many smallmouth of 3-5 lbs. provide diving excitement, good subjects for photographs, and the opportunity to try underwater angling. Since spears are outlawed in many counties of northern Wisconsin that have a heavy fishing and tourist industry, some divers have decided to take the fishing gear underwater, where they can watch the fight firsthand.

The **Spread Eagle Chain of Lakes** in the extreme northeastern corner of the state, near Iron Mountain, Michigan, takes the world prize for largest number of freshwater lakes in a chain — 28. These lakes offer good bottle collecting in clear water.

Wisconsin laws concerning diving: Very complex laws govern the spearing of fish, which is legal only in specified regions, during seasons which vary from section to section. White, striped, and rock bass, crappie, bluegill, perch, and sunfish, as well as rough species, may be speared in some waters. Check locally.

APPALACHIA

KENTUCKY   TENNESSEE

Dozens of large reservoirs have been created by the Army Corps of Engineers and the Tennessee Valley Authority in the Appalachian Mountain states of Kentucky, Tennessee, and West Virginia. Some have become very popular diving areas, drawing divers from many states, while others have yet to see their first scuba system. While summer surface temperatures of up to 84° at many of these lakes might seem warm enough for an uninsulated dive, sharp thermoclines make wetsuits necessary on any deeper dives. As at many reservoirs, diving is most rewarding in the upper 35' of water, where fish congregate and surface light still permeates.

KENTUCKY

Most diving in Kentucky takes place in the southern part of the state. One exception is the **Hanover Quarry**, located north of Louisville, near the small town of Hanover, Indiana, almost on the Kentucky-Indiana line. This quarry is almost tailor-made for scuba diving, with a graduated series of terraces that drop first to 15', then to 40', then 65', and on to a maximum depth of 130'. Photography is good, with water clarity usually 25' in summer, and more in winter. Bass, crappie, bluegill, and catfish make good subjects, and the interesting rock formations provide beautiful backgrounds. Entry is easy, over a sand beach you can drive to, and in summer airfills, equipment rentals, and restrooms are available. To dive on weekdays or in winter, check with Kentucky Diving Headquarters in Louisville.

In southwestern Kentucky, divers visit **Cerulean Springs**, west of Hopkinsville. This 16-acre limestone quarry is reserved exclusively for use by divers who have C-cards and pay a $3.50 admittance charge. Access is easy, with one side providing walk-in access, and the other requiring a jump of 15'. Since there's little silt on the bottom, clarity averages 30'. Several car wrecks, a rock crusher, submerged trees, instructor platforms, and bluegill, bass, and catfish keep the 35' maximum depth interesting. Since this is primitive, with no air or diver facilities for at least 85 miles in either direction, bring all the supplies you'll need.

Dale Hollow Lake is an enormous reservoir spanning the Kentucky-Tennessee line. It offers a variety of diving, with some of the best sites found around **Rock Island**, where pastel slate walls drop to 90'. Other shallower dives can be found off gradually sloping mud bottoms, where you might see big carp, catfish, bass, brim, or drum. Cemeteries, towns, and several boat wrecks also attract divers. Clarity averages 20', and is especially good in early summer. Camping and air are available nearby.

Laurel Lake, near Corbin in southeastern Kentucky, is a beautiful lake set in forested hills that provide a perfect watershed and keep the water clarity high —

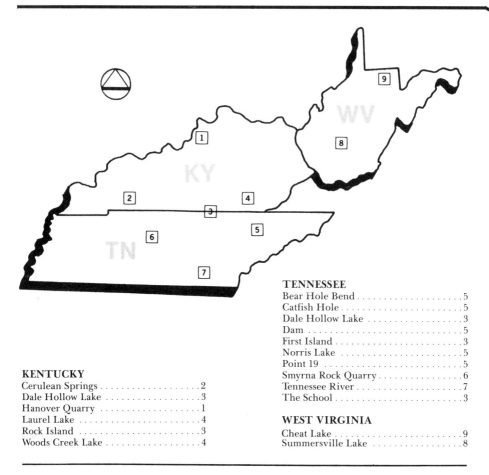

TENNESSEE

Bear Hole Bend 5
Catfish Hole 5
Dale Hollow Lake 3
Dam 5
First Island 3
Norris Lake 5
Point 19 5
Smyrna Rock Quarry 6
Tennessee River 7
The School 3

WEST VIRGINIA

Cheat Lake 9
Summersville Lake 8

KENTUCKY

Cerulean Springs 2
Dale Hollow Lake 3
Hanover Quarry 1
Laurel Lake 4
Rock Island 3
Woods Creek Lake 4

up to 30'. Underwater attractions vary from shallow, sandy coves to deep canyons with fully submerged standing trees. Cliffs of solid rock with crevices and overhangs attract divers from many states. Near the dam a vertical wall drops 290' to the riverbed.

Another lake in the area that offers outstanding diving for all levels of experience is **Woods Creek Lake.** This smaller lake, seven miles north of London, is known for having the best water clarity in the state — sometimes reaching past 40'. Little boat traffic and an excellent watershed of a tree-lined deep ravine creates this good visibility. No spearfishing is allowed, but for the photographer or fishwatcher there's much to see. In addition to the fish, quarter-sized freshwater jellyfish are often seen, rhythmically pumping across the surface waters, often in groups. Maximum depth reaches 150'.

Kentucky laws concerning diving: spearing for rough fish is permitted only in lakes of 1000 acres or larger.

TENNESSEE

With one of the largest man-made lake systems in the country, Tennessee offers a wide variety of diving. Spearing for carp, searching for geodes with their beautiful quartz,centers, treasure hunting for Indian and Civil War artifacts, and photographing freshwater jellyfish are the principal lures drawing divers to Tennessee's lakes and rivers.

Of all the Tennessee dives, none is more famous than **Dale Hollow Lake**, spanning the Kentucky-Tennessee state line in the north-central part of Tennessee. Clarity in this beautiful reservoir nestled in forested hills can surpass 40' in spring and fall. Some of the favorite areas include **First Island**, where spearfishermen find abundant catfish and carp hiding near the shale bluffs, and **The School**, where old foundations are overgrown with wavy green fingers of water grass. Arrowheads and baseball-sized geodes can both be found by searching amongst the clefts in the shale bottom near the shore.

Another fine diving lake is **Norris Lake**, located near Knoxville. At the **dam** area, you can follow an old mooring cable to the depth you choose. Most likely many fish will investigate you, and you might find artifacts ranging from rods and reels thrown off the dam to stolen guns. At **Point 19**, you can drop down a wall lined with small ledges to past 120', where as many as 70 stolen cars have rested at one time. One-half mile out from Point 19 by boat, you'll come to **Bear Hole Bend**, which is one of the last places to silt up in times of heavy boat traffic. Rocky bluffs drop down to past 130', and clarity ranges from 5-25'.

For both spearfishing and interesting bottom terrain, few places can match **Catfish Hole**, located at Norris Lake just across from Anderson County Park. Rocks tower up from the bottom to as high as 15', and catfish of up to 50 lbs. have been discovered hiding amid the pinnacles. Since maximum depth is 50', you'll have plenty of bottom time to explore between the huge rock formations. This spot does lose clarity rapidly if boat traffic is heavy.

Near Nashville, **Smyrna Rock Quarry** attracts many divers. This fish-filled hole has a maximum depth of 40', with the remains of a 15' runabout and a VW adorning the bottom. Beautiful bright green plants hide turtles in the shallower parts of the quarry, and in the center "hole" you can try your hand at feeding 4'-long catfish. Night diving is safe and enjoyable in the clear water, averaging 30' visibility.

In southeastern Tennessee, divers head to the little town of Jasper, near Chattanooga, for a fascinating artifact dive in the **Tennessee River.** Currents can vary from 1-5 knots, depending on whether they're generating above-stream at the dam, so check with divers in Nashville who frequent this area. Advanced artifact divers find the river to be a goldmine. Civil War artifacts, a sunken steamboat from the 1840's, an old ferry crossing where three covered wagons went down in a mishap, and an old fort on the riverbank that has given up hundreds of bottles are the favorite diving areas. The rocky river bed slopes to a maximum depth of 60', and the current has dug out under the banks and created sizable eddy holes. In addition to the more common fish, you might see the famed snail darter.

Tennessee laws concerning diving: Non-game fish may be taken by spear year-round.

WEST VIRGINIA

While diving in West Virginia has not attained the popularity that it has in other Appalachian states, there are suitable diving sites. Divers should be aware that services are few. Well-planned trips with air and equipment obtained in advance are essential.

Summersville Lake, east of Charleston, is the biggest and most popular of the West Virginia lakes. A boat is almost essential to dive this lake, since most of the shore is composed of huge boulders and steep cliffs. Average depth over much of the inshore area is 35', although in spots the lake is much deeper. Clarity averages 10-20', and many small coves provide interesting diving in summer. In winter, the lake is dropped to a low level, resulting in poor clarity and difficult boat navigation.

Other lakes in West Virginia suitable for diving include **Cheat Lake**, near Morgantown, where divers have found a gun cache discarded by paramilitary outfits training for the Bay of Pigs invasion. Clarity in this mud-bottom lake averages 10-20', and depth averages 45'.

West Virginia laws concerning diving: All fish, except game fish and catfish, may be speared in daylight hours from July 1st to October 1st except in certain rivers. A minimum of two diver's flags must be displayed at all times.

YOU NEED DAN
DAN NEEDS YOU!

Join the
DIVERS ALERT
NETWORK

DAN FILLS A NEED

DAN unites hyperbaric chamber facilities into a nationwide communications network to help divers and their physicians arrange consultation, transportation, and treatment by using a single central emergency telephone number.

FOR DIVING EMERGENCIES CALL (919) 684-8111
24 HOURS   7 DAYS A WEEK
FOR INFORMATION CALL **(919) 684-2948** MONDAY-FRIDAY 9-5 E.S.T.

DAN NEEDS YOU

The cost of providing this invaluable national service is high. Startup funding was provided by the federal government but not continued. Do your part by becoming a member of DAN which will help insure the continuing existence of DAN as well as provide you with **diving safety information.**

JOINING DAN — $10

Individual membership in Dan is $10 per year — a small sum to insure there will be somebody able to help you immediately in the event of an accident.
On joining you will receive:

- **MEMBERSHIP CARD** with the DAN phone number and a list of diving injury symptoms.
- **TANK DECALS** with the DAN emergency phone number.
- The DAN **UNDERWATER DIVING ACCIDENT MANUAL** which describes symptoms and first aid for the major diving related injuries plus guidelines a physician can follow for drugs and i.v. fluid administration.
- A **NEWSLETTER**, "ALERT DIVER", presents information on diving medicine and diving safety. Actual DAN case histories and questions are presented in each issue.

NEW
ENGLAND

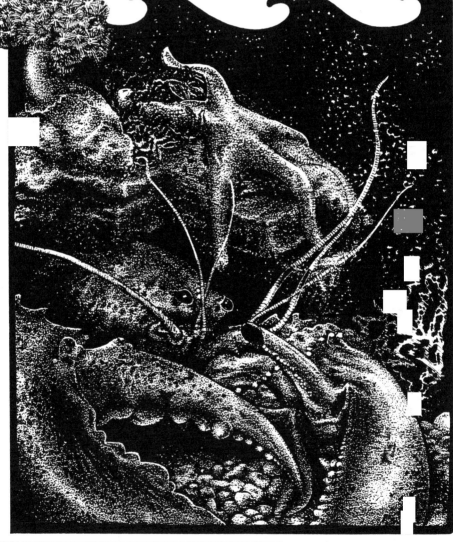

CONNECTICUT   **MASSACHUSETTS**

MAINE   **NEW HAMPSHIRE**

For a long time, divers who enjoyed New England waters felt compelled to defend themselves. After all, the water is cold — never much above 65°. In winter it drops to a low of 30° in places. Clarity is rarely more than 40', and often more like 15'.

But as time goes by, more and more divers are discovering why these cold waters provide such a potent lure. After you've experienced the somber beauty of one of the richest marine environments in the world, you don't mind the cold as much. And you recognize that the characteristic green color of the water, which reduces its clarity, is due to the hordes of plankton that serve as the groundwork for all the incredible life forms.

If you're not adventurous enough to experience New England diving, you'll never know why the goosefish is the most valuable ugly fish in the world. Or how exciting it is to see striped bass, the speedsters of the gamefish world, zoom across the edge of your vision. Or what incredible beauty there is in a wall of cream-colored anemones, accented by smooth, sinuous blood stars and transparent hydroids, as fragile as bubbles as they wave their pink hearts aloft.

Not to mention the king of crustaceans, *Homerus americanus*, the one and only Maine lobster. Or the thousands of exciting shipwrecks.

If you don't want to limit yourself to just tropical diving, visit New England. Maine, Massachusetts and Rhode Island are the most popular states for ocean dives. New Hampshire and Vermont both have great inland diving. A word of caution: treat lobster pots and lobster laws with the utmost respect, since relations between divers and lobstermen are fragile at best, in many places. Of the New England states, only Connecticut allows residents and non-residents to obtain lobster permits. In Massachusetts and Rhode Island, only residents may obtain licenses.

CONNECTICUT

COASTAL

Connecticut has added a great deal to its popularity with out-of-state divers by granting non-resident lobster permits. Since Connecticut fronts Long Island Sound, most dives are shallow and the water clarity can be low. However, pollution control measures have cleaned up the water in recent years, and Connecticut divers stay busy, thanks to rocky reefs and abundant marine life. Swift tidal currents and heavy boat traffic require cautious diving at many sites.

RHODE ISLAND
VERMONT

Divers in western Long Island Sound visit **Sheffield Island** by boat. The best diving areas are the south shore, near the old lighthouse, and along the rocky reef which stretches west from the island. Cunner are very common; blackfish and lobster might be seen. Maximum depth is approximately 30' and, since currents can be very swift, you can only dive at slack tide.

Currents are also strong 300 yards off **Norwalk Light**, where a reef drops to 50'. A prohibition rumrunner is believed to have gone down here, since bottles are recovered on almost every dive. Besides some visible wreckage, you'll see flounder, blackfish, striper, crabs, and lobster. Because of heavy current, this must be a boat dive.

One of the easiest shore dives in western Connecticut is found at **Sherwood Island State Park**. The state park officials have designated the area west of the breakwater as the spot for divers. However, since the bottom at the jetty is mainly silt with scattered rocks, and the principal marine life is millions of crabs, a more exciting dive can be found at **Sherwood Point**, accessible by water only, where you'll see toadfish and flounder amongst the rocks. Clarity rarely reaches over 10'.

MASSACHUSETTS

27-mile obstruction 35
Albert Gallatin 33
Alva 23
Angela 18
Brant Rock Beach 29
Breakwater 22
Burt's Beach 28
California 36
Cape Higgon 21
Cat Island 33
Cathedral Rock 36
Charles S. Haight 36
Chatham 23
Chelsea 36
Chester A. Poling 35
City of Columbus 21
City of Salisbury 32
Cliffs 1 through 4 30
Cohasset Public Beach 31
Corporation Beach 25
Cuttyhunk 19
Devil's Bridge 21
Dry Salvages 36
Edward Rich 36
Folley's Cove 36
Gay Head 21
Gloucester Bay 35
Graves Lighthouse 32
Great Egg Rock 34
Green Island 32
Grouse 36
Gurnet Point 28
Halfway Rock 33
Harding's Beach 23

Hathaway's Pond 22
Henry J. Endicott 26
Herring Cove 24
John Dwight 19
Loblolly Cove 36
Lunet 19
Manomet Point 28
Mars 28
Maryann Rocks 28
Minot's Lighthouse 31
Monomoy Island 23
Naushon Island 19
Pebble Beach 36
Pendleton 23
Pigeon Cove 36
Pinthis 30
Port Hunter 20
Pottstown 27
Provincetown 24
Provincetown Harbor 24
Roaring Bulls 32
Rockport Breakwater 36
Sagamore 21
Sandwich Beach 25
Scusset Breakwater 27
Sengekontacket Pond 21
Strawberry Point 31
Tansy Bitters 19
Tarpaulin Cove 19
The Race 24
Triana 19
USS New Hampshire 34
Vineyard Lightship 21
West Stockbridge 37
Whitehorse Beach 28

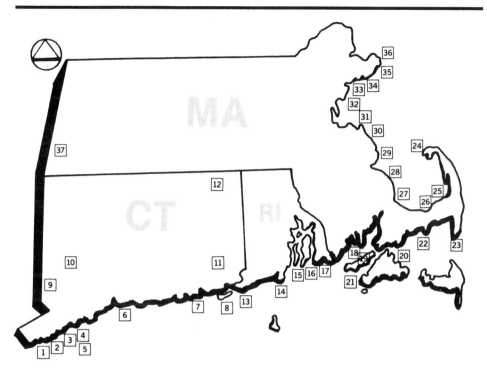

CONNECTICUT

Black Rock Harbor 4
Candlewood Lake 9
Enders Island 8
G-2 submarine 7
Green Falls Pond 11
Hammonaset State Park 6
Harkness Memorial Park 7
Lake Mashapaug 12
Lake Waramaug 10
Middle Ground 5
Mount Tom State Park 10
Norwalk Light 2
Penfield Light 4
Pleasure Beach 7
Seaside Point 7
Sheffield Island 1
Sherwood Island State Park 3
Sherwood Point 3
Squantz Pond State Park 9
Stonington Breakwaters 8
Stratford Shoal 5

RHODE ISLAND

Beavertail Point 15
Belleville 16
Black Point 14
Block Island 15
Brenton Cove 16
Castle Hill 16
Fort Wetherill 15
Gooseberry Island 16
Green Bridge 16
Jamestown Harbor 16
King's Beach 16
Land's End 16
Larchmont 13
Lightburne 15
Lydia Skolfield 16
Montana 15
Pinnacle 15
Point Judith 14
Sachuest Point 16
Sakonnet Point 17
Seal Rock 16
Third Beach 17
U-853 14
USS Bass 15
Watch Hill 13

One of the favorite dives in western Connecticut is found at **Penfield Light**, one mile off Fairfield. Large rock formations around the lighthouse in 15-20' of water provide good lobstering and spearing, mostly for tautog (locally called blackfish) and flounder. Northern corals, mussels, red beard sponges, and anenomes entice macro photographers. Slack high tide offers the best conditions, with average clarity of 5'.

At Bridgeport, divers visit **Black Rock Harbor**, where several small light beacons atop rock piles harbor lobster and some area fish. Only five minutes from shore, it's a convenient dive. For a more advanced dive with better clarity, divers visit the **Middle Ground** at **Stratford Shoal**. A lighthouse over 100 years old alerts you to the shallow area, ten miles off Bridgeport. A wide variety of sea life, including weakfish, striped bass, and schools of bluefish can be seen here. Heavy boat traffic, fishing line, and currents require experienced divers. Clarity can be better than 15'.

For an easy shore dive, visit **Hammonaset State Park**, east of New Haven at the small town of Madison. As at all Connecticut state parks, you need to check with the attendant and dive at the designated area, which, in this case, is east of Meigs Point jetty. Rocks litter the sand bottom, which slopes to a maximum of 20'. Flounder, lobster, cunner, blackfish, anenomes, and sponges can be seen if the clarity is good enough, since it's sometimes less than 5'.

Pleasure Beach, eastward near New London, is another easily accessible shore dive. Depth is very shallow, often less than 10', but clarity can reach 15'. In addition to the more common marine inhabitants, squid can sometimes be seen in late spring.

Just a few miles to the east is **Harkness Memorial Park**, where convenient access is gained to a sandy, rock-strewn area 20' deep. Check with local divers about nearby **Seaside Point**, where depth goes below 70', clarity improves, and a **G-2 submarine** that accidentally sank in the 1920's has been located.

Enders Island, off Mystic, is a good boat dive, since the island provides a lee. Diving around the bridge to the island requires caution, as currents can be strong. Depth in the area is less than 20', and the main attraction is lobstering.

NEW HAMPSHIRE

Clark's Point Cliffs	18
Fort William and Mary	16
Governor Endicott	18
Great Island	17
Great Island Commons	16
Lady of the Lake	18
Lake Spofford	19
Lake Sunapee	17
Lake Winnipesaukee	18
Melvin Village	18
Meredith Bay	18

VERMONT

Champlain	20
General Butler	20
Glen Ellis Falls	23
Lake Champlain	20
Lake Memphremagog	22
Marble quarries	21
Phoenix 1	20
Rouse's Point	20
Water Witch	20
White River	23

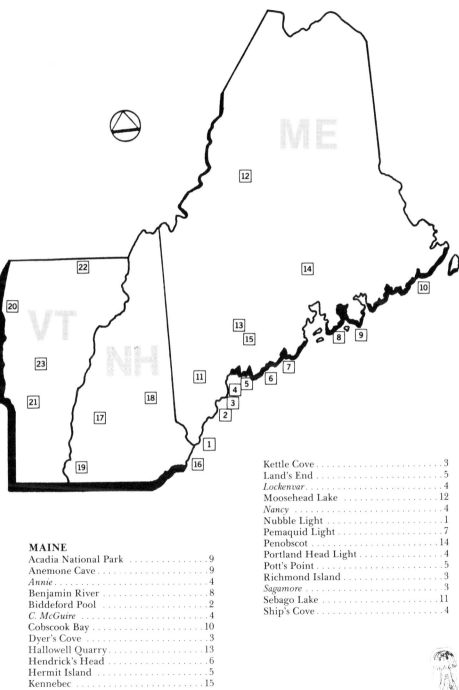

MAINE

Acadia National Park 9
Anemone Cave 9
Annie 4
Benjamin River 8
Biddeford Pool 2
C. McGuire 4
Cobscook Bay 10
Dyer's Cove 3
Hallowell Quarry 13
Hendrick's Head 6
Hermit Island 5
Kennebec 15

Kettle Cove 3
Land's End 5
Lockenvar 4
Moosehead Lake 12
Nancy 4
Nubble Light 1
Pemaquid Light 7
Penobscot 14
Portland Head Light 4
Pott's Point 5
Richmond Island 3
Sagamore 3
Sebago Lake 11
Ship's Cove 4

Off the **Stonington Breakwaters**, near the Rhode Island line, several interesting dives can be made. You can swim out to the first and second breakwaters, where abundant invertebrate life interests macro shooters and sightseers. For lobster, the outer breakwall is best, and you'll need a boat and a flag, since current can be strong.

INLAND

Candlewood Lake, created in 1929, is the largest lake in Connecticut. Clarity is limited — usually 5-20' — but there is a wide variety of diving. Most interesting is the submerged village of Jerusalem, where you can explore the remains of buildings, roads, fences, wagons, a Model-T car, and a 45'-long steel bridge of that lies at a depth of 35'.

Four different state parks allow diving in their lakes. You can dive in **Squantz Pond State Park** at New Fairfield, where you enter the water through the west end of the beach. Squantz is a natural pond that was enlarged when Candlewood Lake was created. Its maximum depth is now 40'. At 20' down stone walls and a row of old tree stumps outlines the former shoreline. Clarity over the mud and silt bottom averages 3-8'.

At **Mount Tom State Park**, the lake is officially titled **Lake Waramaug**, but is usually referred to "Mt. Tom Pond." Clarity reaches 20', with fish life that includes bass, perch, pike, trout, and crayfish. Many antique bottles from the 1800's have been recovered from Mt. Tom. No motor boats are allowed.

Other inland dives include **Green Falls Pond**, at the Pachaug State Forest, near Volountown, and **Lake Mashapaug**, at Bigelow Hollow State Park at Union. Here you enter through the small cove reserved for divers just north of the picnic area. Riddled granite ledges drop off into mud below 60'. Clarity averages 15-20'. Watch for boat traffic near the channel. There are excellent picnic and camping facilities in the forested park.

Connecticut laws concerning diving: Spearing is illegal in fresh water. In salt water, all fin fish except striped bass may be speared. Lobster licenses are available for residents and non-residents. Buddy diving and use of a diver's flag are required by law.

*The brightly colored tilefish (*Lopholatilus chameleon ticips*) lives in caves along the eastern coast of North America. In 1882, the species suffered a major disaster, with an estimated 1.5 billion of them dying, possibly because of a slight shift in the Gulf Stream that year. Contemporary ship captains reported sailing through waters covered with dead tilefish for 69 continuous miles.*

MAINE

COASTAL

An almost unlimited number of coves, bays, and inlets mark the fantastically rugged coast of Maine, while several thousand islands lie just offshore. In fact, a straight line from Cape Elizabeth to Passamoquoddy Bay on the Canada line measures only 200 miles — but there are more than 2500 miles of shoreline in that same distance!

Few coasts offer such exciting, exotic, challenging — and unexploited — diving. The teeming life found beneath the waves spills out of the ocean to blanket the exposed granite rock with a dense covering of barnacles, mussels and rockweeds. Beneath the water, you'll see some of the strangest marine creatures found anywhere. Among these are the knobby and awkward-looking lumpfish, often seen clinging to rocks in the kelp zone with its sucker disc, and the incredibly grotesque goosefish, whose huge, frilled mouth hangs agape as the fish rests on the bottom, hoping to snare a passerby.

In addition to its abundant and bizarre marine life, this region is unique in other ways, too. The Gulf Stream swings away from the East Coast at Cape Cod, causing water temperature to drop dramatically within the Gulf of Maine. 60° is the summertime high, while winter water temperature can drop to 30°. Obviously, adequate thermal protection is essential. Tides, which are usually less than 4' to the south of Cape Cod, double on the north side, and increase the further north you go up the Maine coastline. Clarity averages 20-30', and lessens with the plankton bloom of late summer. Winter offers much greater clarity.

For the adventurous diver, a trip underwater off the Maine coast reveals a wonderland of subtle colors and diverse textures, slowly revealing the presence of a fantastic array of life. Most diving in the state of Maine takes place off the southern coast and in Casco Bay, the southernmost of Maine's three large bays, simply because there are more services in this region.

On a small island just off York is **Nubble Light**, a beautiful landmark, as well as the scene of a former controversy between divers and the town of York. A small channel separates the island from the town park. Besides offering an easy entry into protected water, the channel has an ideal depth of 40'. Marine life abounds over the rock ledges and sandy patches, including pollock, goosefish, skates, lobster, crabs, starfish, scallops, and anemones.

It's little wonder that Nubble rapidly became one of the most popular dives around. However, one spring weekend over 300 divers all showed up at Nubble, and it was more than the parking lot could stand. A scene ensued, with the result being the passage of a law by the town of York instituting an expensive permit system to dive Nubble. Divers appealed the restrictive ordinance, and it was changed to the present law, which still requires a permit — now free — good for any day but Sunday and holidays. You pick up the permits at the police station. Please use consideration when diving Nubble.

Further north at **Biddeford Pool**, about 20 miles south of Portland, many dives can be made. Get permission if entering from private property. The classic rocky shoreline gives way to 30'-deep shoals harboring a variety of fish and invertebrates, including green, brown, and white star tunicates that cluster in colonies, looking like delicate star-shaped flowers. You might also see nudibranches, dining on sea anemones. Somehow the anemone's stinging cells pass undisturbed through the stomachs of the nudibranches, and are deposited on their exposed gills. The anemone's defenses then protect the nudibranches!

Kettle Cove, near Crescent Beach on Cape Elizabeth, provides a good introduction to Maine diving, with paved parking, a fairly easy entry and a maximum depth of 30'. The sand and mud bottom of the cove gives way to rocky outcroppings on each side. A freshwater stream enters the cove, and lures marine life like skates, flounder, pollock, and lobster.

Several varieties of kelp wave gently from their holdfasts on the rocks. While New England kelp isn't as gigantic as California kelp, it can grow to 30'. Many of these species of kelp have tougher stalks than the kelp of California, so you can't free yourself by snapping a stalk — you either have to cut it or methodically untangle yourself.

Nearby, off Prout's Neck, a diver has recently discovered remains thought to be the *Sagamore*. This freighter went aground during a bad storm in 1934. Enormous schools of pollock and mackerel swarm about the boilers and engine. A boat is necessary.

Just offshore from Kettle Cove is **Richmond Island**, known among experienced divers as a great place for fish life. Besides the cunner, a small rockfish commonly seen in every shade from reddish to blue-brown, you'll probably also see dark, thick-bodied tautog. These fish of up to 3' in length can smash crustaceans with their thick-lipped mouths and strong crushing teeth. Flounders are common, lying half-buried in sand. Bizarre sea ravens sit sluggishly on the bottom, often colored bright yellow, red or brown. Schools of striped bass may even speed by.

While you can't dive in Maine's state parks, you can dive adjacent to Two Lights State Park, if you go past the park to **Dyer's Cove**, near the tip of Cape Elizabeth. Park on the gravel adjacent to the cove. In summer, sanderlings and other shorebirds dabble in the sand of the small pocket beach. A sand and rock bottom with varied life leads out to ledges crawling with sea stars, crabs and lobster.

First-time divers in Maine are often surprised to see lobsters out strolling, seemingly aware of their protected status. While such a sight is tempting, stringent and well-enforced laws provide stiff penalties, since lobstering is the state's second largest moneymaker. Almost 9000 lobster trappers depend on the crustacean for their livelihood.

Portland Head Light, one of the most famous of Maine's lighthouses, reaches more than 100' above the entrance to Casco Bay, warning of shallow granite reefs. Several ships — including the *Nancy*, *Annie*, *C. McGuire*, and *Lockenvar* — met their doom on the rocks, and divers often spot stray bits and pieces of the wrecks. While you can't enter from the lighthouse grounds, access is available from either side of the Coast Guard property, or by boat. Maximum depth is 60'.

If the weather's a little rough, less than one-half mile from the lighthouse is **Ship's Cove**. Good parking and easy access off a protected sand beach leads to rock outcroppings on both sides of the cove. Flounder blend with the sand of the bottom. Maximum depth is 50'.

In the Brunswick area, the most popular spot is **Land's End**, 30 miles north of Portland at the tip of Bailey's Island. The gift shop on the left of the sandy beach was rebuilt a few years back, after a ferocious storm washed the first building, which had sat at the water's edge, out to sea. Now you can find many souvenirs decorating the bottom, interspersed with flounders. On the right side of the beach, periwinkles, scallops, and crabs decorate the shallow rock ledges. Stay out of the channel, as rapid tidal currents and some heavy boat traffic occur there.

Pott's Point, just south of Brunswick, is for the more advanced diver, since ledges and currents can make for difficult entries and exits. However, the water teems with life, including scallops.

Hermit Island, just a short way by dirt road from Small Point Beach, is an excellent spot for traveling divers to visit, with a nearby campground, and two miles of sandy beach giving way to rocky headlands. Several islands within snorkeling distance from shore lure the adventurous. Spearfishing for flounder is great along the gently rolling sand bottom, while skates, sea ravens, lumpfish, tautogs, cunners, and crabs inhabit the kelp-covered rock ledges. Maximum depth is 35'. The major difficulty with this dive is the long walk to water, packing gear from the parking area.

A few miles north of Brunswick, near the town of Wiscasset, is **Hendrick's Head**. Easy parking and an easy entry lead out to shallow rock ledges and sand patches. Many green sea urchins, crabs, skates, and lobsters can be seen. A long swim will be necessary to attain any appreciable depth.

Pemaquid Light, northeast of Brunswick, is the favorite dive site in Muscungus Bay. A very beautiful, classic lighthouse setting drops off into an even more beautiful underwater scene. However, a difficult 50' climb down a rocky cliff, as well as treacherous tides and surf, make it a dive for the experienced. During season, there is a small entrance fee. Picnic facilities, as well as restrooms, are available.

Further north along the coast are many more beautiful spots to dive. However, these are generally limited to longtime explorers of the Maine coast, since services are non-existent and the coast becomes even more rugged and desolate. There are some incredible sights underwater. Perhaps one of the loveliest is to come upon a deep cave or clean rock face where colonies of hard star coral have massed together. The delicate pink stars often share the rock expanse with scarlet sea cucumbers, presenting one of the most beautifully colored scenes possible to a diver. In addition, tiny crimson and violet sea stars, beds of horse mussels covered with pink coralline algae, and wispy, stalked hydroids all present fantastic photographic opportunities.

At Blue Hill, where the **Benjamin River** meets the ocean, you can make a difficult entry down a steep 40'-high cliff to a cobble-strewn beach. Green crabs, sea urchins, burrowing anemones, hermit crabs housed in whelk shells, gunnel, and several species of colorful sea cucumbers are the most frequently seen residents. In addition, lion's mane jellyfish, trailing their 10'-long stinging tentacles, sometimes drift close enough to make divers cautious.

At **Acadia National Park**, just outside Bar Harbor, incredibly beautiful dives await those prepared enough to bring all their gear, including full tanks. The National Park Service has a guide to diving within the park available to those who come in season. Many of the rocky outcroppings in this gorgeous park provide exquisite diving. **Anemone Cave**, on Mt. Desert Island, is a favorite site of macro photographers.

In **Cobscook Bay**, almost at the Canadian border, you can see 6" pink-hearted hydroids, eel-like wrymouths that live in burrows, and an amazing variety of colorful invertebrates.

While Maine, with 3000 offshore islands, has more than any other state, there are presently no dive boats taking people out to visit them. Since many of the islands are close enough to shore to be visible, many divers bring their own small boats with them. Plans are being made in the Brunswick area to have a charter boat available for visiting divers. In addition to fantastic underwater scenery and prolific fish populations, harbor seals and a splendid array of seabirds make their homes on some of the offshore islands. (Imagine seeing a puffin underwater.) Many whales, including the extremely rare right and humpback whales, also inhabit the Gulf of Maine, and are sometimes seen from boats.

INLAND

Sebago Lake and **Moosehead Lake** are the biggest lakes in the state. Inhabited by trout, bass, salmon, perch, and snapping turtles, they have generally poor clarity. **Hallowell Quarry**, near Augusta, is deeper than 100'. Tree limbs and monofilament can entangle the diver.

Geoduck clams, besides being huge, are also incredibly long-lived. One individual in British Columbia was found to be 146 years old.

Current divers enjoy Maine's fast rivers, of which the most famous are the **Penobscot** and the **Kennebec**. Pollution control measures have cleaned these rivers up in recent years, and even Atlantic salmon may once again be seen. Unlike Pacific salmon, Atlantic salmon don't die after spawning, but return again to the sea.

Maine laws concerning diving: Absolutely no lobsters may be taken by divers. Spearing is illegal in fresh water, but is legal in salt water. Scallops may be gathered by divers from November 1 to April 15, limited to two bushels per day, for personal use only.

MASSACHUSETTS

Although Massachusetts ranks 45th in size among the states, it's the seventh biggest in diving popularity. Despite its small size, the state offers a staggering variety of diving. The rocky north shore and Cape Ann offer exquisite diving into a glacially carved submarine world of canyons and ridges, teeming with so much marine life it's almost ridiculous. You'll see anemones everywhere, many lobsters and crabs, tomcod, eelpout (also known as blubberlips), starfish, soft corals, and basket stars. Schools of pollock, cod, and even occasional striped bass swim over the rocky bottom, covered with sinuous kelp in the shallows, and rich pink coralline algae in deeper water.

And then there's Cape Cod, which has snared a good percentage of the 2000 shipwrecks found off Massachusetts. Since the Cape extends out so far into the ocean, diving at the tip gives you the rare opportunity to see open ocean rovers like whales or ocean sunfish. In Massachusetts Bay, you can drop into a largely unexplored wilderness and catch a lobster dinner, with the outlines of one of the country's greatest cities visible off in the distance. Off the south shore, there are famous wrecks and kelp-covered rock reefs. And you can't forget Martha's Vineyard, where you'll find rocky ledges, sandy drift dives, and great wrecks — in fact, Martha's Vineyard has almost every kind of diving in Massachusetts.

SOUTHERN MASSACHUSETTS — Buzzard's Bay and Elizabeth Islands

The Buzzard's Bay area of Massachusetts sees fewer divers than the rest of the state, since this backwater has limited visibility due to the summer temperatures that can reach 72°. Plankton takes off in the warm still water, leaving early spring and fall the best diving seasons.

The *Angela*, an old cement barge, is the favorite dive in the area. It takes no special equipment to find it, since you can see it from the surface. You simply tie up to it, drop down the ladder, and you're inside — a welcome change from all the wrecks that take Loran C and luck to locate.

The Elizabeth Islands stretch down from the base of Cape Cod between the mainland and Martha's Vineyard. **Cuttyhunk**, the southernmost of the islands, has snared several ships over the years. The *Triana*, an ocean-going Navy tug, went down in 1895 on the southwest side of the island. Today divers can find pieces of scattered wreckage, but currents can be heavy.

The *John Dwight* started out as a tug, and wound up a Prohibition rumrunner. According to one of many tales, the *John Dwight* was supposed to be carrying a load of whiskey. Instead, the captain substituted cheap beer, pocketed the $75,000 savings, machine-gunned the crew, sank the boat one mile off Cuttyhunk, and was never heard from again. The 125'-long steam-powered vessel was blown up by the authorities to prevent salvage of the illicit cargo. Today her bones, together with pieces of beer bottles, lie at 80'.

On **Naushon Island**, sheltered coves, accessible by boat only, offer interesting diving. At **Tarpaulin Cove**, the old wooden schooner *Tansy Bitters* burned and sank in very shallow water near shore. Planks give the major remaining evidence of the ship's existence. The *Lunet*, a 103' wooden schooner, sank off the south side of the islands during a ferocious gale in 1898.

MARTHA'S VINEYARD

The reefs, beaches, and wrecks of Martha's Vineyard see the most diving south of the Cape. Since the Vineyard is situated between the old shipping lanes connecting Boston with points south, as well as between New England and Europe, it would take a lifetime to explore all the ships that have gone down in the area.

One in particular, though, stands out. In 1918 a British freighter of over 400', the *Port Hunter*, was carrying war goods from Boston to France. A thick fog blanketed the shipping channel and caused a tug to ram the freighter. The captain purposefully ran the freighter aground on Hedgefence Shoal, three miles north of Martha's Vineyard, in hopes of salvaging her.

Now the bow is at 45' depth, and the stern is 80' deep. Marine growth covers the decks. Cod and stripers are common. Inside a cabin, candles float in liquid space. The six-foot stern gun is still intact, and railroad wheels from the cargo are scattered about. The *Port Hunter* is an advanced dive, with heavy currents. Dive on slack tide. Clarity around the ship ranges from 10-40', on a day-to-day basis.

In colonial New England, living lobsters were sometimes used as fertilizer after heavy storms washed multitudes of them ashore. Lobsters were normally so plentiful they were considered a poor man's food.

Another interesting wreck is the *Vineyard Lightship*, which sits on a sand bottom 65' deep between Gay Head and Cuttyhunk. Twelve crewmen went down with their ship in a 1944 hurricane. Photography around the vessel is excellent. Marine life, including tautog and goosefish, is plentiful.

The *Sagamore* was a 219'-long four-masted schooner. In 1907 she was hit and ended up 80' down. Her intact ship's wheel and anchor used to provide great photos until they were removed.

In addition to these wreck dives, the Vineyard is surrounded by interesting, boulder-strewn bottom, particularly around the southwest part of the island, from Gay Head to West Tisbury. You can find access near the colorful cliffs around **Gay Head**, where a parking lot by the lighthouse and a large public beach lead out into waters teeming with life.

A rocky reef known as **Devil's Bridge** juts out into the sea from the base of the cliffs, and offers one of the most scenic dives of Martha's Vineyard. Lobsters hide in crannies between the boulders, while star coral, sea anemones, and sea stars adorn the surfaces of the rocks. It's best to stay close to shore to avoid the current which picks up further out. Devil's Bridge was the scene of a terrible disaster in 1884 when the iron steamship *City of Columbus* ran aground with 97 lives lost.

Gay Head is also a good launch for a visit to the deeper water off the cliffs, or other dive sites around **Cape Higgon** and **Makoniky Head**. One of the most interesting fish you'll see is the curious squirrel hake, which "walks" over the bottom with its elongated ventral fins.

In rough weather, Martha's Vineyard offers alternate, protected sites. **Sengekontacket Pond**, near Oak Bluff, is a large salt pond. Its shallow waters are teeming with life, for the diver curious enough to slow down and simply observe. Dense eel-grass beds support shrimp, delicate hydroids, blue-eyed scallops, and crabs. And when you're tired of focusing your eyes on the wealth of minute life, you can always try the saltwater version of a river run. If you wait until ebb tide, the current will pull you effortlessly for several hundred yards down the channel before it spits you out into the sea, where you can slip around the jetty and exit.

NANTUCKET

Since Nantucket is surrounded by deep water, and has a boring sand bottom, very little diving activity goes on. Of course, the "Everest of wrecks" lies near Nantucket. The *Andrea Doria* has always been for the most experienced of wreck divers. Depths at the famous wreck are well past the no-decompression limits, currents are heavy, and the infamous weather is predictably terrible all but a few days out of the year. Recently, though, another element of danger has entered the picture — the increasingly swift disintegration of the ship.

CAPE COD

The Cape sticks out into the Atlantic like a long flexed arm. It is the boundary line for two distinct marine environments — so distinct that temperatures off the north shore of Cape Cod may be several degrees colder than those of the south shore just a few miles away. Unlike most of New England, Cape Cod is predominantly sand, with a slightly sloping floor extending out for quite a distance. Since the Cape is a very popular summer tourist spot, expect parking fees at most beaches.

The south side of the Cape, bordering Nantucket Sound, isn't as good as the north for shore diving, since the warmer water also has less clarity, and less marine life. Around Hyannisport, an inflatable will be handy to take you out to the end of the **breakwater**, where small lobster, tautog, and flounder can be seen. Depth slopes to 25' and, at best, clarity is 10'. Summer boat traffic is heavy.

If the weather prevents you from going out to the *Port Hunter*, the *Vineyard Lightship* (for detailed coverage see the section on Martha's Vineyard), or any of the other wrecks off the south side of the Cape, you can always dive at **Hathaway's Pond**. Clarity in this freshwater pond near Hyannis usually averages 25'. A vintage cabin cruiser sits on the sand bottom 38' down and provides an interesting dive.

Since **Monomoy Island** is a wildlife refuge, with nobody inhabiting the dunes except beach grass and terns, you'll need to go with a charter to explore the water around it. The wreck of the *Pendleton* draws many divers, although dangerous currents and heavy wave action around the partially exposed vessel require very experienced divers with surface tenders.

Shore diving around **Chatham** is best at **Harding's Beach**, where protected, shallow water harbors a variety of life, including skates and dogfish.

In 50' of water off Chatham is the wreckage of the *Alva*. Built for the Vanderbilts, this was the most luxurious yacht of her day. The three-masted, topsail schooner also had steam, and a steel hull. Built in 1886, the *Alva* sank after being struck while anchored in the shipping lanes.

The tip of Cape Cod, at **Provincetown**, has good diving, especially in August and September, when all kinds of schooling fish, lobster, blue sharks, and even whales can be seem. **Herring Cove** is one of the few areas within the National Seashore where diving is allowed. The sandy beach slopes gently past the surfline. Sea robins, skates, and flounder might be spotted on the sand bottom, which never surpasses 20' deep.

Within **Provincetown Harbor** is an easy dive, safe for novices, where a quick beach entry and a short swim will put you right over a couple of small wrecks that lie near each other at a maximum depth of 70'.

In only one month, a diatom may have a billion descendants.

For divers who enjoy feeling like a bit of flotsam caught up in a powerful current, it's hard to beat **The Race**. Since you'll be drifting in the Gulf Stream, which veers out to sea at the tip of the Cape, it's essential that this be a well-planned dive undertaken by experienced current divers. Besides the thrill of riding a wild sea current, it's also a good opportunity to pick up lobster or flounder, or see open ocean rovers like immense, pig-eyed ocean sunfish. However, you'll have to watch out for the commercial fishermen operating their draggers. Use an extra degree of caution besides towing a flag, since, unfortunately, many of the draggers have no respect for divers.

Farther west, **Corporation Beach** at East Dennis attracts many divers. Clarity goes to 25' or more, and the sloping bottom has an interesting mixture of sand and rock habitats. **Sandwich Beach** is a nice dive site, complete with a bathhouse. The water stays shallow for a great distance.

One of the favorite wrecks visited by charters in Cape Cod Bay is the *Henry J. Endicott*. The four-masted schooner sank in 1910 under gale conditions, and today lies three miles offshore. You can still see much of the cargo of cobblestone paving bricks. If you see part of a railroad engine, don't be surprised — one was loaded on the deck. The wreck rests on its side, 80' down. Often goosefish can be seen around the wreck, where clarity averages 10-40'.

SOUTH SHORE

Stretching all along the south shore from the edge of Cape Cod Canal almost to Boston is a wide variety of dive sites. Currents are rarely a problem, depths are generally less than 40' on shore dives, and summer clarity ranges from 10-40'.

Don't expect to see goosefish at the more popular sites, though. Although those unfamiliar with New England waters are usually shocked to discover it, the goosefish, which is without a doubt the ugliest fish in North America, is also fantastic eating. Ignore the immense mouth, the armlike pectorals, the weird frilling below the lower jaw, and the wormy "bait" projecting over the fish's head. The taste of goosefish is so fantastic that it often retails for twice the price of cod.

Naturally, they're quite rare in popular areas, especially since they have such small territories. Fall seems to be the best time to find them.

But there's more to see along the south shore than goosefish. At **Scusset Breakwater**, beside the Cape Cod Canal, you can dive off the 1/2-mile-long breakwater, but not on the canal side. You'll likely see most every kind of marine life found in the area. Lobster hide in the caves between the rocks, tautog snoop around the jetty, flounder and skate park in adjacent sand, and, if you go further out by boat, you'll find sea scallops.

Just out from the canal is the wreck of the **Pottstown**. This four-masted schooner sank in 1930 in a northeaster. The 190'-long vessel went down in 50' of water with a cargo of coal. Marine life is good around the wreck, with occasional schools of pollock. Recently divers have found the wreck of the ocean-going tug **Mars**, closer to Manomet Point in deeper water.

Within the Plymouth Bay area, at least three easily accessible dives can be made. The southernmost is **Maryann Rocks** on **Manomet Point**. Sand extends out from the shore for about 20', and then a kelp-covered rocky terrain begins. This is a good spot for sightseeing, with a depth of 60' attainable 1/4-mile out. Tautog are plentiful here.

At **Whitehorse Beach** and **Burt's Beach**, on the northern part of the bay, you'll find nearby parking and easy access to sandy, sloping bottoms with scattered small rocks. Flounder are abundant. **Gurnet Point**, enclosing the north side of the bay, is known for good clarity, but some heavy surf and currents make it a more difficult dive.

But it's **Brant Rock Beach** in Marshfield that's the most popular dive around with both novices and experienced divers. Free parking 30' from the water and an exceptionally easy entry lead into sand patches separated by small, kelpy rocks. Depth is 25' at 200 yards from shore and hits a maximum of 40'. Lobster, tautog, flounder, perch, and some large cod hang out around Brant Rock. Night diving and photography are popular.

Off Scituate, **Cliffs 1 through 4** are good dives, especially for lobstering and photography. And for wreck divers, one of Massachusetts' best known is found about six miles east of the fourth cliff.

The **Pinthis** was a steel-hulled tanker, about 220' long, carrying a cargo of gas in June 1930 when a passenger liner rammed her port side. She went down within 20 minutes. More than 45 people died in the collision. The *Pinthis* rests keel up, on a sand and rock bottom 95-100' down. Because of the depth, slight currents, and jagged metal around the wreck, this isn't a dive for novices. Marine life can be plentiful around the wreck, especially in summer.

Strawberry Point in Cohasset offers a nice shore dive, but parking is available for only a few cars, so more divers head to the **Cohasset Public Beach**. A mainly flat sand bottom with scattered kelpy rocks slopes to 40' maximum. In summer, lobsters, clams, and flounder are plentiful. The swim out at high tide may be 300 yards.

Close to the public beach is **Minot's Lighthouse**, a famous historical landmark, as well as one of the most exciting dives in the area. Many ships of the 18th and 19th centuries met with disaster near the lighthouse, which marks the entrance to Cohasset Harbor. You need a boat or inflatable for this dive, and approaching the ledge can be difficult. Currents that can be 3-5 knots mandate advanced divers with careful plans.

Some species of amphipod eat over 100,000 diatoms a day.

The sheer granite wall of the lighthouse drops to 80', with many craggy over-hangs and ledges. As you'd expect, marine life finds the area an excellent habitat, and schools of mackerel and pollock are common. Although the 200-lb. cod reported by early New Englanders aren't seen anymore, Minot's Light is one of the best places around to see today's version of a large cod. In addition, big lobsters and blue sharks are occasionally seen. Diligent searchers are usually rewarded with artifacts.

BOSTON HARBOR

The best diving around Boston is in the outer harbor area, near **Graves Light-house**. The name gives you a clue — the area's so rocky it resembles a graveyard. The glaciers scoured out deep gorges and piled massive boulders about like pebbles. The rugged scene dwarfs a diver; the granite formations leave you feeling miniscule.

Near the northeast side of the Graves Light is the wreckage of the *City of Salisbury*. This 419'-long freighter went down in April of 1938, carrying a load of farm animals. It's best to dive here on a slack tide to avoid the up-to-3-knot current of incoming or outgoing tide. Wreckage of the vessel, which broke in half, has fallen to both sides of the ledge. Although it was salvaged, there are still items of interest over the rocky bottom. Maximum depth is 90'.

Other dives, like **Green Island** or **Roaring Bulls**, are for the experienced only. It's wise to go with local divers since heavy currents and a bewildering underwa-ter terrain can be confusing. Clarity averages 10'.

NORTH SHORE AND CAPE ANN

Famous for dramatic underwater landscapes of gorges, ledges, dropoffs, caves, and canyons, Cape Ann and the North Shore offer radically different dives than those found south of Cape Cod. Clarity improves the farther north you go, from an average of 25' around Marblehead and Magnolia to 30' or more at Cape Ann. Some divers even relate tales of 60' or more clarity at offshore sites in early spring. And the underwater scene is fascinating, with an abundance and great variety of marine life.

The glaciers did amazing things to the seafloor. At **Cat Island**, just out of Marblehead Harbor, a waving forest of kelp grows on a 20'-deep shelf that extends off the island. Hermit crabs and moon snails crawl about in the shadowy, spooky world under the plants. Sudden vertical cuts are randomly spaced in the shelf. They lead into narrow, white-walled gorges that end in gravelly floors 45' deep.

But if you can visit only one site in Massachusetts, make it **Halfway Rock**. This guano-covered rock outcropping sticks up out of the water three miles due east of

Marblehead Harbor, halfway between Boston and Gloucester. Since anchoring can be tricky, go with experienced charter captains. Herring gulls, Wilson's petrels, and cormorants skim and wheel around you as you prepare to drop over the side.

It's quite a shock to pass from the drab world above water to the fabulous richness beneath the surface. On the northwest corner, the walls drop vertically to 110'. On other sides, flat shelves stairstep down to dramatic dropoffs, plunging cuts, and curving walls. In the top ten feet, still within the surge zone, kelp billows with the waves. As you descend, kelp gives way to a rich hard purple algae. Wolf eels, with their big heads, powerful jaws, and vicious-looking teeth, hang close to the rock, looking for mollusks to crunch. Sea ravens, sometimes in bright shades of yellow or red, squat motionless, making great subjects for photos. Schools of pollock glide out of the haze, picking plankton from the water. In deeper water, white, orange, and red anemones grow in colonies on the sheerest walls, lending a soft, blurry touch to the granite. And everywhere, smooth blood stars and bright sea stars wrap their sinuous arms around the rock.

Halfway Rock gives you a great deal of latitude — if you're on your second dive of the day, there's plenty of life in the shallows. If you want an exciting deep dive down curving dropoffs, or if you're hungry for lobster, flounder, or cod, Halfway Rock is the place. It's an especially good site for photographers or those who want to enlarge their horizons by seeing practically the entire spectrum of New England marine life.

The **Albert Gallatin** lies on the BooHoo Ledge, which projects from 75' to within 2' of the surface at low tide. The rusted remains of the 142'-long, iron-hulled steam-sail revenue cutter have been scattered over the ledge at 20-40' depths since 1892. Encrusted cannonballs, hand-painted pottery, and sabers are occasionally found.

There's good beach diving off the North Shore, too, but many beaches are off-limits to divers in the summer months, so it's necessary to seek out rocky headlands. Check locally, since laws restricting diver access change frequently.

For wreck history buffs, few dives can match the **USS New Hampshire**, found just outside Manchester Bay. This sister ship to *Old Ironsides* was built in 1810. She sank off Graves Island, and the remains lie in 30' of water. Often sand covers the wooden wreckage, but occasionally rough winters will wash much of the sand away and expose the ribs. Many divers have found copper spikes and flooring nails, forged in Paul Revere's foundry. Some still remain to be located.

Great Egg Rock, just north of Manchester Bay, is an exciting boat dive. Sheer walls covered with anemones, basket stars, and sinuous little rock eels make great photos, especially in winter.

The bluefin, king of the tuna tribe, is one of the fastest fish, able to attain speeds up to 55 mph. It can swim 100 miles in a single day on its transatlantic migrations. Only the mako shark and the orca can catch it. The record bluefin weighed 1,496 lbs. and was 32 years old.

At the mouth of Gloucester Bay, the wreck of the **Chester A. Poling** lies in a sheltered area at 100' depth. The 300'-long oil tanker broke in half and sank in 1977. Clarity often surpasses 35' around the intact stern, encrusted with invertebrates and surrounded by huge schools of fish. The bow is still undiscovered.

Just inside the breakwater the remains of an unknown schooner, sunk around 1900, are known as the **27-mile obstruction**. Sitting on a mud bottom at 40', only the huge windlass rises above the mud. The anchors, keel, and bilge are partially buried. Clarity averages 1-8'.

Divers also explore **Gloucester Bay** for artifacts and antique bottles, with one of the best finds being a clay smoking pipe from the colonial era 300 years ago.

In the Rockport area, several sites offer good beach diving. The 1/2-mile-long **Pebble Beach** offers several good access points. In summer, long-finned hake, pollock, cunner, and flounder are thick. Winter divers wonder at the fabulous clarity — often 50-100', the bright invertebrates, and the absence of fish. Most move out to the deeper and warmer waters of the continental shelf, returning only when the water warms up.

Loblolly Cove, at the eastern tip of Cape Ann, slopes gently to a shallow bottom covered with colorful pebbles and scattered large rocks. Lobster and sculpin are abundant. Male lumpfish, appearing to wear suits of green knobby armor, guard their egg masses vigilantly, fanning their fins to keep the eggs aerated, and attacking anything that comes nearby. However, very limited parking requires that divers use consideration and forethought.

At **Pigeon Cove**, it's also necessary to use care so as not to rile the many lobstermen using it. Like Loblolly, Pigeon offers a shallow, bright, colorful dive. Sometimes schools of bluefish surround divers in summer. The razor teeth of these fish have bitten chunks out of pilings during feeding frenzies. Schools of mackerel have been seen leaping onto beaches to escape them!

At **Folley's Cove**, you can choose between a shallow boulder-strewn entry on the east side or a wall on the west side that drops to 25'. Bluish cunner peer at you from their hiding places inside the kelp. If you follow the wall out to the point, basket stars, anemones, and hermit crabs combine to create a muted world of pale orange and cream. In deeper water farther out, you'll see schools of pollock and cod, as well as 10-lb. striped bass.

Just north of Rockport Harbor, directly behind the Ralph Waldo Emerson Inn, is a large area known as **Cathedral Rock**. Entry is difficult, with limited parking and a climb down a sloping headland to the beach. Once you're in the water, the rock bottom continues to slope downwards, occasionally broken by overhangs upholstered in somber dark-red and green plant life. From the sandy bottom looking up, the huge granite outcroppings resemble a natural amphitheater. Known for excellent clarity, Cathedral Rock is worth the hike.

Charters in the Rockport area often head out to the **Rockport Breakwater** (also known as the Sandy Bay Breakwater — near Pigeon Cove). Usually those new to the area choose to dive the protected inside. Kelp and other seaweeds billow in the top 40' of the rockpile. Below that, the orderly stacks of huge boulders form small caves where anemones extend hungry snares. Lobster antennae twitch from the deepest recesses of the caves, and many lobster traps sit on the bottom. Maximum depth is 80'.

Experienced area divers, in calm weather, also dive the surgy outside of the breakwater. The battering sea has rearranged the orderly stacks of boulders into piles that create caves big enough to enter. With a good light, you'll see a beautiful array of sponges, crabs, anemones, and tunicates, as well as pelagics like big cod. A large pile of paving stones marks the remains of the two-masted schooner *Edward Rich*, which sank in 1899 after striking the breakwater.

Another interesting wreck can be found on the Flat Ground, offshore. The Liberty Ship *Charles S. Haight* went aground in 1946 when returning to Boston from Europe. Since the vessel has been stripped and dynamited, the remains of the huge ship are scattered across a large area of the 20-40'-deep ledge. Currents are strong during some tides.

Other, smaller wrecks in the vicinity include the remains of the fishing boat *California*, at 40-70' deep, and the minesweeper *Grouse*, which ran aground on a shallow ledge in 1955. Both are very broken and scattered.

The *Chelsea* ranks as a great dive. This wreck lies between Straitsmouth and Thatcher Islands, off Rockport. The bow is intact at 40', but the stern has been dynamited. Down since 1957, the *Chelsea* has become encrusted with an incredible amount of marine life. Cod, pollock, and many other fish swim about the wreck.

The **Dry Salvages**, also in this rocky offshore area, is a granite outcropping where you'll see the entire spectrum of Cape Ann marine life, including some heavy kelp beds, schools of pollock, cod, and striped bass, and invertebrates of every size and description. Clarity is excellent, often 50'.

INLAND

Although Massachusetts has many ponds, most are too shallow and muddy to offer good diving.

For the experienced penetration diver, though, there are old granite and feldspar mine shafts and quarries in the beautiful mountains of western Massachusetts. At **West Stockbridge**, an iron ore mine drops to 60' before the shaft begins. Entering these shafts is less dangerous than entering mining shafts of softer shale or limestone, but it is still a penetration dive requiring training in cave diving. In spring and fall, clarity is excellent, but in summer it goes blackwater below 30'.

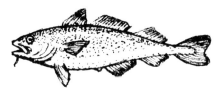

Massachusetts laws concerning diving: Lobsters may be taken with a non-commercial permit only by residents of Massachusetts, or non-residents who own more than $5000 worth of Massachusetts real estate. Striped bass, smelt, shad, and all anadromous fish are protected from spearing. Use of diver's flag is required.

NEW HAMPSHIRE

The best spot for traveling divers along New Hampshire's 26 miles of coast is **Great Island Commons**. For a small fee, this town park is open to divers, and provides rest rooms, showers, and picnic areas. A circular beach provides easy access to a sandy bottom, or you can enter off the rocky breakwater if you prefer.

You can also dive at **Fort William and Mary**, situated on a river inlet, although slippery rocks make for a more difficult entry. Tidal changes combine with the river current to create challenging conditions. Underwater, though, the scene is beautiful, with ledges covered by kelp and starfish, and abundant fish life. Maximum depth is approximately 40'.

Inland New Hampshire has a much wider array of diving in its many clear, natural lakes of glacial origin. **Lake Sunapee** is a nine-mile-long lake with a rock and mud bottom that reaches a maximum depth of 103'. Water temperature reaches 78° above the thermocline, but below 35' it drops to 40°. Clarity averages 25', and is best in spring and fall. Sunapee has several shore accesses but is best explored by boat.

You can enter the water right behind the Newbury town information booth and enjoy a fairly secluded dive along the shoreline. The bottom gradually slopes to 35', dotted with rock piles harboring much life, including bass, perch, suckers, crayfish, and mussels. Photography is excellent; clarity averages 25' in summer, and more in winter.

If you have a boat, the area just north of **Great Island** on Lake Sunapee offers excellent diving. Depth drops rapidly to 90'. A natural reef of huge boulders and rock piles projects off the bottom. Since the lake has been used for years, parts of steamships, huge anchors, scores of very antique bottles, and more modern relics like fishing tackle have all been found. An ancient dugout canoe, found by divers, was removed to go on display at a New Hampshire fort.

For an especially interesting dive, check with local divers in fall. They've located the areas where the landlocked trout and salmon populations spawn, making Sunapee one of the best sites available for photographing the excitement of a trout or salmon run.

Within immense **Lake Winnipesaukee**, you can enjoy a fantastic diversity of diving. At **Clark's Point Cliffs**, you can explore rock ledges, walls, and overhangs in the first 40' of water, and then drop down a sheer cliff to 105'. At **Melvin Village**, you can find Indian artifacts and explore the Indian ruins. You can dive a train wreck of many flat beds and box cars located in **Meredith Bay**, or you can search for the hundreds of lost watercraft ranging from horse-drawn barges, to paddlewheelers, to steamboats, to modern yachts and sailing craft.

Some of the more popular found wrecks include the *Lady of the Lake*, an intact 120' steamboat in 30' of water, and the 100' *Governor Endicott*.

Since Lake Winnipesaukee is the largest glacial lake wholly within the boundary of any state, the diving variety is endless. Many of the caverns, reefs, and ledges remain to be explored, and, since over 350 islands dot the lake, a boat can open up whole new territories to the adventurous diver. In fall, area divers swim amidst migrating salmon. In winter, they ice dive in the crystalline water. Summer clarity at Winnepesaukee averages 30'.

Several lakes exist in southwestern New Hampshire, around Keene. One of the favorites is **Lake Spofford**. This clean, spring-fed lake attracts many divers — including instructors with their classes — because entry is easy, particularly over the north shore beach. Bath houses and food are available. Offshore reefs, rock shelves, and an underwater valley provide interest. Small tame fish beg to be hand-fed, while large trout and bass remain more wary. Depth ranges from 30-65'. Clarity ranges from 15-20' in summer, more in winter. Spofford is popular for night dives.

New Hampshire laws concerning diving: No spearing is allowed in fresh water. It is illegal to take lobsters by diving. Use of diver's flag is required.

Evidence that complex descriptive language exists among orcas is clearly seen in this fact: In 1957, a pack of orcas over 1000 strong was hounding Norwegian fishing vessels. So a nearby whaling fleet was called in, which operated in identical WWII corvettes but for a harpoon mounted in the bow of the whalers. One whale was harpooned and injured. Within 30 minutes there were no whales near the whaling vessels, but they were still catching the prey of the fishing fleet.

RHODE ISLAND

Rhode Island has more to offer the visiting diver per acre than just about any other state in the Union. If you're a lobster fan, you can catch bugs for a nominal fee while you're vacationing in the state. If you're a spearfisher, you can seek the most prized gamefish on the East Coast, the striped bass, and try to beat the record — a 58-lb. striper speared over a decade ago. If you're a wreck diver, you can take your pick of a wide array ranging from wooden schooners to a U-boat and its last victim, sunk within a few miles of each other in one of the closing clashes of World War II. If you like bottle collecting, few places can beat Narragansett Bay. If you're strictly a shore diver, you'll find easily accessible sites ranging in depth from 10-150'.

But for many people the favorite activity is capturing the tropicals that are borne north by the Gulf Stream. Since they're doomed by approaching winter, this is one of the few places divers can feel altruistic about removing sealife! Clarity in Rhode Island varies from nothing to as much as 80'. It's best at offshore sites in late summer when the Gulf Stream swings close to shore. Water temperatures rarely reach past 60° in the hottest part of summer, and deeper dives have sharp thermoclines.

Watch Hill, at the extreme western tip of Rhode Island, offers good diving. Many fish, scattered wreckage, and beautiful plant-covered reefs create excellent diving. Clarity averages 25'.

About 3-1/2 miles southeast of Watch Hill is the wreck of the ***Larchmont***, a steamer that went down in a 1907 collision in which over 200 people died. Since the almost-intact ship sits on a current-swept, low-clarity gravel reef 130' down, it's a site only for the most experienced divers.

Further east is **Point Judith**. Besides the diving available around the breakwater and the point, some of the most famous wrecks in the state lie off Point Judith. One is the *SS Black Point*. This coal hauler was torpedoed by a German sub, the *U-853*, on May 5, 1945. She sank within a few minutes, taking 12 crewmen down with her, but almost immediately two nearby destroyers responded to her alarm. They found the U-boat heading back out to sea, and cut off its escape with well-aimed depth charges that sent the sub with its entire crew to the bottom.

Diving on the ***Black Point*** brings the tragic battle vividly to life. The ship sits in 90' of water. Time has transformed the ship's gun into a garden of pink-hearted hydroids amidst large white anenomes. Cunner, hake, lobster, and numerous sea ravens inhabit the wreck.

The *U-853*, further out in water 130' deep, is a dive for the more advanced. Besides the depth, currents can be strong, particularly as you descend the anchor line. Also, there are unexploded munitions around this wreck. Add to that the enticement of penetration, since the hatches have been removed, and you have a very challenging and eerie dive for only the most experienced of divers.

Just seven miles south of Point Judith is **Block Island**, one of the favorite dives in the state. Besides interesting terrain close to the island, you'll also find some fantastic wrecks offshore. About 1/4-mile off the southeast side lie the remains of the *Lightburne*, a 400'-long oil tanker that ran aground in 1939. Despite dynamiting by the Coast Guard, the ship's remains, scattered over a sandy bottom only 25' deep, still offer a fine dive. Pieces of wreckage are totally covered with marine life — corals, anenomes, and kelp. Species like sea stars, blackfish, and eels are common. Clarity often exceeds 25', making the *Lightburne* a good dive for photographers and novices.

That can't be said about the **USS Bass**, since this sub lies over 150' deep, and harbors almost no life. The sub was one of a class of U.S. Navy subs that had insurmountable design flaws, and so it was deliberately sunk.

The wreckage of the schooner **Montana** is a favorite of photographers, since the wooden rib beams of the old vessel are thickly furred with many macro subjects. In addition, eels often slither around the coal cargo. Eelpout and cunner also live around the "coal pile", which lies on a sloping bottom with a maximum depth of 90'.

For a good natural site for photography, it's hard to beat the **Pinnacle**, a huge pile of enormous boulders that were deposited by a glacier. Many fish, including schools of stripers, swim through the caves and tunnels of the moraine. Clarity is excellent, often over 50', and depth falls to a maximum of 75'.

At the tip of Conanicut Island is a favorite site of spearfishers, **Beavertail Point**. Entry can be difficult at times, as this is an exposed peninsula with swift currents. Diving at slack tide in calm weather is the practice. The rocky entry slopes to past 60', with huge boulders surrounded by kelp, sea stars, hydroids, urchins, blackfish, and stripers. Clarity averages 5-15'.

Around the tip of the island, near Jamestown, is one of the favorite dives in the state, **Fort Wetherill**. Lots of parking and two coves accommodate all the divers using this popular check-out spot. You enter the west cove through a boat ramp. The sandy bottom slopes gently to 40', with rock walls and shallow caves around the perimeter of the cove.

At the east cove, the entry is rocky, and it drops off immediately to 15', and then to 105' outside the cove. Near the mouth is a spectacular wall of sea anenomes extending down to 40'. Within the inner coves, currents are nonexistent, but outside, on an incoming tide, they can reach two knots, so divers planning on going outside the coves wait until high tide. Fort Wetherill abounds with marine life, including kelp, sea robins, northern coral, sponges, anenomes, blood stars, crabs, lobster, blackfish, and even occasional stripers and bluefish. Since it's crowded on summer weekends, weekday and night dives offer the best conditions. Clarity is 5-15'.

Just across the bay, **Castle Hill** stands like a sentinel, guarding the entrance to Narragansett Bay. Register at the inn. The lighthouse side is a steep rock face that drops to 180' at the deepest. Besides the depth, currents can be swift, and require consulting with local divers first. The reward is an incredibly scenic wall dive, with almost all the marine life found in New England, and clarity that can be 50'. The *Lydia Skolfield* ran aground on an outcropping 100 yards offshore from Castle Hill known as Butterball Rock. Poking around the remains of the 190'-long, three-masted schooner may turn up brass deck spikes or copper nails. Depth is only 20'.

Some of the popular dive spots in the state can be found along famous, scenic Ocean Drive. One that is always crowded is **King's Beach**. Divers come here from all over the Northeast, and it is a favorite spot for check-outs. King's Beach offers easy access into a beautiful sheltered cove, with a good variety of marine life. Scattered boulders, and an unbelievable variety of aquatic plants cover the sand bottom and rock walls. Depth reaches a maximum of 35', and clarity averages 10-30'.

Less than a 1/2-mile from the launching ramp at King's Beach is **Seal Rock**, where spearfishing is good. The wreck of the freighter *Belleville* is in shallow water 100 yards from the rock. It's a favorite dive, since clarity is good and it's easy to find.

The next site along Ocean Drive is **Green Bridge**, a cove so shallow it's best dived at high tide. Eelgrass carpets the 8'-deep bottom and many juvenile fish are drawn to its cover. In late summer, many species of tropical fish are swept north by the Gulf Stream. The luckiest ones find the protection of Green Bridge Cove, where quick divers try to catch them for their aquariums. Squirrelfish, sea horses, filefish, puffers, damselfish, butterflyfish, and even grouper have been spotted within the sanctuary of the cove. Catching them, even with a slurp gun or net, is another matter. Since the cold of winter will mean doom to the tropicals, some divers wait until it's just cold enough to slow them down a little.

One-fourth mile offshore is **Gooseberry Island**, where there is always a shelter from the wind. There's also an excellent variety of marine life, including voracious bluefish, and occasional stripers and lobsters. Beautiful invertebrates like hydroids, tunicates, and anenomes carpet the rugged boulders. A 10'-high arch provides fascinating exploring.

Land's End, at the eastern tip of Newport, has a cobble beach leading down into a sandy, shallow cove, protected by a huge barrier rock. Many types of fish spawn within the sheltered area. Hardy divers make the long swim out past the inlet to a kelp-covered reef where big swells result in heavy surge. Huge rock outcroppings are covered with waving seaweeds near the top. Down deeper, caverns and ledges are covered with anemones. During the spring and fall runs this is a great place to catch sight of record stripers and bluefish.

Two rocky points that project out into the ocean, **Sachuest Point** and **Sakonnet Point**, are especially appealing to tropical collectors and spearfishers. In addition, sandy areas such as **Third Beach** on the Sakonnet River lure those who relish shellfish like quahogs and snails (locally called conch).

For bottle collectors, one of the best sites is **Jamestown Harbor**. Although you'll be groping in dirty water, the promise of really outstanding finds might make it worthwhile. **Brenton Cove**, behind Fort Adams, is another good spot, with cannonballs and old bitters bottles found here. Heavy boat traffic in both areas requires use of a flag, and extreme caution.

Rhode Island laws concerning diving: Non-commercial lobster licenses are available for resident divers who take the crustaceans by hand. Spearing is permitted for all fish, including striped bass, which must be 16" long, minimum.

VERMONT

By far the most popular spot for diving in Vermont is gigantic **Lake Champlain**, which has witnessed more early American history than any other fresh water in the country. The French and Indian War and the Revolutionary War were in large part played out upon the waters of Lake Champlain. Divers have found such artifacts as cannonballs, shot, pewter buttons, anchors, and bottles. In addition, several wrecks from the era of steamboats have been located by Burlington divers, who are hoping to establish underwater parks to preserve the vessels as museums.

But Lake Champlain has something for divers who aren't interested in artifacts, also. The vast body of water, with dozens of islands, underwater reefs and ledges, and a maximum depth of 400', has just begun to be explored. At **Rouse's Point**, an abandoned railroad trestle offers a great place for fishwatchers. Schools of perch, large bass, and walleye usually swarm about the pilings. A barge wreck, just 50' to the south, provides great cover for carp and catfish. Clarity within the area averages 25', and depth is less than 20'.

According to John Culliney in The Forests of the Sea, *the mantis shrimp found off the East Coast have evolved to hunt by two different methods — "spearing" or "smashing." The spearers strike at their prey with a chitinous lance, at speeds approaching 1000 meters a second. This is one of the fastest animal movements known. Instead of a spear, the smashers have an enlarged and thickly shelled knuckle. Some smashers have been observed sneaking up on a crab, delivering a karate chop to stun it, and then deliberately smashing both of the crab's claws. Then they drag the disarmed crab off to feast in peace. Since the smashers can strike with a force equal to a small caliber bullet and have been known to break two-layered aquarium safety glass, and since the spearers can impale a finger, it is fortunate for us that the mantis shrimps range in size only from 1.5 to 3.0 cm.*

The 146'-long steamboat *Phoenix 1* burned and sank in the lake in 1819. Recently, the vessel was located, and divers have found the hull to be a very interesting dive. Another interesting wreck is the *General Butler*, lying just off the Burlington breakwater. This 80' canal schooner sank in 1876.

Just one year earlier, the 258'-long *Champlain* ran hard aground on Steam Mill Point, presumably because the captain had been taking heavy doses of morphine for medicinal purposes. The stern broke off and slid down into the lake, where it lies from 7-40' deep.

Recently, the *Water Witch*, a 90'-long steamer built in 1832, was located. The vessel sits upright, perfectly preserved by the cold fresh water. Talk to local dive stores about visiting any of these wrecks. With more than 400 lakes and ponds, Vermont has other diving areas besides Lake Champlain. Around the wooded mountains of Rutland, several flooded **marble quarries** provide deep and clear dives, with patterned rock walls making good backdrops for photography. In extreme northern Vermont, **Lake Memphremagog** straddles the border with Canada, near Newport. While the lake covers a large area, depths are generally less than 40'.

Avid Vermont divers have been known to dive the pools at the base of some of the state's waterfalls, such as **Glen Ellis Falls** in the scenic White Mountains. Winter diving is especially surreal in this pool, since the plunging motion of the water leaves the center free of ice. Incredible clarity lures hardy divers into the 32° water.

For a warmer, but still thrilling, dive, you can drift down some of Vermont's fast, clear rivers in spring. Full wetsuits are still advisable for warmth, as well as buoyancy. The **White River**, near White River Junction, is one of the favorites. Tanks aren't necessary. In fact, they're a hindrance, since they lower your mobility. Even when the water is churned up and visibility is nil, it's a thrill to drift down the White. On clearer days, you can watch suckers rolling stones with their mouths to build triangular nest mounds.

Vermont laws concerning diving: The possession of a spear in or around most Vermont waters is a violation. One exception is Lake Champlain, where carp, bowfin, sucker, pickerel, bullheads, and gar may be speared from March 25 through May 25. From May 25 to June 15, only carp, gar, bowfin, mullet, and suckers may be speared. A hunting or combination license is required.

MIDDLE ATLANTIC

DELAWARE   MARYLAND   NEW JERSEY

It's almost impossible to draw any generalizations about diving in the Middle Atlantic states. The variety of dives is simply tremendous. Ocean dives range from the famous wrecks off New Jersey and Long Island to the artifact and oyster hunts within Chesapeake Bay. And freshwater diving is at least as varied. You can drift down clear streams in the mountains of Virginia or sail down the mighty Niagara in New York. Hundreds of quarries throughout the region provide diving excitement. An even larger number of lakes, especially in New York, attract divers to wrecks and artifacts dating back to the Revolutionary War.

DELAWARE

The **Lewes Breakwater** is the top dive in Delaware. A boat is necessary, since this breakwater is offshore and doesn't connect to land as a jetty would. There are two breakwater structures, each marked by a lighthouse. The outer one has the best diving over its one-mile length. The hard mud and packed shells of the bottom give way to rocks at the breakwater. Currents can reach two knots — dive at high slack tide, and avoid the southern tip. Typical clarity is 6-8', and maximum depth is 40'. Average summer water temperatures are 60-70°. Tautog and flounder are common.

To the south, in the Delaware Seashore State Park, is **Indian River Inlet**, where you'll need permission from the park to dive. Stone jetties extend out from the shoreline on the north and south side of the inlet, just off the coastal highway. Depth goes to 25' about 50 yards off the rocks. Clarity is best on flood tide, and during fall and winter. Heavy boat traffic, especially on weekends, requires cautious surfacing. Don't dive during tidal exchanges as currents are very severe. Good facilities exist for camping, picnicking, and parking, and a boat ramp and refreshment stand are available.

Offshore, there are a few areas such as **Fenwich Shoals**, which is about ten miles out from the Delaware-Maryland line. A clean sand bottom 50' down draws many fish to these shoals, including schools of bluefish, kingfish, and sheephead. Some wreckage has been found in the area, but it takes an experienced captain to locate it.

Delaware laws concerning diving: No scuba diving is permitted in any state-controlled lakes or ponds without written permission. Spearing is illegal in fresh water. Spearing is legal in tidal waters, but no striped bass over 20 lbs. may be taken. Minimum size for stripers is 12", for sturgeon, 4-12'. Only two lobsters per day may be taken by divers.

MARYLAND

COASTAL

The Maryland coast usually sees a great influx of divers on spring and summer weekends. Many come for the unparalleled experience of eating just-picked oysters. Others come to dive amidst stripers and tautog on rocky jetties. And some want to dive for artifacts or fossils within Chesapeake Bay. Although clarity is generally poor, anything might be found within groping distance on the bottom, since Chesapeake Bay has been the thoroughfare to one of the largest East Coast ports for centuries. In addition, one of the country's richest fossil beds is found at Calvert Cliffs. Water temperature on shallow dives can reach 70°, but below the thermocline it will drop as low as 50°.

At **Ocean City Inlet**, you can dive off the jetties, although you need to be prepared for heavy boat traffic on weekends, and severe current during tidal exchanges. A flag is essential. Clarity averages 5' in summer, more in fall and winter. Peak clarity is on a flood tide. At **West Ocean City**, there is fair diving at the old bridge.

At the southern tip of Maryland, where the Potomac River joins Chesapeake Bay, is **Point Lookout**, the former site of a Civil War prison. Now it has been turned into a waterfront park, with camping, boating, and shore diving possible. Artifact divers have found buttons and minnie balls. Oyster divers also find the area rewarding.

The 30-mile stretch from Chesapeake Beach to Drum Point is called **Calvert Cliffs**. These cliffs, up to 100' high, contain some of the best fossil deposits anywhere. Private property limits shore dives, so a boat is necessary for many sites. Ancient 100'-long sharks used to roam these waters, preying on prehistoric whales who bred and calved here. Divers find these sharks' 9"-long fossilized teeth, as well as other sharks' teeth, alligator teeth, dolphin earbones and vertebrae, sand dollars, scallops, and whale bones, by searching the 8'-deep bottom. **Governor Run** is a good spot, and is also good for oysters.

MARYLAND
Bloomington Lake 8
Calvert Cliffs 5
Choptank River 6
Deep Creek Lake 8
Eastern Bay 7
Governor Run 5
Love Point 7
Ocean City Inlet 3
Point Lookout 4
Potomac River 9
Susquehanna River 10
West Ocean City 3

DELAWARE
Fenwich Shoals 3
Indian River Inlet 2
Lewes Breakwater 1

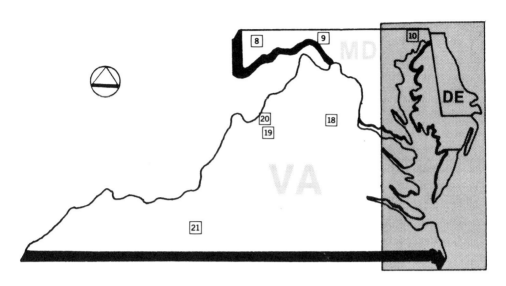

VIRGINIA

Chesapeake Bay Bridge Tunnel 13
Chesapeake Light Tower 13
Dixie Girl 14
Dry River 20
Garrison 15
Gulf Hustler 14
Havilon 15
Haymarket Quarry 18
James River 16
Kingston 13
Little Foxes Islands 11
Luckenbach 15
Morgan 15
Philpott Reservoir 21
Rappahannock River 12
Sherando Lake 19
Sontorre 13
Spring Cove 21
Tiger 13
Todd Lake 19
Trepka 15
Triangle Wrecks 15
Webster 15
York River 17

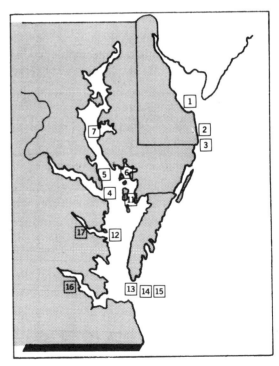

DELAWARE AND CHESAPEAKE BAYS

PENNSYLVANIA

Bainbridge Sportsmen's Club 3
Beaver Dam Quarry 4
Billmeyer Quarry 3
Dutch Springs 1
Fleetwing 10
Isolde 9
Lake Edinboro 9
Lake Erie 9
Lake Pleasant 9
Paper barge 9
Quarries 8
Quest 2
Susquehanna River 5
Willow Springs 2
Youghiogheny River 6
Youghiogheny River Lake 7

NEW JERSEY

19th Avenue Beach 1
Allenhurst T-jetty 2
Almirante 6
Barge 1
Chaparro 4
City of Athens 4
Delaware 3
Eighth Avenue 1
Great Isaac 4
Gulf Trade 4
Lana Carrol 3
Manasquan Inlet 3
Manasquan train bridge 3
Maurice Tracy 6

Mohawk 6
Pinta 2
Pliny 2
Quarry 10
R.P. Resor 5
Rock pile 8
Round Valley 11
San Jose 7
San Saba 4
Sea Hag 4
Shark River Inlet 1
Shrewsbury Rock 9
Spruce Run 11
Stolt Dagali 3
Tolten 6
Vizcaya 4

NEW YORK

Acme 27
Adirondack mountain lakes 17
Alabama 27
Bare Hill 23
Barge 43 27
Blue Mountain Lake 17
Canandaigua Lake 23
Charity Shoals 20
Chautaugua Lake 30
City of Rome 29
Coin pile 27
Crane Neck Point 3
Dacotah 28
Deep Run Park 23
Delaware River 14
Diamond Island 15
Dome Island 15
Duck Pond Point 4
Eaton's Neck 3
Execution Rocks 1

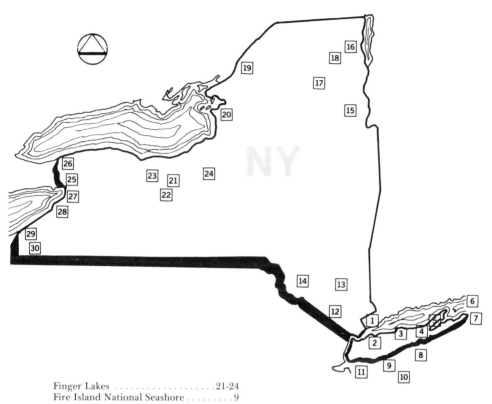

Finger Lakes 21-24
Fire Island National Seashore 9
Fishers Island 6
Greenwood Lake 12
Gwendoline Steers 2
Hart Island 1
HMS Culloden 7
Huntington Harbor Light 2
Iberia 10
Keuka Lake....................... 22
Lake Champlain.................... 16
Lake George 15
Lake Minnewaska................... 13
Lake Ontario 20
Lake Placid 18
Lake Skaneateles 24
Lizzie D. 11
Long Island 2-11
Lower Niagara 26
Mailboat......................... 24
Maine 1
Minne-Ha-Ha 15
Montauk Point jetties 7
Narrowsburg bridge................ 14
North Hill 6
Ohio 5
Oregon.......................... 10
Otter 28

Phoenix 16
Pond Eddy 14
Raleigh Briton 27
Reeves Beach 3
Robert Fulton 28
Rogers Rock 15
Rye Breakwater 1
Sackets Harbor.................... 20
San Diego....................... 10
Seneca Lake 21
Shinnecock Inlet 8
Smithtown artificial reef 3
SS Olinda 6
St. Lawrence River 19
Stone barge 11
Stony Point....................... 20
Taylor warehouse area 22
The Sore Thumb 9
Ticonderoga 15
Upper, "west" Niagara 25
USS Turner 10
Valcour Island 16
W.C. Richardson 27

There are more oysters in the area between Blackwalnut Point and Cook Point, at the mouth of the **Choptank River**. The remains of a Martin P5M submarine are also in the vicinity. Strong currents and zero visibility make diving the sub very dangerous. Only a few local captains, like Capt. Donald Gowe out of Tilghman Island, are able to locate it.

The **Eastern Bay** has many interesting dive spots, but they're accessible mainly by boat. Clarity ranges from 0-20' and is best in spring and fall. Lizardfish, toadfish, blue crab, seahorses, and horseshoe crabs abound in this area. Around Romancoke and Mattapex you'll find good oystering. **Love Point**, on the north end of Kent Island, has especially good oystering around the large stone jetty. Big anchors have also been found here.

INLAND

In western Maryland, divers visit **Deep Creek Lake**. This man-made lake attains a maximum depth of 70'. Patches of grass and some tree stumps cover the silt bottom. Clarity in summer drops to 5', and boat traffic becomes very heavy, so spring and fall are the favorite seasons. Camping, picnicking, and a boat ramp are available. Divers are also interested in nearby **Bloomington Lake**, just constructed in 1981.

You can take a drift down the **Potomac River**, with the best section being the two-mile stretch between Williamsport and the Potomac Fish and Game Club. Don't go after heavy rains or in periods of excessive boat traffic, or the normal 10-15' visibility will drop to zero. The 300'-wide river has a soft mud bottom with a few rock outcroppings. Depth averages 30'. Civil War artifacts, antique bottles, anchors, fishing gear, and motors have all been collected. Use the dive flag. Enter adjacent to the Fish and Game Club and respect property owners' rights.

The **Susquehanna River**, northeast of Baltimore, is one of the main tributaries of the Chesapeake. Diving above the Conowingo Dam isn't the finest, but diving several miles below the spillways can be an eye-opening experience. The best time is during early spring or long dry spells in summer. Aquatic life includes catfish, crayfish, eels, lamprey, white and yellow perch, large and smallmouth bass, walleye, pike, striped bass, bluegill, and freshwater clams.

In low water, when the turbines are closed, the pools formed by the receding waters teem with so much life it's easy to believe you're in a giant fish bowl. Underwater photographers in particular enjoy this dive. Clarity reaches a maximum of 15'. Currents may be very strong when the turbines are opened. You need to use extreme caution, as there is considerable boat traffic.

Maryland laws concerning diving: Dive flag is required.

NEW JERSEY

COASTAL

So many ships have sunk off the New Jersey coast over the centuries that it's surprising the area isn't known as "The New Jersey Triangle." Of course, few of the vessels went down for unexplainable reasons — either terrible storms, collisions in crowded shipping lanes, or German U-boats claim responsibility for most of the sinkings. And while some ships seem to have vanished without a trace (especially to the wreck divers searching for them), many have been located.

Wrecks offer many attractions, including artifact diving, lobstering, spearfishing, photography, or simply admiring the spectacle of immense man-made objects becoming part of the sea. Sand bottom provides little anchorage for marine life so, when a ship goes down, marine creatures flock to it. Most wrecks are covered with huge mussels, sea anemones, and various forms of encrusting life. Fish ranging from bottom-dwelling flounders to cobia cruising overhead can be seen in the vicinity of the wreckage. And you can't forget the lobsters, which are able to extend their range southward by hiding within the wrecks.

Since the shifting sands change with every storm, the wrecks are seldom picked over — new sections and artifacts can become exposed. Artifacts from old schooners and the many torpedo victims of World War II are prized possessions of many divers.

May through October is the most reliable season. Water temperature rises to a high of 70° on the surface in August, but two or three thermoclines drop it to 55° or below on the bottom. On an average day, clarity is 10-20'. On an excellent day, it might approach 50'. Gloves and knives are recommended. It takes special training and equipment to enter a wreck.

Over 3000 ships are estimated lost off New Jersey. Below are descriptions of some of the most interesting.

A short distance off Belmar is the wreckage of a **barge** at the depth of 60'. Tales circulate of a 15-lb. lobster making its home in the jagged metal of the stern. Sea robins, flounder, stripers, and stingrays have been observed around this 60'-long barge. Mussels have installed themselves as a living carpet over the metal. Flat sand in all directions surrounds the wreck.

For more excitement, visit the 194'-long *Pinta*, seven miles off Asbury Park. This Dutch freighter sank after a collision in 1963, but is still intact, listing 90° to port. Clarity averages 20-30'. Marine life is great, with schools of triggerfish and stingrays in late summer.

Ten miles off Manasquan Inlet, the wreck of the **Lana Carrol** sits perfectly upright on a flat sand bottom 90' down. The wheelhouse and holds of this 70'-long intact trawler are easily accessible. Within the stern and wheelhouse you can find many lobster. Mussels, sea anemones, starfish, flounder, blackfish, ocean pout, and stingrays are seen. The trawler creates a surreal setting for photographs.

The **Stolt Dagali**, a 500'-long Norwegian tanker, was rammed early on Thanksgiving morning 1964 by an Israeli liner, which passed completely through the *Stolt*, killing 19 of the tanker's crew. The stern immediately dropped to the bottom, but the bow was salvaged and later welded onto another ship. The stern of the *Stolt Dagali* now looms 70' above the 130'-deep seafloor, 16-1/2 miles out of Manasquan Inlet. It is one of the most compelling wrecks anywhere.

Another popular wreck dive is the 287'-long steamer **Vizcaya**, sunk in 1890 after a tragic collision that took 59 lives. The wreck, covered with growth, sits at 80' depth, eight miles east of Barnegat. Lately, divers have been recovering silverware as well as big bugs.

A Cuban steamer loaded with sugar named **Chaparro** hit a mine in 1918 and dropped to the bottom in less than three minutes. Amazingly, 23 of the 29 aboard were saved. Bizarrely, the steamer **San Saba** had struck a mine and sunk in almost the same spot only one month before. Today, their remains lie at 80-90' between eight and nine miles off Barnegat.

The tug **Great Isaac** collided and sank 10-1/2 miles southeast of Barnegat Inlet after a collision in 1947. Intact on its side at a depth of 90', the 185'-long tug is great for artifacts and marine life, like monkfish, mussels, sea bass, and large ling. Entry is dangerous due to the narrow, silty corridors.

In 1942, the **Gulf Trade**, a massive oil tanker, fell victim to a Nazi torpedo. The immense stern now lies 90' deep 13 miles out of Barnegat. Penetration divers enjoy the wide passageways and easy exits. Food collectors love the big lobster, cod, ling, sea bass, and tautog. Photographers find good subjects in the mussels, anemones, and fuzzy sand dollars. And almost everyone is impressed by the immensity of this piece of the *Gulf Trade*.

The bow of the *Gulf Trade* lies closer to shore, at only 60' depth. Clarity isn't as good but marine life is abundant. This site provides a favorite check-out dive.

The **R.P. Resor**, 32 miles off Barnegat Inlet, was an oil tanker torpedoed by a U-boat in World War II. Although sections have collapsed, some of the wreckage rises 30' from the 120'-deep sand bottom. Big bugs and immense schools of pollock and cod are frequently seen. Shark fishing tournaments are held here.

Other notable wrecks off New Jersey include the **Maurice Tracy** (six miles off Seaside Heights), a 253'-long collision victim now reduced to piles of rubble that shelter bugs; the **Delaware**, sunk 1-1/2 miles off Bay Head in 80' of water, where divers look for bugs and a rumored $250,000; the **Sea Hag**, a 104'-long trawler at 80' depth that rests 4-1/2 miles off Barnegat; the **City of Athens**, 105' deep, popular for majestic scenery, bugs, and artifacts; the **San Jose**, 15 miles out of Atlantic City, with fish, bugs, and even portholes lying in the sand; the **Tolten**, a torpedo victim that went down 13 miles off Island Beach, now famous for its wide corridors and for the 13-lb. claw wrenched from a huge lobster there; the **Almirante**, a freighter sunk in 1918 with a load of flour, now known for great sea life and artifacts; and the **Mohawk**, victim of a collision in 1935 that killed 46, now reduced to 10-20'-high pieces of rubble.

Almost all shore diving off New Jersey takes place around jetties, which lure marine life from the surrounding miles of sand bottom. There are more than 100 jetties, each with its own specialty, shape, and restrictions — check locally. Clarity ranges from 0-20' and depth rarely surpasses 15'. Be cautious of currents and boats.

At the northern tip of the coast, some divers visit the **rock pile** off the Gateway National Recreation Area at Sandy Hook. Dive on an incoming or slack tide to avoid the heavy currents of the exchange. Tautog is the most common fish. The proximity of the beach to New York City means that over two million people a year visit Sandy Hook.

Further south, off Monmouth, **Shrewsbury Rock** is a large area of rocky bottom where depths go to 35' about 400 yards offshore. Clarity can be 20'.

At Allenhurst, just to the south, there are a couple of interesting beach dives. At the **Allenhurst T-jetty**, rocks as high as 10' sit on a sandy bottom of 10-25' in depth. Striped bass, bluefish, blackfish, flounder, and crabs are frequently seen around the jetty. In summer, night diving will usually net a lobster or two. Clarity averages 5-10'. Use a flag and be cautious of boats.

The British steamer **Pliny** sank 200 yards off the beach near Allenhurst in 1882. Today you can find access from the Philips Avenue Bathing Pavilion. Clarity seldom exceeds 5-8', since the remains lie in the surf at 25' deep. Big blackfish visit in spring; striped bass visit in fall. In northeast winds, the dive is impossible due to high surf and strong currents.

The world record bluefish taken by spear was landed just off **Eighth Avenue** in Asbury Park. Access to the shallow water off the beach is limited in summer to before 9:00 am or after 6:00 pm. During the rest of the year, there are no time restrictions. Clarity is usually poor.

The **Shark River Inlet** is a favorite site. From May 1st to October 1st the inlet is closed to divers from 8:00 am to 5:00 pm due to heavy boat traffic. Night diving is popular because of the abundance of marine life — including lobster and flounder. From late July until October the Gulf Stream swings close to shore. Those with saltwater aquariums hunt for butterflyfish, sea horses, squid, angelfish and others that have become trapped in the northward pull of the Gulf Stream. The best dive season is fall, when clarity reaches 25' or more, but Shark River Inlet is diveable all year. Maximum depth is 30'. Current is nonexistent on a slack tide, otherwise reaching 3-4 knots. Watch for boats.

Another popular beach dive at Belmar is the **19th Avenue Beach**. This is a very good novice dive, with a shallow sand bottom sloping to 20-25'. Scattered wreckage is visible from the beach at low tide, but you need to line it up with landmarks and wait until high tide to dive. All the common fish of the coast swim about the wreck, making it a favorite site of spearfishers, especially during summer. However, during summer you can only dive from the beach before 9:00 a.m. or later than 6:00 pm.

The **Manasquan Inlet**, twice the width of Shark Inlet, also presents a good dive, but it is harder. Entry is made from the Pt. Pleasant side or off the beach on the Manasquan side.

Although the current is very strong directly under the **Manasquan train bridge**, the inlet opens into a wide area beyond it that is safe enough for check-outs. Orange sponge grows in abundance.

At conception, a blue whale's egg weighs about a milligram. After the 15-16-month gestation, the newborn calf is from 20 to 27' long and weighs about three tons.

INLAND

The favorite inland dive in New Jersey is the **quarry** at Hamburg in the northern part of the state. This seven-acre quarry is commercially operated for divers, with camping and picnic facilities available. The quarry attains a maximum depth of 40' and has several ore cars, automobiles, and a 32' boat on the bottom. Clarity averages 25-30', and many species of freshwater fish can be photographed.

Near Clinton, divers visit **Spruce Run** and **Round Valley** reservoirs. Since both are in the state park system, you need to register before diving and observe all the regulations. Clarity averages 20' at both sites, and trees and weeds are scattered over the shallow mud bottoms.

New Jersey divers also visit the Delaware River and Greenwood Lake, both on the line with New York State. For more information about these sites, see our section on New York.

New Jersey laws concerning diving: Spearing is permitted for striped bass in the Atlantic — season is March 1st through December 31st. Capturing lobsters while diving is permitted; check for size requirements. No eggbearing lobster may be taken. Use of diver's flag is required.

NEW YORK

New York has more large, deep lakes of glacial origin than any other state in the country. It has shoreline on two of the Great Lakes, several thrilling river runs, and hundreds of smaller clear lakes. And that's just the fresh water. For saltwater diving you can take your pick of the rocky, shallow Long Island Sound, or the deeper wreck dives off the sandy Atlantic coast of Long Island. Temperatures range from a winter low of 32° to a summer surface high of 72°. As many as three thermoclines will drop the temperature on deeper dives.

LONG ISLAND SOUND

At Rye, on the mainland just east of White Plains, divers find the **Rye Breakwater** a good spot for observing the plentiful marine life of Long Island Sound. A sand and mud bottom 20' down is interrupted by the breakwater, where crabs sidle over the rocks, eels slither out from crevices, and blackfish poke about, looking for invertebrates to crunch. Night is the best time to find lobster roaming the rocks. Water clarity averages 5' in summer.

South, along the curve of New York heading out to Long Island, are several other sites. These include **Execution Rocks**, where the steamer *Maine* foundered, and **Hart Island**, where divers pluck lobsters out of the underwater debris. In addition to common hazards like low clarity, dangerous currents, and small boat traffic, you also have to worry about the wake from passing ocean-going vessels. These sites are best left to experienced divers.

Further east on Long Island, there are a variety of good tourist dives, ranging from wreck dives on paddlewheelers and WWI battle cruisers, to drift dives through fish-filled inlets. At **Huntington Harbor Light**, the best dives are on an incoming tide at night, when you'll see fish sleeping and lobster stalking among the rocks. If you turn out your light in the warm water of the late summer, you can detect a faint phosphorescence in the waves. The rocks around the lighthouse drop to a hard gravel and sand bottom 15' down. Fly the diver's flag, dive on the west side, and plan for currents. Within Huntington Bay, the tug *Gwendoline Steers* sits upright and largely intact 55' down.

To the east, **Eaton's Neck** guards one side of Smithtown Bay. While diving on the point itself is difficult due to currents, just inside Eaton's Neck is an area of scattered small boulders sheltering hermit crabs and fish. Within the bay, the **Smithtown artificial reef**, composed of a barge and old tires, serves as a shelter for throngs of cunner and some lobster. Clarity can surpass 20' in dry weather.

But **Crane Neck Point**, on the eastern tip of the bay, is the best dive in the area. On the bay side, marine life is rich, with kelp-covered boulders sheltering the appropriately named oyster toadfish (besides being ugly, they croak loudly in the June spawning season). In shallow water around thick plant growth, look for pipefish, the skinny northern relative of the seahorse and trumpetfish. If you follow the boulders out to a depth of 25', you'll see many large *Metridium* anemones, yellow sulfur sponges, pink-hearted hydroids, and maybe a skate or dogfish. Dive on a low tide to avoid currents.

At Riverhead, you can drive to **Reeves Beach**. A submerged barge in shallow water approximately 150 yards offshore has become loaded with invertebrate life.

Another easily accessible shore dive is found at **Duck Pond Point**, at Mattituck. You can walk into the water off the quiet beach or head up to the rocky point where, if you time it right, the tide will bring you back to the sandy beach. Glacially deposited gravel and boulders dot the bottom of 20' maximum depth. Night diving for lobsters is good here.

At Greenport, there's another easy shore dive out to the wreck of the *Ohio*, a vessel that served in the War of 1812. Depth is 20'. Many small artifacts have been taken from the vessel. Pier dives in the old fishing village of Greenport produce medicine bottles and antique fishing gear. Clarity averages 5'.

Divers also visit the remains of the *SS Olinda* on the south shore of **Fishers Island**. The boiler is the most visible evidence of the ship, which ran aground in 1895. Other sections of wreckage are sometimes exposed by the shifting sand on the 30' deep bottom.

For marine life around Fishers Island, the best bet is **North Hill**. Huge boulders cover the 40'-deep seabed and provide excellent cover for lobster, cunner, blackfish, and American eels. Macro photography is good, since there is a wide array of invertebrate subjects, and clarity can be better than 25'. Slack tide presents the easiest diving.

LONG ISLAND — Atlantic Shore

At the tip of Long Island, the **Montauk Point jetties** offer easy access into water that reaches a maximum depth of 20' at the end of the jetty. Currents can be strong at the end, though, so it's best to stay near the rocks. Night dives are popular for lobster, and both day and night are good for macro photography. Blue-claw crabs can be seen among the grasses of the sandy bottom, while eels and blackfish are common around the jetty. Clarity ranges from 5-20'. The **HMS Culloden**, a British frigate, lies near Montauk and draws experienced divers.

For advanced divers, few spots on the island can beat **Shinnecock Inlet**. Currents of up to five or six knots pour through the inlet on tidal exchanges. Boat traffic can be heavy. Use a flag, dive at slack, and don't surface until you are near the jetty. Large rocks fall away to a sandy bottom. In spring, clarity can be 30'. Lobsters and striped bass begin returning to shallow water. As fall comes, tropicals get swept up by the Gulf Stream and the striped bass make their last run for the year, with individuals of more than 50 lbs. taken at Shinnecock. Permit camping is available on the sandy beaches at the ocean's edge.

All along the **Fire Island National Seashore**, sandy beaches slope gently outward. Flounder and small wrecks are common and, near the light, the wreckage of a paddlewheeler provides interesting exploration. An artificial reef offshore at 60' has a wealth of marine life, including soft coral and anemones.

Just west of the Robert Moses Causeway is a spot known as **The Sore Thumb**. A rock jetty covered with colorful anemones, mussels, hydroids, and sponges lies at a depth of 15'. Below that, a steeply sloping sandy bottom extends out from the jetty. Access is by boat only and, since this is a very active fishing spot, you'll need to watch for lines. Macro photography is good here. This is also an excellent site for check-outs, since there is usually at least 20' visibility.

South of Long Island are some of the most exciting wreck dives on the East Coast. The 518'-long luxury liner *Oregon* sank after a collision in 1886. Today the wreck sits, upright but broken, at 120' deep off Fire Island. The engine and boilers stick up more than 30' from the bottom. The *Oregon* is known for artifacts like silverware, china, and portholes.

The *Iberia*, a tramp freighter from France carrying a cargo of dates, was rammed by the luxury liner *Umbria* in 1888. The freighter dropped to the bottom the next day. The *Iberia* has become a pile of heavy machinery, twisted steel, and cargo cartons, scarely recognizable as a ship, but offering refuge to anemones, lobster, eelpout, and blackfish.

Only one U.S. warship was lost during WWI, and that was the **San Diego**, which fell victim to a U-boat mine off Fire Island. The 504'-long vessel, formerly named the *California*, now lies intact, but upside-down, at 110'. It's 55' down just to the hull. Huge guns protrude from underneath the hull. Rusting pieces of steel plating have fallen, creating many entrances into the vessel, but penetration is dangerous, with live ammo and disorientation problems. Clocks, dinnerware, and lobsters have been recovered.

Other wrecks off Long Island include the Prohibition rumrunner **Lizzie D.**, sunk a few miles off Long Beach; the **stone barge**, 50' deep, off Freeport; and the **USS Turner**, a Navy destroyer that blew up in 1945. For more information on wreck opportunities in this area, see the section on New Jersey.

INLAND

When it comes to deep, clear lakes, few states can match New York. You can take your pick of the Finger Lakes, those long, narrow grooves between the ridgetops; you can dive the many wrecks of Lakes Erie and Ontario, including the old coin pile, where more than 10,000 coins have already been picked up; you can drift down the Delaware or the Niagara River; or you can try to choose which of the hundreds of smaller glacial lakes you want to submerge in. And you can't forget Lake George and Lake Champlain, where you can look for artifacts from the Revolutionary War. Clarity varies at each site, but water temperature rarely surpasses 70°.

SOUTHEASTERN

Divers in southeastern New York head to **Greenwood Lake**, but you'd better try to get there before July 4th, since boat traffic is impossible after that. This small lake south of Warwick, almost on the New Jersey line, is generally shallow in the south end. Deeper holes by the island on the north end of the lake drop to 70' maximum. Beach entry is permitted off the public use area. Greenwood is a favorite site for bottle collecting, with clarity ranging from 0-15'. Watch for boats on every dive.

Lake Minnewaska, west of New Paltz, allows no power boats. Easy access, clarity of up to 25', and rock cliffs dropping to silt distinguish this lake. Maximum depth is 80' but silt is very deep at the bottom. The cold water harbors no fish, but does have two species of rare salamander that are interesting photo subjects.

Besides an abundant and varied collection of marine life including bass, trout, carp, suckers, shad, pickerel, muskie, eels, and crayfish, the **Delaware River** also offers underwater salvage. Heavy canoe traffic, combined with two or three rapids, has created an underwater shopping spree for divers. Camping and camera equipment, coolers, money, clothing, and all the other items that inexperienced canoeists lug with them can be picked up from the bottom.

At the **Narrowsburg bridge**, the Delaware attains a maximum depth of 115'. Further south, just above the bridge at **Pond Eddy**, maximum depth is 80'. Clarity over the rocky bottom river ranges from 15-25' in summer. It's important to check on current conditions and canoe traffic before planning your drift dive. Use of a flag is essential.

NORTHEASTERN

Lake George seems tailor-made for scuba, with water clarity that ranges from 25-60', depths that reach 130' in many areas of the lake, 150 rocky islands to explore, and artifacts from the French and Indian or Revolutionary Wars to find. (Because of their age, many relics are very fragile — if you find something of historic importance, notify authorities before attempting salvage.) Because of boat traffic, it's important to use a flag and ascend cautiously.

Rogers Rock at Rogers State Park and Campground drops to 70' in a sheer wall marked by large boulders. Excellent clarity and fish life that includes northern pike and salmon make this a popular area.

Other good sites include **Dome Island**, where depth goes past 190'; **Long Island**, where many relics can be found on the sloping rock bottom that drops to 85'; and **Diamond Island**, where you'll find good exploring, but heavy boat traffic.

The wreckage of the ***Minne-Ha-Ha*** lies at 15' deep at Black Mt. Pt. At Hawkeye Pt., the ***Ticonderoga*** burned and sank. Other good sites for artifacts include the rock cribs where steamboats used to dock.

Lake Champlain, the largest deep freshwater lake in the country (after the Great Lakes), appeals to all divers, but especially to history buffs and wreck divers. Among the most famous finds from the battle at **Valcour Island** in 1776 is the warship ***Philadelphia***, located in 1934 and now on display in the Smithsonian. Since many other flagships sank from both the British and American fleets, Valcour Island is a treasure trove to the underwater researcher.

If you'd rather enjoy the fruit of someone else's research, dive the steamboat ***Phoenix***, which sank over 150 years ago. It was recently located on the slope of Colchester Shoal at depths from 60-95'. Even at that depth, water clarity can be excellent. As you gaze at the charred timbers of the hull, it's easy to imagine the terrifying fire that sank the *Phoenix*. For more information about diving Lake Champlain, see our section on Vermont.

Also located in beautiful upstate New York are thousands of **Adirondack mountain lakes**. **Blue Mountain Lake**, near the town of Blue Mountain, has clear water and depths that fall past 140'. **Lake Placid**, more famous for skiing, also has good water clarity and depth past 100'. Literally hundreds of smaller lakes, like **Mirror Lake**, invite divers with brilliant blue water set in the midst of rugged mountain scenery. Unfortunately, many of these lakes have been adversely affected by acid rain. Most lakes in the Adirondacks are heartbreakingly blue, and extremely clear, but some are so acidic that they're devoid of life.

CENTRAL

Divers in upstate and central New York sometimes visit the **St. Lawrence River**, especially the Thousands Island area. Wreck and artifact diving are the principal attractions, with wrecks varying from old sailing boats to 300' steel freighters. However, since the St. Lawrence Seaway rapidly drops to below 100', clarity is usually less than 10', currents can be severe, and the channel is used by ocean-going ships, diving here is difficult.

The south shore of **Lake Ontario** also sees some diving activity, although clarity is usually less than 15'. Block-shaped rocks cover the shallows along the shoreline. Further out, the bottom goes to sand and mud. Although a long swim is necessary at many sites to find depth, beach diving is good for observing trout and salmon.

Charity Shoals, off Cape Vincent, is a large area of shallow gravel bottom where divers have recovered many anchors. Within **Sackets Harbor**, you'll find several small wrecks partially buried in mud. If you're lucky, you might spot cannonballs or other relics from the War of 1812 on the shallow rock ledges of the cliffs. **Stony Point**, just south of the harbor, has excellent sightseeing, with much fish life around the rock slabs, as well as a couple of demolished wrecks. Boat traffic can be heavy in most areas of Lake Ontario.

But some of the best diving in central New York is found at the **Finger Lakes**. These long, slender lakes were created by the retreating glaciers, which scraped grooves into the valleys between the mountains. At up to 300', they are surprisingly deep. Clarity can reach 50'. Summer water temperature averages 55°. Beautiful scenery of rolling hills, ravines, and waterfalls has made the Finger Lakes into a top vacation area.

At **Seneca Lake**, a barge wreck is just out from a water treatment plant on the west side of the lake. These barges were used to bring coal to salt plants; often they returned north with a load of scrap metal. This barge sits on a flat silt bottom 65' down. Schools of perch emerge out of the haze and then disappear again. But the most interesting thing about this wreck is the large wooden rudder, approximately 4' by 6', with a two-man steering arm. Clarity averages 14-20'.

When females of several crustaceans, such as Jonah crabs and lobsters, are molting, they use powerful pheromones to entice males to mate. They thus gain protection during their most vulnerable period. For some species, mating is impossible once the shell has hardened.

At **Keuka Lake**, one of the most interesting dives is found at Hammondsport on the south end of the lake, in the **Taylor warehouse area**. You can make an easy beach entry over a rock bottom that slopes rapidly to a flat shelf 50' down. Old pilings and weed beds support a large array of life including bass, rock bass, perch, carp, suckers, pike, large trout, brown trout, crayfish, and snails. If you tire of observing the abundant creatures, you can look for an iron boiler head and other remains of a turn-of-the-century paddlewheeler. There are also bottles and other artifacts to be found from local wine producers. Clarity sometimes reaches 30'.

At **Canandaigua Lake**, one of the favorite spots is **Deep Run Park** on East Lake Road. Entry is off the southern end of the beach, where a pipeline can be found at a depth of 12' and followed to 55'. The bottom drops away in a series of staircasing shelves. Bass and yellow perch often follow as you descend.

On the east side of the lake, the cliffs at **Bare Hill** are an interesting dive to those who have a boat available. The sheer cliffs above the water staircase beneath into several plateaus extending past 45'. Windy weather creates rough water conditions at this site. Geode rocks are strewn over the ledges. There is good bottle collecting in several junkpiles.

Lake Skaneateles, like most of the Finger Lakes, has limited beach access due to private property. The wreckage of a **mailboat** at 50' depth and fossilized coral at the southern end attract divers.

WESTERN

Between Lake Erie and the Niagara River, divers in western New York stay busy. For excitement, it's hard to beat the drift dive down the Niagara River. On the **upper, "west" Niagara**, the favorite drift starts about two miles above Six-Mile Marina and Grand Island. An hour's drift will take you to the marina. The actual depth towards Grand Island is 20', but in the middle of the river the current is stronger and there are a few deep holes that reach 40'. Clarity is usually 5-10' but, like the current, it varies on a daily basis.

Besides shooting downstream past black bass, sturgeon, muskie, and, in summer, many pike, this is a great artifact dive, with clay bottles, blob-top bottles, clay pipes, old anchors and guns to be found. On a single dive, over 30 different bottles, some dating back to the early 1800's, were found. Since boat traffic can be very heavy, it's essential to use the flag. And since the swift current can surpass six knots, it's also essential that this dive be made under the supervision of local divers. For the experienced, few dives are more thrilling. Other spots on the upper Niagara are much more dangerous, with currents that can exceed 13 knots.

The total present population of northern elephant seals is descended from one small herd of 100 animals overlooked by sealers.

On the **lower Niagara** where it empties into Lake Ontario, excellent artifact dives may be made. Since the current is much slower, local instructors conduct check-out classes here. The best diving is near Old Fort Niagara. You can't dive within 1000' of the fort, so a boat is necessary. The flat bottom varies from grassy to rocky, and the deepest spot is 60'. There were many battles between Fort Niagara and Fort George in the early 1800's. Cannonballs, musket balls, bottles, brass buttons, and barrel rings are a few of the items recovered. Clarity averages 20', with heavy boat traffic presenting the main danger.

There are numerous dives available in Lake Erie's New York shoreline, but probably the most famous is the **coin pile**, found just outside the north Buffalo breakwater. Even novices can enjoy this dive if the weather is calm and they're using a flag. Flat solid rock 15-20' deep, covered with a thin layer of sand, hides an incredible array of artifacts. Found items include over 10,000 coins from 1800 to 1880, silverware, leg irons, clay pipes, jewelry, guns. And more items are uncovered each year. A boat is necessary, and it's important to wait for calm weather since high waves make it a dangerous dive. Current is generally less than one knot, and clarity averages 10'.

Most of the other Lake Erie diving takes place on shipwrecks like the **W.C. Richardson**, **Raleigh Briton**, **Barge 43**, **Alabama**, and the **Acme**. Most are well broken up, and at depths of less than 40'.

Further south, off Angola, the sailing vessels **Dacotah**, **Otter**, and **Robert Fulton** all went down on the same reef in the 1860's. While little is to be found of these ships, divers still bring up artifacts and items of cargo like horseshoes, wheel hubs, flat irons, pottery, and ornamental stove parts. A rock bottom in the area is usually less than 40' deep, and clarity averages 20-25'.

The **City of Rome** is accessible from shore off the town of Ripley, but you need permission to use the stairs down to the beach. Since this is an exposed sandy beach, the weather must be calm. The steam-powered, wooden-hulled vessel lies at a depth of 12-15'. Ice and waves have taken their toll on the vessel, and so have some divers, who attempted to take the propeller, but never got it up the cliff. Clarity averages 10'.

In the southwestern corner of the state, near Jamestown, divers visit **Chautauqua Lake**. Spring and fall are the best seasons, with clarity of 10-15'. Two old cruisers and the burned-out hulls of steamers provide havens for an incredible variety of fish including huge muskie, bass, perch, pickerel, and sunfish. Bottle diving is great around the old steamboat docks, with frequent discoveries of valuable bottles. Maximum depth is 70'.

New York laws concerning diving: Residents may take lobsters for noncommercial purposes. Spearing is allowed in salt water for game fish including striped bass. Check size limits and license rules. Dive flag is required.

PENNSYLVANIA

A variety of quarry, river, and lake dives span the state of Pennsylvania. **Dutch Springs**, in the southeastern corner of the state, attracts as many as 7000 divers a year to its 50 acres of spring-fed waters. Located just out of Bethlehem, this quarry drops in a graduated series of shelves to a maximum depth of 120'. Standing trees, steel girders, a cement tanker, and underwater islands with plane and cabin cruiser wrecks are just a few of the interesting subjects to be explored on the bottom of this quarry. Submerged platforms at 25' make good sites for novice divers. Clarity ranges from 12-30'. A thermocline 30' down drops the temperature to 46°.

Further west in Richmond is one of the most famous quarry dives in the state. **Willow Springs** (also called Myerstown) is such a popular site that over 170,000 students have taken their openwater training here. The quarry was originally hand-dug for traprock until an underground spring was tapped. Now, 44,000 gallons of water per minute flow into this 25-acre lake. Although the main underwater attraction is the 72'-long *Quest*, a former racing boat/patrol boat/trawler, there are other items of interest on the 55'-deep bottom, like submerged platforms, a steel mining crane, and an underwater habitat where stress tests were performed. Clarity ranges from 10-35', and Willow Springs is free of ice in winter. Camping is available, and a dive store is just across the road.

A new attraction for divers, the **Bainbridge Sportsmen's Club**, has opened in the beautiful hills around Lancaster. This 100-acre site has been developed around **Billmeyer Quarry**, which offers 23 acres of spring-fed water. Because of the limestone and dolomite bottom, clarity is good, often 30-50'. Depth over most of the bottom averages 60' but one area drops below 100'. Abandoned buildings and mining machinery provide underwater interest, as do the many large fish including trout and bass. The summer surface temperature of 80° drops below the thermocline to 40°. Restrooms, changing areas, and a dive store on site make this a convenient dive.

Many other quarries and lakes in Pennsylvania lure divers, including **Beaver Dam Quarry**, which drops to 90' and is located just off I-83 halfway between York and Baltimore. Other sites are **Edenville Quarry, Blue Hole Quarry, Pinola Quarry, Lake Raystown**, and **Blue Marsh Lake**. Check with local dive stores for current conditions.

In central Pennsylvania, a favorite dive is found at the Jay Street Bridge on the **Susquehanna River** at Lock Haven. Artifact hunting is popular, since heavy logging formerly took place in this area, and yearly ice floes scour up new items every year. Very old coins, bottles, gold and ivory watches, and antique tools have all been found. Depth is 15' maximum, and clarity in winter improves from the summer average of 25' to past 50'. Currents of two knots and heavy boat traffic make a flag essential.

The **Youghiogheny River** south of Pittsburgh is another fast river ride. Some sections are too fast, so check with local dive stores about good areas. A beautiful scene of rocky banks winding through tree-covered hills is matched underwater by good clarity and many fish.

Below the dam, the **Youghiogheny River Lake** offers a fun dive, with shore access from the swimming area across from the dam. Clarity ranges from 5-20'. Spring and fall have better clarity and less boat traffic. Perch, bass, and freshwater sponges appeal to photographers. A 375'-long arched stone bridge, built in 1818, has been submerged. It's 60' to the top of the bridge, and 90' to the base.

Just across the border from Youngstown, Ohio, are several **quarries**. Located less than a mile south of Hillsville, Pennsylvania, these quarries together cover 20 acres. Clarity ranges from 5-20' in the shallow water, where maximum depth is 20'. Hundreds of bluegill swim above the plant-lined bottom.

In the northeastern part of the state, near Erie, divers visit at least four different sites. The largest is **Lake Erie**. Off Presque Isle State Park, the wrecks of the steamer *Isolde* and a **paper barge** sit on a stony bottom less than 10' down. The boiler from the steamer is almost awash in low water. Around the barge, you can search amongst the old rigging and tackle blocks for personal artifacts from the crew.

Other dives in the Erie area include **Lake Pleasant**, a small natural lake with an average depth of 30' and clarity of 5-10', and **Lake Edinboro**, with similar depth and clarity. Besides seeing many muskie, you might also find old bottles in Edinboro.

At Lake Conneat, you need to wait until early spring or late fall to dive, since boat traffic limits diving in the summer to only the suicidal. Within this 928-acre lake — the largest natural lake in the state, divers have found the remains of an old wooden ferry, the *Fleetwing*, that sank in the 1920's. Maximum depth is 80', but most areas average 35' or less. Clarity is 10'.

Pennsylvania laws concerning diving: No diving is permitted in Fish Commission or State Park lakes. Hand-propelled spears may be used in taking carp, gar, suckers, and eels. Catfish may also be taken by spear from the Delaware River. Diver's flag is required.

The tsunamis (also known as tidal waves) that hit Hawaii in 1946 and 1957 arose more than 2000 miles away, in the Aleutian Trench. Today scientists can usually predict the seabed earthquakes and eruptions that cause them.

VIRGINIA

In addition to the clearest water in the Del-Mar-Va peninsula, Virginia also has some intriguing freshwater dives in the Shenandoah Valley — but it's the coastal waters that see the most divers. Artifact diving with underwater metal detectors, oyster diving, visiting offshore wrecks where the clarity can be more than 50' and where summer temperatures range from 50-80°, and diving the Chesapeake Bay Tunnel with its hordes of fish are some of the most popular activities.

In the northern part of Chesapeake Bay the **Little Foxes Islands**, almost on the Maryland line, are favorite dive sites. Underwater photographers find these small islands ideal, with clarity of 15-20' year-round. Some of the most striking subjects are stingrays with 4' wingspans; they seem to thrive in the area. Since tidal currents in the cut between the islands can be very strong, this makes an excellent drift dive, if well-planned. The nearest boat ramp is at Crisfield, Maryland.

Throughout the Chesapeake are many opportunities for oyster diving from shore, since the mollusks are usually found on a rock bottom, often only 10-30' deep. However, oysters are getting scarce. Catches are only a fraction of what they used to be. If you don't find oysters, you can always look for old anchors instead. The **Rappahannock River**, near Windmill Point, is a good spot to find both.

Much shore diving in southern Virginia takes place at **Ocean View**, where you can enter off the beach into water less than 10' deep, and search (most easily with a metal detector) for relics left from a turn-of-the-century hotel that burnt down. Modern artifacts like diamond rings and gold necklaces are also found. **Buckroe Beach** is a similar dive, mainly for artifact hunters, since the shallow sandy bottom is easily stirred up by the surf.

For better clarity and more exciting life, you need to go offshore. The Norfolk side of the **Hampton Roads Tunnel** sees some divers, but the **Chesapeake Bay Bridge Tunnel** is more popular. Marine life abounds around the rock piles supporting this massive structure. Flounder, tautog, bluefish, striped bass, and a wide assortment of sea stars, whelks, mussels, oysters, and clams are common. Black sea bass, sharks, and rays are sometimes seen. Current can be very heavy toward the boat passageways between the islands. Be sure to check with local divers, who know the safe spots away from the boat lanes. Clarity is seasonal, best in fall and winter, when it may surpass 30'.

Another favorite dive in the area is the **Chesapeake Light Tower**. This 60' tower · supports heavy marine growth on its stone base. Depth in the sand around the base averages 40'. Many fish are drawn to the site, including abundant tautog.

Near the tower, the wrecks of the *Sontorre*, *Tiger*, and *Kingston* lie at 50'. An artificial reef of sunken barges and landing craft, also near the tower, is marked with buoys.

Local divers have created an informal marine sanctuary around the wrecks of the *Gulf Hustler* and *Dixie Girl*, a little further offshore. The wreckage attracts a great variety of fish, with schools of bluefish, tautog, stripers, and flounder joined by butterflyfish and blennies in late summer.

If you're willing to take a longer boat ride, you can visit the **Triangle Wrecks**. The *Morgan* is the most exciting. This fully intact, penetrable ship was carrying a cargo of tanks, aircraft, ammunition, and motorcycles when she collided and sank in 1942. The *Luckenbach*, *Trepka*, and an old paddlewheeler are also in the area. Depth is 100' at most.

An artificial reef created from the wreckage of the *Garrison*, *Webster*, and *Havilon* isn't visited frequently due to its distance from shore. Sitting upright on the sand bottom, these wrecks are still good for artifacts.

Marine life is plentiful and unused to divers at these distant sites, with amberjack, black sea bass, bluefish, and lobsters — either spiny or Maine.

The **James River** and the **York River** in Chesapeake are also good oyster and artifact dives. However, since the kepone chemical pollution scandal on the James a few years ago, most divers stick to artifact-hunting rather than oyster-picking within that river. Clarity is low, only 5-10' in the very best fall and winter conditions, but that doesn't bother determined artifact hunters. Both rivers saw much activity during the Civil War, and divers have found evidence in the form of cannonballs and other military equipment. The Virginia Institute of Marine Science is attempting to erect a cofferdam around one of the three Civil War wrecks in the area, in the hopes this will allow the public to view the historic vessel. And although you can't dive from the grounds of Civil War forts, many explore the waters around them by boat, and some are rewarded with historical artifacts.

Other inland sites include **Haymarket Quarry**, at Haymarket, less than an hour from Washington D.C. This site is so popular that as many as 200 divers a month submerge in the quarry. A rugged rock bottom drops away to a maximum of 100', with shelves at 30', 50', and 70'. Various underwater sights include school buses and an array of autos. Clarity is usually 20' or more, and bluegill, bass, turtles, frogs, beaver, swans, and geese all reside in the clean water. Surface water temperature rarely exceeds 70°. Camping is available.

To the southwest, in the beautiful Shenandoah Valley, you'll find several interesting dives. You can dive **Sherando Lake** or nearby **Todd Lake**, southwest of Harrisonburg. Shallow depth, clear water, and abundant fish characterize these lakes. Camping is available at each site. Around Todd Lake is a variety of mountain streams. Check with rangers at the recreation area to find out which of these rushing, clear, cold rivers is the current favorite.

The highest waves known in the Pacific reach 100'. In the Atlantic, the highest waves reach 75-90'. However, tsunamis (tidal waves caused by earthquakes or volcanic eruptions) have been known to approach heights of almost 200'.

Dry River, nearby, in the rugged country almost on the West Virginia state line, is a great dive for the seasoned creek explorer. Since depth is generally less than 15', scuba isn't essential to experience the exhilaration of a run down the rapids. For those who prefer less movement, there are plenty of slow pools where you can lie quietly and watch the intricate system of fish life found in a mountain stream. Tiny darters coexist with monster catfish. Since Dry River is in the heart of Mennonite country, don't be surprised to see black-cloaked farmers in horse-drawn buggies.

To the south, between Roanoke and Martinsville, you'll find **Philpott Reservoir**, which stands out from the many man-made lakes in the area because of its clearer water. Clarity averages 25' below the thermocline 40' down. Boat divers have the freedom to explore the entire rugged shoreline of rocky points and coves; shore divers usually stick to **Spring Cove** on the south side. The rock bottom drops off gradually into a forest of tree stumps. Fish weave through the maze, and if you find freshwater mussels for them, you'll soon have an admiring audience.

Virginia laws concerning diving: Check locally, as the state didn't answer our request for information.

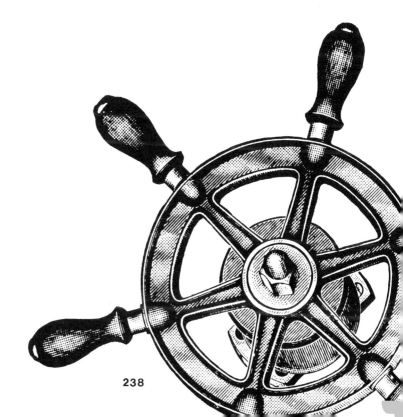

SOUTH EAST

GEORGIA   NORTH CAROLINA

The southeastern states are primarily famous for the wreck dives off North Carolina. With some of the best wrecks anywhere, North Carolina has earned its reputation as the "Graveyard of the Atlantic."

But both South Carolina and Georgia also have interesting offshore diving. Gray's Reef, off Georgia, is an extensive area of reefy ledges covered with corals and sponges. Besides porgy, mackerel, sheephead, and grunts, loggerhead turtles are often seen. The southeastern coast of the United States is probably the second largest remaining breeding ground in the world for these endangered sea turtles. On all the offshore dives, luck with the weather will be necessary. Wetsuits are worn for protection, since summer water temperatures can surpass 85°.

GEORGIA

Although many sport divers don't yet realize it, one of the few National Marine Sanctuaries in the U.S. is 16 miles off Georgia's Sapelo Island. **Gray's Reef**, one of the largest live-bottom areas in the nearshore waters of the Southeast, encompasses 17 square miles of limestone ledges lying at depths from 70-110'. Rock reefs 6' high are heavily coated with corals, sea whips, sea fans, basket sponges, anemones, and tube worms. Blue angelfish, beau gregories, triggerfish, and schools of spadefish and snapper browse above the reef top, while grouper and cardinalfish lurk in the caves and recesses that undercut the ledges. Amberjack, cobia, and barracuda patrol the upper water. Gray's Reef is also important to loggerhead turtles, who are frequently seen here. Jewfish, rays, and huge spiny lobsters also drop by periodically. Clarity is extremely variable, attaining a maximum of 50'.

The other major area of natural live bottom off Georgia's 100-mile coast is **Snapper Banks**. While visibility is consistently 50' or better, the distance from shore — 40 miles — and the minimum depth of 90' means that far fewer divers visit the banks.

In addition, Georgia has a large system of artificial reefs. Diving is recommended on those further than 12 miles offshore, since strong tidal currents and estuary conditions, like zero clarity, mark the nearshore shelf. **"G" Reef**, created from the remains of the 424'-long Liberty Ship *E.S. Nettleton*, and the 100'-long tug, *Tampa*, lies 23 miles offshore. Another Liberty Ship, the 424'-long *A.B. Daniels*, as well as a 65'-long wooden vessel and a 100'-long tug, comprise **"J" Reef**, 17 miles off the coast. Scattered rock ledges can be found south of the buoy marking "J" Reef.

Both of these artificial reefs are at depths of less than 75', giving you sufficient bottom time to explore the fish-infested area. Sea bass, porgies, grouper, and

SOUTH CAROLINA

snapper are year-round inhabitants, while Spanish and king mackerel, cobia, bonito, barracuda, and jacks are common in summer. Divers have even reported seeing sailfish and schools of iridescent, blunt-headed dolphinfish in the water above the encrusted wrecks.

INLAND

Diving in freshwater Georgia is considerably hampered by that famous red clay, which turns most dives into exercises in limited visibility. One lake, though — **Lake Lanier** — about 30 miles north of Atlanta, has decent clarity, sometimes attaining 20' in summer. A gentle slope leads down to a sand and rock bottom, inhabited by fields of mussels. Around the dam, maximum depth is 130'. Thermoclines at 30' and 70' can lower the water temperature from a surface high of 90° down to just 40°.

In addition, there are several springs in southwest Georgia, near Bainbridge. Since most are on private property, check with local dive stores for information.

Georgia laws concerning diving: Freshwater spearing is permitted for non-game fish only, with license. Use of dive flag and buddy system recommended by the Department of Natural Resources.

NORTH CAROLINA

From the early 1500's through the Civil War, the shifting sands of North Carolina's Outer Banks earned the fear and respect of every sailor who knew the area. Clashing currents, roving shoals, natural magnetic irregularities, wars, and wild storms have created one of the most hazardous shipping lanes in the world. But it wasn't until the 1940's that an additional deadly element was added to this melting pot of sea disasters — submarine warfare. Of 87 vessels lost along the North Carolina coast during World War II, 29 were victims of the Nazi submarine wolfpacks.

And it's these relics of the greatest war ever fought that primarily lure modern divers. Of all the 2000 vessels entombed in the "Graveyard of the Atlantic," none hold as much fascination as the victim ships of World War II and their submarine enemies.

The wrecks themselves can't take all the credit for North Carolina's great diving — the Gulf Stream is also responsible. Swinging close to the coast, the Gulf

Stream improves the water clarity from 10-30' inshore to 80-100' at offshore sites. It brings summer water temperature of 85°, and carries north with it such a tropical assortment of marine life that most wrecks resemble an outpost of the Caribbean stuck in the sandy barren seafloor. Beautiful corals, sponges, moray eels, angelfish, butterflyfish, spiny lobster, anemones, arrow crabs, grouper, amberjack, sharks, manta rays, starfish, sea turtles, and triggerfish are all visitors.

NAG'S HEAD

Since the Labrador Current flows south and meets the Gulf Stream around Cape Hatteras, water temperatures north of the Cape are colder — 55° at depth. The clarity is less — 15' average — and tropical sea life isn't common. Nevertheless, exciting wrecks lure divers.

ROD FARB

*The rudder steering wheel at the stern of the **Proteus**.*

The most notable is a German submarine, the ***U-85***, which lies 100' down, 15 miles east of Oregon Inlet. Unlike the hapless *U-352*, which never hit an enemy vessel in 13 attempts, the *U-85* had a more notorious record. On the night the *U-85* attacked the U.S. Navy destroyer *Roper*, though, luck was with the Allies, and the

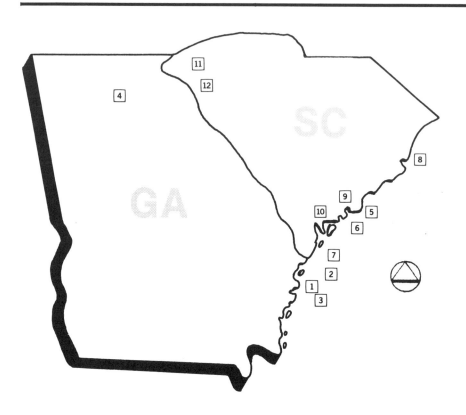

GEORGIA

A.B. Daniels 3
E.S. Nettleton 3
"G" Reef 3
Gray's Reef 1
"J" Reef 3
Lake Lanier 4
Snapper Banks 2
Tampa 3

SOUTH CAROLINA

Betsy Ross 7
Caper's Island Reef 5
City of Richmond 8
Cooper River 9
Devil's Fork 11
Edisto River 10
Georgeanna 5
Hinton 6
Kiawah Island Reef (4KI) 6
Lake Hartwell 12
Lake Jocassee 11
Martin's Landing 10
R-8 5
Strawberry Landing 9
Sullivan's Landing 9

NORTH CAROLINA

Ashkhabad 6
Atlas 4
Badin Lake 14
Benson 1
Caribe Sea 4
Cassimer 10
Ciltvaira 2
Hutton 7
John D. Gill 12
Modern Greece 13
Naeco 8
Normannia 11
Norvana 1
Papoose 8
Portland 6
Proteus 3
Suloide 7
Tamaulipas 5
U-352 9
U-85 1
USS Shur7 9
USS Tarpon 3

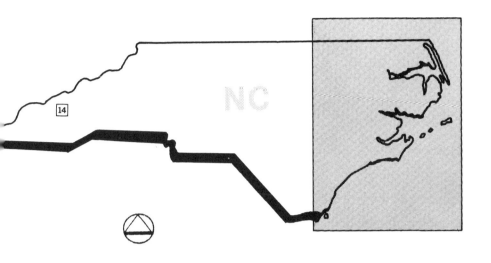

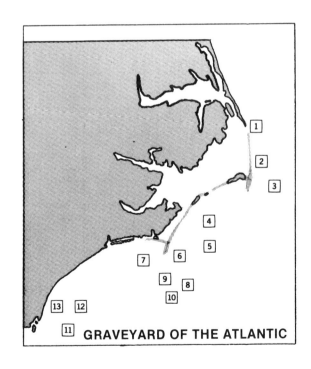

GRAVEYARD OF THE ATLANTIC

destroyer sent the sub with its entire crew to the bottom. A swim around this 220' vessel today reveals torpedo tubes, deck gun, and 88mm shells sharing the 100' depths with flounders. The sub lists 45° to starboard.

Nearby lie the remains of two tankers that fell victim to U-boats. The *Norvana* lies in pieces at 100'. The *Benson* is larger and more intact, and provides an interesting dive.

To the south, off Avon, the favorite wreck is the *Ciltvaira*, which was also sunk in 1942 by the wolfpacks. Since this wreck lies south of the Labrador Current, it is covered with the corals, sponges, and fish life associated with the Gulf Stream. The tanker lies at 105' maximum depth, with upper parts at 80'.

CAPE HATTERAS

Although at least eight wrecks lie off Cape Hatteras, two have gained special renown — the *Proteus* and the *Tarpon*. The *Proteus* was a passenger ship built in 1899 that suffered a collision and sank in 1918. Lying in 130' of water, the *Proteus* is dominated by three boilers and a portion of the starboard stern that rises 30' above the sand. Artifacts like portholes, stained glass windows, anchors, and machinery are scattered about the sand. Tropicals like lobster, sponges, barracuda, grouper, and sand tiger sharks are common.

ROD FARB

*The compressor of the **Proteus** is upholstered in purple encrustation.*

The **USS Tarpon** was a 300'-long WWII submarine that survived twelve Pacific war patrols, with the sinkings of several Japanese and German ships to its credit. After the War, the *Tarpon* was being towed to Baltimore for scrap when a storm sent it to the bottom. Lying at 130', the *Tarpon* is a majestic memorial, with the conning tower reaching up to 115'. Clarity around the *Tarpon*, like the *Proteus*, is excellent, averaging 80'. There's much marine life around the *Tarpon*, especially since it has only recently been discovered by divers.

OCRACOKE ISLAND TO CAPE LOOKOUT

Five tankers that fell victim to German U-boats lie offshore in the warm, clear water between Ocracoke Island and Cape Lookout. Charters from Morehead City and Beaufort regularly visit these classic shipwrecks.

The **Caribe Sea** was a 250' freighter carrying manganese ore when it fell prey to a night-roving German submarine. Now, it's 40' down to the top of the wreck, and another 85' to the hard sand bottom. Since the superstructure has been blown apart, you can peer down into the upper deck. Two bow anchors still in place make good photographs. Marine life is fantastic, with corals, sponges, amberjack, large grouper, and manta rays often seen.

Further offshore than the *Caribe Sea* is the wreck of the **Atlas**, lost to a U-boat the following month. This is a deeper dive, 80' just to the upper part of the wreck, and 120' down to the bottom. Bathed in the warm water of the Gulf Stream, the *Atlas* is known for excellent clarity, often 80-100'. With boilers, machinery, holds, hatches, pipes, bulkheads, and several decks to explore, the *Atlas* is fairly intact. Strong currents and a huge fishing net snagged on the ship present hazards. Abundant marine life helps make the *Atlas* one of the most exciting dives on the coast.

The **Tamaulipas** is strictly for serious wreck divers, as it's past sport diving depth and subject to strong currents. And the other two wrecks in this area lie close enough to the Cape Lookout Shoals that clarity is poor and surge a problem. The American tanker **Portland** and Russian tanker **Ashkhabad** lie widely scattered at 55' depth; a cross-wreck line and compass are essential.

CAPE LOOKOUT TO CAPE FEAR

This southern area of North Carolina boasts some of the most exciting wrecks anywhere, often arrayed in a tropical regalia worthy of Florida's Keys. In addition, there are natural rock reefs and many inshore wrecks.

One such wreck, the **Hutton**, was torpedoed in 1942 and sank in 70' of water only 10 miles offshore. A year later, the freighter **Suloide** struck the wreck of the

Hutton and sank about a mile away in 65' of water. Both vessels are broken and scattered, with boilers providing the most structure. Clarity ranges from 10-70'.

On the same night that the *Hutton* was torpedoed — March 18, 1942 — the **Papoose** also was sunk, along with three other vessels. The *Papoose* sank after getting a torpedo from Germany's *U-124*, which went on to blaze the notorious record of being singlehandedly responsible for more than 63 Allied sinkings in little over a year.

All the grim bloodshed seems far away when you're exploring the *Papoose*. It lies upside-down, 35 miles offshore, with the keel at 80'. Maximum depth is 130'. Gaping holes in the side and bottom of the ship allow limited penetration. Water clarity is excellent, often 70-100'. Morays, lobster, amberjack, cobia, grouper, sheephead, angelfish, Spanish mackerel, porgies, spadefish, and sea turtles are attracted to the wreck.

The **Naeco**, ten miles further offshore, is seldom visited due to the minimum depth of 120', as well as the distance. Broken in half with a fairly intact stern, the *Naeco* offers much marine life and many artifacts to the few experienced divers who visit her.

The **USS Shurz** was a German cruiser confiscated by the Navy and used for submarine duty during the First World War. In 1918 she collided and sank in 110' of water. Twisted girders and machinery almost disappear under schools of baitfish which sometimes throng the vessel. Brass artifacts and great water clarity make the *Shurz* a popular dive.

One of the greatest controversies yet seen by the diving world swirled around the remains of a German sub, the **U-352**, that was discovered in 1975 in 115' of water 26 miles out of Beaufort. Before the controversy ended, our Navy, a U.S. Senator, the West German government, and countless divers had entered the uproar, each with their own opinions about the sub's safety, and whether it was salvage or pilfering to remove souvenirs from the vessel. When the displayed souvenirs from the sub extended to bones from the bodies of the German crewmen, the government of Germany reacted angrily to this despoilation of one of their war memorials and cemeteries.

Today, almost a decade after its discovery, the controversy has died down. You can dive the *U-352* without feeling either ghoulish or self-destructive, since the human remains have been removed, and the Navy has disarmed the dangerous torpedoes outside the hull. Since the *U-352* is the most dived-upon wreck off North Carolina, don't expect artifacts or marine life. Even minus a propeller and its deck gun, the *U-352* remains an eerie dive to a majestic war memorial.

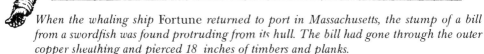

When the whaling ship Fortune *returned to port in Massachusetts, the stump of a bill from a swordfish was found protruding from its hull. The bill had gone through the outer copper sheathing and pierced 18 inches of timbers and planks.*

*The conning tower of the famed **U-352**.*

Yet another tanker, the **Cassimer**, fell victim to the U-boats in 1942. Lying in two sections in 120' of water, the *Cassimir* allows limited penetration on the stern end, which rises 35' high. Clarity usually betters 50', unless a current is running. Filefish, blue angels, and morays inhabit the remains.

The **Normannia** was a Danish freighter that foundered in a storm and sank off Cape Fear in 1924. Rated one of the top five wrecks of the state, the *Normannia* has collapsed into the sand amidships, while the bow and stern tilt upwards at 45° angles. The pair of boilers, propeller, and engine are intact. Antique beer bottles are buried in the sand just inside the stern. Clarity ranges from 50-100'. Depth is 110' maximum. Currents can spring up. Marine life is fantastic — sharks, sea turtles, slipper and spiny lobster, manta rays — as well as more ordinary fish.

The largest ship sunk off North Carolina is also one of the most popular dives, especially for newcomers to this coast — the **John D. Gill**. To the German submarine lying in wait offshore, the massive tanker of more than 500' was clearly silhouetted against the lights of Wilmington. It took only one torpedo ripping into the petroleum-filled hull to ignite an inferno so intense that rescue efforts were thwarted by the heat. The tanker rapidly broke in half and slipped beneath

*Soft corals and sponges in every color blanket the deck of the **John D. Gill.***

ROD FARB

the waves. The bow section extends from 55-90' deep, even without the superstructure, which was dynamited off. Jagged sections of the stern litter the seabed further out in deeper water. A huge anchor still hangs from the bow. The immensity of the ship is so great that, even in 100' visibility, you can see only a fraction of the wreck. Large cracks in the hull can be entered by experienced divers.

But it's the density of the sea life that really makes the wreck of the *John D. Gill* a classic. Branching red soft corals and clusters of bright flat sponges adorn every inch of steel. In summer, tropicals hide around the bulkheads, and thousands of tiny baitfish cascade over the wreckage like silvery waterdrops. From the upper reaches, amberjack and barracuda come diving in on the clouds of fish, causing grunts to huddle nervously in the gunnels. Around the pieces of stern, you'll see schools of spadefish and groupers.

Since Wilmington was the principal port for the Confederates during the Civil War, a large number of Confederate blockade runners met their doom in the area. Many were run aground to avoid letting the Union Army get the cargo. Today, their well-battered remains usually lie in shallow water close to surf zones.

Of the dozen discovered sites, the ***Modern Greece*** remains the favorite. Lying in 25' of water 1000 yards from shore, the *Modern Greece* still gives up artifacts, even though two massive salvage efforts have already recovered more than 14,000 items including rifles, ingots, and tools. To dive the *Modern Greece* or any other Civil War wreck requires a permit — see the North Carolina laws listed at the end of this section.

Although at 210' deep it isn't in the realm of sport diving, many await the day when improved diving technology will make the **USS Monitor** accessible. This historic ironclad has been preserved as a National Marine Sanctuary. Scientists who have visited the famous ship report that it rests upside-down, and that it appears to have been damaged in World War II by depth charges.

ROD FARB

*Forward hold of the **John D. Gill**.*

INLAND

Diving in the inland waters of North Carolina can't begin to match the excitement of oceanic wreck diving. But for family recreation, practice, or just an easy dive with no boat trip, divers head to quarries, including **Goldston Quarry**. Check with local dive stores about conditions, as clarity varies on a seasonal basis.

Another type of diving — for gold — is becoming popular and profitable. **Badin Lake**, in the Smoky Mountains near Asheville, is one of the most likely spots.

North Carolina laws concerning diving: In inland waters, spearing is permitted only for non-game fish. Dive flag is required. Hobby permit is needed for artifact recovery; write to: Underwater Archaeology Branch, Division of Archives and History, P.O. Box 58, Kure Beach, NC 28449.

SOUTH CAROLINA

The wrecks of Civil War blockade runners and modern steel vessels, as well as artificial reefs and broad tidal rivers loaded with artifacts, comprise the best dive sites in South Carolina.

At first glance, the murky water off Charleston might not seem like the most appetizing dive site in the world. But once you get a few miles offshore, the picture changes dramatically. The silt and topsoil flushing out of all the rivers is what causes the zero visibility right offshore, but it only takes a few miles for the dirt to settle out. Clarity can be anywhere from 15-60' or more at most sites off the coast.

For most sport divers, the best dives are made on the reefs intentionally created to attract fish. A chain of these reefs stretches along the coast from 3-13 miles offshore. All lie at ideal sport diving depths of 40-75'. One of the most popular is the **Caper's Island Reef**, also known as **R8**. Only ten miles out of Charleston, this reef is built around the carcasses of a landing craft, a trawler, and several other old vessels. At the **Kiawah Island Reef (4KI)**, 20 miles south, the wreckage of a tug named the *Hinton* provides the most excitement, as the intact galley and cabin allow exploration. Thousands of auto tires in heaps around the wrecks expand the live bottom area.

Pairs of triggerfish weave around the reefs, looking both graceful and ridiculous as they move their big flat bodies with delicate ripples of their upper and lower fins. Sometimes schools of bluefish attack clouds of baitfish, and the diver who witnesses their ferocious feeding will come away repulsed by the carnage and glad that bluefish usually weigh less than 10 lbs. Small tropicals like blennies and hawkfish dart into the sanctuaries of coral-covered tires at your approach and, if you peer closely at the sand as you swim over, you will often be able to pick out the shape of a flounder.

In 1979 the Artificial Reef Program delighted the diving community by sinking the *Betsy Ross*, a 442'-long Liberty Ship, 16 miles off the popular resort island of Hilton Head. The upper deck is 75' deep, with 110' the maximum depth. Big fish are attracted to this immense vessel, with droves of cobia in spring.

Hilton Head Island also offers great artifact diving, with finds dating back to 1600, and many others of Civil War origin. Winter is the best season for artifact diving, with clarity of up to 25'.

Another favorite shipwreck is the ***City of Richmond***. This large steel vessel went down in a hurricane in 1964 while being towed. It sits on a sand bottom 40' deep, 17 miles out of Georgetown. Although it is upright, the sea is beginning to take its toll, and pieces of the vessel break down and fall periodically, making it hazardous to penetrate. Variable currents sweep the area and require cautious and experienced divers. The wreck has more marine life than most sites, with 30-lb. amberjack common. In addition, barracuda, sea turtles, and sharks often visit.

The ***Georgeanna***, a steamer that succumbed to the Union Navy while trying to pierce the blockade around Charleston, now lies in a scrambled mess covered by only 20' of water at high tide. Tidal exchanges and poor water clarity restrict diving this wreck to the serious artifact hunter.

Artifact hunters also find the rivers south of Charleston very rewarding, with finds of Revolutionary and Civil War artifacts, Indian relics, fossilized sharks' teeth, and more "modern" relics such as 200-year-old bottles. Probably the best-known site is the **Cooper River**, at **Strawberry Landing**, also known as **Sullivan's Landing**. Clarity is never more than 10' in the dark water stained tea-color by tannin. Tidal currents can be up to four knots, and boats pass the landing at 60 mph, so this isn't the place for a relaxed easy dive. A permanent line extends out 100' from the pier piling into the middle of the river, where a 60'-wide crater drops to a depth of 65'. Beds of fossilized sharks' teeth are just a few of the finds made here. Octopus regulators, double knives, and going with knowledgeable local divers on a slack tide are all recommended procedures.

For an easier dive, try the **Edisto River** at **Martin's Landing**. The Edisto fits the perfect image of a romantic Southern river, winding through moss-draped cypress and live oak, and sheltering hundreds of bird species, including brilliant wood ducks. The tannin-stained water looks black from above. But at noon on a sunny day, when you're 10' down looking up, the water is the color of those faded rose satin drapes you see in the windows of old ladies' homes. The Edisto is never deeper than 20' in this section. Since a 2-to-3-knot current runs to the sea, watching tide tables and practicing good buoyancy control is essential. Divers usually skim the bottom in case an old bottle or artifact is spotted.

In addition, divers in the western part of the state also enjoy **Lake Jocassee**, near Greenville, and **Lake Hartwell**, near Anderson. At Jocassee, you can beach dive at **Devil's Fork**, or do a wall dive along the dam, where depths go below 350'. At Lake Hartwell, spearing is good, and large catfish are abundant around the underwater forests of the 170' maximum depth lake. Clarity at both sites averages 10-15' in summer.

South Carolina laws concerning diving: A hobby license must be purchased from the state for $5.00 by anyone recovering submerged artifacts noncommercially. Dive flag is required.

FLORIDA

Florida has more coastline than any other state besides Alaska, the densest concentration of the largest freshwater springs in the world, the only living coral reef in North America, the greatest collection of fossils accessible to divers of any state in the Union, the only remaining population of sea cows in North America, and the world' shortest river, the Ichetucknee.

The list of Florida's unique attractions could go on and on. But one statistic tells it all as far as diving is concerned: 57% of all divers traveling within the continental U.S. make Florida their destination.

With tropical coral reefs bursting with color, the Keys are a snowbound diver's dream of paradise. Jewfish of 400 lbs. and an incredibly varied collection of wrecks lure divers to the Gulf. For excitement, it's hard to beat drifting with the Gulf Stream over the turtle-filled reefs of the Gold Coast. And nowhere else in the world will you find better freshwater diving than in Florida's inland springs, where you can share the crystalline water with such bizarre creatures as the gentle and critically endangered manatee.

EAST COAST

NORTHERN — Jacksonville to Daytona Beach

While many divers overlook the northeast coast of Florida in their hurry to reach the more acclaimed spots further south, if you're willing to take a little time, you'll find good diving in the summer months. In summer, clarity improves from its winter low of less than 15' to an average of 30', and the water warms up to 80°. Plan on a long boat ride, since most spots are well offshore. You'll be rewarded with lobster and abundant game fish. Depths, occasional currents, and open ocean conditions call for experienced divers.

The **P.M. Reef** is one of the favorite dives in the area and, at 10 miles out, is the closest to shore. A natural ledge from 2-4' high has been supplanted with several wrecks, including an upright ocean-going tug at 60' depth. Lobster hide out under the ledge. Some decent-sized jewfish, plentiful grouper and snapper, and schools of baitfish create interesting scenes against the backdrop of the wreck.

Nine Mile Reef, just to the north, has a natural reef that juts up as high as 6' off the sand bottom, where depths average 65'. You might see deer cowries or giant Atlantic murex, and you'll definitely see many small tropicals.

Butterflyfish and many other tropicals also hang out around **Rabbit's Lair**, approximately 12 miles off the Mayport jetties. Clarity averages 30' at the lair, where rows of ledges provide interesting bottom relief that attracts fish from the surrounding miles of sand flats. As you drop out of the boat, often you'll see crowds of amberjack or cobia in the upper waters. When you reach the bottom of the ledges at 80', grouper and snapper will be the most common fish, with occasional schools of spadefish sweeping by.

Nurse sharks are the highlight at **Ponte Vedra Ground**, a ledge area 16 miles southeast of the jetties. At **Southeast 16-17**, five miles further out, food gatherers have better luck, with both lobster and gamefish commonly taken from the low-relief area 95' deep.

Another favorite dive for the hardy is **Blackmar's Reef**, 25 miles offshore. A scattered area of broken bottom, combined with the wrecks of a barge, a ferry, and a tug have made this area a fish haven. Depths dropping to 110' require that you be experienced with deep diving and open ocean conditions. Clarity is better this far offshore, usually at least 45' in summer, and fish throng around the cover. Many barracuda, big jewfish, grouper, and snapper have been seen, and tropicals like beau gregories and queen angels are usually observed hovering over their chosen territories.

The *Casa Blanca*, 4-1/2 miles further out, is an enormous transport sitting upright with its hull resting at 115'. You begin to see the wheelhouse and the upper deck at 65', and if you limit your dive to the upper reaches of the wreck, you'll have a little time for exploration. Inside the dim interior, jewfish are common.

DAYTONA BEACH AREA — Ormond Beach to Cocoa Beach

With Liberty Ships, WWII bombers, a 19th-century gunrunner, and both natural and artificial reefs offshore, Daytona Beach promises interesting diving. As at Jacksonville, summer is the dive season, and novices should go with experienced local divers. Clarity averages 25' in summer, when water temperature approaches 78°.

The most popular dive in the Daytona area is also the newest. The Liberty Ship **USS Mindanao** saw extensive WWII experience. In October of 1980, the *Mindanao* was sunk 10-1/2 miles offshore to begin civilian duty as an artificial reef. Unlike Florida's other Liberty Ships which were so gutted that they resemble football stadiums more than ships, the *Mindanao* had only her superstructure and top decks removed, leaving a hulk 35' high and 441' in length. The ship sits 85' down on the hard sand bottom. Holes were cut in the sides to allow current flow and access, and the local fish have taken up residence in the new habitat. Around the top of the vessel, barracuda and amberjacks patrol; inside the maze of compartments within the three separate decks, grouper and jewfish hide. The *Mindanao*, like all wrecks, shouldn't be penetrated except by divers trained and equipped for wreck diving. For those divers, though, the hold is very interesting. Many nautical items like the control wheel and brass gauges were left in place.

For that rarity in northeastern Florida — a dive that doesn't require a boat — check with local divers about the current conditions at the **North Jetty**. If the current is down, you can dive off this mile-long granite jetty at Ponce Inlet. Besides thriving fish populations, you might find stone crabs or lobster, if the water is clear enough.

At **Nine Mile Hill**, nine miles offshore, an artificial reef of old cars, cement pipes, and tires has been placed on the seabed at a depth of 60' maximum. Water clarity varies from 10-30'.

A few miles further out, the **12 Mile Wreck** is marked by a black flag. This historic wreck was finally decided to be the remains of a gunrunner that sank during the Spanish-American War of 1898. Piles of Gatling-gun ammunition clued divers to the wreck's identity. Enormous schools of spadefish throng around the highly broken and scattered remains, and large barracuda and amberjack occasionally swim above.

For a look at the relics left from a more recent war, try a trip 16 miles offshore to look at the **twin bombers**. These two WWII torpedo bombers crashed 200 yards apart in 72' of water. Now sheephead, snapper, and grouper inhabit the planes.

Scattered areas of natural relief break up the flat sand bottom further offshore from Daytona. Since these spots lie from 24-28 miles out, they aren't as frequently visited, and the fish life is fantastic. Both **East Eleven** and **Turtle Mound** drop to 75' deep and provide homes for angelfish, beau gregories, grunts, and occasional nurse sharks. At **East Ridge**, small caves and overhangs in the 15'-high ledges hide big grouper and lobster.

And if you really want to go far out, visit the remains of a freighter torpedoed during WWII. The **Liberty Ship** rests over 50 miles off the coast. The jeeps and equipment it carried have been scattered over a wide area, and gigantic jewfish and snapper swim about the relics. Strong currents call for drift diving.

FT. PIERCE AREA — Vero Beach to Stuart

Famous as the "Treasure Coast," with priceless finds from the 1715 Spanish Silver and Gold Fleet discovered just offshore, the Ft. Pierce area is also gaining additional fame as a fantastic center for sport diving. Three major reef lines lie within 300 yards of shore, making Ft. Pierce the main place in Florida for easily accessible beach diving. The deeper reefs begin only 12 miles out from the Ft. Pierce inlet. They harbor an abundance of larger marine life. Summer clarity ranges from 10-50', and summer water temperatures reach 80°.

The 22-mile stretch of beach from Sebastian Inlet to Ft. Pierce Inlet has numerous access points to clean, sandy beaches where good diving is just a short swim offshore. While there are dozens of dive spots, a few have gained recognition as the most interesting.

Around Vero Beach, reef lines can be found 75-200' offshore from the many public beaches. Depth doesn't surpass 20' and clarity is only 15' due to surf action. On calm days, visit the reefs off the public parks at **Sebastian Inlet Recreation Area**, **Wabasso Beach Park**, **Indian River Shores**, **Jaycee Beach**, or **Round Island Beach**.

About 150 yards off the beach at the end of SR 60 East, you'll see a boiler poking above the surf. This clues you to the remains of the *Breconshire*, which has rested at this spot for more than 100 years. Natural ledges nearby help create good fish and lobster populations.

The **Paddlewheeler**, three miles north of the Ft. Pierce Inlet, appeals to all divers, and especially to novices. The remains of the 19th-century ship can easily be seen from the beach, since it lies only 100 yards offshore. It's a great spot for an introductory dive, or a late afternoon dive if you haven't had quite enough, since the wreck lies in only 15-20' of water. Wooden ribs and the huge boiler provide shelter for clouds of tropicals, tame enough to feed and photograph.

Another popular, relaxed dive is **Pepper Park**, just a couple of miles north of Ft. Pierce Inlet. It's a good spot to familiarize yourself with the unusual rock structure found around Ft. Pierce. The brown, heavily textured reef is known as a sabecom worm reef. At Pepper Park, the reef drops from 15' to 30'. It provides many ledges and crevices for spiny lobster, nerites, gray cowries, and top shells to hide in. Spearing is prohibited around the park, which provides showers and other facilities.

Inlet Park also pampers the visiting diver with picnic tables, showers, and restrooms. There's lots of room to explore in the many rock ledges and reefs that parallel the beach, starting just 75 yards offshore. The remains of a small fishing boat adorn the bottom a 1/4-mile to the north of the inlet. Around all the ledges and rocks, tropicals thrive, and you can easily spot such varieties as rock beauties, porkfish, and sergeant majors.

At **Jaycee Park**, two miles south of the inlet, the offshore ledges continue, with the furthest ledge attaining a maximum depth of 60'. Since it's 300 yards out, weak swimmers should use an inflatable or a kick board. Marine life gets more abundant and varied on this furthest ledge, with a fantastic variety of shells, some lobster, grouper and snapper. Spots of live coral spangle the rocks. Since the current is non-existent on these inshore reefs, they make excellent night dives.

To visit the offshore reefs, you'll need to ride with a knowledgable, well-equipped charter captain. The best sites can be hard to find and the diving is complicated by the Gulf Stream, whose current ranges from 1-3 knots, depending on how close it's swinging to shore. Depths on these offshore reefs range from 30-100'. Often drift dives are planned so you can cover the most area in your limited bottom time.

The closest spot to visit by boat is the **Old South Bridge**. The artificial reef was created from the rubble of an old bridge. The piles of concrete create many holes for grouper and other bottom dwellers. Depths go to 40'.

One of the most often visited of the natural reefs is the **Fingers**, only 12 miles offshore. The rock fingers of the reef stretch for over 10 miles in widely separated ledges. Tropicals of every type flit around the surface of the reefs. Brilliant blue chromis mingle with the blue-spotted young of the yellowtail damselfish. Color is everywhere. Sponges and patches of live coral dot the rocks. In the sand troughs between reef ledges, big loggerhead turtles often swim. Food collecting is great, with frequent catches of lobster, snapper, grouper, and scallops.

A spot even more famous for big lobster, though, is the **Horseshoe**, nearby. This large area of U-shaped reef ranges in depth from 50-65'. Besides being the source of many lobster catches, the Horseshoe has a thriving population of grouper, moray eels, and tropicals.

The *Amazon*, 16 miles out, was the victim of a WWII torpedo. Broken up into several big chunks, it offers protection for much marine life.

At **Two Freighters**, 13 miles southeast of the Ft. Pierce Inlet, you'll find one of the largest concentrations of fish around, despite heavy charter boat fishing. These two large freighters were sunk during WWII and came to rest three miles apart at a depth of 90'. In addition to the throngs of game fish, hammerhead sharks and large turtles sometimes put in appearances. The depth, open ocean conditions, and possibility of strong currents call for experienced divers.

Diving the reefs off Stuart and Jupiter can be described in two words: BIG BUGS! Huge lobster and abundant fish crowd the reefs, which don't see many divers, since the Gulf Stream swings out to sea north of Palm Beach and water clarity is poor.

Good shore dives on Hutchinson Island include the **House of Refuge Museum**, where the framework of an old schooner lies 100 yards off the beach, and **Bathtub Reef** and **North Jetty Reef**, where reefs hide lobster as well as stone crab.

On Jupiter Island, **Blowing Rocks Preserve** is a great dive on calm days, with the craggy rocks below water attracting grunts and snook. **Carlin Park** is also an easy beach dive, only 15' deep, with tropicals uncounted swimming over the rocks.

The *Gulf Pride* split and sank one mile offshore after a collision during WWII. In calm weather, clarity is decent, and fish are fantastically varied for a site so close to shore.

Jupiter Reef, 1-1/2 miles north of the inlet, drops to 80'. The favorite season for diving here is during grouper migration in winter, when the fish seek refuge in the blowholes and tunnels of the reef.

PALM BEACH AREA — Riviera Beach to Lake Worth

Without a doubt, Palm Beach offers the wildest and most exciting diving on Florida's Atlantic coast. One factor accounts for this — the Gulf Stream. This mighty current comes closer to shore along Palm Beach than anywhere else, bringing with it marine life so rich it can only be described as "teeming."

And unlike diving locations farther north, Palm Beach divers go out year-round. There are advantages to each season. In summer, weather and seas are more predictably calm and, since the Gulf Stream swings closer to shore, the water warms up and the current speeds up. Winter, although prone to higher seas and colder water, is considered by many the best dive season since prevailing northeast winds slow down the current, and big pelagics move in. Palm Beach is a great place to see sea turtles, leopard rays, big schools of amberjack, and bar jack.

Add to excitement like that the fact that most diving requires only a short boat ride of 15 minutes. And that water clarity almost always surpasses 50' and often exceeds 80'. And that Palm Beach is a famous resort area, with regularly running charters and plenty of facilities for visiting divers. It's no surprise that Palm Beach is one of Florida's fastest growing dive centers.

At almost every site near Palm Beach, current requires special procedures. In high currents of 4-5 knots, drift diving will usually be practiced. If not, you'll be given a lead line attached to the anchor line so when you fall over backwards you won't have to fight to reach the anchor line. However, maverick currents, counter currents, and wind currents do spring up with less predictability than the always north-running Gulf Stream, so you need to be prepared for anything.

It takes a boat ride of only 10 minutes to get to the wrecks of the *Mizpah* and the *Amaryllis*. These vessels were deliberately sunk over 15 years ago to form an artificial reef and total marine life preserve just 1-1/2 miles out from the inlet. The **Mizpah**, a 189' Greek luxury yacht, lies in 90' of water, nestled against a **patrol craft**, also right-side-up.

The *Mizpah* is a great wreck for those who aren't hardcore wreck divers, as all doors, cables, and other obstructions have been removed. Surface light penetrates easily into the vessel. Two stairways lead to an engine room intricate enough to satisfy even the most experienced wreck diver.

Three hundred yards to the north, the 389' **Amaryllis** rests on a sand bottom. Although all has been removed save the the hull and lower deck, and exploration is therefore limited, the *Amaryllis* is an incredible sight due to the hordes of fish that throng around the wreck. At the **barge**, nearby, the life is even more dense. Grouper of 100 lbs. rise to meet you as you descend to the bottom. Morays peer around spiny oyster clumps. Amberjack, snapper, and porkfish all rotate between the barge and the adjacent natural rock bottom.

PANHANDLE

INLAND

see detail maps

GULF

ATLANTIC

KEYS

At **Second Gully** in winter, you can see everything from nurse sharks, leopard rays, barracuda, and sea turtles to such unusual tropicals as lookdowns, filefish, and boxfish. And as you pass over the low, rolling ledges, you'll come to areas so thick with porkfish they seem to be upholstered in 3-D yellow.

The reefs to the north of Palm Beach Inlet are deeper and wilder, with colder waters and fantastically abundant fish. On the outside of one reef a deep ledge drops from 110-160' in short order. It's on this dropoff that **The Cave**, one of America's most exciting dives, is found. You're cruising the edge of the cut, 130' down, when you come to an immense yawning tunnel that cuts into the reef and veers right back out again. Since you can see the exit as soon as you enter, lights aren't essential, but recommended. The fast current propels you past sharks, jewfish that seem big enough to swallow Jonah, and snapper that can weigh as much as 50 lbs.

A closer and tamer — but still exciting dive — is found on one of the innermost of the northern reefs, at **Seashell City**. Rolling, Pennsylvania Dutch-type hills spawn enormous basket sponges and space colonies of gorgonians. Grunts galore group in the ledges and valleys and various mollusks like murex and cones creep about on slimy feet. Formerly, Seashell City was a prime collecting ground for shells, but in recent years area divers have tried to discourage collecting the lovelies, in hopes that the name will always be an accurate description.

Just east of Seashell City is **The Valley**, where you can soar down a 75'-deep gully between ledges up to 10' high, surprising thousands of tropicals as you drift into their midst. **Koller's Reef**, known in some circles as Turtle Ledge, parallels The Valley, a little further out, with meandering snapper-infested ledges. Logger-heads rest in the gullies that reach down to 85'. Some parts of the reef are heavily furred with coral.

But it's on the reefs to the south of the Palm Beach Inlet that coral really takes off. The southern reefs feature shallower depths, less current, and more coral growth. On the innermost reef track, at **Cable Crossing**, depth reaches only 30', making this a prime snorkeling spot. Purple sea fans, brilliant tropicals, and thick sponge growth keeps the dive interesting.

On the deeper reefs, photography is a favorite pastime. **Breaker's Reef** winds toward the south for some distance. The pockmarked reef face drops from 45-60' and harbors an incredible density of life. If you can take your eyes off the abundant barracuda, you might find a lobster or surprise an octopus from its den.

Halfway down the reef a cut has been made across the reef face. This **trench** drops 15' into the reef and for some reason has become a focus area for fish populations. Porkfish spangle the 100-yard trench with yellow and black. Sea turtles, not too uncommon a sight around Palm Beach, are ordinary here, and rays often put in an appearance.

Even further south, off Lake Worth, the reefs resemble those you'd expect to find in the Keys. Depths rarely go below 60' and coral growth is extensive. Soft and delicate gorgonians, bristle worms, sponges, and hard corals coat the honeycombed rock. Large blue parrotfish nose about the reef, while leopard rays sometimes sail by, like spaceships in formation. Barracuda show their toothy grins, and if you're willing to explore the white sand flats around the reef, you might see conchs or helmets out exploring. **Horseshoe Reef**, the most famous of the Lake Worth reefs, has many small caves in the 10-15' ledge. These make good backdrops for photography.

For years, scientists have been puzzled by the large spermaceti organ found in the heads of sperm whales. Recent discoveries of sonar abilities among other cetaceans have led many to believe that the spermaceti organ is a sonar weapon, capable of focusing sound waves to stun prey such as giant squid.

LAKE WORTH TO DEERFIELD BEACH

Just 2-1/2 miles north of the southern Lake Worth Inlet is **Hogfish Reef**, a large area of low-profile bottom. Small patch reefs smothered in basket sponges and swarming in tropicals, especially hogfish, interrupt expanses of the sea grass that carpets the valleys down to 75'. Shells, lobster, and juvenile tropicals hide amongst the grass.

Sea turtles often swim through the area. If you see one eating sea grass, you've probably spotted a rare green sea turtle, distinguished from the loggerhead by its vegetarian habits and smaller head. The loggerhead, much more common to the East Coast, chooses to dine on sponges, crustaceans, and jellyfish.

Green sea turtles were once common as far north as Massachusetts, but now are seldom seen even in Florida.

The **Boynton Ledge** extends southward from Boynton Beach almost to Delray Beach. Less than one mile offshore, the ledge is popular, with several favorite spots along the expanse of the reef. **Lynn's Reef**, on the northern tip, is one of the best. Since boat traffic can be heavy, the diver's flag is a necessity. The reef begins in only 40' of water, and drops to a sand bottom 80' deep. Sea whips, soft corals, huge sponges, and hard coral mounds landscape the reef. Undercuts and crevices provide plenty of hiding spots for the abundant fish life.

FLORIDA ATLANTIC COAST

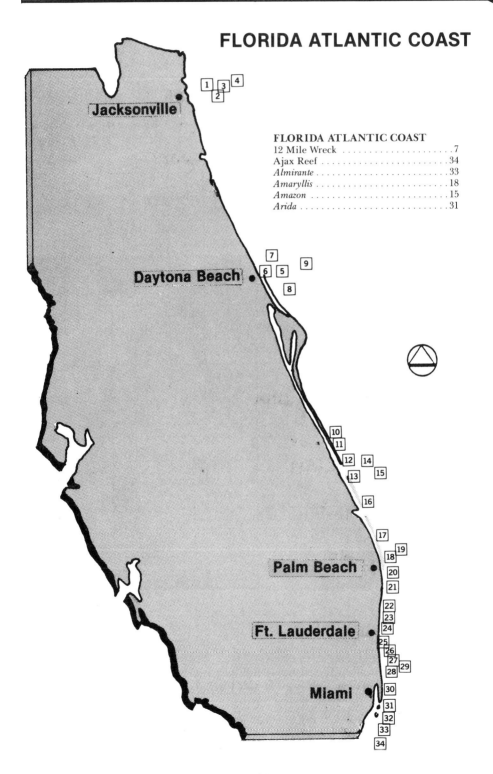

FLORIDA ATLANTIC COAST

12 Mile Wreck 7
Ajax Reef 34
Almirante 33
Amaryllis 18
Amazon 15
Arida 31

263

Barge	31	Labonte Reef	24
Bathtub Reef	16	*Lakeland*	31
Becky's Ledge	26	Liberty Ship	9
Blackmar's Reef	4	Long Reef	33
Blowing Rocks Preserve	17	*Lowrance*	29
Blue Fire	32	Lynn's Reef	22
Boca Reef	24	*Mizpah*	18
Boynton Ledge	22	*Monomy*	28
Breaker's Reef	20	Nine Mile Hill	7
Breconshire	11	Nine Mile Reef	1
Brewster Reef	32	North Jetty	6
Cable Crossing	20	North Jetty Reef	16
Carlin Park	17	Oakland Ridge	27
Casa Blanca	4	Old South Bridge	12
Copenhagen	25	*Orion*	31
Cuda Reef	26	Osborne Reef	28
Deep Freeze	30	P.M. Reef	1
Delray Ledge	23	Pacific Reef	34
Delray Wreck	23	Paddlewheeler	12
East Eleven	8	Patch Reefs	33
East Ridge	9	Patrol craft	18
Emerald Reef	31	Pepper Park	12
Fingers	14	Ponte Vedra Ground	2
First Reef	25	Rabbit's Lair	1
Four Barges	27	*Rio Bravo*	29
Fowey Rocks	32	Sailboat	29
Grouper Hole	24	Seashell City	18
Gulf Pride	17	Sebastian Inlet Recreation Area	10
Halfway Heads	33	Second Gully	18
Hammerhead Reef	27	Second Reef	26
Harbor House Reef	30	Shrimper	31
Hogfish Reef	21	*South Seas*	31
Hopper Barge	32	Southeast 16-17	3
Horseshoe	14	Spotfin Reef	27
Horseshoe Reef	21	Star Reef	33
House of Refuge	16	The Cave	19
Houseboat	28	The Valley	18
Indian River Shores	10	Third Reef	27
Inlet Park	12	Trench	20
Jap Rock	24	Triumph Reef	33
Jaycee Beach	11	Turtle Mound	8
Jaycee Park	13	Twin bombers	7
Jupiter Reef	17	Two Freighters	15
Key Biscayne Wreck	31	*USS Mindanao*	5
Koller's Reef	18	Wabasso Beach Park	10

Just 1/4-mile off the south end of the public Delray Beach is one of the most popular dives in the area. The **Delray Wreck** provides a great introduction to diving Florida's southeast coast. It's so popular that weekdays are the best time to visit if you want to see more fish than divers. A steel-hulled freighter from the 1920's lies in two distinct pieces on a sand bottom, 25' down. Triggerfish, snapper, barracuda, and large parrotfish have all been seen swimming around the coral-encrusted wreck, since it's the closest thing to a reef this close to shore. Night divers visit the Delray Wreck for lobster. Clarity usually averages 50', and heavy boat traffic makes a flag necessary.

After the Delray Wreck has piqued your interest in this area's diving, visit **Delray Ledge**. You'll find better clarity, usually 70', greater depth, dropping to 75' or more, and some of the most exciting topography around. The reef, thickly furred with waving fingers of soft coral, drops off into one of the most spectacular ledges on this stretch of coast. Entire sections of ledge have broken off and created small rooms and tunnels. As you'd expect, sea creatures have taken swift advantage of such cover. Morays slink out of rock piles; twitching lobster antennae protrude from crannies. And under some of the larger overhangs hide nurse sharks and grouper.

If you haven't the time or inclination for a boat dive, check with local dive shops about conditions at **Jap Rock**. If the weather's calm, this big rocky area, jutting out from the north end of Boca Raton's public beach, can be excellent snorkeling. Since depth is less than 15', any surf makes contact with the rough-edged rock unpleasant. Many tropicals live amongst the pot-holed rock.

The **Boca Reef** parallels the coast off Boca Raton about one mile offshore. Lobster and morays typify the reef, which slopes from a coral-covered crown at 50' to 65' or deeper. Juvenile Spanish hogfish, looking remarkably similar to fairy basslets, share the shallow caves with grouper.

For grouper fans, though, a visit to **Grouper Hole** is essential. You have to be experienced enough to drift on a fast current over a 140'-deep reef crowded with grouper and jewfish. Clarity is best on an incoming tide, when it can exceed 75'.

Less experienced divers can check out the reefs just off Deerfield Beach, where depths don't exceed 50', currents are negligible, and the marine life is great for such a close-in spot. You can see tropicals swimming practically in the surf line. **Labonte Reef** is the favorite boat dive, with a hole-pocked inner ledge supporting angelfish, lobster, and grouper.

FT. LAUDERDALE AREA — Pompano Beach to Hollywood

Ft. Lauderdale is another fast growing diving center. Long famous as a haven for college students in desperate need of spring recreation, the Lauderdale strip is starting to gain fame as a diver's smorgasboard, with hundreds of dive sites along three distinct reef lines, as well as an interesting variety of shipwrecks to explore. Summer's the season, with 80° water.

The **First**, or **Poor Man's Reef**, starts anywhere from 100-300 yards off the beach. Since you can't beach dive south of Oakland Park Blvd., Pompano Beach is the center for scuba diving the first reef. Free divers can enter anywhere. Depths don't go below 30' and clarity is variable, depending on whether the wind is blowing inshore and kicking up the sand or not.

*One of the largest giant squid (*Architeuthis longimanus*) ever found was 57' long. It washed ashore in Lyall Bay, New Zealand, in 1887.*

But the ease of access — just a swim off the beach — guarantees the popularity of first reef dive sites. Big sea fans and sponges cover the low reefs, with patches of hard coral swarming with spiny sea urchins. Tropicals thrive and present unbelievable color accents, swimming amongst the purple sea fans. Lobster hide in the holes of the shallow reef, but usually large game fish aren't present.

One of the favorite sites close-in has long been known as the Cumberland Barge. Recently it was discovered that the remains are really those of the **Copenhagen**, a coal freighter that sank in 1899. Only 20 minutes out of the Hillsboro Inlet, the old wreck attracts good fish life for such a close-in site. The remains of the barge reach from the shallow sand floor almost to the surface, festooned with waving fans. Crabs and other small invertebrates make great close-up photographs.

The **Second Reef**, about 3/4-mile offshore, is the most popular with beginning divers, and is also great for night dives, since the current is moderate at worst and depths only fall to 50' or 60'. Water clarity is usually 50' in summer. The advanced coral growth and huge schools of grunts and goatfish surprise many people, who forget that the Bahamas are only 60 miles due east.

Becky's Ledge, north of Oakland, looms up to meet you 40' below the waves. Tiny arrow crabs teeter on the huge basket sponges that share the reef crown with scattered heads of brain and star coral. The sloping ledges along the sides of the reef are guarded by immense schools of grunts, who barely part to let you swim by. At Becky's Ledge and other dive spots along the Second Reef, lobster are so common that a dive doesn't seem complete without spotting one.

To the south, a favorite site is **Cuda Reef**, only 1/2 mile offshore. It has a reputation as a great game reef, and also sustains a growth of rare pillar coral.

The **Third Reef**, lying from 1 to 1-1/2 miles offshore, promises the most big fish action, with barracuda, jacks, sea turtles, and even dolphin described in logbooks. However, current does pick up on the third reef edge. Facing east, the ledge drops 15' to depths ranging from 60-90'. Looking up at the silhouetted ledge presents a dramatic scene, with large vase sponges and corals outlined against the clear blue water.

Spotfin Reef, less than a mile north of the Port Everglades Inlet, has the most exciting relief found along the third reef line. Rugged and undercut, its caves and crevices house morays and a great variety of tropical fish. Hard and soft coral in abundance covers the 60'-deep reef.

Sometimes wind shifts bring jellyfish with 15'-long tentacles as far south as New Jersey, with the highest concentration blown together along the Rhode Island and Connecticut shores. These are actually immatures of a North Atlantic species whose tentacles may be over 50' long.

DON PETERSON

Spiny lobsters, some of the most sought-after denizens of the coral reefs, can grow to more than 10 pounds.

Another favorite site just north of the Port Everglades Inlet is known as **Four Barges**. Drifting over the largest barge, 100' long and almost intact, will reveal barracuda, blue parrotfish, and jacks. Experienced wreck divers find octopus inside the sediment-floored rooms.

South of Port Everglades, the reef lines become more distinct. Sites like **Hammerhead Reef**, loaded with coral, and **Oakland Ridge**, known for its 15'-high, cavern-riddled reef are famous. Feather plume worms project through holes in the coral covering. Parrotfish, hogfish, and triggerfish, as well as smaller tropicals like angelfish, damselfish, and the elusive spotted drum swim over the coral.

Further out, on the outer edge of the Third Reef, the wreck of the *Monomy* is snuggled down into a niche at 70' depth. The old wooden yacht, 80' long, is well broken up, but its remains offer the local fish a diversion from the natural reef that surrounds the yacht. Barracuda, snapper, cobia, and bar jacks swim above the wreck.

Less than a mile due south of the Monomy is the **Osborne Reef**, a pile of old barge sections and tires that has fostered an incredibly dense swarm of fish. Goatfish schools coalesce with the grunts, chubs, and snapper into an army of fish. Depth reaches 75'.

Of the thirty wrecks offshore from Pompano Beach to Ft. Lauderdale, the following are the most attractive to divers. A **houseboat** offers an excellent site for both deep and wreck diving practice, since the intact ship sits 90' down. A luxuriant covering of soft corals hides blennies and tiny tropicals. Silver baitfish envelop the sides in a soft mist and barracuda shoot in every now and again to pick one off.

The wreck of a **sailboat** lying on its side at 100' has created legends of monster lobster, since a lobster of 11 lbs. was recently evicted from its dwelling within the wreck.

Further out, a tugboat called *Rio Bravo* sits 140' down, so it's for the experienced only. Sunk in 1982 by an explosion that blew the bridge right off the ship, this is a good dive for penetration, without silt buildup or confusing passages. Marine life is already developing well around the *Rio Bravo*.

A 435'-long freighter was sunk even further out to create a huge and well-populated fish home. Originally called the *Mazon*, the freighter was renamed the *Lowrance* in honor of the corporation that helped finance her sinking. It's a long descent down the anchorline to the 130'-deep upper decks. Since the bottom sits at 210', this is an easy place to get bent. Penetrating the interior can be very dangerous.

MIAMI AREA

Miami has long been known for its shallow areas of extensive coral and exciting deeper reefs. Recently, thanks to an artificial reef project of the local government, it has become a mecca for wreck divers. With many huge and intact vessels in deep water (rarely above 70'), and visibility that can approach 100', Miami offers some of the most exciting wreck dives in the USA.

The best reef off northern Miami is called **Harbor House Reef**. Located just off an apartment complex of the same name just south of Haulover Inlet, it's easy to find. The reef top begins at 45' and drops rapidly to 85'. Soft corals and large sponges are characteristic of Harbor House. Occasional turtles, resident grouper and moray eels keep the dive interesting. Clarity, good for this close to shore, can be 70'.

To the south, near Government Cut C, the wreck of the **Deep Freeze** attracts divers. It's 110' down to the main deck and 135' to the base of the 210'-long vessel. Sunk in 1976, the ship has silted heavily. Besides the depth and silt, fishing line presents a hazard, so carry a knife. Photogenic, and with a great ecosystem that includes such large fish as grouper and amberjacks, as well as spiny oysters, this wreck is worth it for the advanced.

Key Biscayne offers a great introduction to Miami diving. Patch reefs and huge coral heads dot the white sand bottom northeast of the Key at depths of 15-50'. Easy diving lures novices to the abundant sea life and scattered wreckage of an old schooner.

For more excitement, visit the **Key Biscayne Wreck** lying in 60' of water east of the Key. One of the most popular dives in the area, the 120'-long vessel sits upright on the white sand. Schools of baitfish are so thick they hide the steel vessel. Black coral thrives in one of the holds. Just to the east, a **barge** with a 65'-long **shrimper** alongside attract cobia and grouper.

Within the Key Biscayne Artificial Reef Site, the variety of great wreck dives is astonishing. The **Arida** lies on her side 88' deep, looming up for 25'. Big grouper hide within the 170'-long freighter.

Broken wreckage of six wrecks surrounds the **South Seas**, a 175'-long steel yacht that swarms with baitfish and grunts. Depth around this cluster of wrecks reaches 100'.

The **Lakeland** rests upside-down at a maximum depth of 140'. The steel freighter of 200' in length lures the big ones, which includes a shark every once in a while.

But it's the **Orion**, also in the Key Biscayne Artificial Reef Site, that provides one of the most photogenic and popular dives in the area. Complete with twin engines and propellers, the 128'-long tug sits intact, with stacks and superstructure rising 30' off the floor. In the clear water of Miami, the *Orion* seems to be cruising along perpetually.

A little closer to Key Biscayne is one of the most popular natural reefs in the area, **Emerald Reef**. This small reef is amazingly scenic, with colorful tropicals, beautiful sponges in every hue, and a moray that has lost its need to lurk in holes and instead swims about divers bearing food. Only 20' deep, Emerald offers some of the best color anywhere.

Spearfishers are the main ones to brave the difficulties in diving the **Hopper Barge**. Hard to hook, with a maximum depth of 165', and swept by the strong currents common to deep water off Miami, it takes the lure of big fish to make this dive worthwhile.

A better dive is the **Blue Fire**, which rises 30' feet off the white sand bottom 115' deep. Upright, intact, and majestic, this ship offers beautiful red soft coral, midnight parrotfish, cobia, grouper, amberjacks, and barracuda, as well as a safe and easy spot to learn penetration.

A large area of shallow patch reefs around an 110'-high lighthouse, known as **Fowey Rocks**, is a charming spot for a shallow repetitive dive. This is the northern edge of the reef line that runs into Pennekamp, and diving is much what you'd find within the park, with beautiful corals and tons of tropicals. East of the lighthouse, a dropoff goes to 90'.

South of the Fowey Rocks lighthouse are a series of reefs that range from 10-70'. Since most of these reefs are in the Biscayne National Park, mollusks, coral, and tropical fish are protected. Conch may be taken for human consumption, within game limits.

Brewster Reef, three miles south, is over a mile long, with the reef crowning at 20'. Clarity on good days can surpass 60' and is best at high tide. The outer edge of the reef drops to 75', where you come upon scattered chains, boilers, nurse sharks, and morays.

Star Reef, to the south, lies just north of the Biscayne Monument Marker. It's an all-time favorite due to its rugged relief, which offers so many hiding places that morays seem almost as common as angelfish! **Patch Reefs** two miles west of the Monument's north marker are especially favored by photographers. Brilliant sponges that are almost translucent and many large puffers provide great shots.

Triumph Reef, just south of Sands Cut, is popular as much for its reliably clear water as for its rugged terrain. Depth runs the gamut from 10-120', and fish life is healthy.

Halfway Heads, between Triumph and Long Reef, drops to 140'. Huge heads as much as 20' high dot the white sand bottom. Big fish, good clarity, and strong currents distinguish this dive.

Long Reef, further south, is an extensive area of shallow reef less than 40' deep that gives way in a series of undercuts and ledges to a deeper reef 90' down. Staghorn forests mark the shallows, where beautiful sponges shelter a wide variety of tropical fish, including high hats and beau gregories.

Less than a mile from Long Reef is the wreck of the **Almirante**, sunk in 1974. You descend 110' just to reach the top deck. The sharp outlines have given way to soft, waving red corals and groups of spiny oysters. Barracuda, jacks, and schools of small fish are always present, and some lucky divers chance upon visiting jewfish. Maximum depth is 135', and clarity around the 210'-long freighter is good — often 100'.

Ajax Reef and Pacific Reef are the southernmost reefs in Biscayne Park, which shares a boundary with Pennekamp Park. These southern reefs have the widest coral variety, with many staghorn and elkhorn clumps. Diving ranges from very shallow to below 100', with steep dropoffs, large ledges, and sea caves sheltering a wide variety of life. Night diving offers a great chance to see an interesting variety of invertebrates. You might see the juvenile hawk-wing conch, which cunningly resembles a cone during its vulnerable, thin-shelled youth. Thus it gains a measure of protection, since the poisonous cone has few predators. By the time the hawk-wing becomes an adult, it gives up the impersonation, since its shell has hardened.

FLORIDA KEYS

If popularity with divers is the criteria, then Florida's Keys win first place as the best diving in America, with more than a half-million divers and snorkelers visiting the Keys each year. These flat, sandy islands, covered with low mangroves, dive stores, campgrounds, and motels, and connected by a 100-mile long highway, give little idea of the magnificence that lies under the water a few miles to the east. The only living coral reef off North America parallels the Keys four to seven miles offshore, and creates a large, surreal world of elaborate coral structures, dazzling fish, and untold shipwrecks.

One reason so many divers relish the Keys is the warm water — 85-88° in summer, and 69° minimum in winter. While good diving days can occur year-round, late spring through fall promises the most predictably clear weather. On calm days, clarity can reach 100', although 40-60' is the norm. January through March are the least reliable months, with spells of 6-high seas occurring during the cold fronts.

Of course, the ease of access, coupled with the abundant tourist facilities — including some of the most modern and competitively-priced dive boats in business — are other reasons divers return again and again to the Keys, the islands you drive to.

JOHN PENNEKAMP UNDERWATER PARK

For many, Pennekamp and the Keys are synonymous. Thanks to Dr. Gilbert Voss of the University of Miami, and John Pennekamp, editor of the *Miami Herald*, 78 square miles of coral reef became the Pennekamp Underwater Park in 1960. Over 40 species of coral and 650 varieties of fish flourish in the fringing reefs which lie from four to seven miles offshore. All spearfishing is prohibited, although line fishing is permitted. Recently a system of mooring buoys was installed to decrease anchor damage to the corals.

Male sperm whales can detect the path of a school of female sperm whales, even several hours after the females have passed by.

At the northern edge of the park is a reef that the dive boats often skip, since it's a greater distance from the cuts and harbors most often used. **Carysfort Reef**, marked by a 125'-high tower, is an immense area ranging from acres of shallow elkhorn and staghorn to large patches of dome corals.

Northwest of the tower, you'll find two huge anchors from sailing ships that lost out to the reef before the lighthouse was built. And to the northeast, one of the most beautiful staghorn forests in the park slopes down gently to a depth of 75'. Wavy sheets of lettuce coral and pillowy mounds of star coral interrupt the staghorn thicket, and an immense mixed school of grunts and goatfish cascades down the face of the reef.

The **HMS Winchester** went down southeast of the light in 28' of water in 1695 but, in the centuries since, the process of disintegration has made the remnants hard to pick out from the reef.

Between Carysfort and The Elbow is an area almost untouched by charter boats, as navigation is tricky due to the shallow corals, and clarity is less predictable. For those skillful boaters who like to get off the beaten track, **Racetrack Reef** and **Leopard Reef** offer good opportunities. Macro shooters love the small oval patch reef at Racetrack, with its steep wall riddled with holes sheltering anemones, crabs and shrimp. A coral arch smack in the center of Leopard Reef forms a 35' tunnel, often home to lobster.

At small **Watson's Reef**, nearby, dense schools of glass minnows in summer throng around **Harrison's Cave**, bouncing off your bare skin and creating a peaceful fantasy scene until hungry grouper and jacks turn it into a carnage. This cave winds 75 feet under a huge stand of elkhorn, marked by an anchor. Halfway in, the tunnel widens into a large space lit by a crevice in the reef, where nurse sharks often rest, and butterflyfish hang upside-down, grazing the ceiling.

The Elbow, midway down on the outer boundary, is marked by a 36'-high steel tower. A shallow spur and groove elkhorn reef runs for almost 1/2-mile in front of the tower. Oceanward, there's a sloping dropoff from 60-100' where a great variety of sponges and corals, including the rare pillar coral, are sometimes visited by large pelagics wandering in from the Gulf Stream.

At least four wrecks around the Elbow make good diving. *The City of Washington* was a steel-hulled freighter of 200' that foundered in 1917. Today it's a flattened and twisted pile of encrusted rubble, a suitable dwelling for tame spotted and green morays.

Other, even less intact wrecks include the **Barge Wreck**, which has scattered its steel girders and pieces of hull plating over the shallow seafloor. While you're touring this underwater junkyard, don't be surprised if angelfish, ocean triggerfish, or even barracuda approach you with a hungry look — they're just pets, waiting for handouts.

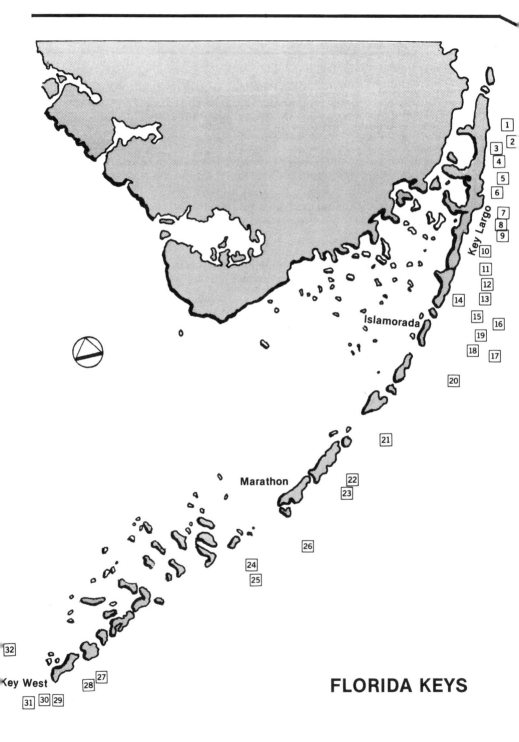

FLORIDA KEYS

FLORIDA KEYS

Alexander 32
Alligator Reef 18
Aquanaut 28
Barge Wreck 5
Beans 19
Benwood 7
Cannabis Cruiser 17
Carysfort Reef 1
Cathedral Cave 6
Christ of the Abyss 6
Christmas Tree Cave 8
Coffin Patch 21
Conch Reef 11
Crocker Reef 13
Davis Reef 12
Delta Shoals 22
Eastern Dry Rocks 29
Eastern Sambo 27
El Bargo 14
El Capitan 12
El Infante 11
French Reef 8
Grecian Rocks 6
Harrison's Cave 4
Hens and Chickens 14
HMS Winchester 2
Hole in the Wall 9
Horseshoe 6
Ignacio 21
Islamorada Coral Gardens 14
Ivory Wreck 22
Klem's Wreck 5

Leopard Reef 3
Little Conch Reef 11
Little Grecian 6
Looe Key 24
Matecumbe Dropoff 20
Middle Sambo 27
Minnow Hole 6
Molasses Reef 9
No Name Reef 15
North Horseshoe 6
Pickles Reef 10
Racetrack Reef 4
Raspberry 20
Rock Key 30
Sambo Reefs 27
San Jose 11
Sand Key 30
Seven Mile Bridge Reef 26
Sombrero Reef 23
Spiny Oyster Barge 16
Ten Fathom Bar 30
Ten Fathom Ledge #1 31
Ten Fathom Ledge #2 28
The City of Washington 5
The Elbow 5
The Rocks 14
Tile wreck 30
USS Alligator 18
Watson's Reef 4
Western Sambo 27
Windlass Wreck 9

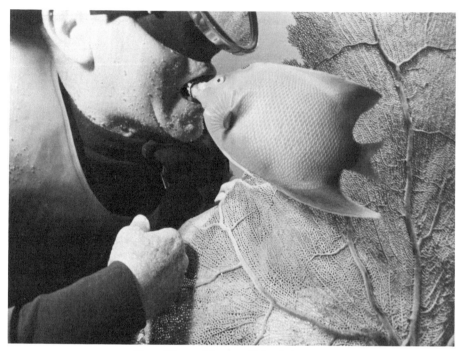

Steve Klem with one of his piscine pets.

Where you'll really see the pets is at **Klem's Wreck**. This old work barge foundered in the early 1900's, while working on Flagler's Folly, the railroad that took over eight years and 100 lives to build. It stretched to Key West but was washed out by a hurricane only 23 years after its completion. Now the wooden beams are furred with big sea fans and waving sea whips. Yellowtails and cottonwicks guard the wreck. Not only are tropicals like queen and gray angels tame, but even spotted morays, green morays, big grouper, margates, and stingrays have been trained to take food from the hand.

Also found in the area around the Elbow is the world-famous statue of *Christ of the Abyss*, presented to the Underwater Society of America by Egidi Cressi, the Italian manufacturer of diving equipment. The statue, created by Guido Galletti, reaches upward for 11' from the sea floor. The shallow area around the statue is a favorite snorkeling site, with some of the largest brain coral heads in the park — at least 20' across — located nearby.

There are sponges which, after being pressed through a cloth filter to separate the cells, will reassemble themselves and continue to grow.

Only 300 yards north of the statue is **Minnow Hole**, where summer finds glass minnows so thick they are liable to disorient you. Groupers, jewfish, and even a tame cuda called "Old Smokey" have been known to take advantage of the easy pickings. Further north, two shallow, interesting patch reefs known as **Horseshoe** and **North Horseshoe** have coral caves with swarms of both silversides and larger baitfish.

Less than one mile south of the statue is **Grecian Rocks**. This shallow area provides excellent snorkeling over a tropical-packed reef. Navigation is very difficult because the reef averages only 6' deep and may be awash in low tide. To the north 250 yards is **Little Grecian**, a small patch reef that has the most diverse relief found on the inner reef line. A huge formation of star and brain coral known as "Skyscrapers" opens up on its ocean side to reveal majestic **Cathedral Cave**.

The most popular wreck in Pennekamp lies just 1-1/2 miles northeast of French Reef. The ***Benwood***, torpedoed by a German sub during WWII, became a navigational hazard and was blown apart. Today the superstructure is scattered about the broken hull, which stretches for 285' from the bow in only 25' of water to the stern 55' deep. A spectacular collection of fish adorns the wreck, from schools of glassy sweepers and porkfish to grouper and snook. Beautiful invertebrates like Christmas tree worms and sponges add more motionless color.

While **French Reef** might have lesser clarity and fewer fish than the more popular Molasses, it remains for many people the best dive in the park due to its outstanding bottom configuration. There's more variety of landscape than anywhere else in Pennekamp, with coral buttresses riddled by holes separated by winding sand canyons. Some of the holes even open up into full-fledged caves. **Christmas Tree Cave** opens into a broad, sand-floored room, with schools of glassy sweepers creating a copper wall of shimmering streaks that bends and regroups around you as you swim through the cave. There's also a deeper reef off

Over 90 percent of all marine life is concentrated on the coastal margins. Almost 98 percent of the world fish catch is taken within 200 miles of land.

*The scarlet sea star (*Henricia sanguinolenta*), besides having a depth range varying from shallows to the abyss, is also one of the few starfish to guard its eggs until hatching.*

French, where advanced divers can take advantage of the up to 2-1/2-knot current to sail along a low-profile reef, 120' down. Black coral, large jewfish, and even sailfish have been seen.

Marked by a 50' steel tower, **Molasses Reef** is the workhorse of Pennekamp. Fortunately, Molasses is so big that it can withstand enormous diving pressure well, as long as boaters use mooring buoys or anchor in sand, and divers practice good buoyancy control. With the most predictably clear water in the park (often 25' more visibility than at other spots), and simply incredible numbers of tropical fish inhabiting the dense coral, Molasses is the most dependably gorgeous reef in the park.

In 1984, more than 19,000' of shallow, ancient coral heads were sheared off by a freighter, which somehow missed the shipping lanes and came more than 20 miles inland to run aground at Molasses.

One of the favorite spots within Molasses is the **Windlass Wreck**, where heavily encrusted wreckage scattered throughout a sand canyon provides great backdrops for photography. Just to the east is **Hole in the Wall**, where a buddy team can swim together through a 15'-long tunnel in the coral wall. Due to its ease of access, Molasses is a great spot for night diving if the current which sometimes washes it is down. Many divers have gotten their first taste of night diving at Molasses, where lights make the reaching arms of elkhorn seem mysteriously graphic.

UPPER KEYS

Just because Pennekamp Park stops, the reefs don't. Islamorada has become the relaxed headquarters for the varied diving that characterizes the Upper Keys. Shallow, vivid reefs, deeper dropoffs, and the wrecks of modern-day vessels as well as Spanish treasure galleons are the highlights.

Gorgeous little coral reefs like **Pickles Reef** can be found less than two miles outside Pennekamp. Shallow depth and many shells, including abundant conch, characterize Pickles.

And at **Conch Reef**, 2-1/2 miles further south, you'll find conch on the shallow land side. Oceanward, there's a rugged dropoff that gradually slopes to 115'. The reef is known for its lovely 10'-tall spires of pillar coral, and its sponges, so enormous you can hide inside them. In addition, outstanding clarity means that divers can look up from the base of the reef and clearly see the silhouetted sponges, often with magnificent creatures such as loggerheads, eagle rays, or pompano cruising by.

That part of the ocean that is below 12,100' accounts for 90 to 95 percent of the ocean's volume. It is an unchanging environment characterized by great pressure, almost total darkness, extreme cold, and currents so slow that they're measured in inches per hour.

Little Conch Reef, one mile to the southwest, houses pillar coral and tropical fish along its gentle slopes. The famous *El Infante* met doom at Little Conch. This ship and 19 others formed the famous 1733 Spanish Plate Fleet, which a hurricane scattered over the Keys from Largo to Vaca. At the *San Jose* site, professional salvors discovered over $30,000 in gold and silver on the first day of their operation in 1973. Ask Islamorada dive stores about trips to the sites of the Plate Fleet, including the vessels *Lerri*, *San Pedro*, *Tres Puentes*, *Chaves*, and *Herrera*. A common site for a second dive is **Davis Reef**. The reef ledge rises from 6-8' above the seabed; depth ranges from 15-28'. Although for years only piles of ballast stones marked the wreck of the *El Capitan*, recent storms have uncovered structural timbers and divers have recently recovered cannonballs, spikes and nails, musketballs, pottery, coins, and a bronze cannon.

Running for 500', Davis Reef is upholstered in purple seafans, big brain coral heads, and bright orange sponges. No one knows why, but Davis attracts more schooling fish than any other reef around. Besides the huge schools of goatfish, golden grunts, porkfish, yellowtail, and schoolmaster snapper, you'll see sergeant majors, yellowtail damsels, stoplight parrotfish, Spanish hogfish, and trumpetfish. And if that wasn't enough, a pair of 6' green morays weave out of the reef holes like cobras and a sea turtle occasionally stops by.

Crocker Reef, nearby, is a very popular dive. The reef top lies from 45-55' deep. Spurs of coral separated by winding sand grooves run perpendicular to the reef top, and slope gently down, until, at 55', a sheer coral wall drops to 95'. Red finger sponges highlight the huge basket and vase sponges. Delicate seafans soften the hard edges of the elkhorn. Spearfishermen appreciate the mutton snapper, sightseers and photographers love the sea turtles and eagle rays that sometimes cruise by, and tropical aficionados delight in the rare deepwater species like blackcap basslets and jackknife drums that can be seen hiding under the deep ledges.

Huge heads of brain coral just below the surface distinguish **Hens and Chickens**, about 2-1/2 miles closer to shore than Crocker Reef. Depths of less than 30' make this a good spot for novices or snorkelers. The encrusted remains of *El Bargo*, a steel barge, accent the beauty of the coral heads. Other shallow reefs nearby include **The Rocks**, and **Islamorada Coral Gardens**.

Three Peaks is the name given to three massive coral buttresses lifting 55' off the seafloor at 90'. Big grouper, schools of African pompano, and a stray shark make this an exciting dive. **Teepee Reef** is a beautiful 50'-deep reef marked by narrow sand channels and sheet, starlet, and flower corals. And **No Name Reef** is another favorite site, similar to Teepee but with greater fish concentrations.

Wreck divers drawn to Islamorada find themselves hard pressed to choose between the *Cannabis Cruiser* and the *Spiny Oyster Barge*. The little-visited barge lies in 105' of water beyond the outer reef line, affording great visibility. The upper deck of the mostly intact barge is 90' down, and it is plastered with spiny oysters. Huge stoplight parrotfish, angelfish, grouper, snapper, yellowtail, and amberjack are commonly seen. Divers looking in the bashed-in side usually catch sight of the resident 200-lb. jewfish.

The *Cannabis Cruiser* is another deep dive, five miles off the southern tip of Islamorada. Smugglers apparently decided things were getting too hot, so they ditched their boat, complete with Loran-C, radar, and a full load of marijuana — unfortunately, nothing is salvagable. Divers discovered her after she'd been down about five years. Upright and heavily encrusted, she is shrouded by tons of baitfish. Schools of jack and snapper, grouper, gray angels, hogfish, and a 300-lb. tame jewfish have all been regularly seen, and some even report sighting sharks and sawfish around the *Cruiser*.

Tame jewfish can be vulnerable to hook and line fishing and spearfishing.

KLAUS KARWATH

For history buffs, a dive on the wreck of the *USS Alligator* is essential. The highly broken remains lie in the sand between coral fingers 100 yards in front of the Alligator lighthouse. Congress commissioned Commander Allen to fight the pirates who were ruining ocean-going commerce in the Keys. Although the *Alligator* and her captain both meet their doom in a skirmish in 1822, they had effectively ended the pirates' reign.

For those more interested in coral than wreck history, **Alligator Reef** (also called "The Gully") will still be fascinating. The large area of high-profile reefs sloping down into deep gullies makes a great setting for photography. Marine life of every type — fish, mollusks, crustaceans, corals — is abundant.

Taming sharks takes time, patience, and strong nerves.

Along the outer edge of the reef system, on a level with Crocker, are several deep, sloping dropoffs including **Beans**, **Raspberry**, and **Matecumbe Dropoff**. Often their location is a guarded secret of the dive boat captain who discovered them. If you go to the Upper Keys in fall and get to know a divemaster well, you might get to visit one of these more virgin reefs, where large lobster, grouper, rays, sharks, turtles, jewfish, sailfish, and even newly discovered species of shells have been reported. Depths of past 100' and strong currents call for experienced divers.

MIDDLE KEYS

The Middle Keys, centered around Marathon, include everything from acres of shallow coral gardens to spectacular Looe Key, one of the few National Marine Sanctuaries in the entire country. You'll also find a palm-lined, sandy beach, rare in the Keys, at Bahia Honda.

At **Coffin Patch**, 3-1/2 miles off Key Colony Beach, you'll find six distinct reef areas at depths of less than 30'. Mounds of brain coral that surpass 20' in diameter, abundant gorgonians and tropicals (including certain angelfish who've assumed the role of Coffin Patch mascots), sand dollars, and ledges alive with lobster are some of the more memorable sights.

Perhaps the most exciting thing at Coffin Patch is the amorphous clumps of pillar coral, with spires beginning to take shape and grow upwards. New growths of pillar coral are extremely rare, and since this area lost many beautiful specimens years ago to collectors, it's exciting to see the coral returning. The *Ignacio*, one of the ships in the famous 1733 Plate Fleet, broke open and scattered its cargo over a wide expanse of grassy flat near Coffin Patch.

Delta Shoals, straight out of Vaca Key, is as famous for its wrecks and fish life as it is for its coral. The reef is a narrow patch system, less than 20' deep, with fingers that extend oceanward and clutch the remains of vessels that went aground on the shoals. Some of the wreckage is thought to belong to a slaver that ran aground here in the 1850's. Elephant tusks led to the name **Ivory Wreck**. Further offshore, a deeper reef drops to 100'. Besides decent-sized grouper, nurse sharks also inhabit the craggy ledges and reef holes.

Sombrero Reef, marked by a 140' light tower south of Delta Shoals, is a large and magnificent area of coral heads that rise as much as 25' from the sand floor. Winding sand channels separate the reefs, which seem to have more brain coral heads and moray eels than anywhere else. The diving is best above 30', where you'll see many fish cleaning stations among the star coral mounds, sheets of lettuce coral, and waving gorgonians. On these gorgonians exist a species of flamingo tongue, Sedlack's flamingo, found nowhere else.

Over 30 other species of shells inhabit only the central Florida Keys. Because of their geographic isolation, the Keys have served as an evolutionary laboratory for both terrestrial and marine creatures, with the result being the creation of entirely new species, native only to the Keys, as well as the survival of fossil forms that have died out elsewhere. The Keys dove shell and the Florida button shell are examples of this; they were assumed to be extinct fossils until live specimens were discovered quietly lurking in the Keys. Examples of species that evolved uniquely in the Keys includes such beauties as the Clapps tower shell, the two-colored crown conch, and the splendid Burry's cone.

But the best examples of all are the flamingo tongues. Nine species of flamingo tongues are found in the Keys, thanks to one of the richest concentrations of gorgonians (their food staple) anywhere. Two of these species are found nowhere else.

It's because of biological splendor like this that **Looe Key** was made a National Sanctuary by President Carter. It's also the most spectacular and easily accessible reef in the Keys. A V-shaped shoal (all that's left since a hurricane blew the island away 150 years ago) shelters an incredibly dense spur and groove coral system, extending from the surface down to 35'. Over 40 species, including elkhorn, star, flower, pillar, saucer, and leaf corals, create overhangs and holes that shelter octopus, sea stars, and hundreds of shells and tropicals. Fish life grows more abundant and varied constantly under complete protection.

At one spot in the reef, an anchor has become interlaced with the coral that grew around it. It could be from the *HMS Looe*, a British frigate that ran aground here in 1744, but more likely it's from one of the many other vessels lost to the reef.

Schooling baitfish in the Florida Keys.

Approximately 1/4-mile to the southeast, the sloping bottom suddenly plunges down to 90' in a vertical dropoff. Huge coral boulders create a rugged scene, enhanced by the presence of large grouper, lobster, and morays peering out from the clefts. Currents and depth demand experience.

Another, very different, deep dive in the Middle Keys is the **Seven Mile Bridge Reef**. The three-story-high steel shafts of the old bridge were dumped at 120' just south of Marathon. You can sit on a girder and watch yellowtail and bonita strike at the glass minnows swirling around the rubble. Jumbo grouper and jewfish keep things exciting, along with the possibility of swift current.

KEY WEST

Key West has it all: great reefs easily reached in half-day trips, charter services to remote, untouched areas like the Marquesas, Cosgrove Shoal, and the Dry Tortugas, and — unique in this island chain — the excitement of a lively city at night. I usually wonder what non-divers do on their vacations. But at Key West, I know: they ride the Conch train, they gorge on Key lime pie and other gourmet fare, they admire the architecture, the galleries, the museums, the boutiques, the sunset, and they drink and dance all night.

The dive sites themselves are varied, ranging from shallow reefs to deep dropoffs to wrecks. In 1972, an intact 600' WWII cruiser was sunk 14 miles off the Boca Chica Channel as part of an artificial reef program. Unfortunately, the shallowest section is in 140' of water. Those hardcore deep divers who have visited report giant guns still in the turrets, and schools of pelagics, including sharks.

The **Sambo Reefs** are subdivided into three sections. **Eastern Sambo** is famous for lobster. The bugs shelter amongst many small coral heads and undercuts. At **Middle Sambo**, a well-defined reef is the top attraction, with huge heads of brain and star coral 15' or more across, as well as a gorgeous growth of fuzzy pillar coral. The 30'-deep reef top drops to 60' on the seaward edge. **Western Sambo** has good snorkeling with shallow, high-profile coral heads that are home to schooling goatfish, pink conch, flamingo tongues, and thousands of tropicals.

Ten Fathom Ledge #2, about one mile southwest of Western Sambo, is a deeper reef, dropping to 115' on the seaward side. Big grouper hide out in shallow caves. The decayed wreckage of an old tugboat at 90' lures snook and jacks.

Another wreck usually visited on the way out to the Sambos is the ***Aquanaut***. This 65'-long steel tug sits totally upright and intact on a flat sand bottom 80' down. Barracuda, blue runner, and bar jack often hover around the superstructure. Inside the wheelhouse you might see a resident grouper. It's hard to imagine a more unwrecked looking wreck, as the *Aquanaut* looks functional enough to be afloat.

DOUG COOK

Steve Klem, the original "Pied Piper of Pennekamp", visiting one of his pets.

Barracuda feeding in Pennekamp Park.

Eastern Dry Rocks, marked by a steel beam, is a straight five-mile shot out of Key West. Large coral heads, including a growth of 4' pillar coral, jut out of the shallow sand bottom. This is a good area to observe shells, with figs, tuns, whelks, and tulips all found in the vicinity. You might see ballast stones from an old wreck.

Rock Key, nearby, is a more intriguing dive, with narrow, 20'-deep cracks separating the huge mounds of star and brain coral. An exceptional amount of color makes this a good spot for both photography and night diving. In addition, you might notice a few remnants still left from ancient shipwrecks in the area. One, the **tile wreck**, went down centuries ago, and carried a load of Spanish tiles to the bottom, which divers have been recovering off and on for years.

One mile straight west of Rock Key is one of the favorite sites in the area, popular as much for its altitude view (a rare thing in the Keys) and all-weather diving, as for its underwater beauty. **Sand Key** is a small island with a 110'-high steel light built in 1853. Inside, it looks like any other abandoned tower until you climb the spiral staircase, where you can gaze far off into the distance and pick out the Marquesas, or look straight down into the aquamarine shallows that suddenly turn indigo where the Gulf Stream passes. Brown pelicans will probably be diving into the water as you watch, and the enormous wings of the frigatebird will be gliding on some thermal out in the distant sky.

Underwater, the scene is nice, too, with staghorn and elkhorn thickets in the shallows giving way on the ocean side to massive heads of brain and star coral that ride the ledges down to 75'. Large grouper hide in the canyons and ledges of the slope. Sometimes an enormous school of mullet covers the cove shallows like an iridescent blanket. At these times, the diving is especially exciting, with barracuda swooping into the mass to snatch one of the members, while the rest barely move aside.

Just 1/2-mile to the south is **Ten Fathom Bar**, one of the deeper and more challenging dives close to Key West. Heavy current marks the first 30' of the dive; once you drop below that, the current usually slows down. The Gulf Stream flowing by so closely means more than just current, though. It also means exceptional clarity and a chance to see some really big sea creatures. Schools of rays and occasional loggerheads are sometimes spotted along the wall, which drops rapidly from 30' to 135'.

Not to be confused with Ten Fathom Bar is **Ten Fathom Ledge #1**, about five miles southwest of Sand Key. Charters frequent this ledge because it's known for clear water due to its closeness to the Gulf Stream. The maximum depth of 50' gives you plenty of bottom time, and the interesting caves, undercuts, and peaks of the reef provide lots to explore. March to June sees the most traffic here, as black grouper converge on the ledge in huge numbers.

Wreck divers head for the Gulf side of Key West to visit the *Alexander*, a WWII destroyer escort sunk in 1970. Broken in half and lying on its side in 40' of water, the battered wreck swarms with baitfish. Clarity can be poor, depending on the weather.

North of Smith Shoals, also on the Gulf side, are the remains of at least four freighters that went down in 1942. Clarity is poor, but abundant fish still lure divers.

GULF COAST

Few areas in this country can surpass the Gulf Coast of Florida when it comes to both wreck diving and big fish life. The scattered natural reefs offshore have been supplanted with a great variety of wrecks, both accidentally and intentionally placed. Summer offers the most predictable diving conditions, with generally calm seas from March through September. Water temperature during these months stays around 80°, and clarity averages 50', with occasional days up to 100'. During winter, storms limit the predictable diving days, clarity falls, and the water temperature drops to 55°. Nevertheless, many divers find winter dives the most exciting of all, since more big jewfish move in.

The average ocean swell travels at about 35 mph in the Pacific, and slightly more slowly in the Atlantic

PENSACOLA

Although you can make a shore dive around the jetties at Fort Pickens to see many of the local tropicals, for more exciting diving you need at least a small boat. The **USS Massachusetts**, a WWI battleship, was sunk by the Navy in 1927 about one mile off the jetties. Best diving here is on a rising tide, since the deteriorated ship is partially exposed in only 25' of water.

For more interesting marine life, visit the **Coal Barges**, less than two miles off the beach. These three barges were placed in 50' of water to form an artificial reef 600' long. Spadefish and triggerfish are notable in the crowd of fish surrounding the barges; out in the sand, you can find shells, including sand dollars, olives, and augers.

Other artificial reefs include a 130'-long **air transport plane**, just a few miles past the barges, and a **Liberty Ship**, whose 20'-high hull was placed in 80' of water about 10 miles southeast of Pensacola. Since natural reefs — known as **Big Rocks** — are nearby, fish life is pretty good.

But the **Old Toll Bridge** rubble has created a fish haven that surpasses any of these sites. Dumped in 80' of water seven miles southeast of town, the rubble piles are the haunts of tropicals, snapper, grouper, flounder and an army of small baitfish.

At the wreck of the **San Pablo**, nine miles off the beach, barracuda, cobia, and amberjack patrol the upper waters, while black grouper might be seen hiding inside the stern. The *San Pablo* was a 400' Russian freighter torpedoed in WWII that went down while being towed in. The stern section and boilers, lying at 80' depth, are all that remain intact.

DESTIN — FORT WALTON BEACH

With more abundant natural rock reefs closer to shore than any other area of the Gulf, Destin has become a very popular diving area. Many reef lines lie less than 10 miles offshore. These aren't true coral reefs, although you might be fooled at first, since a tropical current brings such southern species as large basket sponges and colorful encrusting corals and bryozoans. Hard coral in small patches also contributes to the thick fur covering the limestone ledges.

At **Amberjack Rocks**, only three miles south of Destin, a rock uplift has thrust 10-15' off the sea floor. Depths reach a maximum of 85'. Ledges and undercuts covered with big sponges hide grouper and a variety of shells, including some, like the beautiful 5" striped Branham's tulip, that are found only on the Gulf Coast.

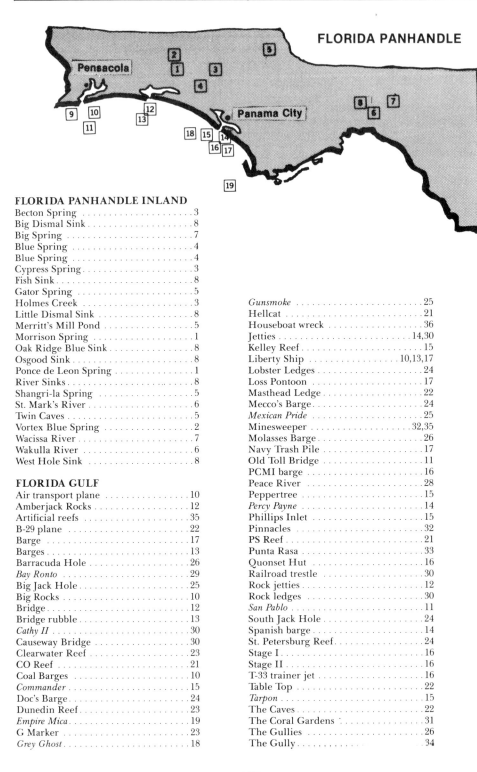

FLORIDA PANHANDLE

FLORIDA PANHANDLE INLAND

Becton Spring 3
Big Dismal Sink 8
Big Spring 7
Blue Spring 4
Blue Spring 4
Cypress Spring 3
Fish Sink 8
Gator Spring 5
Holmes Creek 3
Little Dismal Sink 8
Merritt's Mill Pond 5
Morrison Spring 1
Oak Ridge Blue Sink 8
Osgood Sink 8
Ponce de Leon Spring 1
River Sinks 8
Shangri-la Spring 5
St. Mark's River 6
Twin Caves 5
Vortex Blue Spring 2
Wacissa River 7
Wakulla River 6
West Hole Sink 8

FLORIDA GULF

Air transport plane 10
Amberjack Rocks 12
Artificial reefs 35
B-29 plane 22
Barge 17
Barges 13
Barracuda Hole 26
Bay Ronto 29
Big Jack Hole 25
Big Rocks 10
Bridge 12
Bridge rubble 13
Cathy II 30
Causeway Bridge 30
Clearwater Reef 23
CO Reef 21
Coal Barges 10
Commander 15
Doc's Barge 24
Dunedin Reef 23
Empire Mica 19
G Marker 23
Grey Ghost 18

Gunsmoke 25
Hellcat 21
Houseboat wreck 36
Jetties 14,30
Kelley Reef 15
Liberty Ship 10,13,17
Lobster Ledges 24
Loss Pontoon 17
Masthead Ledge 22
Mecco's Barge 24
Mexican Pride 25
Minesweeper 32,35
Molasses Barge 26
Navy Trash Pile 17
Old Toll Bridge 11
PCMI barge 16
Peace River 28
Peppertree 15
Percy Payne 14
Phillips Inlet 15
Pinnacles 32
PS Reef 21
Punta Rasa 33
Quonset Hut 16
Railroad trestle 30
Rock jetties 12
Rock ledges 30
San Pablo 11
South Jack Hole 24
Spanish barge 14
St. Petersburg Reef 24
Stage I 16
Stage II 16
T-33 trainer jet 16
Table Top 22
Tarpon 15
The Caves 22
The Coral Gardens 31
The Gullies 26
The Gully 34

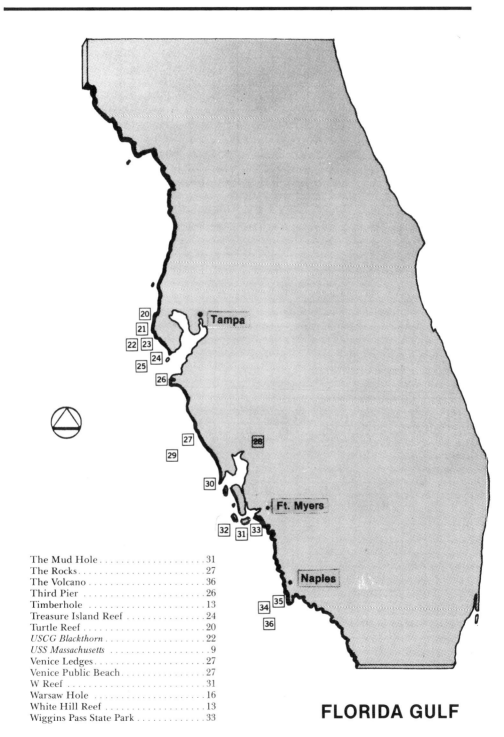

The Mud Hole 31
The Rocks 27
The Volcano 36
Third Pier 26
Timberhole 13
Treasure Island Reef 24
Turtle Reef 20
USCG Blackthorn 22
USS Massachusetts 9
Venice Ledges 27
Venice Public Beach 27
W Reef 31
Warsaw Hole 16
White Hill Reef 13
Wiggins Pass State Park 33

FLORIDA GULF

White Hill Reef, eight miles offshore, is a deeper and wilder dive, reaching 100' at the base of the ledges. Many tropicals, triggerfish, and grouper of up to 60 lbs. swim around the soft corals and anemones of the reef. Cowries, cones, tulips, and turbans hide in cracks in the rock and under sponges, often with thick growth obscuring their shells.

Further offshore, the ledges continue, and reach heights of up to 18' at sites like **Timberhole**, where many round holes pocket the 110'-deep reef. Lobster as well as shells take advantage of this cover.

You can also dive a 500'-long **Liberty Ship**, sunk 80' deep off Ft. Walton Beach, as well as several **barges** 65-90' deep. You'll find many more fish on the **bridge rubble** deposited in about 20 different spots, all within three miles of shore. These rubble piles make good introductory dives for students, and since they generally have good clarity and great fish populations, they still appeal to the experienced. Flounder, snapper, and even a few Warsaw grouper inhabit the piles of concrete.

And the clear, blue-green water around Destin extends far enough inshore to make diving or snorkeling two **rock jetties** and under the **bridge** appealing. These easy, beach-access dives will show you a surprisingly good time, with flounder, tropicals, and even snapper or grouper often present. Watch the dive tables and dive on the slack to avoid the current of an outgoing tide.

PANAMA CITY

Some of the most famous wrecks in Florida are found around Panama City, which has become headquarters for Panhandle diving, thanks to both fantastically varied Gulf dives and beautiful inland springs, some only 30 minutes out of town.

Within St. Andrews Bay, you can make a beach dive off the **jetties** or visit the remains of the **Spanish barge**, where you'll see many shells and schooling baitfish in the 18'-deep water if clarity's good. The *Percy Payne*, just 100 yards off the St. Andrews State Park beach, is mainly sand-covered, but occasionally divers find brass spikes among the old timbers.

For better visibility, though, you need to get outside the bay into the open waters of the Gulf, where you'll find wrecks and natural reefs to tempt you, with clarity averaging 50'. Depths in the area range from 55-110'. Thirteen miles offshore, the low reefs of **Phillips Inlet** drop from 65-110', and harbor big lobster, game fish, and great shells. Knowledgable skippers visit spots like *Peppertree and **Kelley Reef** to see the entire spectrum of Gulf marine life.

The continental shelf, which represents only about three percent of the ocean, varies from a few feet wide to as vast as 800 miles wide, as in the Artic off Russia. The world average is 44 miles wide.

Warsaw Hole is the most famous natural structure off Panama City. It lies nine miles southwest of the St. Andrews jetties. The hole starts in 85' of water and drops 12' into the reef floor. Ledges hide much marine life.

At least nine different **barges** have been scattered offshore, at depths ranging from 40-90'. While their size and degree of intactness varies, they all have made great habitats for a wide variety of fish. And in 1977, a 441' **Liberty Ship** was sunk 9-1/2 miles offshore at a depth of 74'. Already it's become a favorite dive, attracting grouper, jacks, snapper, and angelfish. Pink anemones carpet the 20'-high hull, which is a good introductory wreck dive.

A variety of Navy structures underwater attract divers. The **Navy Trash Pile**, three miles off Shell Island, is an especially good dive for those who like to poke around garage sales and junkyards, with old chains, airplane parts, and much other Navy equipment junked over a large area.

For a more focused dive, visit the **Loss Pontoon** several miles south of the jetties. This 80-ton salvage tool was sunk in 60' of water. (Sealab I, the first manned saturation habitat of the Navy, has been taken up recently.) Spearfishers especially relish a huge metal cylinder known as the **Quonset Hut** which is 90' deep for, despite the poor clarity, big jacks and snapper can be found.

In addition, the Navy operates two huge laboratory structures known as **Stage I** and **Stage II** that are similar in appearance to oil rigs. Technically you can't dive them without official permission, but on occasion dive stores conduct tours. Stage II, 50' deep, can be seen from the beach. The placement of a **PCMI barge** just west of Stage II has enhanced fish life in the area.

Stage I has better fish life since it's 11 miles offshore and at a depth of 107'. Natural reefs in the area as well as a **deep barge** nearby lure many fish.

In 1977, the Navy submerged a **T-33 trainer jet** near Stage II, only to find later that someone had moved the plane secretly. After wasting much time and money on fruitless searches, the Navy offered a reward through local dive shops to anyone who could turn up the small jet. Finally the culprit confessed the new location anonymously, and the Navy, in its haste to return the jet to its original location, flipped it belly-up. It now lies in 50' of water and is a great checkout dive.

But for most people diving Panama City, shipwrecks are the highlight. The 65' tug *Commander* was sunk in 1980, and has become very popular. The wreck presents a dramatic sight, upright and intact on a hard sand bottom. Marine life loves the many porthole openings. Sand dollars speckle the hard sand floor.

The *Tarpon* lies at 92', with its hull broken and the boilers, gears, valves, and pipes spilling out from the interior. Beer bottles can be found scattered around the wreckage, since the *Tarpon* was a coastal freighter carrying a load of empties to

Panama City in 1937, when a hurricane gusted up and caused the 160' vessel to founder 9-1/2 miles west of the jetties. Many tropicals, including spotted drums and a resident spotted moray, and good gamefish make the *Tarpon* a perennial favorite.

Although the **Grey Ghost** has only been under since 1978, the wreck's already become a fish haven. Clouds of baitfish disorient you as you descend. Amberjack and grouper stop by for the easy pickings. The 105'-long intact tug rests on its starboard side 105' down. Since the doors have been removed, you can enter the wheelhouse. Lying 22 miles offshore on the edge of a natural reef covered with soft corals and large sponges, the *Grey Ghost* gives you an opportunity to see virtually any marine life in the Gulf.

But for real open ocean Gulf diving a visit to the **Empire Mica** is essential. Recently, charters have begun running from Indian Pass (12 miles south of St. Joe) and this has knocked the time out to 2-1/2 hours. It's well worth it. History seems tangible because of the presence of this huge ship. The *Empire Mica* was a 465' British tanker returning home in 1942 from her maiden voyage to Texas when a German submarine, lying 23 miles off Cape San Blas, sent two torpedoes into her port side. A lifeboat full of 14 crewmen was rescued that night but the rest of the crew of 47 died.

Visiting the wreck today is an awesome experience. Since the freighter rests almost intact on the bottom at 110', you have to carefully watch your bottom time. You can't take the entire ship in during the few minutes you have, so you come away with a hazy, surreal image of a huge shape looming more than 60' up from the bottom, surrounded by thousands of tiny flashing streaks of silver, and inhabited by thick-lipped grouper with staring eyes and immense mouths. Barracuda, snapper, schools of huge amberjacks, and bull sharks all visit the *Mica* regularly. The huge prop has been taken up and now resides at a Panama City restaurant.

From Apalachee Bay almost to Clearwater is a vast meadow of turtle grass, starting right offshore, and extending out for miles into a gradually sloping shallow plain. Because of this monotonous (but immensely productive) field, there isn't any offshore diving to speak of until you reach the St. Petersburg/Tampa area.

HUDSON TO ST. PETERSBURG

The Tampa area is probably the most overlooked diving region in the state. A vast underwater plain is broken occasionally by natural rock outcroppings, artificial reefs, and numerous shipwrecks, usually making a Loran-C equipped boat necessary, with some long rides to the favorite sites.

The fiddler crab of the Atlantic is so well-timed in its daily color changes that, even when transplanted to the Pacific, it maintains its internal clock and changes colors in correspondence to the tides on the East Coast.

Unpredictable weather, especially in winter, causes widely varying clarity which can range from inches to 60', averaging 20' and improving the farther offshore you go. To compensate for the sometimes difficult conditions, the southern Gulf Coast has some of the most exciting fish life around. Huge jewfish, barracuda, jacks, grouper, cobia, kingfish, and many others swarm around the dive sites with a density few other areas can match. For adventurous divers, the Tampa Bay area offers what only a few other spots still do — the chance to dive with incredible populations of big fish on remote reefs and wrecks.

Around Hudson, the favorite diving area is known as **Turtle Reef**. This limestone ledge ranges from 1-5' in height, protruding up from a 35'-deep sand bottom. Many types of hard and soft corals decorate the ledge. Starfish and sea urchins, along with stone crabs and horse conch, crawl around the rock, while tropical fish, pinfish, sheephead, grouper, and schools of baitfish swarm around the ledge top.

Just to the south, out of New Port Richey, artificial reefs and plane wrecks are favorite sites. **PS Reef** is composed of four 200' barges and concrete culverts lying 11 miles offshore. **CO Reef**, 15 miles out of New Port Richey, has augmented the small natural ledges in the area with a broken barge. Like PS Reef, fish life is healthy.

A short trip three miles off Anclote Key gives you the chance to see an intact WWII **Hellcat**, resting on a flat sand bottom 25' down. Further out, visit the wrecks of a **tug** and **barge** lying within 1/4-mile of each other at 85'. They went down together in high seas about 30 miles offshore. Now they shelter gamefish, enormous nurse sharks, and milling tropicals, including filefish.

The most popular live bottom off Clearwater is **Masthead Ledge**, 16 miles offshore. Running for more than a mile, this ledge juts up from the flat seafloor for eight feet. Craggy relief provides homes for marine life, especially shells like helmets. Sea whips, sponges, and fire coral cover the rock ledge. The scattered wreckage of a **B-29 plane** lies nearby at a depth of 50'. Eight-foot barracuda, giant cobia, and sea turtles are some of the more memorable creatures reported in the area.

But Clearwater also has good sea life on its shallow, close-in artificial reefs, too. **Clearwater Reef**, only 3-1/2 miles offshore, is composed of tires and rubble. **Dunedin Reef** has concrete culverts and some natural rock bottom; gamefish thrive at both sites.

But it's at **G Marker** that you have the best chance of seeing the big ones close to shore. Sea turtles, jewfish, and even nurse sharks sometimes cruise this area of 5'-high scattered rock reefs. Located less than five miles offshore, depth ranges from 25-30'.

One of the most famous wrecks on the Gulf Coast is the ***USCG Blackthorn***, 27 miles from St. John's Pass. This 108' cutter was hit broadside in the winter of 1981 by a freighter. Twenty-two Guardsmen died in the accident. The wreck was moved to create one of the best dive sites around, with weekly charters usually making the trip out to the site. The vessel top starts at 30' and the hull sits on a sandy bottom at 80'. Thousands of baitfish swarm around the wrecked cutter in clouds so thick they're disorienting. Penetrating the *Blackthorn* can be hazardous, and requires wreck diving experience, although all companionway doors have been removed.

Within 1/2-mile of the *Blackthorn*, rock juts above the seabed in a couple of spots. At **Table Top**, a wide plateau lifts several feet above the sand. At **The Caves**, a ledge 7-8' high interrupts the flat sand seabed 80' down.

A variety of artificial reefs off St. Petersburg keeps divers busy. In the 35' depth range, **Treasure Island Reef** and **St. Petersburg Reef** are the favorites. Tropical fish flit around the old tires and culverts at each site. For maximum depths of 60', visit **Mecco's Barge** or **Doc's Barge**. Near Doc's Barge, 16 miles offshore, is a bit of rock relief to break the sand monotony. **South Jack Hole** uplifts about 8'. Undercuts in the rock hide everything from shovelnose lobster to black grouper.

At the even bigger **Lobster Ledges**, only 12 miles offshore, a ridge of 12' high extends for 1/2-mile. Schools of angelfish, big lobster, and even a sea turtle now and then are attracted to the relief in the otherwise flat scenery.

A wreck of fairly recent origin is the ***Gunsmoke***. She went down in a cloud of mystery in 1977, leaving behind several floating bales of marijuana as tantalizing clues. The intact vessel bears more evidence of her former respectable life as a shrimper, with nets still hanging above the decks. Jewfish sometimes hide deep in the hold, and barracuda are usually seen around the rigging. Lying 24 miles offshore at a depth of 85', the 65' vessel lists slightly to starboard.

For big wreck excitement, dive the ***Mexican Pride***, 37 miles out of St. Petersburg. The more than 200'-long wreck rests upright at a depth of 120'. It's 80' down just to the top deck. Both the depth and the occasional strong currents call for experienced divers, cautious of bottom time.

The incredible throngs of fish around the *Pride* have to be seen to be believed. Huge schools of mackerel, jacks, and cuda cruise the water above the ship. Inside, your lights might startle grouper and red snapper. Jewfish here are big enough to scare you. Shells like spiny oyster, hairy triton, and tulips are common on the wreck. The superstructure is gone, but openings allow experienced divers some exploration into the vessel in the limited amount of bottom time.

Big Jack Hole is almost as far out as the *Mexican Pride*. Try to visualize a sink like Catfish Hotel sitting right in the middle of the ocean floor and you get a good idea of this dive. The "big" in Big Jack refers to the size of the jacks that swim around it, not the size of the hole — it's only 25' across. Since the top of the hole starts at 110', be a deep diver before you try this one.

BRADENTON TO NAPLES

Along this stretch of southwest Florida, dives vary from shallow, murky trips after stone crab claws, to expeditions out to deep water where a lone jewfish is ho-hum — it's the families of 20 or so that startle you!

A 100-yard swim off the Bradenton beach leads to the remains of the **Molasses Barge**, 20' down on a sand bottom. Conch, olives, and sand dollars are common around the old barge, which is easy to find since the bow breaks the surface. Fire coral thrives here and at nearby **Third Pier**. This reef, only 200 yards off the beach, loses all clarity on a west wind since it too is a shallow dive.

Barracuda Hole, about 10 miles out of Bradenton, is a series of rock ledges that drop from 40-50'. Corals and shells provide good subjects for photography, while red snapper, hogfish, and other edible species attract spearfishers.

The Gullies are usually the second dive after Barracuda Hole. A little deeper (maximum 60'), this rocky area provides lots of cover for grouper and lobster.

Around Venice, divers look for fossil sharks' teeth off the **Venice Public Beach**, and usually find them. **The Rocks** require a walk of more than a mile, and since depth over the flat rocks doesn't pass 18', snorkeling is preferred. Rocky bottom extends from just west of the Venice Fishing Pier out for five miles. Called **Venice Ledges**, the outer edge of this area drops to 50'. Clarity at all these sites averages 5' due to the runoff from the Peace River.

The **Peace River** itself, near Arcadia, lures confirmed artifact and fossil hunters who grope around (with gloves) in the soft mud at the bottom of the dark shallow river to turn up huge fossil sharks' teeth and arrowheads. Clarity varies from nothing to 2'. No diving is done between June and October, due as much to the abundant alligators as to the rainy season.

Go 30 miles offshore to find excellent clarity — it takes that long for the sediment from the Peace to settle out. The ***Bay Ronto*** provides a good excuse. This 400' freighter went down in a storm back in 1919. Now the hull rests upside-down at a depth of 110'. Experienced wreck divers enter the huge hull. Photographers love the wreck, but not as much as they did before the propeller was removed. Spearfishers go ape over the big jacks. Tourists love the jewfish lurking inside.

Around Port Charlotte, the best diving is found at Boca Grande on Gasparilla Island. Both the **Causeway Bridge** and the adjacent **railroad trestle** offer good spearing and crabbing. Depth doesn't surpass 25', and clarity is usually about 5' on the slack before high tide.

Rock ledges off 17th Street in Boca Grande and **jetties** off the beach on the Gulf side of the island are easy, shallow dives that offer little clarity but many stone crabs.

For better visibility, go offshore. Five miles off the north end of Boca Grande, at the wreck of the *Cathy II*, clarity can be more than 40'. The broken up shrimper lies at 42' depth.

Ft. Myers divers head out about 7 miles to **The Coral Gardens** where small fish swarm and sponges and soft coral grow thick. Depth averages 25'. Two miles further out, **The Mud Hole** is actually a small fissure 40' down issuing enough fresh water to create a boil on the surface. Besides enjoying the surreal wavy effect of fresh and salt mixing, this dive offers a good opportunity to see big jewfish or sea turtles.

Further offshore, divers visit **W Reef**. A wide area of rocky bottom 50' deep supports soft corals, shells, and gamefish. At the **Pinnacles**, 22 miles off the coast, spires more reminiscent of California rise 15' or more off the seabed. Depth averages 55'. The battered hull of a 60'-long **minesweeper**, 25 miles out, sits on a flat bottom 70' down. Grouper, snapper, and occasional spearfishers visit the wreck.

Just south of Ft. Myers is **Punta Rasa**, where the old Sanibel Island ferry used to dock. Before that, the site served as anchorage for Civil War vessels and even Spanish galleons, so the wealth of artifacts found spans the centuries. Depths go to 20', and clarity may hit 10' in winter but is commonly below 5'.

Twenty miles to the south is **Wiggins Pass State Park**, where you can enjoy an easy dive over a shallow reef 100 yards offshore. There won't be any clarity at all unless you go on high tide, but on those occasions when it is decent you might see tropicals, small octopus, or squid around the rocky, coral-covered reef. Complete bath facilities and a lifeguard make this a good area for novice divers, and beautiful shell-covered beaches will entertain the non-divers.

Naples, on the west end of Alligator Alley, is the headquarters for diving some wild areas of the southern Gulf. **The Gully**, 40 miles offshore, is the name for a couple of ledges that protrude 2-8' above the surrounding flat sand bottom, 80' down. Since these ledges run for miles, some areas are still packed with both red and black grouper. Huge jewfish roam the bottom in packs, and divers pet the 400-lb. monsters. Enormous schools of snapper and grunts can be so thick they block surface light. Arrow crabs, flaming clams, helmets, and a large variety of tropicals can be seen around the rocks, bedecked with many types of sponges and soft corals. Sea turtles also commonly visit this oasis in the midst of the sand desert, where clarity ranges from a low of 25-60'.

The wreckage of a **minesweeper** 11 miles out of Naples is so broken up that the main reason divers visit is to take advantage of the abundant snapper and other

In the strictest sense, plankton ("that which is made to wander") includes not only the microscopic animals and plants, but also such giants as ocean sunfish (Mola mola) which have been hit several times by ships as they drift passively on the surface.

gamefish around the 45'-deep wreck. A **crater** in the ocean floor about 22 miles northwest of Naples forms a 15'-deep depression that fish seem to love, as do spearfishers.

Another wild dive out of Naples that takes Loran C and an experienced skipper to find is called either **The Volcano**, or **The Hole**. It lies 30 miles offshore. As soon as you drop out of the boat you know this will be an unforgettable experience. A flat sand bottom 70' down opens suddenly into an eerie spring mouth of more than 85' across. As you float in the throat of the hole, you can see ledges lining the sides of the hourglass-shaped hole. Freshwater emergence can't be detected, but something draws fish. Schools of amberjack, spadefish, and lookdowns; snapper, grouper, jewfish, turtles, cobia, pompano, and tropicals all visit the hole regularly. Since this is in the middle of nowhere, surrounded by miles of open ocean, and the lure of great depth exists (estimates of the Volcano's depth vary from 210' to more than 250'), careful safety measures are essential, and buddy teams must closely watch bottom time.

Nearby rock ledges and a **houseboat wreck** four miles to the north also lure marine life. Families of jewfish have taken over the houseboat, providing an unmatched thrill.

Recently there have also been some **artificial reefs** created off Naples. The closest, just two miles off the fishing pier, is made of tons of concrete rubble. Clarity averages 5-10' but is best in summer, when it reaches as much as 20'. The other reefs, also of concrete rubble, lie from 2-5 miles off Marcos Island, and, like the one off Naples, they are shallow — 30' maximum. Marine life is already starting to move in, and time will tell if divers will soon be able to see the exciting fish Naples is famous for this close to shore.

INLAND

Nowhere in the world has better freshwater diving than the state of Florida, where you'll find dozens of gin-clear springs in which standard descriptions of visibility become meaningless because it seems you can see forever.

Nowhere else in the world are there as many springs, connected by such an intricate system of underwater passageways. Either of Florida's two largest springs could supply a city of 1,000,000 with water, while 17 of the smaller springs could each supply a city of 500,000. Florida contains the world's biggest spring, Silver Spring, pouring out over 500 million gallons of water a day (mgd). And Florida contains the world's deepest spring, Wakulla, where water gushes from a cavernous mouth over 185' down. Florida also contains almost 1/4 of the first-magnitude (releasing more than 100 cubic feet a second) springs in the country.

FLORIDA INLAND

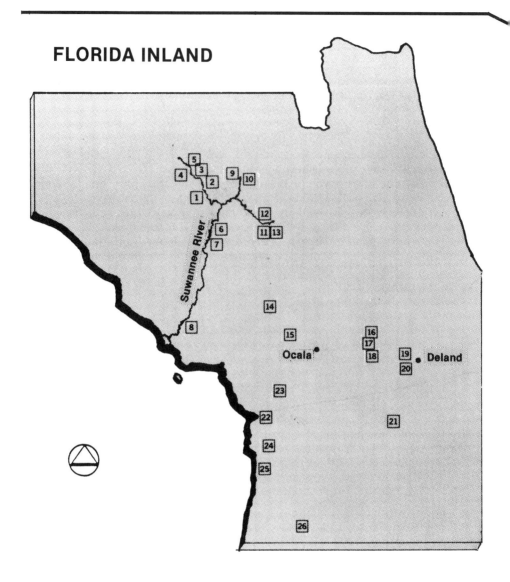

FLORIDA INLAND

Alexander Springs 18
Big Spring 22
Blue Grotto 14
Blue Hole Spring 10
Blue Springs 13,20,24
Blue Spring, Lafayette County 4
Catfish Corner 22
Catfish Hotel 8
Challenge Sink 3
Charles Spring 5
Chassahowitzka River 24
Cistern Sink 3
Crab Creek Springs 24
Crystal River 22

Crystal Springs 26
Devil's Eye 11
Devil's Punch Bowl 24
Dogwood Spring 11
Forty Fathom Sink 15
Gator Hole 22
Ginnie Springs 11
Grand Canyon Spring 22
Hart Spring 7
Hospital Hole 25
Houseboat Springs 24
Ichetucknee River 9-10
Ichetucknee Spring 9

Idiot's Delight	22	Rainbow River	23
July Spring	12	Rainbow Springs	23
Juniper Creek	17	Rock Bluff Springs	6
Juniper Springs	17	Rock Springs	21
King's Bay	22	Royal Spring	2
Little Blue Spring	13	Salt Springs	16
Little River Spring	2	Shark Sink	22
Manatee Spring State Park	8	Silver Glen Springs	16
Mullet's Gullet	22	Snake Sink	4
Naked Spring	13	Sun Spring	7
Olson Sink	3	Three Sisters	22
Orange Grove Sink	3	Troy Springs	1
Otter Spring	7	Uncle John's Sink	24
Peacock Springs	3	Weeki Wachee River	25
Ponce de Leon Springs	19	Wekiwa Springs State Park	21
Pothole Sink	3	Yana Spring	4

All these statistics are due to the enormous aquifer of fresh water that underlies the state and boils up in the form of springs, where water temperatures rarely vary more than 5° from an average of 72°. It's hard to think of a more inviting dive than floating effortlessly in one of these jewels of the woods.

The variety of diving in the springs is amazing. You can content yourself with fast-action snorkeling down the spring runs, or watch for fish or manatees in the clear water, or explore the caverns, or search for fossils under the white sand.

Florida is one of the premier fossil areas of the country. Giant sharks' teeth have been found in the same spring with fossils of prehistoric mastodons and sloths. There's also great relic hunting, since everyone from primitive man to the Spanish explorers has congregated around the springs.

Unfortunately, few other areas contain as great a potential for disaster as do many of the Florida springs, for nowhere else is the line between a novice dive and an advanced dive so hazily drawn. At most places, you know before you ever enter the water that surge, or currents, or depth limits the diving to the experienced. But in many springs, a distance of only a few feet separates an easy dive from a cave dive where free ascent to the surface is impossible.

Obviously, diving into the innards of the earth shouldn't be undertaken as a lark, but, strangely enough, many people who are totally untrained in cave diving have been tempted to explore back just a few more feet ... and the results are almost invariably disastrous. Only proper training and equipment can make cave diving safe. For the untrained, diving beyond the realm of natural light is a recipe for disaster. For more information on cave diving, read the article at the end of this section.

INLAND — Panhandle Area

With several large and popular springs located conveniently close to northern states, the Florida panhandle rates as a top vacation area for divers.

Morrison Spring, nearly five miles south of the town of Ponce de Leon, is one of the favorite dives in the state. The huge spring basin, surrounded by cypress trees, dwarfs even commercial springs like Weeki Wachee, so it can handle large numbers of divers well. The first cavern entrance opens up at 30' to a well-lighted, horizontal room. You can clearly see the surface, and you can look down into a smaller, mouth-shaped opening at a depth of 50'. Forcing yourself against the flow of the water will lead you into a large, very dimly-lit room that spirals down to 90'. Formerly, the cave continued past this point, but it was dynamited in 1962 after many divers had drowned.

Since the run to the warm and muddy Choctawhatchee River is only 1/2-mile long, it's easy for high water in the river to back up and destroy Morrison's clarity. Inquire about water conditions first, especially in spring. Dressing rooms, air, and primitive camping are available.

No scuba is allowed at **Ponce de Leon Spring**, just outside the town of the same name. Snorkeling is allowed, and that's all you'll need to appreciate this lovely little spring, since depth never goes below 15'. An underwater natural bridge at the base of the pool keeps things interesting. The state operates the spring and the adjacent forest as a day-use area, and recently encircled the spring with concrete retaining walls. On hot weekends, local people use the spring and forest trails heavily. There is a bathhouse and picnic area.

Vortex Blue Spring, four miles north of Ponce de Leon, is another large, commercially operated spring. The spring pool has a diameter of 200', and the run flows for over four miles, with excellent snorkeling. Training platforms have been installed 20' down in the pool itself. At 50', you enter the mouth of the cavern into a large room, still lit from the surface, where schooling bass, redhorse, and eels often swim. Experienced divers can continue down a garage-sized tunnel with a safety rail for another 100 yards until, at 115' depth, a steel grate blocks any further penetration. Water flows from the spring at a rate of 25 mgd, and ripples the white sand floor. A dive store, camping, and a dormitory make Vortex an easy and convenient dive.

Holmes Creek, to the east of Ponce de Leon, is one of the favorite runs in the area for relic hunters. In addition, at least three springs near its banks provide hours of entertainment for divers.

At **Cypress Spring**, some of the clearest water anywhere boils out from a series of springs at the rate of 55 mgd to create a fish-filled pool 25' deep, and at least 155' across. The run goes 1/2-mile to Holmes and is very shallow. **Becton Spring**, nearby, flows from crevices in the rocks 35' down to create a beautiful pool of 100' diameter, with a shallow, plant-filled run to the creek. And **Blue Spring** has a little cave 35' down in its small, cypress-lined pool.

Absolutely no trespassing or diving is now allowed at Gadsden Spring.

Further east of Marianna, **Merritt's Mill Pond** attracts all divers. The pond originates in a large, bluff-lined headspring, named **Blue Spring**, commercially operated with a bathhouse and picnic tables. Only snorkeling is allowed in Blue Spring. You can use scuba in the rest of the pond but, since average depth is less than 18', it isn't essential. The bright sand bottom is covered with aquatic plants and darting fish. The pond is about five miles long, ending at a dam on Hwy. 90. Since the water is continually moving through, it remains clear and cold and clean.

Several small caves and ledges can be found in the banks. **Twin Caves**, just 1/2-mile downstream, has two openings in the rock, about 20' apart, that connect to form a large room where depth reaches 35'. Since natural light enters, this is a safe spot for trained cavern divers.

At **Gator Spring**, you'd better be a cave diver, as lights and a line are necessary. The partially air-filled cave takes a sharp left bend and loses all surface light. Deep silt covers the floor of the 5-10'-deep run from the cave. And at **Shangri-la Spring**, you need to be accustomed to tight places, since the shaft down to the cave has a diameter of only two feet.

Below the dam at Hwy. 90, the speed picks up as Merritt's Mill Pond transforms into a narrow spring run down to the **Chipola River**. This river is a favorite hunting ground for relic collectors. **Bozell Springs** are a series of small, shallow springs found about a mile up the Chipola from Florida Caverns State Park.

Florida Caverns State Park, located just north of Marianna, contains some of Florida's few dry caverns. Besides the spectacular pin cushions, soda straws, flowstones, and translucent draperies of the small caverns, the park also allows diving in **Blue Hole**. The spring has a beautiful run down to the Chipola River through a thick woods of magnolia and beech trees that seem more reminiscent of the Appalachians to the north than they do of the more tropical vegetation that predominates in other sections of Florida.

INLAND — Tallahassee Area

Diving around Tallahassee is mainly done in either beautiful clear rivers like the Wacissa or St. Mark's, where a canoe will lead you into prime fossil grounds surrounded by primeval woods, or in steep, silty sinks that present challenges to cave divers.

Anyone who is interested in springs should make **Wakulla Spring** their first stop in the Tallahassee area. Even though the well-run nature sanctuary (complete with beautiful old hotel and four-star restaurant) allows no scuba in the spring, Wakulla will be unforgettable. It is one of the deepest and clearest springs in the world. You can snorkel or ride a glass-bottomed boat to get an idea of its immensity. Through the 100'-wide mouth of the cavern, over 183 million gallons of water pour each day. Since the cavern mouth drops down to a depth of nearly 200', it is beyond the realm of the sport diver. However, in the 1950's, a group of divers explored the immense spring, penetrating a distance of 950' at depths that went below 240'. On this incredible journey, they discovered the fossilized bones of mastodons, bears, camel, deer, and giant ground sloths. At one point, the divers were at a depth of 235' when they entered a cathedral-sized room whose ceiling soared over their heads for 170', finally ending in a fissure only 60' below the surface.

The beautiful **Wakulla River** is a great canoe-snorkel trip (it was the setting for the old Johnny Weismuller *Tarzan* movies). Enter below the U.S. 219 bridge to skim over a white sand bottom only 8-10' deep, with relics and fossils hidden amidst the thick vegetation.

St. Mark's River, nearby, at Newport, is strictly for the fossil hunter. This river, averaging 15-18' deep, has one of the oldest histories in the state. Spanish ship-building yards from the 16th century supposedly operated along St. Mark's. Along with Spanish relics, divers have found artifacts from the Civil War and early trading vessels, as well as fossilized bison bones. Residences surround the headspring near Tallahassee.

The **Wacissa River**, just south of the little town of the same name, is a favorite place to combine a canoe and snorkel trip. A six-hour canoe trip down the 15 miles of navigable river will take you through some of the most beautiful and primitive country in Florida, where paper companies own the densely forested banks. At least twelve springs feed the upper mile and a half of river, including **Blue**, **Buzzard Log**, and **Big Spring**, which is the one most suitable for scuba. A park at the head of the river has a boat launch and picnic tables, and camping is available at several sites along the banks.

Of the many sinkholes just south of Tallahassee, **Osgood Sink** stands out as the most interesting site for cavern divers. Beautiful limestone cliffs line the sink and contain a fossilized history of life in the area. Even the concentric age rings from ancient trees have been preserved in the rock walls. Depths at Osgood reach 105', with a large ledge entrance on the east wall leading back 100' into a cavern. Brim, turtles, and freshwater eels are all commonly seen at Osgood.

At least 15 other sinkholes cluster within a few miles of each other just south of Tallahassee. **Oak Ridge Blue Sink** has two caves with limited exploration within its 100' depths. **Fish Sink** is actually a spring-syphon with an advanced cave dive in the syphon end. **River Sinks** is a combination of two sinks, upper and lower, although the lower sink is now on private land. Within upper River Sinks, use caution in the syphon on the south end of the pool, as current into the ground can be strong.

West Hole Sink also appeals mainly to longtime explorers of Florida springs. Entering the water at this sink can be difficult. Many fossils exist in the abnormally soft walls. You should refrain from touching the walls, as sections of them have broken away. A deep layer of silt on the bottom discourages going too deep. On the south side of the sink a large ledge opens back for 100'.

Other springs and sinks in the area include **Big Dismal Sink** (this sink just formed in the early 1900's), a large pit surrounded by steep walls where ropes are required to enter and exit from the water, and **Little Dismal Sink**, where a large cave extends for over 400' at a maximum depth of 60'. Promise and Go-Between Sinks are now closed to divers and posted no-trespassing.

INLAND — Suwannee River System

Branford is the headquarters for some of the finest freshwater diving in Florida, with one of the heaviest concentrations of springs anywhere in the world. Dozens of beautifully clear springs spangle the length of the Suwannee River like beads on a necklace. The Peacock Slough system alone contains close to 20 different outlets, all within 1-1/2 miles of each other! Little wonder that the Suwannee River springs are one of the most popular groups in Florida.

But even though many of the springs along the Suwannee are advanced cave dives, they all aren't. You don't have to be a cave diver to enjoy **Troy Springs**, one of the best springs around Branford for non-cavers to visit. Located five miles north of Branford on the west bank of the Suwannee, Troy is a very wide-mouthed pool that can accommodate many divers without losing its beautiful water clarity, thanks to its strong flow of 66 mgd. Rugged, almost vertical limestone walls cut back 15' under an overhang 60' deep. From there, the bottom slopes gradually to 80'. At the deepest point, water gushes forcefully from a small opening in the rocks.

For many people, the best part about Troy Springs is the run to the river. The wide run averages 6' deep and has a textured limestone bottom with crevices and small arches to explore. If you notice some old timbers lying in a pattern reminiscent of a ship's ribs in the sand near the river, don't disturb them. They're the remains of an old Suwannee River steamboat, the *Madison*, that was scuttled during the Civil War.

Also north of Branford, but on the opposite side of the river, are a couple of other interesting springs. **Royal Spring**, about 16 miles northwest of Branford, is surrounded by steep banks. A concrete apron with steps has been built for easy entry down to the 120'-wide pool. Underwater, a smooth bluff slopes to about 50', where spring water very slowly issues from a small and silty cave entrance that is not worth exploring. The spring has a short and shallow run to the Suwannee.

But **Little River Spring**, also on the east side of the Suwannee near Branford, has little to offer the non-cave diver. You need to be a certified cave or cavern diver even to enter the water at Little River, since the cave begins in only 10' of water and the basin itself has little of interest in the way of plants or fish.

For the advanced cave diver, though, Little River is one of Florida's most challenging dives. The small cave entrance slopes down to 60' where it veers off sharply to the left, losing all surface light. A permanent sign at this point reminds cavern divers not to go any further, because, around this turn, the cave drops to the 100' level, and leads into a maze of tunnels.

Many of the other springs on the Suwannee River are found clustered around the Peacock Slough, to the north of Branford, near Mayo. Besides being one of the most popular diving spots with cave divers in the world, Peacock also holds the distinction of being the longest explored underwater system anywhere. Over 20,000' of underwater passageways have been mapped in the Peacock Slough system. Any cave diver (must show proof of cave certification) attempting exploration of this surreal system of interconnecting underground passageways should obtain a detailed map of the system from the NSS Cave Diving Section, 10259 Crystal Springs Road, Jacksonville, FL, 32221.

Peacock Springs is a series of three springs that forms the headwaters of the slough. The slough itself provides excellent snorkeling through lilypads for 1-1/2 miles to the Suwannee. The first spring opens up at a depth of 18', with a large mouth providing access into the horizontal Blue Room. On the north wall of the cavern, a sign warns that a potentially dangerous cave system begins, and that cavern divers should turn back. Advanced cave divers slip through a crack, where they can either follow a corridor that leads 400' to an ascent up a narrow shaft into Pothole Sink, or investigate other sections (some of which are blind alleys) of the cave system. The other two openings in the slough are strictly advanced cave dives.

Pothole Sink is a small and narrow sink that has an unstable entrance through sand. Besides connecting with Peacock, Pothole also has a side tunnel that wanders underground for more than 1200' before coming out in a tunnel on the south side of **Olson Sink** at a depth of 70'. Of course, like the rest of this system, this dive is strictly for advanced cave divers, who have been trained to deal with situations like blackout where silt is so thick you can't see your own light in front of your face.

Other, even more difficult, cave dives in the system include **Challenge Sink**, a very small sink that only goes 10' deep, before an extremely narrow, silty, and confusing tunnel drops off the 70' depths and wanders away; and **Cisteen Sink**, where a cave opening starts only 10' down, and leads to a dangerous, silt-plagued room known as the Witches Kettle, and, from there, to who-knows-where, the bowels of the earth probably.

The waves breaking on the California coast in summer have often traveled more than 6000 miles from their origin in winter storms east of New Zealand.

Orange Grove Sink, a large sink in a beautiful wooded setting near Cisteen Sink, can be enjoyed by the diver with cavern training. Orange Grove, like many other of the slower-moving sinks and springs in the area, sometimes develops a heavy layer of tiny duckweed plants in summer months. This growth usually occurs only in the top 20', with clear blue water underlying it. In winter, the duckweed dies off, and surface clarity is again 100'.

Fifty feet down on the north wall, a cavern entrance opens up into an area, still fed by natural light, in which depths go from 60-100'. A small corridor at a depth of 70' leads back for 50' into a cave. (Only experienced cave divers should enter this corridor as it is beyond the realm of natural light.) The cave, known as the Coliseum, is 130' long and 60' wide, but in places the ceiling is only 25' above the floor. Since the clay floor silts easily, the Coliseum is subject to blackout.

Located just west of the Peacock System on the Suwannee River is **Blue Spring, Lafayette County,** which is actually a chain of three pools that share underground connections. The first basin is a small, beautiful spring pool with a maximum depth of 30' that lies at the base of a limestone cliff. A natural bridge bisects the short run to the Suwannee, and creates a long shallow pool called **Snake Sink.** Two caves open up within Snake. One leads back to Blue Springs, and the other cave entrance leads you to the third basin in the chain, **Yana Spring.** This sink, besides connecting with Snake, has another cave opening which leads into the Dome Room, known for its solution domes. From this room, advanced cave divers have explored more than 20,000' back into the Green Sink cave system, which ultimately connects to more than 15 different sinks.

Charles Spring, on the opposite side of the Suwannee farther upstream, offers a good chance to get off the beaten path, explore a small — 50' diameter — rustic spring, and practice up on freediving. Although a cave does open up 10' down in the pool, it is not frequented by cave divers due to its extreme siltiness and instability. The run to the Suwannee is the most appealing aspect of Charles, with two natural bridges that are fun to free-dive.

There are also several springs lining the east bank of the Suwannee River south of Branford. Reached most easily by canoe, these springs are wonderful places to stop and freedive. **Rock Bluff Springs** is surrounded by private property, so you can't set foot on the land around the wide spring basin. Water gushes out of a small cave 30' down. Since the cave is tight and the force of the water makes it difficult to enter, it is not a favorite site for cave divers. The 150'-long run to the river is more enjoyable, with mullet schooling amidst the cypress roots along the banks.

Other beautiful and shallow springs in the Wilcox area accessible by canoe or road include **Sun Spring** and **Hart Spring.** Located in Gilchrist County Park, Hart Spring has an area set aside for swimming and snorkeling, but no diving is allowed in the boil.

Catfish Hotel, in beautiful Manatee Springs State Park.

HENRY NICHOLSON

At **Otter Spring**, the run is beautiful and tree-shaded, but the spring itself was in a degraded condition when I last visited it, with bare dirt banks and high school kids fishing and throwing their beer cans in the water. The spring itself has two fissures in the rock, somewhat like the roots of a tooth, but clarity isn't the best due to the weak flow. Camping is available.

Two of the best dives along the entire Suwannee River are found on the downstream end, just north of Chiefland. At **Manatee Spring State Park**, a gorgeous large spring boils water out at a rate of 96 mgd. Beautiful green plants sway over white sand. Bluegill, brim, and other fish dart amongst the fronds. Snorkelers love the spring basin itself, with its limestone bluff dropping to 40'. Water pours out of a small cave entrance below the bluff with enough force to make entry into the cave from this outlet difficult. Once past the ledge, the flow slacks as you enter a huge room, which doesn't silt up because of the constant exchange of water. Walkways around the spring provide easy entrance and preserve plant life. Camping facilities are secluded, a snack bar and boat launch are available, and a full-service dive store is right at the entrance to the park.

Cavern and cave divers seek out **Catfish Hotel**, a sink on the other side of the picnic area at Manatee Park, which offers a great dive. Ignore the duckweed on the surface, as it's crystal clear a few feet down. At 40' down, a ledge entrance leads into a wide cavern that offers a safe site for cavern training. Beyond the cavern, you eventually enter a huge room crowded with fish — especially catfish of 1-10 lbs. Experienced cavers catch a ride on the current to emerge under the ledge at Manatee!

Diving (including cave diving) is encouraged if you're certified. Always inform the park ranger of your intent to dive. The Florida Park System has rules for cave diving. One of the most sensible prohibits anyone from carrying lights into a cave system unless the holder has a cave diving certification, thereby guaranteeing that only the trained will be able to proceed beyond the realm of natural light.

INLAND — Ichetucknee River

The unbelievably clear waters of **Ichetucknee Spring**, **Blue Hole Spring**, and other smaller side springs form the beautiful **Ichetucknee River**, one of the most popular rivers in the country. Florida has preserved nine named springs along with 3-1/2 miles of the river — more than half its length — in a pristine condition, together with 2250 acres of adjacent hardwoods and river swamp.

You can snorkel, canoe, or tube down the river for about three hours, ending at the park boundary at Hwy. 27. Or, you can take a shorter trip down only the upper river to the newly-opened access at Mill Pond Spring, or down the lower river from Mill Pond Spring to Hwy. 27. The primeval woods, the beautiful pure river, and the crystalline springs have become so popular that the state even operates a bus shuttle service in summer.

If you're the kind of person who finds solitude — or at least a semblance of it — necessary to enjoy a river, then you'd better plan on visiting Ichetucknee on a weekday in winter. On a rainy weekday in October, with the river mostly to yourself, it's hard to believe that the Ich could ever be wall-to-wall tubers, but on summer weekends, the park frequently meets its 3000-person limit before noon.

The credit for the still-pristine condition of the river, despite such heavy use, goes to the Florida State Park System, which guards this natural treasure vigilantly. The aquatic plants are most susceptible to damage from all the traffic, so take care everywhere on the Ichetucknee, and especially around the springs, not to uproot plant life. Ichetucknee, the headspring, bubbles out of a cavern ledge to fill a basin over 100' in diameter and 13' deep.

The second major spring on the river, **Blue Hole** (or Jug) is now closed, with a wire fence across the run. Formerly, it was a favorite dive but multiple drownings combined with destruction of plant life caused its closing. It may reopen at any time. The azure water, surrounded by huge old cypresses, pours with relentless force from a jug-shaped shaft. The shaft begins in only 12' of water and drops to a white sand bottom at a depth of 32'. A small corridor opens up on the south side of the shaft bottom, but the force of the flow makes penetration almost impossible. A wetsuit top is advisable year-round at Ichetucknee, since the water, like most Florida springs, averages 72°, and you'll likely be spending several hours watching the beautiful sandy bottom slide by. Hunting for relics and fossils is popular, as the area was the site for numerous Indian dwellings and a Spanish mission, and has also been popular with wildlife for at least 50 million years. Giant armadillos, beavers, and ground sloths were among the first to appreciate this region, which was once a coastal bayou. The portion of the Ichetucknee below Hwy. 27 is not included in the park. Although private property along this portion of the river restricts access, a wonderful 3-hr. trip can be made to the junction with the Santa Fe. The park closes at 8:00 pm, with no camping allowed. Rangers search all gear, checking for anything that might become litter.

INLAND — Santa Fe River

Some of the clearest water in the world can be found at the dive resort of **Ginnie Springs**. Divers from all over the country make Ginnie their headquarters for exploring inland Florida. It's easy to see why. Centrally located off I-75, just west of High Springs, Ginnie Springs contains six separate springs as well as 200 acres of cypress, pine, and oak woods bordering a two-mile section of the Santa Fe. Every facility a visiting diver could ask for has been provided, including hot showers, camping (with tent camping thoughtfully isolated along the river bank), and a full-service dive store offering courses in cavern and cave diving.

Cypress decks lead right to the basin of Ginnie Spring. As you walk up, you can see silvery bubbles escaping from a fissure in the 5'-deep limestone shelf that edges the basin. It then drops abruptly to a white sand floor, dotted with swaying eelgrass, at a depth of 20'. A horizontal mouth 6' across leads into a chamber

The mysticism of cavern diving is revealed at Ginnie Springs.

WES SKILES

307

almost 10' high and 30' wide. A permanent lifeline leads you down a gentle slope as this chamber then opens into the Cathedral, a large, sloping room that's 78' long, 72' wide, and 38' high. The room slants down to a maximum depth of 60', where a steel grating was placed years ago to block the entrance into two narrow tunnels. Surface light is still visible due to the bright sand floor, even though you're 114' away from the surface. Ginnie is an excellent place to practice cavern or cave diving skills safely, as the trained staff keeps close track of diving activity.

Certified cave divers find **Devil's Eye** to be a beautiful and challenging cave dive. Snorkelers and canoeists simply admire its beauty, awestruck. Devil's Eye really does look like an immense blue eye viewed from above. The "pupil" is an absolutely round shaft that opens up 6' down, and drops to 20'. On the north side, a mouth-shaped opening 3' high leads into a dark-walled room, the Devil's Dungeon. Mineral content in the water has stained the walls of the 20'-high room. Advanced cavers who don't mind tight spots squeeze through a tiny opening on the north end of the Dungeon. This leads into a tight corridor that goes under the river, widening to 10' and then narrowing again before a steep chimney finally allows you to rise into the daylight zone once more.

Other, smaller springs in the Ginnie Springs resort include **Dogwood Spring**, bordered by a cypress deck. Snorkeling is great in the beautiful pool and run, since depth never exceeds 12'. **July Spring**, across the river, has a short run to the Santa Fe, bordered by lily pads and schools of bream. The spring itself is only 15' deep, emerging from a narrow crevice.

The preponderance of springs in this area will make the normally brown-stained Santa Fe run clear in low water. The river contains an interesting assortment of large turtles, gar, and bass, usually found hiding amidst gnarled tree roots or lily pads. Relics and fossils can be spotted in cracks in the limestone floor, especially if you spend a little time fanning the silt.

The other popular site in the vicinity of High Springs is **Blue Spring**, also on the Santa Fe. This private campground and picnic area has a sign reading "No aqualung," but don't let that stop you from freediving this dramatic underwater scene. The spring pool drops 25' down rounded limestone bluffs to reveal water issuing from two small caverns forcefully enough to perpetually ripple the eelgrass. Yellow-spotted catfish lurk under the bluff, fins waving in the current. Within the crystalline water of the spring, hundreds of tame bream nibble bread crumbs from your hands. The setting is great for photography.

A boardwalk borders the 1500' run. Although the run is shallow enough that the grass will tickle as you pass by, it's worth doing to see the spooky border where the clear spring water meets the dark gloomy water of the Santa Fe. Fish love the junction. Two smaller adjacent springs, **Naked Spring** and **Little Blue Spring**, are also fun to explore.

INLAND — Ocala Area

Twenty miles northwest of Ocala, near the town of Williston, is **Blue Grotto**. This privately owned and operated cavern dive can be visited by reservation only. Tom McQuarrie, the owner, is a certified scuba instructor. He leads visitors on tours of the cavern, which has underwater guide lines, an air bell, equipment rentals, rough camping, and hot showers. **Forty Fathom Sink**, eleven miles northwest of Ocala, is operated by Hal Watts, especially for deep training.

Salt Springs, 28 miles northeast of Ocala in the Ocala National Forest, is a commercially operated spring 100' in diameter, and offers fine snorkeling down a 5-mile run to Lake George. Heavy eelgrass growth, many small ledges, and abundant mullet and crabs make the basin and run interesting. Salt Springs is an artesian spring that derives its slight salt content from dissolved sediments in the underlying rock layer. Snorkeling equipment is available for rental.

Another fine snorkeling area is found at **Silver Glen Springs**, on the west side of Lake George. This first-magnitude spring is so large that its 1/2-mile run to the lake is classified as a navigable waterway. The pool, 150' in diameter, drops down a "natural well" to open into a small cave, but scuba diving in the spring itself is not allowed. Snorkeling alone is very rewarding, with bright creamy sand, thriving tame fish, and thick eelgrass beds. In addition, divers have found many relics from the 400-year old Indian shell mounds in the area. Camping, cabins, and boat rentals are available.

In 1932, the Civilian Conservation Corps dug out a tiny sand-choked pit, circled it with concrete, and thereby created one of the most popular National Recreation Areas in the country. **Juniper Springs**, just south of Silver Glen Spring in the Ocala National Forest, doesn't allow scuba, but snorkelers are thick in the 100'-wide, clear pool. Camping, with isolated sites for tents, is available.

The run, **Juniper Creek**, makes a fine snorkel trip below Hwy. 19 (you'll be fined for entering the water above this point), winding through crystalline water over several boils in the white sand. Beautiful tropical forest, including the rare needle palm, lines the banks all the way down to Lake George. Canoe rentals are available.

If snorkeling a spring run isn't enough for you, then visit nearby **Alexander Springs**, where scuba is allowed. Water of 74° pours out of several springs in a chasm 27' down, with enough force to create a hump on the surface. A sandy swimming beach fringes one side of the 200'-diameter pool, while lily pads and cypress trees creep into the water on the other side.

Both sexes of green sea turtles sometimes spend their days basking in the sun on Hawaiian beaches. This behavior has been observed in no other species of sea turtle, anywhere in the world.

Evening dives around the lily pads give you glimpses of hiding fish, including enormous schools of mullet and bream, and the bass and small gators that prey on them. Alexander Spring Creek flows almost 15 miles to the St. Johns River, but take-outs on the creek allow you to snorkel for as little as one hour, or go all the way in four to five hours. Canoe traffic can be heavy.

The **Ponce de Leon Springs**, eight miles north of Deland, were seized from the local Indians by Don Juan Ponce de Leon in the 16th century, who thought he'd found the legendary fountain of youth. Although they've been closed to diving for many years, they are again open to scuba, but absolutely no cave diving is permitted. The 170'-diameter pool is enclosed by concrete walls and drops to a single cave opening at 35'. Since you can't enter the cave, the favorite activity by far at the springs is searching the bottom for relics. Divers have turned up Indian artifacts like pottery bowls, fossils, including many sharks' teeth, and Spanish relics, but they are still searching for the legendary Spanish treasure supposedly abandoned there.

The treasure at yet another **Blue Springs**, this one just southwest of Deland, isn't Spanish. Rather, it's manatees, for Blue Springs is one of the best places to watch these huge sea cows. This park was acquired by the state primarily for the purpose of protecting the critically endangered beasts, who have been driven almost to extinction in Florida due to collisions with motorboats and habitat degradation. Scuba and snorkeling are allowed, although strict diving regulations are necessary to protect these sirenians.

The spring, one of Florida's 17 first-magnitude springs, is the largest in the St. Johns River basin, with a flow of 121 mgd. The basin, only 85' in diameter, conceals a funnel-shaped shaft that begins 15' down, dropping to 50', where it narrows drastically and angles sharply to 125'. Water pours out of the shaft with such force that it produces a boil on the water surface. To push yourself down the funnel against the velocity of the water requires an experienced diver. The run to the St. Johns, only half a mile long, is a great place to search for sharks' teeth, marine fossils, or just watch the abundant fish. Camping and a general store are available.

Although the majority of people who visit **Wekiwa Springs State Park**, east of Apopka, go to swim in the headspring, the park also offers 6000 acres of river swamps, hardwood hammocks, sandy pine woods, and sinkhole-pocked lowlands. No scuba is allowed but the spring is interesting enough to snorkel, with 75° water emerging from fissures 20' down a kidney-shaped pool. Fossilized sand dollars dot the blue limestone walls. Depth at most of the pool averages less than 10'. The spring run is one of the main headwaters of the Wekiwa River.

The flow issuing from **Rock Springs**, at nearby Kelly Park, is another main headwater of the Wekiwa River. This spring is unusual for Florida, because it emerges from an air-filled cavern at the base of a limestone bluff. Access into the spring cave has been blocked by the installation of a permanent grating, so the only activity left is to snorkel the 1-1/2-mile run to the Wekiwa. The bright blue water, filled with fish and plant life, provides a fascinating run.

INLAND — Gulf Coast

Known for broad, shallow, spring-fed rivers surrounded by subtropical scenery with a profusion of wildlife unmatched in Florida, the Gulf Coast offers spectacular and easy diving, both for those who want luxurious accommodations, as well as for back-country explorers.

Without a doubt, **Crystal River** is one of the best freshwater dives in the world. Thousands of divers will attest to the fantastic diving found in **King's Bay**, where eight famous springs belch out 72° water year-round, attracting an amazing congregation of fish, and groups of as many as 40 manatees. Since weather and tides don't affect the springs, Crystal River has attained the reputation of being a foolproof vacation center where you're always guaranteed at least 100' visibility.

But by far the most popular diving season is from November to March, when manatees make their way out of the cold Gulf to spend the winter munching on aquatic vegetation around the warm freshwater springs. Since Crystal River has one of the largest herds of sea cows left in existence, it has been declared a manatee sanctuary, with stringent laws designed to protect the huge mammals. Swimming is illegal. Since boats are necessary to visit the springs (Big Spring is just a few dozen yards offshore) rentals are necessary. All of King's Bay is an idle speed zone. Boat drivers are cautioned to watch out for manatees. Since they are likely to loll just beneath the surface, they have often been unintentionally struck and killed by propellers.

The other major law that divers need to be aware of regarding the manatee is the one that prescribes a maximum penalty of a year in prison and a $20,000 fine for harassing or disturbing a sea cow. While it is human nature to swim after a manatee for a better look, that does constitute harassment, since the guileless creatures can be chased into water too cold for them. And since they're often afraid of scuba, snorkeling presents the best method of seeing one fairly close-up. Accepted manatee protocol permits you to swim near the beast, letting it decide whether to approach you or not. If it swims away, don't follow. Often they'll swim up to investigate you.

The most popular of the springs flowing into King's Bay is **Big Spring**, also called **Diver's** or **King's Spring**. It is located just off the south side of Banana Island. You anchor in 5' of water surrounding the spring. A rocky basin with a diameter of 75' drops vertically to 30' where you'll find two separate openings yawning back into a cavern. You can penetrate into the cavern to a depth of 60', until piles of jumbled boulders mark the bottom.

The CIA distilled Gonyaulax catenella, *the organism responsible for the deadly red tides along the Northwest Coast, and used it on assassination darts.*

The half-moon toenails on the manatee's front flippers are evidence that they are related to elephants.

Ethereal views of light slicing through the crystal water and illuminating the jagged silhouettes of the cliff walls make Big Spring an underwater photographer's paradise. Besides the freshwater fish like catfish, bass, bluegill, and bream, you can see many saltwater varieties that are attracted to the warm water, like mangrove snapper, jacks, mullet, redfish, sheephead, and even occasional snook or tarpon. Since the fish are easily approached, spearing is illegal here and throughout King's Bay.

Mullet's Gullet, just east of Big Spring, is another favorite dive of photographers. A series of small springs ripples out from wavy crevices in the rock bottom, 25' down.

Grand Canyon Spring, west of Big Spring, is closed from 15 November to 31 March. But in summer diving you'll find a 25'-deep crevice in the rock, with a powerful surge of water flowing out of a hole at the west end of the canyon.

On the east wall of the bay, in a canal system, you'll encounter the springs of **Idiot's Delight**, **Three Sisters**, and **Gator Hole**. Gator Hole is another sanctuary, also closed from 15 November to 31 March. This formerly extensive cave system collapsed in 1963. At present, access into the fish-filled entrance room is allowed only in summertime. However, both Idiot's Delight and Three Sisters are open to year-round diving. Idiot's Delight consists of three vertical shafts that drop from 8-20', with the largest shaft having a diameter of four feet. Very clear water and abundant fish make these shafts interesting to explore. Three Sisters, located up a small creek north of Idiot's Delight, is a group of five of the most beautiful springs in the area, ranging from 18-25' deep.

Catfish Corner, near shore on the north side of King's Bay, is appropriately named, since hundreds of catfish live in the hole. You enter a 4'-diameter shaft, which then opens into a room that's 10' by 20'. Lights are a good idea. At **Shark Sink**, on the west side of the bay, several springs feed an irregularly defined depression of 42' maximum depth. The surrounding area is very shallow and weed-choked, and clarity at Shark's Sink isn't good, compared to the rest of the area.

You can also dive the rest of Crystal River, where water clarity stays remarkably good for at least eight miles. About three miles downriver from Big Spring, you'll notice 30'-high Indian mounds. All along the bottom of this area, you can find artifacts such as arrowheads, pottery, and bone tools. And for at least four more miles, clear down to the Indian mound island (which makes a great spot for tent camping) you'll discover clear water, abundant fish, and fine snorkeling.

But even though Crystal River is the most popular great dive on Florida's west coast, it isn't the only one. **Rainbow River**, to the north near Dunnelon, is a beautiful, large, clear river, born in one of the two biggest spring groups in the world. A popular resort haven in the 1940's, Rainbow Springs is now surrounded by housing development, and inaccessible except by boat from the K.P. Hole Recreation Area. This launch is right in the middle of the 5-mile river.

A 2-1/2-mile ride upstream will take you to **Rainbow Springs** with its huge semi-circular basin, 400' in diameter. Sunlight striking through the crystalline water reflects off the numerous vents boiling the sand, and creates rainbow patterns on the bottom of the basin, where the maximum depth is 30'. Many other smaller springs boil through rock vents, attracting hordes of fish to the crystal-clear run. Depths in the river reach 20'.

Chassahowitzka River, near the town of the same name south of Crystal River, has long been famous among naturalists as one of the best places left to experience the unbelievable profusion of life that was subtropical Florida years ago. Although the majority of the canoeists you'll see along this broad, shallow river will be scanning the scenery with binoculars and uttering triumphant cries as they check new species on their birding lists, growing numbers of divers are also discovering this nature preserve.

The Steller's sea cow weighed up to 11,000 lbs. and subsisted entirely upon seaweed. They were the largest vegetarian marine mammal to live in frigid seas. Within only 27 years of their discovery in Alaska, they were extinct.

You can swim to the main spring, called the **Devil's Punch Bowl**, since it's only about 160' offshore from the fish camp. Almost 150' in diameter, it drops to 32'.

If you rent a boat at the fish camp, you can explore **Crab Creek Springs**, about 200 yards downstream. Follow the eelgrass-choked run on the right side until boils on the surface clue you to the presence of three chimney holes spewing water from 20' down.

Springs dot the entire river downstream. **Houseboat Springs** fills a wide bay with crystal water, attracting hordes of fish. **Blue Springs**, further downstream, is famous more for its fast, intimate run, surrounded by a jungle setting echoing with bird cries like something out of a Disneyland fantasy. The deepest point on the river is **Uncle John's Sink** on the west side of the run. A long chasm drops off to 60'. Saltwater intrusion at the bottom means clarity falls and you get the eerie, smeary Vaseline look of fresh and salt water mingling. Besides renting boats, there is a canoe ferry service, a general store, and a campground at the fish camp.

Although you can't interrupt the "mermaids" at Weeki Wachee, who descend 117' down into 74° water, legs bound, without regulators, buoyancy control, or even wetsuits, and only taking occasional breaths from a hose — all for the delight of tourists — you can enjoy the **Weeki Wachee River** outside of the tourist attraction.

Many of the manatees seen by divers bear scars from their encounters with careless boat operators.

Entering at Rodgers Park near the bridge gives you access to vodka-clear water, flowing through tunnels of trees for ten miles to the Gulf. Although a boat launch is at the park, rentals aren't available, so an inflatable or canoe will come in handy to take you up to the Weeki Wachee property line.

Three hundred yards upstream from Rogers Park on the south bank is **Hospital Hole**. A crevice opens up into the white limestone bank eight feet down, dropping to below 150'. However, a layer of foul-smelling hydrogen sulfide begins at 90' and makes going deeper dangerous. In the shallower reaches, fossilized sea biscuits can be seen in the elegant white limestone walls.

Crystal Springs,   just west of the town of the same name,   has been dammed to form a concrete-lined pool, bent in the middle to an L shape. Clusters of springs at a maximum depth of 15' issue a combined flow of 65 mgd. Fish thrive in the clear water, and so do many varieties of aquatic plants. Picnic areas and a swimming beach are available. **Lithia Spring**, a tributary of the Alafia River, also offers a clear, shallow snorkel run. Several sinks in the Tampa area provide sites primarily for local divers.

Florida laws concerning diving: The taking of any freshwater fish by diving is prohibited. Spearing in salt water is limited to bag limits and other regulations of the angler. Snook, striped bass, porpoises, and manta rays are protected. No spearing allowed around public beaches, piers, jetties, or fishing bridges. Diver's flag is required.

CAVE DIVING

Cave diving is a specialized scuba sport in which divers penetrate a water-filled cave. (Cavern divers also penetrate into water-filled cave entrances, but never go beyond the reach of natural light.) Since cave diving combines the hazards of ordinary scuba with the special conditions of a cave environment — total lack of light, inability to ascend to the surface for air, and, often, presence of deep silt — specialized training and equipment are essential. This cannot be emphasized enough. Because of its potential danger, cave diving is one of the most controversial aspects of scuba. Much of this controversy has resulted from negative publicity surrounding the many deaths of ill-prepared and untrained divers.

Since the cave diver, like the astronaut, is traveling into what is essentially an alien, hostile environment, he is totally dependent on his man-made life support system, his training, and his buddy. Although no guarantee of absolute safety ever exists in any aspect of scuba, certified cave divers can effectively minimize the dangers of the sport through adherence to responsible cave diving practices.

Cave and cavern divers throughout the United States explore sumps (completely water-filled passages within a cave) and springs in Kentucky, West Virginia, Missouri, and New Mexico. In addition, the lava tubes of Hawaii, the sea caves of the Pacific, and the blue holes of the Bahamas and Central America also attract divers.

But nowhere is the sport more popular than in the springs and sinkholes of north-central Florida. Because of the beauty of the sites, the crystalline water, and the easy accessibility, thousands of divers each year experience the thrill and adventure of diving this cavers' mecca. Some of these divers lose their lives because they didn't bother to take the time to learn cave diving. Analysis of cave diving accidents reveals that, in almost every case, at least one of the four cardinal rules of caving was violated.

1. Two-Thirds Air Rule: Always exit the cave system with at least 2/3 of your air supply. Constantly monitor your pressure gauge.

2. Guidelines: Use a line from the cave entrance throughout the dive. It is the cave diver's most important piece of gear.

3. Stay within Depth Limits: Remember, the maximum sport diving depth is 130'.

4. Obtain Training First: Cave divers need adequate training in emergency procedures and techniques. Buddy-breathing, good buoyancy control, and good "buddymanship" are essential to know and practice regularly.

In Florida (and other states as well), spring water appears endlessly clear, and in heavy-flow springs, it may stay that way, leaving the diver with only a heavy current as the major problem. But in many springs of average or low flow, a much more dangerous phenomenon is encountered — SILT.

The presence of silt within a cave system rarely manifests itself at the surface. What many divers have ignored (at risk of their lives) is that the floors and walls of many caves are covered with fine sand, mud, or clay silt. Careless fin movement, or even bubbles bumping against the ceiling, can stir this silt into clouds that reduce clarity to nothing in a matter of seconds. Not even the most powerful light available can penetrate some kinds of clay silt. Such silt can take several weeks to settle. In situations like this where you can't see your light when it's literally in front of your face, it's easy (but often too late) to understand why cave divers have such need of rigorous training.

Equipment, too, is important. No one should enter a cave with just the basics for the open-water sport diver. Specialized and properly maintained equipment is essential for this sport. To delete one piece of required gear is to jeopardize the safety of the entire team.

There are no shortcuts to safe cavern and cave diving. Sound judgement, the use of common sense, and competent training followed by patience in gaining experience is the only way to become a safe cave diver.

* Stay away from silt.

* Be honest with yourself — know your limits.

* Use proper equipment.

* Avoid stressful situations.

* Allow for the unexpected.

* Safety first.

* Exercise good judgement.

Interest in cave and cavern diving has grown rapidly during the past ten years. The following organizations all offer certification in cave and cavern diving. For more information, conduct one or more of these groups:

National Association of Cave Diving
General Manager — Jim Kasserman
P.O. Box 14492
Gainesville, FL 32604

NSS — Cave Diving Section
Wes Skiles, Training Chairman
P.O. Box 73
Branford, FL 32008

NAUI Headquarters
P.O. Box 14650
Montclair, CA 91763

PADI Headquarters
1243 East Warner Avenue
Santa Ana, CA 92705

National YMCA Center for U/W Activities
P.O. Box 1547
Key West, FL 33041

Sources of information obtained for this article were NACD "Concepts for Safe Cave Diving" and NSS-CDS "Cave Diving Safety."

Yellowtail snappers and a French angelfish in a feeding frenzy in Florida. ▶
DON PETERSON

DIVE STORE DIRECTORY

ALABAMA

RIPP TIDE DIVE CENTER
2805 S 18TH ST HOMEWOOD AL 35209

SKINNY'S SCUBA SHACK
1215 CENTER PT RD BIRMINGHAM AL 35215

BIRMINGHAM SCUBA CENTER
1409 MONTGOMERY HWY BIRMINGHAM AL 35216

TANT'S SOUTHERN SKIN DIVERS
506 S 45TH ST BIRMINGHAM AL 35222

TOM'S DIVE SHOP
206 HARGROVE RD E TUSCALOOSA AL 35401

DIVING UNLIMITED
116 LEE STREET DECATUR AL 35601

SOUTHEASTERN DIVERS INC
325 S COURT ST FLORENCE AL 35630

OUTDOOR WORLD DIVERS
1525 BROADWAY SHEFFIELD AL 35660

SPORTS ODYSSEY
1815 INSPIRATION LANE HUNTSVILLE AL 35801

AQUASPACE SCUBA SCHOOL
7250 GOVERNORS DR W HUNTSVILLE AL 35805

CAPITOL DIVE CENTER
5163 Atlanta Hwy
Montgomery AL 36109
205/279-8002.
Full-service store, open til 6:00 pm on Friday.
Closed Sunday. Ask us about local diving:
205/279-8002.

AQUA SPORTS
527 GLADE PARK DR MONTGOMERY AL 36109

ANNISTON SPORTING GOODS
805 S QUINTARD ANNISTON AL 36201

KEY WEST DIVING CO
PO BOX 788 JACKSONVILLE AL 36265

HYDROSPACE SCUBA SCHOOL
1605 S OATS DOTHAN AL 36301

DIVERS DEN INC
2803 SW ROSS CLARK CIR DOTHAN AL 36301

LA DIVERS
PO BOX 129 ELBERTA AL 36530

PLEASURE ISLAND DIVE CENTER
PO BOX 1730 GULF SHORES AL 36542

TROPICAL EXPRESSION
RT 1 BOX 650 GULF SHORES AL 36542

GULF GATE MARINA & DIVE SHOP
PO BOX 308 ORANGE BEACH AL 36561

DAVEY JONES LOCKER OF AL INC
1857 GOVERNMENT ST MOBILE AL 36606

DISCOUNT DIVERS INC
7140 AIRPORT BLVD MOBILE AL 36608

DIVE WORLD
708 OAK CIRCLE DR MOBILE AL 36609

GULF COAST DIVERS SUPPLY
1284 HUTSON DR MOBILE AL 36609

ADVENTURE SPORTS INC
212 N GAY ST AUBURN AL 36830

SEA DIVERS
121 WALNUT DR ENTERPRISE AL 36930

ALASKA

ALASKA MINING & DIVING SUPPLY
3222 COMMERCIAL DR ANCHORAGE AK 99501

ALASKAN PROSPECTORS
4409 SPENARD ST ANCHORAGE AK 99503

SUNSHINE SPORTS
1231 W NORTHERN LIGHTS ANCHORAGE AK 99503

DIVE ALASKA
3002 SPENARD RD #2 ANCHORAGE AK 99503

ARCTIC DIVE CO
PO BOX 507 EAGLE RIVER AK 99577

SCUBA DO INC
BOX 2285 1219 KOUSKOV ST KODIAK AK 99615

PENINSULA WATER SPORTS
PO BOX 583 SOLDOTNA AK 99669

SOUTH CENTRAL DIVING
PO BOX 1531 VALDEZ AK 99686

DENALI DIVE & SPORTS CENTER
PO BOX 872147 WASILLA AK 99687

BEAVER SPORTS
2400 COLLEGE RD FAIRBANKS AK 99701

ALASKAN PROSPECTORS SUPPLY
504 COLLEGE FAIRBANKS AK 99701

DOLPHIN TOO
101 COLLEGE #353 POB 60454 FAIRBANKS AK 99706

SCUBA CRAFTS
4485 N DOUGLAS HWY JUNEAU AK 99801

JUNEAU DIVING
14 MARINE WAY JUNEAU AK 99801

NELSON'S DIVING AND CHARTERS
Box 203
Auke Bay AK 99821
907/789-9510
Specializing in sport fishing, diving trips, and
charters throughout southeastern Alaska. We can
handle all your diving, fishing, and travel needs.

SUNSHINE SPORTS
203 LINCOLN ST SITKA AK 99835

BUNESS DIVING
BOX 66 WRANGELL AK 99929

ARKANSAS

SCUBA HUT
SUNSET SQ HWY 68W SPRINGDALE AR 72764

OZARK DIVERS
620 W DICKSON FAYETTEVILLE AR 72701

PANTHER BAY MARINA
RT 6 BOX 508 MT HOME AR 72653

INLAND DIVERS
PO BOX 514 BULL SHOALS AR 72619

JORDAN DIVING SERVICE
JORDAN LNDG KLAUS MARINA JORDAN AR 72548

PROFESSIONAL SKI & SCUBA
HWY 25 PO BOX 831 HEBER SPRINGS AR 72543

101 BOAT DOCK
RT B BOX 164 GAMALIEL AR 72537

J&T DIVE SHOP
Route 7 North Culberhouse Rd
Jonesboro AR 72401
501/935-3289
Scuba instruction. Sales. Service. Rentals. Trips.
501/935-3289.

SWAN'S SCUBA INC
9010 HILARD SPRINGS RD LITTLE ROCK AR 72209

CRAWDADDY'S SCUBA
102 N MONROE LITTLE ROCK AR 72205

LYNN'S SKI & SCUBA
3408 S UNIVERSITY LITTLE ROCK AR 72204

ARKANSAS AQUATICS
1608 W 14TH ST LITTLE ROCK AR 72202

CULLUM & BOREN
3929 MCCAIN BLVD N LITTLE ROCK AR 72116

RICK'S PRO DIVE N SKI
4701 JFK BLVD N LITTLE ROCK AR 72116

CENTRAL ARK DIVERS SUPPLY
38 WHITE OAK CONWAY AR 72032

JS DIVE SHOP
MT HARBOR RESORT MOUNT IDA AR 71957

MIKES SCUBA
BOX 68 AMITY AR 71921

DIVERS DEN
3498 ALBERT PIKE HOT SPRINGS AR 71901

SOUTH ARK DIVE SHOP
601 E 8TH ST EL DORADO AR 71730

ARKANSAS SPORT DIVERS
2510 E HARDING PINE BLUFF AR 71601

ARIZONA

ARIZONA DIVERS SUPPLY
2348 N 7TH ST PHOENIX AZ 85006

AQUA-SPORTS
4230 E INDIAN SCHOOL RD PHOENIX AZ 85018

SCUBA SCIENCES INC
8502 N BLACK CYN HWY PHOENIX AZ 85021

SUN DIVER WATERSPORTS
13835 N TATUM BLVD #7 PHOENIX AZ 85032

EL MAR DIVING CENTER
2245 W BROADWAY MESA AZ 85202

MAXIMA DIVERS
316 S ALMA SCHOOL RD MESA AZ 85202

SCUBA SCIENCES
1825-2 N SCOTTTSDALE RD TEMPE AZ 85281

DESERT AQUA SPORTS
1236 E FRY BLVD SIERRA VISTA AZ 85635

REBEL ENTERPRISES
4837 SIOUX AVE SIERRA VISTA AZ 85635

TUCSON SCHOOL OF SCUBA DIVING
3575 E SPEEDWAY BLVD TUCSON AZ 85716

SILENT EXPERIENCE
2901 E SPEEDWAY TUCSON AZ 85716

THE DIVE SHOP
2505 N CAMPBELL TUCSON AZ 85719

OCEAN ADVENTURES
833 DOUGLAS LN PRESCOTT AZ 86301

CALIFORNIA

MARINA DEL REY DIVERS
312 W 2ND ST LOS ANGELES CA 90012

NEW ENGLAND DIVERS
11830 W PICO BLVD W LOS ANGELES CA 90064

SUNLAND SPORTS INC/DIVE SHOP
8677 WILSHIRE BLVD BEVERLY HILLS CA 90211

AL'S OUTBOARD SERVICE
4043 SEPULVEDA BLVD CULVER CITY CA 90230

DIVERS CORNER
11200 S OLD RIVER SCHOOL RD DOWNEY CA 90241

EZ DIVERS
530 6TH ST HERMOSA BEACH CA 90254

MALIBU DIVERS INC
21231 PACIFIC COAST HWY MALIBU CA 90265

DIVE N SURF
504 N BROADWAY REDONDO BEACH CA 90277

MARINA PACIFIC DIVERS
2539 LINCOLN BLVD MARINA DEL RAY CA 90291

SCUBA HAUS
2501 WILSHIRE BLVD SANTA MONICA CA 90403

BLUE CHEER WATER SPORTS
1731 WILSHIRE BLVD SANTA MONICA CA 90403

CHUGAI INTERNATIONAL
20695 S WESTERN AVE TORRANCE CA 90501

DIVEMATICS USA INC
2909 OREGON CT C12 TORRANCE CA 90503

LAGUNA SEA SPORTS
22767 HAWTHORNE BLVD TORRANCE CA 90505

SPORT DIVING WEST
11501 E WHITTIER BLVD WHITTIER CA 90601

SCUBA TOYS
9547 VALLEY VIEW CYPRUS CA 90630

JON HARDY — ARGO DIVING SERVICE
Box 1201
Avalon CA 90704
213/510-2208
Personalized guided tours of Catalina Island.
Photography, wreck, and night diving. Fish feeding.
Updating diving skills.

CATALINA DIVERS SUPPLY
PLEASURE PIER CATALINA ISLAND CA 90704

NEW ENGLAND DIVERS
4613 BRIERCREST AVE LAKEWOOD CA 90713

AMERICAN INST OF DIVING
1901 PACIFIC COAST HWY LOMITA CA 90717

BOLSTAD SALES SERVICE
505 N PACIFIC AVE SAN PEDRO CA 90731

KEYSTONE MARINE
PO BOX 3951 SEAL BEACH CA 90740

PACIFIC SPORTING GOODS
11 39TH PLACE LONG BEACH CA 90803

SCUBA SCHOOLS OF LONG BEACH
4740 E PACIFIC COAST HWY LONG BEACH CA 90804

HYDROTECH
2424 WALNUT AVE SIGNAL HILL CA 90806

NEW ENGLAND DIVERS
4148 VIKING WAY LONG BEACH CA 90808

ARCADIA POOL & DIVE
21 W DUARTE RD ARCADIA CA 91006

SPORT CHALET INC
920 FOOTHILL BLVD LA CANADA CA 91011

PASADENA DIVERS WEST
2695A E FOOTHILL BLVD PASADENA CA 91107

ALOHA DIVING SCHOOLS
7626 TAMPA AVE RESEDA CA 91335

SCUBA DUBA DIVE
7126 RESEDA BLVD RESEDA CA 91335

THE SCUBA STORE
17723 CHATSWORTH GRANADA HILLS CA 91344

SCUBA LUV INC
712 THOUSAND OAKS BD THOUSAND OAKS CA 91360

FAR WEST MARINE
3233 THOUSAND OAKS BD THOUSAND OAKS CA 91362

CAL AQUATICS
22725 VENTURA BLVD WOODLAND HILLS CA 91364

LAGUNA SEA SPORTS
6959 VAN NUYS BLVD VAN NUYS CA 91405

WEST COAST DIVERS SUPPLY
16931 SHERMAN WAY VAN NUYS CA 91406

ALOHA DIVING SCHOOLS
2910 W MAGNOLIA BL BURBANK CA 91505

PROFESSIONAL SCUBA REPAIR
5725 CAHUENGA BLVD N HOLLYWOOD CA 91601

GATEWOODS BEACH DIVERS
7584 AMETHYST CUCAMONGA CA 91730

OSHMAN'S SPORTING GOODS
218 PUENTE HILLS MALL INDUSTRY CA 91744

CAL PRO DIVE SHOP
1009 S HACIENDA BLVD HACIENDA HTS CA 91745

GUCCIONES SCUBA HABITAT
3220B BREA CANYON RD DIAMOND BAR CA 91765

CAL PRO DIVE SHOP
850 S GREAT BEND DR DIAMOND BAR CA 91766

ALTA SPORTS
9034 HUNTINGTON DR SAN GABRIEL CA 91775

CHAMPION AIR SALVAGE
3080 BLENKARNE CARLSBAD CA 92008

SAN DIEGO DIVERS SUPPLY
1084 BROADWAY CHULA VISTA CA 92012

AMRON INTL DIVING
751 W 4TH AVE ESCONDIDO CA 92025

DIVING LOCKER
348 E GRAND AVE ESCONDIDO CA 92025

SAN DIEGO DIVERS SUPPLY
7522 LA JOLLA BLVD LA JOLLA CA 92037

SPORTLAND
8076 LA MESA BLVD LA MESA CA 92041

DIVING INSTITUTE
105 W 18TH ST NATIONAL CITY CA 92050

U/W SCHOOLS OF AMERICA
707 OCEANSIDE BLVD OCEANSIDE CA 92054

SCUBA SPECIALTIES
BOX 1156 OCEANSIDE CA 92054

DIVING LOCKER
405 N HWY 101 SOLANO BEACH CA 92075

FERERS
PACIFIC HWY & MARKET SAN DIEGO CA 92101

ANY OCEAN DIVING UNLTD
2040 HARBOR ISLAND DR SAN DIEGO CA 92101

SURF N SEA
1863 BACON SAN DIEGO CA 92107

DIVING LOCKER
1020 GRAND AVE PACIFIC BEACH CA 92109

DIVING LOCKER AQUATICS
4619 MISSION GORGE PL SAN DIEGO CA 92109

NEW ENGLAND DIVERS
3860 ROSECRANS ST SAN DIEGO CA 92110

SAN DIEGO DIVERS SUPPLY
4004 SPORTS ARENA BLVD SAN DIEGO CA 92110

WATERMARK
6484 MT ADELBERT DR SAN DIEGO CA 92111

Diving·Adventure·Fun

Get the most out of your diving adventure with the latest in "Dive-Tech" gear from Dacor ...easy breathing PACER XL regulators; comfortable and stylish silicone masks and snorkels; convenient, high-performance BCX SEACHUTE jackets; powerful, lightweight thermal plastic fins; handy, accurate console gauges; fitted wetsuits...a total integrated system that gives you the confidence to enhance the experience of every dive.

DACOR CORPORATION Manufacturer of Diving Equipment
161 Northfield Road, Northfield, IL 60093, Phone: (312) 446-9555

Dive Dacor The Professional's Choice

Send $2.00 for Dacor Divers Kit. Includes catalog, cloth patch, decomp table, decals.

OCEAN ENTERPRISES
4646 CONVOY ST SAN DIEGO CA 92111

WARDS DRY DOCK
2198 HWY 86 EL CENTRO CA 92251

SEA TO SEA SCUBA SCHOOL
10950 S MT VERNON COLTON CA 92324

LAGUNA SEA SPORTS
6343 MAGNOLIA AVE RIVERSIDE CA 92501

LEISURE TIME SERVICES
8099 INDIANA AVE RIVERSIDE CA 92504

LUXFER USA LTD
1995 THIRD ST RIVERSIDE CA 92507

LAGUNA SEA SPORTS
2146 NEWPORT BLVD COSTA MESA CA 92627

JACK'S SURF AND SPORTS
34318 COAST HWY DANA PT CA 92629

BLACK BART'S AQUATICS
34145 COAST HWY DANA POINT CA 92629

UNDERSEA SERVICES
3141 E YORBA LINDA FULLERTON CA 92632

SPORT CHALET DIVERS
16242 BEACH BLVD HUNTINGTON BEACH CA 92646

OCEAN SPORTS LTD
5046 EDINGER HUNTINGTON BEACH CA 92649

LEISURETECH INC
920 GLENNEYRE SUITE X LAGUNA BEACH CA 92651

LAGUNA SEA SPORTS
925 N COAST HWY LAGUNA BEACH CA 92651

U/W EDUCATORS
1221 W COAST HWY NEWPORT BEACH CA 92660

AQUATIC CENTER
4535 W COAST HWY NEWPORT BEACH CA 92663

SCUBA WORLD
1706 N TUSTIN ORANGE CA 92665

DEL MAR SUPPLIES
1141 N CITRUS ORANGE CA 92667

OPENWATER HABITAT
417 S MAIN ORANGE CA 92668

SCUBA UNLIMITED
3721 W PARK BALBOA ORANGE CA 92668

ISLAND DIVE SERVICES
PO BOX 4465 SAN CLEMENTE CA 92672

ADVENTURES IN DIVING
31678 PACIFIC HWY S LAGUNA CA 92677

U/W SCHOOLS OF AMERICA
27601 FORBES RD #19 LAGUNA NIGUEL CA 92677

FOUR SEASONS SCUBA
13762 NEWPORT AVE TUSTIN CA 92680

THE DIVE SHOP
312 N HARBOR BLVD SANTA ANA CA 92703

INTERNATIONAL DIVERS EXCHANGE
1840 S GRAND AVE SANTA ANA CA 92705

DEE SPORTS
14252 CULVER DR SUITE A342 IRVINE CA 92714

SCUBA SCHOOLS
1640 W LINCOLN AVE ANAHEIM CA 92801

VENTURA SCUBA SCHOOLS
1559 SPINAKER DR 108 VENTURA CA 93003

AQUA-VENTURES INC
2172 PICKWIELL DR CAMARILLO CA 93010

SEAFARERS DIVE SHOP
1001 HARBOR BLVD OXNARD CA 93030

AQUATICS
244 MARKET ST PT HUENEME CA 93041

DIVERS DEN
22 ANACAPA ST SANTA BARBARA CA 93101

U/W SPORTS
BREAKWATER HARBOR SANTA BARBARA CA 93109

AQUATICS OF SANTA BARBARA
5370 HOLLISTER AVE #3 SANTA BARBARA CA 93111

BOB'S DIVING LOCKER
500 BOTELLO RD GOLETA CA 93117

DIVERS SUPPLY OF SANTA BARBARA
5854 HOLLISTER GOLETA CA 93117

VISALIA SCUBA CENTER
202 S BURKE VISALIA CA 93291

INNERSPACE
1305 N CHESTER BAKERSFIELD CA 93308

WATER PRO SPORTS SHOP
280 HIGUERA SAN LUIS OBISPO CA 93401

BILL'S SPORTING GOODS
AT THE PIER CAYUCOS CA 93430

SEA WINK SPORTING GOODS
750 PRICE ST PISMO BEACH CA 93449

ALL AMERICAN SPTG GOODS
213 TOWN COURT E SANTA MARIA CA 93453

DIVE WEST SPORTS
123 W MAIN ST SANTA MARIA CA 93454

ADVENTURE DIVING
3142 E BELMONT FRESNO CA 93702

BOB'S DIVE SHOP OF FRESNO
4374 N BLACKSTONE FRESNO CA 93726

AQUARIUS DIVE SHOP
2240 DEL MONTE AVE MONTEREY CA 93940

BAMBOO REEF ENTERPRISES
614 LIGHTHOUSE AVE MONTEREY CA 93940

OUTDOOR RECREATION
BUILDING 3109 4TH AVE FT ORD CA 93941

WALLIN DIVESTORE
517 E BAYSHORE RD REDWOOD CITY CA 94025

PENINSULA DIVE CENTER
1015 W EL CAMINO REAL MT VIEW CA 94040

ANDERSON'S SCHOOL
541 OCEANA BLVD PACIFICA CA 94044

NEW ENGLAND DIVERS
398 5TH ST SAN FRANCISCO CA 94107

BAMBOO REEF ENTERPRISES
584 4TH ST SAN FRANCISCO CA 94107

APOLLO SPORTS CO LTD
PO BOX 77247 SAN FRANCISCO CA 94107

AQUA GEAR SCHOOL OF DIVING
1254 9TH AVE SAN FRANCISCO CA 94122

DIVERS EXCHANGE
649 PACIFIC AVE ALAMEDA CA 94501

PACHECO SKIN DIVING CENTER
5775 PACHECO BLVD PACHECO CA 94520

OSHMAN'S SPORT CHALET
3303 N MAIN PLEASANT HILL CA 94523

O'BRIENS SCUBA DIVING SUPPLY
37313 MAPLE FREMONT CA 94536

FREMONT SCUBA
37313 MAPLE ST FREMONT CA 94536

THE ORIGINAL STEELE'S INC
571 JACKSON ST HAYWARD CA 94544

TRI-VALLEY SCUBA SCHOOL
21310 SAN RAMON VALLEY BD SAN RAMON CA 94583

SAND WIND AND SEA
1645 BROADWAY VALLEJO CA 94590

HYDRO SPACE DIVE SHOP & SCUBA
4345 SONOMA BL #D-2 VALLEJO CA 94590

OLYMPIC SCUBA SCHOOL
2595 N MAIN ST WALNUT CREEK CA 94596

DIVERS SUPPLY
2875 GLASCOCK ST OAKLAND CA 94601

DIVE TECH INTL
290 6TH AVE OAKLAND CA 94606

STEELE'S SKIN & SCUBA
60TH & TELEGRAPH OAKLAND CA 94609

BAMBOO REEF ENTERPRISES
1111 UNIVERSITY AVE BERKELEY CA 94702

LORD BYRON LTD
1825 LINCOLN AVE SAN RAFAEL CA 94901

MARIN SKIN DIVING
3765 REDWOOD HWY SAN RAFAEL CA 94903

PINNACLES DIVE CENTER
875 GRANT AVE NOVATO CA 94947

THE OUTRIGGER DIVE SHOP
2110 WINCHESTER BLVD CAMPBELL CA 95008

STEELE'S SKIN & SCUBA
2350 EL CAMINO REAL SANTA CLARA CA 95051

O'NEILL'S DIVE SHOP
2222 E CLIFF DR SANTA CRUZ CA 95060

ADVENTURE SPORTS UNLTD
303 POTRERO #15 SANTA CRUZ CA 95062

FINSTADS SCUBA ADVENTURES INC
2222 E CLIFF DR SANTA CRUZ CA 95062

OCEAN ODYSSEY
2345 S RODEO GULCH RD SANTA CRUZ CA 95062

U C SANTA CRUZ
COASTAL MARINE ST SANTA CRUZ CA 95064

AQUATIC SPORTS
4195 OLD SAN JOSE RD SANTA CRUZ CA 95065

SOUTH VALLEY SKIN DIVING
3888 MONTEREY RD SAN JOSE CA 95111

GO-DIVE PRODUCTS
2136 THE ALAMEDA SAN JOSE CA 95126

BAMBOO REEF ENTERPRISES
1617 W SAN CARLOS SAN JOSE CA 95128

STAN'S SKINDIVING SHOP
554 S BASCOM AVE SAN JOSE CA 95128

VALLEY SKINDIVING
7831 THORNTON STOCKTON CA 95207

LODI S/D SCHOOL
430 W LOCKFORD ST LODI CA 95240

DIVING CENTER OF SANTA ROSA
2696 SANTA ROSA AVE SANTA ROSA CA 95401

PINNACLES DIVE CENTER
2100 AMORY DR SANTA ROSA CA 95401

STEELE'S SKIN & SCUBA
4020 SANTA ROSA AVE SANTA ROSA CA 95401

COONEY'S SPORTING GOODS
32760 N HARBOR DR FT BRAGG CA 95437

SUB-SURFACE PROGRESSION
18601 N HWY 1 #5 FT BRAGG CA 95437

UKIAH SKIN & SCUBA
1178 N STATE UKIAH CA 95482

DIVERS CORNER
2940 BROADWAY #B EUREKA CA 95501

TJ MARINE DIVE INST
2338 ALBEE ST EUREKA CA 95501

PRO SPORT CENTER
508 MYRTLE AVE EUREKA CA 95501

AUBURN SKI HUT
585 HIGH ST AUBURN CA 95603

SKI STALKER
5740 WINDMILL WY CARMICHAEL CA 95608

SCUBA SPORTS
509 L ST DAVIS CA 95616

OCEAN VENTURES
9172 GREENBACK LANE ORANGEVALE CA 95662

CASSOTTA DIVING INC
4930 PACIFIC ROCKLIN CA 95677

SPORTS COVE
896 ALAMO DR VACAVILLE CA 95688

OUTDOORSMAN
HWY 50 S LAKE TAHOE CA 95705

MOTHER LODE DIVE SHOP
2020 H ST SACRAMENTO CA 95814

DOLPHIN SWIM SCHOOL
1530 EL CAMINO AVE SACRAMENTO CA 95815

KEENE'S AQUA SHOP
2801 P ST SACRAMENTO CA 95816

KEENE'S AQUA SHOP
3036 AUBURN BLVD SACRAMENTO CA 95821

HONANS MINING AND DIVING SUPPLY
2810 HWY 32 CHICO CA 95926

SCUBA HUT
472 PALORA AVE YUBA CITY CA 95991

AQUA DIVERS INC
980 GRAY AVE YUBA CITY CA 95991

THOMAS DIVE SHOP
415 GARDEN HWY YUBA CITY CA 95991

COLORADO

MILE HIGH DIVERS
12330 W 58TH AVE ARVADA CO 80002

HIGH COUNTRY DIVERS
1605 South College
Fort Collins CO 80525
303/493-8562

HIGH COUNTRY DIVERS
60 South Havana St #611
Aurora CO 80012
303/341-5735
PADI 5-star facility. Recompression chamber on site. Complete education program from basic through instructor.

A-1 DIVING CO
4730 S LIPAN ENGLEWOOD CO 80110

DIVERSIFIED MARINE
8919 E UNION ENGLEWOOD CO 80111

DENVER DIVERS SUPPLY
557 MILWAUKEE ST DENVER CO 80206

SCUBA DEN
5055 W 44TH AVE #3 DENVER CO 80212

ROCKY MT DIVING CENTER LTD
1920 WADSWORTH LAKEWOOD CO 80215

FUN DIVING & TRAVEL
75 S ELM ST DENVER CO 80222

SCUBA SHOPPE LTD
85 S UNION BLVD LAKEWOOD CO 80228

THE VISIONARY
3005 S PARKER RD DENVER CO 80231

ROCKY MOUNTAIN DIVING CENTER
1737 15TH ST BOULDER CO 80302

WEAVER'S DIVE CENTER
623A S BROADWAY BOULDER CO 80303

COLORADO SCUBA SCHOOL
29573 PAINTBRUSH DR EVERGREEN CO 80439

HIGH COUNTRY DIVERS
1605 S COLLEGE FT COLLINS CO 80525

MIDWEST DIVERS SUPPLY
1634 S COLLEGE AVE FT COLLINS CO 80525

DIVERS REEF INC
3014 N NEVADA COLORADO SPRINGS CO 80907

SCUBA COLORADO
PO BOX 26082 COLORADO SPRINGS CO 80936

PUEBLO DIVERS SUPPLY
4400 THATCHER AVE PUEBLO CO 81005

NEPTUNES WORLD
1823 GLENISLE DURANGO CO 81301

BLUE MESA SCUBA CTR
500 N TOWNSEND MONTROSE CO 81401

HIGH DESERT DIVERS
1121A N AVE GRAND JUNCTION CO 81501

HIGH COUNTRY MARINE SUPPLY
BOX 997 VAIL CO 81658

CONNECTICUT

JACK'S DIVE CENTER
RT 10 PLAINVILLE CT 06062

WIN-SUM SPORTS
27 HARTFORD TPKE VERNON CT 06066

SCUBA SHACK
1845 SILAS DEANE HWY ROCKY HILL CT 06067

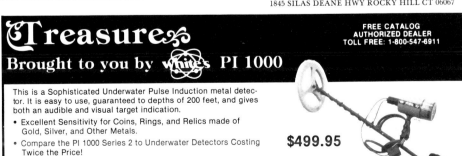

Freshwater diving offers many surprises, like this brilliant rainbow darter in ▲ spawning colors, photographed in Swan Creek, Missouri.

▼ *Every inch of surface is covered with marine life in the beautiful reefs of the Florida Keys.*

Black coral thrives under a lava rock ledge in the clear water of Hawaii. ▶
ED ROBINSON, Tom Stack & Associates

ODYSEA DIVING SCHOOLS INC
286 BROAD ST WINDSOR CT 06095

INNERSPACE DIVING
598 CENTER ST MANCHESTER CT 06110

ODYSEA DIVING SCHOOLS INC
1053 NEW BRITAIN AVE W HARTFORD CT 06110

EASTERN CT SCUBA SCHOOL
27 HOLBROOK AVE #1 WILLIMANTIC CT 06226

AQUA SPORTS DIVING CTR
LONG COVE RD GALES FERRY CT 06335

PAGE'S SPORT SHOP
1000 MAIN ST BRANFORD CT 06405

SEA WOLF DIVERS SUPPLY
TOWN ST RT 82 E HADDAM CT 06423

ART SPORT SHOP
15 BOSTON POST RD MADISON CT 06443

INTERNATIONAL SCUBA CENTER
758 MAIN ST RT 10 PLANTSVILLE CT 06479

ORBIT MARINE
FOOT OF BROAD ST BRIDGEPORT CT 06497

SKI & SCUBA SHOPPE
STRATFORD MARINA STRATFORD CT 06497

BAT LIZ PROV DIVERS SUPPLY
20 RUSSELL RD STRATFORD CT 06497

U/W SWIMMERS
526 MAIN ST WEST HAVEN CT 06516

ORBIT MARINE SPORTS CENTER
3273 FAIRFIELD AVE BRIDGEPORT CT 06605

CENTRAL SALES SCUBA
136 CARTER RD THOMASTON CT 06787

THE DIVING BELL
782 FEDERAL RD RT 7 BROOKFIELD CT 06804

DELAWARE

FIRST STATE SPORTS INC
2150 NEW CASTLE AVE NEW CASTLE DE 19720

REHOBOTH DIVE CENTER
106 MIDWAY DR REHOBOTH BEACH DE 19803

NATIONAL DIVING CENTER
4932 WISCONSIN AVE NW WASHINGTON DC 20016

FLORIDA

BRANFORD DIVE CENTER
BOX 822 BRANFORD FL 32008

ATLANTIC SCUBA
114 E FAIRVIEW DAYTONA BEACH FL 32014

ADVENTURE DIVING INC
3127 S RIDGEWOOD AVE S DAYTONA FL 32019

N FLORIDA SPORTS WORLD
RT 7 BOX 52 LAKE CITY FL 32055

DIVING DON'S DIVE SHOP
333 S YONGE ST ORMOND BEACH FL 32074

AMERICAN DIVERS CO
386 STATE RD 16 ST AUGUSTINE FL 32084

SEA HUNT ENTERPRISES
275 VILANO RD ST AUGUSTINE FL 32084

AQUIFER DIVE CENTER
4564 ATLANTIC BLVD JACKSONVILLE FL 32207

AMERICAN SCUBA SCHOOLS
6255 MERRILL RD JACKSONVILLE FL 32211

MATHENYS AQUATICS UNLIMITED
11300 BEACH BLVD JACKSONVILLE FL 32216

NATIONAL U/W EDUCATION
13639 BEACH BLVD JACKSONVILLE BEACH FL 32250

THE SCUBA DISCOVERY
220 F W THARP TALLAHASSEE FL 32303

DIXIE DIVING SHOPPE
2015 N MONROE ST TALLAHASSEE FL 32303

BARRY'S DIVE CENTER
1362 LAKE BRADFORD TALLAHASSEE FL 32304

CARTERS DIVE CENTER
3001 W TENNESSEE TALLAHASSEE FL 32304

C&G SPORTING GOODS
137 HARRISON AVE PANAMA CITY FL 32401

DIVERS DEN
4720 E BUS HWY 98 PANAMA CITY FL 32401

HYDROSPACE DIVE SHOP
3605 THOMAS DR PANAMA CITY FL 32407

PANAMA CITY DIVE CENTER
3853A THOMAS DR PANAMA CITY BEACH FL 32407

VORTEX SPRING Inc.
Route 2 Box 18A
Ponce de Leon FL 32455
904/836-4979

**Crystal-clear water, 50'-deep basin, large cavern
and cave. Group lodging, camping, RV hook-ups.
Full-service dive shop.**

MORRISON SPRINGS INC
PO BOX 95 PONCE DE LEON FL 32455

SKIPPERS DIVING CENTER INC
408 E WRIGHT ST PENSACOLA FL 32501

SCUBA SHACK INC
719 S PALAFOX ST PENSACOLA FL 32501

DIVE WORLD OF FL
3090 N PACE BLVD PENSACOLA FL 32505

RAY MANUEL DIVING
3624 W FAIRFIELD PENSACOLA FL 32505

PENSACOLA DIVE SHOP INC
PO BOX 16164 PENSACOLA FL 32507

AQUANAUT SCUBA CENTER
PO BOX 651 DESTIN FL 32541

FANTASEA SCUBA HEADQUARTERS
#1 Hwy 98
Destin FL 32541
904/837-6943

**Gulf charters, instruction, sales & service. Rentals,
air. Discover Destin — One Call Does It All!!!**

WET SPORTS INC
PO BOX 1536 DESTIN FL 32548

BAKER MARINE
45 MARILYN AVE NW FT WALTON BEACH FL 32548

THE SCUBA SHOP
230 N ELGIN PKWY FT WALTON BEACH FL 32548

OCEAN TECH
185 MIRACLE STRIP PKWY FT WALTON BEACH FL
32548

FATHOM'S WAY
129 MIRACLE STRIP PKWY SE FT WALTON BEACH
FL 32548

SEA LEVEL SCUBA
4323 NW 6TH ST GAINESVILLE FL 32601

SCUBAPRO
4175 NW 12TH AVE GAINESVILLE FL 32601

WATER WORLD DIVE CENTER
1518 N 13TH ST GAINSVILLE FL 32601

ALLEN'S AQUATIC & TRAIL CENTER
99 SW 34TH ST GAINESVILLE FL 32607

AQUATIC CENTER INC
2126 SW 34TH ST GAINESVILLE FL 32608

WATER WORLD DIVE CENTER
RT 2 BOX 35C24 ARCHER FL 32618

MANATEE SPRINGS DIVE SHOP
PO Box 1699
Chiefland FL 32626
904/493-2124

**Sales, rentals, charters. Groups welcome with
special discounts on air. Right outside of the
gate of Manatee Springs.**

SAND DOLLAR DIVERS DEN
HOLIDAY INN HWY 19 N CRYSTAL RIVER FL 32629

PLANTATION INN MARINA
Hwy 44 W (PO Box 1093)
Crystal River FL 32629
904/795-5797

**Guided Rainbow River trips. Openwater dives
for certification. Boat and scuba rentals. Open
8:00-6:00 daily.**

CRYSTAL LODGE DIVE CENTER
PO BOX 456 CRYSTAL RIVER FL 32629

PALMETTO SCUBA PORT PARADISE
1610 PT PARADISE CIR CRYSTAL RIVER FL 32629

Manatee Springs

P.O. Box 1699
Chiefland, FL 32626

Tel: (904) 493-2124

DIVE SHOP

Sales • Rentals • Charters
Groups Welcome with
Special Rates on Air

GINNIE SPRINGS Inc.
Route 1 Box 153
High Springs FL 32643
904/454-2202 (For out-of-staters: 1-800/874-8571)
A unique recreational resort. Six crystal-clear
springs, RV and tent camping. Full-service dive
specializing in cavern instruction.

BLUE SPRINGS
PO BOX 331 HIGH SPRINGS FL 32643

THE DIVERS LOCKER
3088 NW BLITCHTON RD HWY27 OCALA FL 32675

BLUE GROTTO
RT 2 BOX 460-B WILLISTON FL 32696

JIM HOLLIS SCUBA WORLD
935 W HWY 436 ALTAMONTE SPRINGS FL 32701

FLORIDA STATE DIVE & SKI
380 E HIGHWAY 436 CASSELLBERRY FL 32707

TOMMIES SCUBA CENTER
1650 S WOODLAND BLVD DELAND FL 32720

DIVE AND TOUR
1403 E NY AVE DELAND FL 32724

SUN AQUA SPORTS
304 W OAK ST KISSIMMEE FL 32741

SOUS MARINE
449 MCDONALD ST MOUNT DORA FL 32757

THE DIVE SHOP
1325 S WASHINGTON AVE TITUSVILLE FL 32780

HAL WATT'S SCUBA & SKI
2215 E COLONIAL DR ORLANDO FL 32803

SCOTT'S SWIM & SCUBA
3465 EDGEWATER DR ORLANDO FL 32804

JIM HOLLIS SCUBA WORLD
5107 E COLONIAL DR ORLANDO FL 32807

THE DIVE STATION
4930 LAKE UNDERHILL DR ORLANDO FL 32807

SPORTS WORLD
2712 N PINE HILLS RD ORLANDO FL 32808

REID UNDERSEA CONCEPTS
PO BOX 13033A ORLANDO FL 32809

ODYSSEA SCUBA CENTER
PO BOX 13226 ORLANDO FL 32859

HATT'S DIVING HQTRS
2006 S FRONT ST MELBOURNE FL 32901

SEA VENTURES INTL
PO BOX 3271 INDIALANTIC FL 32903

76 FISHING'AND DIVING
6300 N ATLANTIC AVE CAPE CANAVERAL FL 32920

OCEAN ADVENTURES DIVE SHOP
748 MULLET RD SUITE 124 PT CANAVERAL FL 32920

LAND & SEA SPORTING GOODS
293 N COCOA BEACH CSWY COCOA BEACH FL 32931

PROFESSIONAL DIVING IND
1693 N US 1 MELBOURNE FL 32935

AMERICAN DIVERS INT
691 N COURTENAY MERRITT ISL FL 32953

DIVE CENTER OF SEBASTIAN
1716 N US 1 SEBASTIAN FL 32958

DEEP SIX DIVE SHOP
1550 OLD DIXIE HWY VERO BEACH FL 32960

ATLANTIS MARINA & DIVE
PO BOX 708 LONG KEY FL 33001

AQUATIC DIVING SHOP
1340 STIRLING SHOP DANIA FL 33004

TARPOON DIVING CENTER
3200 PALM AVE HIALEAH FL 33012

HYDROEYE UNDERSEA PHOTOGRAPHIC
6001 NW 153RD ST #160 MIAMI LAKES FL 33014

California diving offers many beautiful sights, like these chestnut cowries and ▲
Corynactis *anemones surrounding a red* Tealia *anemone.*

▼ *The cabezone of California relies on its camouflage ability for protection.*

This giant kelpfish assumes it's hidden by hanging upside-down amidst kelp ▶
fronds. DON PETERSON

UNDERWATER USA

America's First Newspaper for Divers

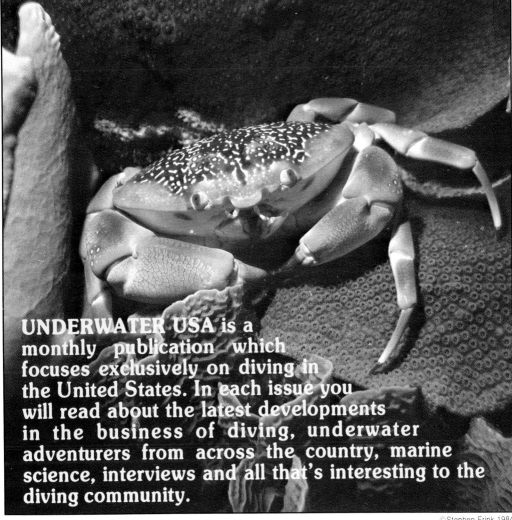

COASTAL MARINE DIVING SUPPLIES
1004 N OCEAN DR HOLLYWOOD FL 33019

BLUE WATER DIVE CTR
4429 HOLLYWOOD BLVD HOLLYWOOD FL 33021

BOB'S SPORT SHOPS
1816 HARRISON ST HOLLYWOOD FL 33021

AQUA SAFARI
5300 WASHINGTON ST #E302 HOLLYWOOD FL 33021

DIVERS UNLIMITED
6023 HOLLYWOOD BLVD HOLLYWOOD FL 33024

PLEASURE DIVERS INC
1509 NW 113TH AVE PEMBROKE PINES FL 33026

PIRATES COVE DIVE CENTER
160 N HOMESTEAD BLVD HOMESTEAD FL 33030

THE SPORTSMAN
407 PARK PLACE HOMESTEAD FL 33030

HOLIDAY ISLE DIVE SHOP
PO BOX 482 MM 84 ISLAMORADA FL 33036

BUDDY'S DIVE SHOP
PO BOX 409 ISLAMORADA FL 33036

LADY CYANA DIVERS
PO Box 1157
Islamorada FL 33036 MM 85.9
305/664-8717
Daily reef trips aboard our 40' custom dive boat.
Rentals, air, sales, service, instruction, group
rates, packages.

THE REEF SHOP
RT 2 BOX 7G ISLAMORADA FL 33036

STEVE KLEM UNDERWATER
GUIDE SERVICE
PO Box 1803
Key Largo FL 33037
305/451-1831
Dive Pennekamp with the "Pied Piper." u/w
photography & fish-feeding guide service.

BILL CRAWFORD'S TROPIC ISLE
PO BOX 755A KEY LARGO FL 33037

ATLANTIS DIVE CTR
51 GARDEN COVE DR KEY LARGO FL 33037

SUNDIVER STATION
RT 3 BOX 289-A KEY LARGO FL 33037

SEA FEVER DIVING CRUISES
PO BOX 1335 KEY LARGO FL 33037

AMERICAN DIVING HEADQUARTERS
RT 1 BOX 274B KEY LARGO FL 33037

DIVER'S WORLD Inc.
MM 99.5
Key Largo FL 33037
305/451-3200
Call 305/451-3200. Scuba-snorkel. PADI
instruction. Full pro store — Bahama cruises
aboard 60' "Prime Time." Spearfishing, shell
collecting, fishing, sailing. Excellent group rates.

SOUTHBOUND
PO BOX 637 MM 106.5 KEY LARGO FL 33037

CAPT BOB KLEIN'S SCUBA SHOP
PO BOX 1849 KEY LARGO FL 33037

PENNEKAMP PARK CONCESSION
MM 102.5 Box 13M
Key Largo FL 33037
305/451-1621 (In Florida: 800/432-2871)
The only dive shop located directly in
Pennekamp Park. Scuba, snorkeling, and
glassbottom boat tours daily.

QUIESCENCE DIVING SERVICES
BOX N-13 KEY LARGO FL 33037

OCEAN DIVERS INC
BOX 1113-A KEY LARGO FL 33037

SEA DWELLERS SPORTS CENTER INC
99850 OVERSEAS HWY KEY LARGO FL 33037

PENNEKAMP DIVING HQS
99696 OVERSEAS HWY UNIT 1 KEY LARGO FL 33037

ISLAND SPORT DIVERS
98474 S OVERSEAS HWY KEY LARGO FL 33037

CAPTAIN CHAMBERS TRIANGLE
DIVE CENTER
PO Box 2258
Key Largo FL 33037
305/451-1805
For reservations, call 305/451-1805. Six-passenger
custom boat, guided dives & u/w camera, N/C.
Reader-recommended "Undercurrent" of 5/82.
Deep, drift, wreck, & night dives in Pennekamp.

KEY WEST PRO DIVE SHOP
1605 N ROOSEVELT BLVD KEY WEST FL 33040

EVANS DIVE SHOP
509 SOUTHARD ST KEY WEST FL 33040

WATERSPORT PEOPLE
508 SOUTH ST KEY WEST FL 33040

REEF RAIDERS DIVE SHOP
109 DUVAL ST KEY WEST FL 33040

PROMETHEAN ADVENTURES
975 S ROOSEVELT BLVD KEY WEST FL 33040

SEASPORTS DIVING CENTER
101 MARGARET ST KEY WEST FL 33040

REEF RAIDERS DIVE SHOP
US #1 STOCK ISLAND KEY WEST FL 33040

TRIANGLE WATERSPORTS
US #1 BOX 321 SUMMERLAND KEY FL 33042

LOOE KEY RESORT & MARINA
PO BOX 5096 RAMROD KEY FL 33042

SUMMERLAND DIVE SHOP
PO BOX 321 MM 24.5 SUMMERLAND KEY FL 33042

KEY SEA CENTER
PO BOX 515 BIG PINE KEY FL 33043

UNDERSEAS
US 1 BOX 319 BIG PINE KEY FL 33043

TARPON LODGE DIVING CENTER
4990 OVERSEAS HWY MARATHON FL 33050

CORAL LAGOON DIVE SHOP
12399 OVERSEAS HWY MARATHON FL 33050

DIVERS HQS
11511 OVERSEAS HWY MARATHON FL 33050

HURRICANE AQUA-CENTER Inc.
10800 Overseas Hwy
Marathon FL 33050
305/743-2400
Lowest prices in the Keys. U.S. Divers, Parkways,
Seatec. Boat trips. PADI instruction.

DIVERS UNLIMITED
HOLIDAY INN MM 53 MARATHON FL 33050

REEF ROVER II
4680 OVERSEAS HWY MARATHON FL 33050

HALL'S DIVING CENTER
1688 OVERSEAS HWY MARATHON FL 33050

THE DIVING SITE
12399 OVERSEAS HWY MARATHON FL 33050

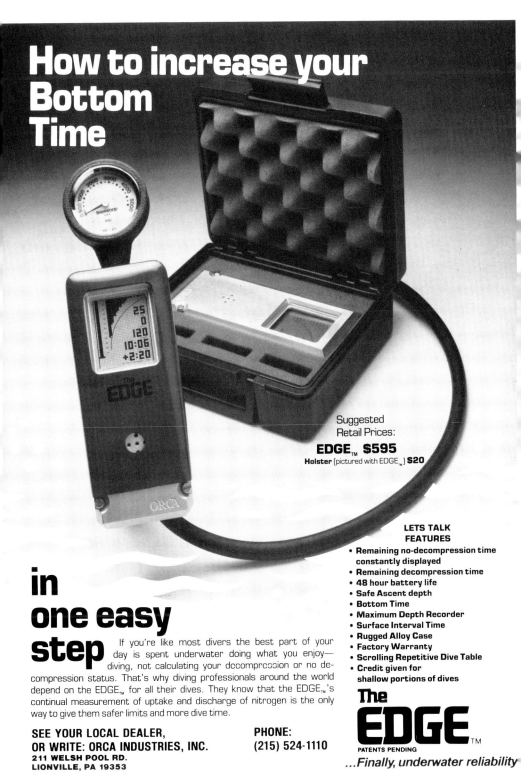

A collection of stupified gar in the tailwaters of the Oahe Dam, South Dakota. ▲

▼ *Looking up the massive side of the* **Papoose** *from 130'.*

Rudderfish and lemon butterflyfish swarm to meet divers under a boat at Molokini.   ED ROBINSON, Tom Stack & Associates   see page 333

Explore the depths with Casio's watersport watches.

DW-1000
200M

MQ550CW
100M

MQ551CW
100M

LQ351CW
100M

Casio's watersport watches can take you for a dunk in a hot tub or a dive in the open sea.

The rugged DW-1000 gives you regular timekeeping functions, as well as stopwatch, countdown alarms, daily alarm, hourly/half-hourly signal and calendar. The MQ-550CW and MQ-551CW feature regular timekeeping functions and give you the date and day in English and Spanish. The LQ-351C ladies watch features hour, minute and second hands. There are over 40 Casio watersport watches, both analog and digital, depth tested from 30 to 200 meters. Prices range from $9.95 to $59.95, so even your wallet won't get soaked.

CASIO®
Where Miracles Never Cease

Casio, Inc. Timepiece Division: 15 Gardner Road, Fairfield, N.J. 07006 New Jersey (201) 575-7400, Los Angeles (213) 803-3411.

UNDER SEA WORLD
521 North US #1
Fort Pierce FL 33450
305/465-4114

Oldest & largest scuba facility on the Treasure Coast. Equipment sales & service. Scubapro dealer. Great lobster diving and spearfishing.

JENSEN BEACH DIVERS
1991 NE DIXIE HWY JENSEN BEACH FL 33457

SCUBA SHACK
2485 NE DIXIE HWY JENSON BEACH FL 33457

LOXAHATCHEE BOAT WORKS &DIVE SHOP
940 N DOLPHIN DR JUPITER FL 33458

JUPITER TEQUESTA SCUBA SPORTS
150 N US 1 TEQUESTA FL 33458

COASTAL SPORT & DIVING
2407 10TH AVE N LAKE WORTH FL 33460

AMERICAN DIVERS INT
409 LAKE AVE LAKEWORTH FL 33460

WORLD OF SCUBA
902 S FEDERAL HWY LANTANA FL 33462

REEF DIVE SHOP
304 E OCEAN AVE LANTANA FL 33462

DIXIE DIVERS
1843 SE FEDERAL HWY STUART FL 33494

BRUNER SPTG GOODS
145 SW MONTEREY RD STUART FL 33494

ROMORA BAY CLUB
PO BOX 216M STUART FL 33495

TREASURE COAST DIVERS
413 S FEDERAL HWY STUART FL 33497

ROBBYS SPORTING GOODS
225 32 D AVE W BRADENTON FL 33505

SUB-MARINER SPORTS
5421 14TH ST W BRADENTON FL 33507

GULF VIEW DIVERS
101 BRIDGE ST BRADENTON FL 33510

MAC'S SPORTS INC
2126 DREW ST CLEARWATER FL 33515

NAUTICAL DREAMS
766 ELDORADO AVE CLEARWATER BEACH FL 33515

POP'S SCUBA SCHOOL
1754 DREW ST CLEARWATER FL 33515

AQUATIC ETC INC
2410 SR 580 CLEARWATER FL 33515

FLORIDA SCUBA CTR
2807 GULF-TO-BAY BLVD CLEARWATER FL 33519

AQUATIC SCUBA
2410 SR 580 CLEARWATER FL 33519

KIEFER'S SPORTING GOODS
306 E PASCO AVE DADE CITY FL 33525

THE BOSUN'S LOCKER
1289 BAYSHORE BLVD DUNEDIN FL 33528

AQUARIUS PRO DIVE SHOP
1450 BEACH RD ENGLEWOOD FL 33533

DENNY'S SPORTS WORLD
1271 BEACH RD ENGLEWOOD FL 33533

LAND O'LAKES SCUBA CENTER
171 US HWY 41 #3 LAND O' LAKES FL 33539

SUNSHINE SCUBA
1901 West Bay Dr
Largo FL 33540
813/585-0938

Professional diving instruction. Continuing education & specialty programs, classes day & night. Air, rentals, charters, trips. PADI, YMCA, NSS certifications.

JIMS DIVE SCHOOL
9047 STARKY RD SEMINOLE FL 33542

THE BOSUN'S LOCKER
3400 US 19 N PALM HARBOR FL 33563

TACKLE SHACK INC
7801 66TH ST N PINELLAS PARK FL 33565

BILL JACKSON INC
9501 US 19 N PINELLAS PARK FL 33565

SCUBA WEST
14213 US 19 NORTH HUDSON FL 33567

TARPON SPORTING GOODS
1406 US 19 N #13 PT RICHEY FL 33568

OCEAN PRO DIVE SHOP INC
2259 BEE RIDGE RD SARASOTA FL 33579

ECONOMY TACKLE
6018 S TAMIANA TRAIL SARASOTA FL 33581

CORAL KINGS PRO DIVE SHOP
5770 S TRAIL SARASOTA FL 33581

FLORIDA DOWN UNDER INC
4658 ARDALE ST SARASOTA FL 33582

GULF MARINE WAYS
950 ROOSEVELT BLVD TARPON SPRINGS FL 33589

TARPON SPORTING GOODS
272 US HWY 19 TARPON SPRINGS FL 33589

SOUTHERN SHORES DIVE SHOP
2357 S TAMIANA TRAIL VENICE FL 33595

WORLD OF WATER INC
2917 W KENNEDY BLVD TAMPA FL 33609

OSHMAN'S SPORTING GOODS
2154 UNIVERSITY SQ MALL TAMPA FL 33612

TAMPA PRO DIVER
1028 W BUSCH BLVD TAMPA FL 33612

TAMPA SPORTS UNLTD
4545 W HILLSBOROUGH AVE TAMPA FL 33614

THE BOSUN'S LOCKER
9735 W HILLSBOROUGH AVE TAMPA FL 33615

TERRACE WATERSPORTS
9228 N 56TH ST TEMPLE TERRACE FL 33617

UNIQUE SPORTS CORP
11209 N DALE TAMPA FL 33618

WOODS & WATER
8514 BLUE RIDGE DR TAMPA FL 33619

JIM KETROW DIVING
225 54TH TERR N ST PETERSBURG FL 33703

SCUBA NAUTICS
801 49TH ST S ST PETERSBURG FL 33707

DIVERS WORLD
13613 GULF BLVD MADEIRA BEACH FL 33708

IRVS SCUBA
5950 34TH ST S ST PETERSBURG FL 33711

DIVERS DEN-SKYWAY
6701 34TH ST S ST PETERSBURG FL 33711

GREEN TURTLE DIVE SHOP
4401 HARDEN BLVD LAKELAND FL 33802

SAND DOLLAR DIVE CENTER
4805 HWY 60 W MULBERRY FL 33860

DEEP SIX DIVERS SERVICE
2710 W LAKE ELOISE DR WINTER HAVEN FL 33880

ABC SPORTS
1915 LINHART AVE FT MYERS FL 33901

BULLSEYE SPORTS SUPPLY
1214 N TAMIANA TRAIL N FT MYERS FL 33903

KENS TOP SPORTS
4600 CLEVELAND AVE FT MYERS FL 33907

U/W EXPLORERS DIVING CTR
6020 MCGREGOR BLVD FT MYERS FL 33907

SEALANDIA OF NAPLES
625 8TH ST S NAPLES FL 33940

SCUBA-SKI INC
118 9TH ST S NAPLES FL 33940

Bald eagles prey on baby sea otters who lie on the surface, wrapped in kelp, while the mother dives.

MID KEYS MARINE SUPPLY
2735 OVERSEAS HWY MARATHON FL 33050

KEY COLONY DIVE CENTER
PO BOX 49 KEY COLONY FL 33051

PRO DIVING SCHOOLS
1540 N FEDERAL HWY POMPANO BEACH FL 33062

NAUTILUS DIVE SURF AND SKI
2700 E ATLANTIC BLVD POMPANO BEACH FL 33062

AQUATIC GATEWAYS DIVING CENTER
15 N FEDERAL HWY POMPANO BEACH FL 33062

SCUBA DIVERS INC
1799 N STATE RD 7 MARGATE FL 33063

OCEAN DIVING SCHOOLS
4301 N FEDERAL HWY LIGHTHOUSE PT FL 33064

DIVING SPECIALTIES
10115 W SAMPLE RD CORAL SPRINGS FL 33065

AQUATIC GATEWAYS SCUBA CENTER
10115 W SAMPLE RD CORAL SPRINGS FL 33065

FLORIDA KEYS DIVE & SKI
PO BOX 391 TAVERNIER FL 33071

PRIDE DIVER
PO BOX 523290 MIAMI FL 33129

US AQUANAUTS
677 SW FIRST ST MIAMI FL 33130

COCOANUT GROVE SCUBA SHOP
2809 BIRD AVE MIAMI FL 33133

SCUBA SPORTS
16604 NE 2ND AVE N MIAMI BEACH FL 33133

U/W LTD
4633 SW LEJEUNE BLVD CORAL GABLES FL 33134

DIVERS DREAM INC
919 SW 87TH AVE MIAMI FL 33135

NEW ENGLAND DIVERS INC
2945 NE 2ND AVE MIAMI FL 33137

UNLIMITED PRESSURES INC
5214 NW 35TH AVE MIAMI FL 33142

KEY DIVERS INC
200 CRANDON BLVD #202 KEY BISCAYNE FL 33146

BAYFRONT DIVERS
4225 PONCE DE LEON BLVD CORAL GABLES FL 33146

U/W UNLIMITED
4633 LE JEUNE RD CORAL GABLES FL 33146

EAGLES NEST
3301 RICKENBACHER CSWY KEY BISCAYNE FL 33149

CALYPSO DIVE CENTER
8449 SW 40TH ST MIAMI FL 33155

NEW ENGLAND DIVERS
9820 S DIXIE HWY KENDALL FL 33156

AUSTINS DIVING CENTER
10503 S DIXIE HWY MIAMI FL 33156

SCUBA SPORTS OF PERRINE INC
1707 PERRINE PLAZA MIAMI FL 33157

THE DIVING LOCKER
295 SUNNY ISLES BLVD MIAMI BEACH FL 33160

AMAROK CHARTERS
PO BOX 611235 N MIAMI FL 33161

DSG INC
2050 NE 151ST ST N MIAMI FL 33162

DIVERS PARADISE
10740 SW 24TH ST MIAMI FL 33165

PISCES DIVERS INC
14328 BISCAYNE BLVD N MIAMI FL 33181

DIVERS DEN SOUTH
12614 N KENDALL DR MIAMI FL 33186

CUTLER RIDGE DIVING CENTER
20850 S DIXIE HWY MIAMI FL 33189

DIVE N SALES CENTER
1339 NE 4TH AVE FT LAUDERDALE FL 33304

UNDERSEA SPORTS INC
1525 N FEDERAL HWY FT LAUDERDALE FL 33304

U/W EXPLORERS SOCIETY
PO BOX 5608 FT LAUDERDALE FL 33310

NAUTILUS DIVE SURF AND SKI
2104 W OAKLAND PARK BLVD
FT LAUDERDALE FL 33311

DIVING SPECIALTIES INC
2139 STIRLING RD FT LAUDERDALE FL 33312

BRENT FEINMAN'S SCUBA WORLD
3932 DAVIE BLVD FT LAUDERDALE FL 33312

SCUBA TOO
4565 SW 37 AVE FT LAUDERDALE FL 33312

WALKERS CAY DIVE SHOP
700 SW 34TH ST FT LAUDERDALE FL 33315

LAUDERDALE DIVERS
1334 SOUTHEAST 17TH ST FT LAUDERDALE FL 33316

PRO DIVE SHOP/BAHAI MAR YACHT CLUB
PO BOX 3030 FT LAUDERDALE FL 33316

ADVENTURE DIVERS
923 SOUTHEAST 20TH ST FT LAUDERDALE FL 33316

DIVERS HAVEN
1530 CORDOVA RD FT LAUDERDALE FL 33316

SUNRISE SCUBA AND SPORTS
2700 N UNIVERSITY DR SUNRISE FL 33322

WEST BROWARD WATERSPORTS
9146 ST RD 84 DAVIE (FT LAUDERDALE) FL 33324

SCUBA SPORTS
1802 N UNIVERSITY DR PLANTATION FL 33324

DIVERS DEN
8280 STATE RD 84 DAVIE FL 33324

SCUBARIFIC INC
4282 S UNIVERSITY DR DAVIE FL 33328

DEEP ENTERPRISES
820 NE 59TH ST FT LAUDERDALE FL 33334

SCUBA II
5060 N DIXIE HWY OAKLAND PARK FL 33334

THE AQUA SHOP DIVING CENTER
1940 BROADWAY RIVIERA BEACH FL 33403

SEAPRO SCUBA CENTER
US 1 AT 37TH ST RIVIERA BEACH FL 33404

DIVERS WORLD UNDERSEA CENTER
2525 LAKE DR RIVIERA BEACH FL 33404

FRANK'S DIVE SHOP
301 E BLUE HERON BLVD RIVIERA BEACH FL 33404

GULF STREAM SCUBA CHARTERS
2315 CAROMA LN WEST PALM BEACH FL 33406

NORINE ROUSE SCUBA CLUB
4708 N DIXIE HWY W PALM BEACH FL 33407

MOTHER OCEAN
152 NW 20TH ST BOCA RATON FL 33432

NAUTILUS
877 E PALMETTO PARK RD BOCA RATON FL 33432

AMERIC DIVE
18232 104TH TERRACE S BOCA RATON FL 33434

INLET DIVE SHOP
1940 N FEDERAL HWY BOYNTON BEACH FL 33435

NAUTILUS INC
286 SW 12TH AVE DEERFIELD FL 33441

ATLANTIS ADVENTURE
1621 SE 3RD CT DEERFIELD BEACH FL 33441

OCEONICS INC
250 DIXIE BLVD DEL RAY BEACH FL 33444

DELRAY DIVE SHOP
3645 N FEDERAL DELRAY BEACH FL 33444

HELENE'S SHOPPE
1906 ORANGE AVE FT PIERCE FL 33450

DIXIE DIVERS INC
1717 S US 1 FT PIERCE FL 33450

FLORIDA DIVERS SUPPLIES
1700 STEADLEY AVE PUNTA GORDA FL 33950

CHARLOTTE DIVER
4549-F Tamiami Trail
Charlotte Harbor FL 33952
813/629-2722
Scuba instruction. Air station. Rentals.
Equipment repair. Boat cleaning service. In the
David Hill Bldg between Arby's & McDonald's.

CHARLOTTE DIVER
4549 F TAMIANA TRL CHARLOTTE HARBOR FL 33950

AQUA SCUBA DIM IN DIVING
4336D TAMIANA TRAIL PT CHARLOTTE FL 33952

MSA SCUBA RESALE
DRAWER 940 BLDG 154 APO MIAMI FL 34004

ATLANTIC PACIFIC SCUBA
PO BOX 882 APO MIAMI FL 34008

ZEAGLE SYSTEMS
PO BOX 1144 ZEPHYR HILLS FL 34248

GEORGIA

ATLANTA DIVERS SUPPLY
4144 East Ponce de Leon Ave
Clarkston GA 30021
404/296-7513
NAUI pro facility. Sales, instruction, air, service.
Cave diving specialists. Diving travel worldwide.

DIXIE DIVERS INC
1945 CANDLER RD DECATUR GA 30032

BRIARLAKE DIVERS
3561 LAVISTA RD DECATUR GA 30033

SPORTCO INC
1696 COBB PKWY SE MARIETTA GA 30061

DIVERS LOCKER INC
1475 TERRELL MILL ROAD MARIETTA GA 30067

LANIER DIVE MASTERS
102 BUFORD DAM RD CUMMING GA 30130

DIVERS SALVAGE & SERVICE INC
14 ELLIOT CIR ROME GA 30162

OCEAN QUEST DIVERS ACADEMY INC
7488 TARA BLVD JONESBORO GA 30236

DIVEMASTERS UNLIMITED
1042 Hwy 19 North
Thomaston GA 30286
404/648-6700
Sales, service, instruction, rentals. PADI
certifications. Air, specialties . CPR, first aid.
Local diving, Flint River tours. Trips. Family owned
& operated.

VENTURE OUT SPORTS
PO BOX 14285 ATLANTA GA 30324

DIVE SALES
1925 PIEDMONT CIRCLE NE ATLANTA GA 30324

INLAND REEF DIVE SHOP
2546 MELLVILLE AVE DECATUR GA 30325

SANDY SPRINGS DIVERS
6445 ROSWELL RD NE #106 ATLANTA GA 30328

DIVING WORLD U.S.A.
2945 Buford Hwy NE
Atlanta GA 30329
404/634-4354
Twenty-six years in Atlanta. All brands — sales,
service, rentals, air. Trips — Florida, Bahamas,
Cayman. Two recompression/hyperbaric chambers.

BERRY SCUBA ATLANTA
3443 STEWART AVE HAPEVILLE GA 30354

USDS
3306 SIMS ST HAPEVILLE GA 30354

AQUA SPORTS DIVERS SUPPLY
1766 GREEN RD BUFORD GA 30518

DIVING LOCKER
1490 BAXTER ST ATHENS GA 30606

JONAH'S DIVING WORLD
2610 PEACH ORCHARD RD AUGUSTA GA 30906

THE DIVE SHOP
201 S COMMERCIAL CIR WARNER ROBINS GA 31093

OUTDOOR ADVENTURES UNLTD
5208 MERCER UNIVERSITY DR MACON GA 31206

ADVENTURE BOUND SPORTS
21 E DE RENNE AVE ATLANTA GA 31406

GOLDEN ISLES AQUATICS
123 BEL AIR CIR BRUNSWICK GA 31520

PSI
203 A OSBORNE ST ST MARYS GA 31558

ODYSSEY DIVE CENTER
2501 RADIUM SPRINGS RD ALBANY GA 31706

PLANET OCEAN SCUBA CENTER
3865 MILLER RD WINDSOR VLG CTR
COLUMBUS GA 31904

HAWAII

SEA URCHIN SCUBA SHOP
98-025 HEKAHA ST AIEA HI 96701

HAWAII SEA ADVENTURES
98-316 KAM HWY AIEA HI 96701

HONSPORTS
PEARLRIDGE CENTER AIEA HI 96701

CORAL KING DIVE SHOP
921176 HOOKEHA ST EWA BEACH HI 96706

HONSPORTS
393 KILEAUA AVE HILO HI 96720

NAUTILUS DIVE CENTER
382 KAMEHAMEHA AVE HILO HI 96720

HONSPORTS
KAAHUMANU CENTER KAHULUI HI 96732

AARON'S DIVE SHOP INC
39 MALUNIU AVE KAILUA HI 96734

SANDWICH ISLE DIVERS
73-1263 LIHAU ST KAILUA KONA HI 96740

FAIRWIND INC
78-7128 KALEOPAPA RD KAILUA-KONA HI 96740

GOLD COAST DIVERS
75-5660 PALANI RD KAILUA KONA HI 96740

JACKS DIVING LOCKER
KONA INN VILLAGE-BOX 5306 KAILUA KONA HI 96740

DIVE MAKAI CHARTERS
PO BOX 2955A KAILUA KONA HI 96740

HAWAIIAN DIVERS
BOX 572 KAILUA KONA HI 96740

SEA DREAMS HAWAII
PO Box 4886
Kailua-Kona HI 96745
808/329-8744
A private charter service. One to four divers.
One trip daily & nights. YOU select the spots —
we'll take you there!

KONA COAST SKINDIVER
PO Box 1780
Kailu-Kona HI 96740
808/329-8802
The one-stop dive shop. Professional experience
since 1968. Write for free color brochure, map,
& package tours info.

KONA REEF DIVERS
PO BOX 1409 KAMUELA HI 96743

PROFESSIONAL DIVERS HAWAII
PO BOX 1252 KAMUELA HI 96743

SEA URCHIN SCUBA SHOP
46-216 KAHUHIPA ST KANEOHE HI 96744

KONA COAST ACTIVITIES
PO BOX 5397 KAILUA-KONA HI 96745

HI PRO DIVERS--AQUATICS KAUAI
4-901 KUHIO HWY KAPAA KAUAI HI 96746

SEA SAGE DIVING CENTER
4-1378 KUHIO HWY KAPAA HI 96746

AQUATICS KAUAI LTD
733 KUHIO HWY KAPAA KAUAI HI 96746

OCEAN ODYSSEY
4-363 KUHIO HWY KAPAA HI 96746

MOLOKAI FISH & DIVE
PO BOX 576 1-800-553-5926 KAUNAKAKAI HI 96748

OCEAN ACTIVITIES CENTER
3750 WAILEA ALANUI D-2 WAILEA HI 96753

HAWAIIAN WATERCOLORS
PO BOX 616 KIHEI MAUI HI 96753

THE DIVE SHOP OF KIHEI
1975 S KIHEI RD KIHEI HI 96753

MAUI DIVE SHOP
PO BOX 1018 AZEKA'S PLACE KIHEI HI 96753

KAUAI DIVERS
RR1 BOX 56 KOLOA KAUAI HI 96756

FATHOM FIVE DIVERS
PO Box 907
Koloa/Kauai HI 96756
808/742-6991
Condo, car, unlimited diving packages, 5-day
certifications. Daily charters, introductory dives,
sales, air, photography. NAUI, PADI, SSI.

U/W ADVENTURES
PO BOX 11244 LAHAINA HI 96761

CENTRAL PACIFIC DIVERS
780 FRONT ST LAHAINA MAUI HI 96761

BLUE CHIP CHARTERS
PO BOX 5159 LAHAINA HI 96761

CAPT NEMO'S OCEAN EMPORIUM
PO BOX 11267 LAHAINA HI 96761

SCUBA SCHOOLS OF MAUI
1000 LIMAHANA PL #A LAHAINA HI 96761

MAHANA NA I'A ADVENTURES
PO BOX 11323 LAHAINA HI 96761

SUN DIVERS
LAHAINA MARKET PLACE LAHAINA MAUI HI 96761

LAHAINA DIVERS
710 FRONT ST LAHAINA MAUI HI 96761

DIVE MAUI INC
LAHAINA LUNA RD LAHAINA HI 96761

CUSTOM DIVE SERVICE
PO BOX 1056 PAIA MAUI HI 96779

SEA URCHIN SCUBA SHOP
1652 WILIKINA WAHIAWA HI 96786

OCEAN SPORTS HAWAII
PO BOX 3291 WVS KAMUELA HI 96787

OAHU SCHOOL OF DIVING
95 S KAM HWY WAHIAWA HI 96787

LEEWARD DIVE CENTER
85-979 Farrington Hwy
Waianae HI 96792
808/696-3414
Air, classes, charters, rentals, repair.
Three charter boats daily. Dives — ledge, turtle,
porpoise, cave, night, photography, shipwreck,
and much more!

BOJAC AQUATIC CENTER
94-801 FARRINGTON HWY WAIPAHU HI 96797

BOJAC SWIM & SCUBA SCHOOL
94-366 PUPUPANI ST WESTGATE WAIPAHU HI 96797

CLARK SALES INC
94-054 LEOKANE ST WAIPAHJ HI 96797

DAN'S DIVE SHOP
660 ALA MOANA BLVD HONOLULU HI 96814

HONSPORTS
ALA MOANA CENTER HONOLULU HI 96814

SCUBAPRO
1020 AUAHI HONOLULU HI 96814

SOUTH SEAS AQUATICS
1050 ALA MOANA BLVD HONOLULU HI 96814

BIG MIKE'S WAIKIKI DIVE SHOP
2131 KALAKAUA #212 HONOLULU HI 96815

STEVE'S DIVING ADVENTURES
1860 ALA MONA BLVD HONOLULU HI 96815

AMERICAN DIVE HAWAII
PO Box 88161
Honolulu HI 96815
808/732-2877
PADI 5-star shop that offers anything you need
in diving. Wreck & drift dives, caves, dropoffs,
& more.

WAIKIKI DIVING
420 NAHUA ST HONOLULU HI 96815

THE SCUBA SHOP
20 SAND ISLAND RD HONOLULU HI 96819

HAWAIIAN DIVERS
2344 KAMEHAMEHA HWY HONOLULU HI 96819

HONSPORTS
2868 KAIHIKAPU HONOLULU HI 96819

ALOHA DIVE SHOP
KOKO MARINA SHPG CNTR HONOLULU HI 96825

IDAHO

POCATELLO DIVING SCHOOL
1332 S 3RD AVE POCATELLO ID 83201

INTERMOUNTAIN DIVE SHOP
559 West Main
Twin Falls ID 83301
208/734-9275
PADI training facility. Air, rentals, instruction,
specialty courses. Only master instruction in Idaho.
Lots of local diving.

SCUBA IDAHO
306 OVERLAND AVE W HANSEN ID 83334

TREASURE DIVING
PO BOX 582 MERIDIAN ID 83642

THE SCUBA DIVING CO
208 E 37TH ST #9 BOISE ID 83704

BOISE WATER SPORTS
3204 OVERLAND RD BOISE ID 83705

LEE'S OUTDOOR OUTFITTERS
1675 W APPLEWAY COEUR D'ALENE ID 83814

ILLINOIS

PROSPECT DIVE SHOP
1709 E CENTRAL ARLINGTON HEIGHTS IL 60005

ANCHOR IN SCUBA CENTER
1790 ALGONQUIN RD ARLINGTON HGTS IL 60008

DARKENS FOR SPORTS
202 S COOK ST BARRINGTON IL 60010

EMMY TRAVELS INC
8700 W DEMPSTER DES PLAINES IL 60016

AQUAVENTURE INC
1655 OAKTON ST DES PLAINES IL 60018

FROG POND DIVE SHOP
148 GREENBAY RD HIGHWOOD IL 60040

PROSPECT BIKE N DIVE SHOP
506 E NORTHWEST HWY MT PROSPECT IL 60056

BERRY SCUBA
1717 RAND RD PALANTINE IL 60067

BLACK MAGIC DIVE SHOP
202 E MAIN ST ROUND LAKE PARK IL 60073

OM COYNE SCUBA SYSTEMS
3919 OAKTON ST SKOKIE IL 60076

DARCO MARINE
PO BOX 1014 WAUKEGAN IL 60085

VENTURE FORTH SPORTS
817 W LINCOLN HWY DE KALB IL 60115

THE GUN ROOM
161 N EDISON AVE ELGIN IL 60120

BERRY SCUBA
26A YORKTOWN CON CEN MALL LOMBARD IL 60148

SUN & SNOW LTD
18 W 431 ROOSEVELT RD LOMBARD IL 60148

UNDERSEAS SCUBA CENTER
626 N ADDISON RD VILLA PARK IL 60181

THE CREATIVE WHALE
940 E ROOSEVELT RD WEST CHICAGO IL 60185

MIDWEST DIVING ACADEMY
1027 N ROSELLE RD HOFFMAN ESTATES IL 60195

ELMER'S WATERSPORTS INC
707 HOWARD EVANSTON IL 60202

POPE'S DIVING SUPPLY
1828 222ND PL SAUK VILLAGE IL 60411

GOOSES SCUBA SHACK
19507 GOVERNORS HWY FLOOSMOOR IL 60422

AQUARIANS INC
2450 W JEFFERSON JOLIET IL 60436

AAA SCUBA INC
PO BOX 117 PALOS PARK IL 60464

AQUANAUTS ODYSSEY PRO DIVE CENTER
538 East 147th St (Sibley Blvd)
South Holland IL 60473
312/331-3372
Sales, rentals, repairs. Instruction, specialty courses
Trips, charters. Friendliest service in Chicagoland
area.

AQUA CENTER INC
43 E DOWNER AURORA IL 60506

HINSDALE SPORT & SKI
26 E 1ST HINSDALE IL 60521

ANCHOR IN SCUBA CENTER
315 W OGDEN AVE WESTMONT IL 60559

VERN'S SCUBA CENTER
3917 N ASHLAND AVE CHICAGO IL 60613

ANCHOR IN SCUBA CENTER
732 W FULLERTON AVE CHICAGO IL 60614

REEF & WRECK DIVERS
1920 N LINCOLN AVE CHICAGO IL 60614

BERRY SCUBA CO
6674 N NORTHWEST HWY CHICAGO IL 60631

THE GEAR BAG
1605 N NEWLAND CHICAGO IL 60635

DIVE AND SKI SHOP
2958 W 95TH ST EVERGREEN PARK IL 60642

SCUBA EMPORIUM
12003 S CICERO AVE ALSIP IL 60658

PETRIE'S SPORTS & SCUBALAB
1617 N ALPINE RD ROCKFORD IL 61107

VENTURE FORTH
2424 S ALPINE RD ROCKFORD IL 61108

THORNE'S MARINE CENTER
7928 N 2ND ST ROCKFORD IL 61111

COURT N SPORT
316 S MAIN MORTON IL 61550

BLUE HOLE DIVE SHOP
4817 FARMINGTON RD PEORIA IL 61604

DO DIVE IN
7 SHERRY LANE BARTONVILLE IL 61607

DO DIVE IN
5509 SW ADAMS ST BARTONVILLE IL 61607

SPORT DIVERS INC
130 WRIGHT LANE E PEORIA IL 61611

THE AQUA SHOP
319 NORTH ST NORMAL IL 61761

MIDWEST DIVING SPECIALISTS
203 S LINDEN NORMAL IL 61761

MIDWEST SCUBA CENTER
700 S NEIL ST CHAMPAIGN IL 61820

THE OUTDOOR STORE
2224 W MAIN ST BELLEVILLE IL 62221

WINDWALKER DIVE & TRAVEL
1423 W MAIN BELLEVILLE IL 62221

MID AMERICA SCUBA
RT 127 AT KANE ST CARLYLE IL 62231

SOUTHERN ILLINOIS DIVERS SUPPLY
RT 6 BRUSH HILL CARBONDALE IL 62901

WATERSHED DIVE SHOP
1028 E WALNUT CARBONDALE IL 62901

T & S DIVE SHOP
1108 N WASHINGTON ST MARION IL 62959

INDIANA

LAYTON'S CENTRAL SCUBA
200 N MORTON ST FRANKLIN IN 46131

CENTRAL SCUBA
403 GRANADA ST WHITELAND IN 46154

DIVERS SUPPLY CO
3315 N ILLINOIS ST INDIANAPOLIS IN 46208

MIDWEST SCUBA CENTER Inc.

9508 Ross Ln

Indianapolis IN 46268

317/872-2522

**PADI 5-star training facility. Sales, service, air.
Indoor training pool on site. Local diving &
Caribbean charters.**

QUALITY DIVERS SUPPLY
601 SIBLEY HAMMOND IN 46320

HANSEN'S SPORTS
3750 RIDGE HIGHLAND IN 46322

MAD DOG'S SCUBA
307 E MCKINLEY US 20E MISHAWAKA IN 46545

J R AQUATIC CENTER
5133 US 31 N SOUTH BEND IN 46637

MICHIANA SCUBA

51400 U.S. 31 North

South Bend IN 46637

219/277-7288

**Sales, rentals, repairs, lessons, in-store pool.
Wreck dives, Bahama trips, group sailing trips.**

PRO DIVE SHOP INC
3203 COVINGTON RD FT WAYNE IN 46804

ANCHOR DIVE SHOP

1001 Leesburg Rd

Fort Wayne IN 46808

219/432-6288

**PADI training facility. Local diving, Great
Lakes diving, Florida diving, exotic travel.
Instruction, air, rentals.**

U/W ADVENTURES
1509 GOSHEN RD FT WAYNE IN 46818

DIVING DEN INC
2229 E CR 00 NS KOKOMO IN 46902

TOM LEAIRD'S U/W SERVICE
216 S MARTIN ST MUNCIE IN 47303

SOUTHERN INDIANA SCUBA
1106 S WALNUT ST BLOOMINGTON IN 47401

DIVERS WORLD INC
1271 E MORGAN AVE EVANSVILLE IN 47711

JOES DIVE SHOP
5620 UPPER MT VERNON RD EVANSVILLE IN 47712

OUBACHE OUTFITTERS
2831 S THIRD TERRE HAUTE IN 47802

SCUBA LAND
1632 WABASH AVE TERRE HAUTE IN 47802

AQUA NUT DIVERS
RR1 BOX 153C CLINTON IN 47842

LAFAYETTE DIVERS SUPPLY INC
901 MAIN ST LAFAYETTE IN 47901

*Certain deep-sea prawns and fishes emit luminous clouds of glowing mist when startled;
this slowly dwindles into a grayish fluid.*

IOWA

MIDWEST DIVERS SUPPLY
807 ALLEN ST BOONE 50036

LEYDEN'S DIVE SHOP
1213 LOCUST ST DES MOINES IA 50309

IOWA STATE SKIN DIVING SCHOOLS
7500 UNIVERSITY #C DES MOINES IA 50311

KING NEPTUNE'S SCUBA SHOP
521 FLOYD BLVD SIOUX CITY IA 51101

CHRIS'S WATER WORLD LTD
223 W 7TH ST SPENCER IA 51301

DUBUQUE YACHT BASIN
1630 E 16TH ST DUBUQUE IA 52001

WILDERNESS SPORTS LTD
117 W 11 ST DUBUQUE IA 52001

FRYMOYER'S WATERWORLD
414 GARFIELD OTTUMWA IA 52501

DUKE'S DIVER SHOP
333 N MADISON ST OTTUMWA IA 52501

D & M DIVE SHOP
BASBURY CIRCLE OTTUMWA IA 52501

RADAR SCUBA
2704 GLENN BETTENDORF IA 52722

DIVERS PRO SHOP
628 S DUBUQUE ST IOWA CITY IA 52776

MAR'S MARINE & DIVE SHOP
3808 S CONCORD ST DAVENPORT IA 52802

KANSAS

SUNFLOWER DIVERS
923 HOLLAND GREAT BEND KS 67530

MIDWEST DIVING CENTER INC
156 GREENWOOD WICHITA KS 67211

TOPEKA DIVE SHOP
3032 SE 6TH ST TOPEKA KS 66607

THE DIVE SHOP INC
3606 W 95TH ST LEAWOOD KS 66206

KENTUCKY

LOUISVILLE DIVE SHOP
2478 BARDSTOWN RD LOUISVILLE KY 40205

KY DIVING HQS
3928 SHELBYVILLE RD LOUISVILLE KY 40207

DIVERS INC
4807 DIXIE HWY LOUISVILLE KY 40216

AQUATIC WORLD-LIFE SUPPORT
8056 LA GRANGE RD LOUISVILLE KY 40222

LEXINGTON DIVE SHOP
8198 EUCLID AVE LEXINGTON KY 40502

LAUREL DIVING HQS
RT 4 BOX 146B CORBIN KY 40701

AQUARIUS DIVE SHOP
800 W ELM LUDLOW KY 41016

NORTHERN KY DIVING CENTER
225 MAIN ST FLORENCE KY 41042

THE SCUBA CENTER
BOX 180B LOST CREEK KY 41348

PIKEVILLE DIVE SHOP
PO BOX 2856 PIKEVILLE KY 41501

MOUNTAIN DIVERS SUPPLY
ROUTE 1 BOX 114 BETSY LAYNE KY 41605

NEMO'S DIVING
PO BOX 1149 HYDEN KY 41749

ADVENTURE WORLD
1207 31 W BYPASS BOWLING GREEN KY 42101

U/W ODYSSEY
2709 PARRISH AVE OWENSBORO KY 42301

DALE HOLLOW LAKE DIVE SHOP
SULPHUR CREEK MARINA KETTLE KY 42752

LOUISIANA

UWSR DIVE SHOP
RT 1 BOX 220A LEESVILLE LA 71446

GREGS DIVE SHOP
4007 N BOLTON ALEXANDER LA 71303

U/W WORLD PRO DIVE
419 PAULINE DR ALEXANDRIA LA 71301

AGUA SPORTS
715 B TRENTON ST W MONROE LA 71294

TWIN CITY MARINE INC
1001 TONEY BAYOU ROAD W MONROE LA 71291

AQUA SPORTS
609 PARK AVE MONROE LA 71202

DIVING UNLTD
2200 CLOVIS 'A' PO BOX 5014 BOSSIER CITY LA 71171

AQUA CENTER
223 MERRICK SHREVEPORT LA 71104

ADVENTURE SPORTS ARK-LA-TEX
1817 TEXAS SHREVEPORT LA 71103

GOLDEN DIVER
RT 2 BOX 7-H GREENWOOD LA 71033

AQUA CENTER
117 BOSSIER CROSSROADS BOSSIER CITY LA 71010

GULF STREAM DIVERS
7978 ANTIOCH RD BATON ROUGE LA 70817

STEINBERG'S SPORT CTR
CORPORATE MALL BATON ROUGE LA 70808

SEVEN SEAS DIVING
3625 PERKINS RD BATON ROUGE LA 70808

SKI & SCUBA INC
7122 FLORIDA BLVD BATON ROUGE LA 70806

STEINBERG'S SPORT CTR
832 ST PHILLIP BATON ROUGE LA 70802

AIRLINE DIVING
PO BOX 1721 GONZALES LA 70737

BAYOU SCUBA
108 1/2 CITIES SERVICE HWY SULPHUR LA 70663

DIVE TOLEDO SHOPPE
PO Box 761
DeRidder LA 70634
318/286-5457(Shop) 462-2361(Office)
J&L Marina, Toledo Bend Lake, LA. Full-service lakeside. March through November. Call ahead for winter/summer hours.

HOUSE FOR SPORTS
4411 COMMON LAKE CHARLES LA 70605

VENTURE SPORTS INC
1409 RYAN ST LAKE CHARLES LA 70601

LAND & SEA SPORTS INC
802 WELDON ST NEW IBERIA LA 70560

FRANKLIN MARINA & YACHT SALES
PO BOX 261 FRANKLIN LA 70538

DARRELS DIVE SHOP
RT 2 BOX 234 EUNICE LA 70535

SA-NOOK SPORTS AND TRAVEL
1800 E MAIN ST NEW IBERIA LA 70506

AQUATIC DIVE SHOP
1903 JOHNSTON ST LAFAYETTE LA 70503

SKI & SCUBA
3801 JOHNSTON ST LAFAYETTE LA 70503

LA STATE SCHOOL OF DIVING
427 RENA DR LAFAYETTE LA 70501

OUTDOOR WORLD
1123 12TH LAFAYETTE LA 70501

SLIDELL DIVE CENTER
2316 FRONT ST SLIDELL LA 70458

OCEANS I SCHOOL OF DIVING
1300 W 21ST AVE COVINGTON LA 70433

WATER SPORTS DIVE SHOP
908 COLUMBIA ST BOGALUSA LA 70427

GULF S DIVING ACADEMY
1001 N OAK ST HAMMOND LA 70401

BAYOU VENTURES
809 BRASHEAR AVE MORGAN CITY LA 70380

SCUBA HUT
1537 W PARK AVE HOUMA LA 70364

SANTA FE U/W SERVICES
PO BOX 2518 HOUMA LA 70361

HOUMA WATERSPORTS INC
3219 W MAIN ST HOUMA LA 70360

SEA PHOTO
502 HIBERNIA PLACE HOUMA LA 70360

SEA HORSE DIVING ACADEMY
5400 Crowder Blvd — Unit E
New Orleans LA 70127
504/246-6523
PADI 5-star training facility. Instruction, sales, rentals, repairs, and dive trips. Full-service dive store offering 12 specialty courses.

MARINE DIVING SUPPLY
1043 SENA ST NEW ORLEANS LA 70124

CARIBBEAN DIVING CO
7350 W BROADWAY ST NEW ORLEANS LA 70124

ROLANDS NEW ORLEANS SKINDIVING
4417 DRYADES NEW ORLEANS LA 70115

DEEP WATER SUPPLY INC
330 BERMUDA ST NEW ORLEANS LA 70114

CULLUM & BOREN
4100 GEN DE GAULLE NEW ORLEANS LA 70114

TEMENTOS SKIN & SCUBA
435 SALA AVE WESTWEGO LA 70094

AMERICAN AQUATIC SUPPLY
PO BOX 159 MARRERO LA 70073

AQUA TECH DIVE CENTER
6119 WESTBANK EXPWY MARRERO LA 70072

PJ'S SCUBA SHOP
529 AIRLINE HWY LA PLACE LA 70068

VAL'S DIVE SHOP
522F HWY 45 LAFITTE LA 70067

VINEYARDS DIVE SHOP
1400 W ESPLANADE AVE KENNER LA 70062

AQUA AIR IND INC
221 BARK DR HARVEY LA 70058

DIVER'S EXCHANGE
2245 BREAUX AVE HARVEY LA 70058

SCUBA ADVENTURES
PALMER AVE NEW ORLEANS LA 70018

HARRY'S DIVE SHOP
4709 AIRLINE HWY METAIRIE LA 70001

SEA SAFARI INC
2315 N WOODLAWN METAIRIE LA 70001

THE DIVE SHOP
4901 ARGONNE ST METAIRIE LA 70001

MAINE

DIVER'S WORLD
47 MAINE ST BRUNSWICK ME 04011

AQUA DIVING ACADEMY
1183 CONGRESS ST PORTLAND ME 04101

TOMMY'S DIVE SHOP
273 CONGRESS PORTLAND ME 04101

AQUA SPORTS
1183 CONGRESS ST PORTLAND ME 04102

SKIN DIVERS PARADISE
RD 3 TURNER RD BOX 817 AUBURN ME 04210

NORTHEAST SCUBA EQUIPMENT
347 WILSON ST BREWER ME 04412

AQUA CITY SCUBA
11 WATER ST WATERVILLE ME 04901

MARYLAND

SPORTSMAN
ARLINGTON RD & BETH AVE BETHESDA MD 20014

AMERICAN WATERSPORTS
6217 LIVINGSTON RD OXON HILL MD 20021

CATALINA INC
176 GREAT MILLS RD LEXINGTON PARK MD 20653

DYNAMO INC
8906 RHODE ISLAND AVE COLLEGE PARK MD 20740

THE SCUBA SHOPPE
1053 E GUDE DR ROCKVILLE MD 20850

DIVEMASTERS
506 CALVIN LANE ROCKVILLE MD 20851

DIVERS WORLD
923 61ST AVE SILVER SPRINGS MD 20910

CHESAPEAKE DIVERS
537A BAY DRIVE CHASE MD 21017

SEA WORLD DIVERS INC
1808 BEL AIR RD FALLSTON MD 21047

THE SCUBA IIUT INC
7649 CRAIN HWY SOUTH GLEN BURNIE MD 21061

EAST COAST DIVERS
311 ST JOHN ST HAVRE DE GRACE MD 21078

SEA COLONY DIVE SHOP
8470 FT SMALLWOOD RD PASADENA MD 21122

STAMMER'S SPORT MARINE
1175 FT SMALLWOOD RD PASADENA MD 21122

PARK'S DIVING SUPPLY
8027 LIBERTY RD BALTIMORE MD 21207

SCUBA SHOP II
1113G OLD N POINT RD BALTIMORE MD 21222

THE SCUBA SHOP
7976 E BALTIMORE ST BALTIMORE MD 21224

DIVERS DEN Inc.
8105 Harford Rd
Baltimore MD 21234
301/668-6866
Large Enough to Serve You — Small Enough to Know You.

KING NEPTUNE DIVE SHOP
909 W STREET ANNAPOLIS MD 21401

SEA COLONY DIVE SHOP
RT 50 & CASTLE MARINA RD CHESTER MD 21619

CALYPSO DIVE SHOP
RT 50 AT KENT NARROWS GRASONVILLE MD 21638

MASSACHUSETTS

HOLYOKE U/W SUPPLY
354-356 HIGH ST HOLYOK MA 01040

HAMPSHIRE SCUBA SUPPLY
52 MAIN ST FLORENCE MA 01060

WESTFIELD WATER SPORTS
4 MEADOW'ST WESTFIELD MA 01085

SPRINGFIELD SCUBA SUPPLY
876 SUMNER AVE SPRINGFIELD MA 01108

PIER 136
136 OAKLAND ST SPRINGFIELD MA 01108

AQUATIC ADVENTURES
11 MELVILLE ST PITTSFIELD MA 01201

ANDY'S SPORT SHOP
216 DANIELS ST FITCHBURG MA 01420

FOUND ENTERPRISES
61 AUBURN ST AUBURN MA 01501

INLAND DIVERS
100 S MAIN ST LEICESTER MA 01524

CENTRAL SCUBA CENTER
50B LAKE AVE WORCESTER MA 01604

EAST COAST DIVERS
280 WORCESTER RD RT 9 FRAMINGHAM MA 01701

NATICK OUTDOOR STORE
38 NORTH AVE NATICK MA 01760

AL'S ROD & GUN SHOP
400 BROADWAY LAWRENCE MA 01849

EASTERN DIVERS SUPPLY
453 GORHAM ST LOWELL MA 01852

LOWELL SCUBA CENTER
477 GORHAM ST LOWELL MA 01852

NORTHEAST SCUBA Inc.
125 Liberty St
Danvers MA 01923
617/774-7296
Sales, service, rentals, air. Boat charters, scuba instruction, u/w photo instruction, hydro testing, regulator repairs. Carry all major lines. Open seven days a week, 8:00am-9:00pm.

NORTH ATLANTIC SCUBA
1293 OCEAN ST RT 139 MARSHFIELD MA 02050

DIVING HORIZONS
446 SOUTH ST WRENTHAM MA 02093

EASY DIVER CHARTERS
BOX 291 BACK BAY ANNEX BOSTON MA 02117

AMERICAN DIVERS
149 1ST ST CAMBRIDGE MA 02142

BOSTON SCHOOL OF DIVING
59 WASHINGTON ST SOMERVILLE MA 02143

EAST COAST DIVERS
213 BOYLSTON ST BROOKLINE MA 02146

AQUA LUNG CENTER
663 EASTERN AVE MALDEN MA 02148

NORTHEAST SCUBA INC.

"A Full Service Dive Shop"

SALES - SERVICE - HYDRO TEST
RENTALS - BOAT CHARTERS
INSTRUCTION – U. W. PHOTOGRAPHY
AIR STATION
MON. SAT. 8 A.M. - 9 P.M. — SUN. 8 A.M. - 6 P.M.

125 LIBERTY STREET   DANVERS, MA. 01923

SOUTH SHORE SKIN DIVER CO
511 WASHINGTON ST QUINCY MA 02169

DIVER JIMS
404 TRAPELO RD BELMONT MA 02178

PRO DIVERS USA
236 WOOD RD BRAINTREE MA 02184

AQUA-DIVE SCUBA CENTER
561 MAIN ST RT 18 WEYMOUTH MA 02190

M & M SPORTING GOODS CO
35 MAIN ST PLYMOUTH MA 02360

CAPE COD DIVING
134 MAIN ST BUZZARDS BAY MA 02532

CAPE MARINE
304 SHORE RD MONUMENT BEACH MA 02553

THE SUNKEN SHIP
12 BROAD ST NANTUCKET MA 02554

SUNKEN SHIP
BROAD ST NANTUCKET MA 02554

MARTHA'S VINEYARD SCUBA HQS
PO BOX 486 VINEYARD HAVEN MA 02568

HYANNIS SCUBA CENTER
303 IYANOUGH RD HYANNIS MA 02601

EAST COAST DIVERS
237 FALMOUTH RD RT 28 HYANNIS MA 02601

SPORTS PORT
149 W MAIN ST HYANNIS MA 02601

SHIPMATE DIVE SHOP
PO BOX 498 SESUIT HARBOR E DENNIS MA 02641

DIVING ENTERPRISES OF CAPE COD
815 MAIN ST HARWICHPORT MA 02646

DIVING ENTERPRISES
815 MAIN ST RT 28 HARWICHPORT MA 02646

GOOSE HUMMOCK SHOP
RT 6A ORLEANS MA 02653

MARINE SPECIALTIES
235 COMMERCIAL ST PROVINCETOWN MA 02657

THE SCUBA CENTER
11 HORTON AVE S ATTLEBORO MA 02703

WHALING CITY DIVING CENTER
39 MAIN ST FAIRHAVEN MA 02719

CAPE COD SKIING & DIVING
39 MAIN ST FAIRHAVEN MA 02719

FALL RIVER MARINE SPORTS
122 PLYMOUTH AVE FALL RIVER MA 02723

MA SCHOOL OF SKINDIVING
484 S MAIN ST FALL RIVER MA 02724

FAMILY DIVING CENTER
2205 S MAIN ST FALL RIVER MA 02724

PISCES DIVING SERVICE
14 HALL ST FALL RIVER MA 02724

JONES LOCKER
38 SCADDINGS ST TAUNTON MA 02780

MICHIGAN

LAKE ORION DIVERS DEN
879 CENTRAL LAKE ORION MI 48035

DEEP SIX ENTERPRISES
1650 NEW HAMPSHIRE AVE MARYSVILLE MI 48040

BRUNO'S DIVE SHOP
34740 GRATIOT AVE MT CLEMENS MI 48043

PONTIAC SCUBA CENTER
220 S TELEGRAPH PONTIAC MI 48053

THE SPORT SHOP
210 HURON AVE PT HURON MI 48060

BLUE WATER DIVING
1722 LAPEER AVE PT HURON MI 48060

REC DIVING
4424 N WOODWARD ROYAL OAKS MI 48072

ADVANCED AQUATICS LTD.
25020 Jefferson
St. Clair Shores MI 48080
313/779-8777
PADI TRAINING FACILITY. Openwater,
advanced, rescue, divemaster, & specialty courses.
Sales & service. All major brands. Air to 3500.
Rentals. Group/individual tours, local &
international.

U/W OUTFITTERS
2579 UNION LAKE RD UNION LAKE MI 48085

MACOMB DIVE SHOP
28869 BUNERT WARREN MI 48093

RECREATIONAL DIVING SYSTEMS
3380 WASHTENAW AVE ANN ARBOR MI 48104

DEONAS DIVE SHOP
410 GOLFORE ST DEARBORN MI 48124

TOM & JERRY'S SPORT SHOPS
20318 VANBORN DEARBORN HEIGHTS MI 48125

MI U/W SCHOOL OF DIVING
3280 FT LINCOLN PARK MI 48146

SEA-SIDE DIVING
12440 MORANG DETROIT MI 48224

DON'S DIVE SHOP & EQUIP CO
26934 W 7 MILE RD REDFORD MI 48240

FOUR FATHOMS DIVING
75 E ARGYLE ST SANDUSKY MI 48471

DIVERS SUPPLY
4084 CORUNNA RD FLINT MI 48504

THE SCUBA CENTER
64155 FENTON RD BURTON MI 48529

HIGGINS LAKE SPORTS CENTER
9982 W HIGGINS LAKE DR HIGGINS LAKE MI 48627

SEAQUATICS INC
28 ASHMAN CIRCLE MIDLAND MI 48640

DEEP SIX SCUBA SCHOOLS
884 N PINE RD ESSEXVILLE MI 48732

THE DIVE SHOP
505 E GRAND RIVER LANSING MI 48906

ZZ U/W WORLD INC
1806 E MICHIGAN AVE LANSING MI 48912

KALAMAZOO DIVE HQS
1622 BLOOMFIELD AVE KALAMAZOO MI 49001

SUB-AQUATIC SPORTS LTD
1483 W MICHIGAN AVE BATTLE CREEK MI 49017

WOLF'S ENTERPRISES
1207 ANN ST ST JOSEPH MI 49085

SPORTSARAMA
114 W CHICAGO RD STURGIS MI 49091

DIVERS MAST
2900 LANSING AVE JACKSON MI 49202

SCUBA PLUS
126 N BROAD HILLSDALE MI 49242

NEWAYGO COUNTY DIVERS SUPPLY
8697 S MASON NEWAYGO MI 49337

ROCK DIVER INC
850 S STEWART FREMONT MI 49412

GRAND HAVEN DIVE CENTER
216 N THIRD GRAND HAVEN MI 49417

WEST MICHIGAN DIVE CENTER
2367 W SHERMAN BLVD MUSKEGON MI 49441

A & C DIVING ACADEMY
918 E FULTON GRAND RAPIDS MI 49503

LEN'S DIVE SHOP
924 W FULTON GRAND RAPIDS MI 49504

SKAMT SHOP
5055 PLAINFIELD NE GRAND RAPIDS MI 49505

SHIP N SHORE INC
214 DEXTER ELK RAPIDS MI 49629

SCUBA NORTH
13258 W BAYSHORE DR TRAVERSE CITY MI 49684

BILMAR SPORTS
212 E FRONT TRAVERSE CITY MI 49684

THE SKI RACK/SUMMIT SPORTS
224 E CHISHOLM ALPENA MI 49797

LAKELAND SPORTS
408 N 3RD MARQUETTE MI 49855

NORTH STAR DIVING SCHOOL
737 1ST ST MENOMINEE MI 49858

MINNESOTA

THE PEARL DIVE SHOP
216 N CEDAR OWATONNA MN 55060

THE ARGONAUTES INC
1040 UNIVERSITY AVE ST PAUL MN 55105

NORTHLAND DIVERS INC
3000 WHITE BEAR AVE MAPLEWOOD MN 55109

U/W SCHOOLS OF AMERICA
2280 MAPLEWOOD DR MAPLEWOOD MN 55109

SMITH DIVING
14354 BURNHAVEN DR BURNSVILLE MN 55337

THE SUPERIOR DIVER
4833 HANOVER RD MOUND MN 55364

U/W SCHOOLS OF AMERICA
1300 E WAYZATA BLVD A WAYZATA MN 55391

SCUBA OUTLET STORE
4741 Chicago Ave
Minneapolis MN 55407
612/823-7210
PADI training facility. Full service. Hydro instruction. Sales. Trips to Lake Superior, the Caribbean, Central America. Intro to commercial diving career.

SMITH DIVING
2835 CENTRAL NE MINNEAPOLIS MN 55418

SCUBA CENTER
5015 PENN AVE S MINNEAPOLIS MN 55419

CLUB SCUBA SOUTH
9429 LYNDALE AVE BLOOMINGTON MN 55420

LAND OF THE LOON DIVE SHOP
410 CHESTNUT ST VIRGINIA MN 55792

LAKE SUPERIOR DIVERS SUPPLY
3028 W 3RD ST DULUTH MN 55806

ROCHESTER SCUBA
220 SW 1ST AVE ROCHESTER MN 55901

AUSTIN SKIN DIVING SHOP
701 NE 10TH ST AUSTIN MN 55912

HAZELTON SCUBA SHOP
1055 W 7TH ST WINONA MN 55987

ALBERT LEA SKIN & SCUBA
1913 KEYSTONE ALBERT LEA MN 56007

NORTH SHORE DIVERS SUPPLY
539 PACIFIC WILLMAR MN 56201

CENTRAL MN DIVERS
102 E ST GERMAIN ST ST CLOUD MN 56301

ARGONAUTES
9 SE WILSON ST ST CLOUD MN 56301

MICKS SCUBAPRO DIVE SHOP
416 N 14TH ST MOORHEAD MN 56560

SUPERFROG ENT
116 21ST ST S MOORHEAD MN 56560

NORTHWEST DIVERS SUPPLY
1701 N 11TH ST MOORHEAD MN 56560

NORTHWEST DIVERS SUPPLY
1330 ROOSEVELT RD BEMIDJI MN 56601

MISSISSIPPI

SYDNEYS DIVE
PO BOX 98 PONTOTOC MS 38863

SKIPPERS DIVE & SKI
4441 N STATE JACKSON MS 39206

OCEAN TREK DIVE SHOP
1200 ROEBUCK DR MERIDIAN MS 39301

SPORTS LTD
1510 W PINE ST HATTIESBURG MS 39401

WALTER'S SPORTING GOODS
PO BOX V RICHTON MS 39476

EARL'S DIVE & SPORT SHOP
401 BOULSLOG ST GULFPORT MS 39501

DIVEMASTER DIVING CENTER
3309 JODY NELSON DR GULFPORT MS 39501

GULF COAST DIVING ACADEMY
1 COLONIAL PLAZA BAY ST LOUIS MS 39520

THE DIVE SHOP
1312 1/2 W HOWARD BILOXI MS 39530

MISSISSIPPI DIVERS
2518 DENNY AVE PASCAGOULA MS 39567

NEPTUNE SCHOOL OF SCUBA
PO BOX 1413 MCCOMB MS 39648

HUNTERS DIVE SUPPLY
ROUTE 9 BOX 107 COLUMBUS MS 39701

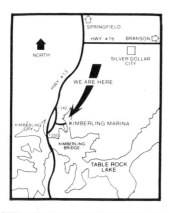

MISSOURI

AQUASPORTS INC.
5601A South Campbell
Springfield MO 65807
417/883-5151 or 739-2704
Kimberling City Marina, Table Rock Lake. Air,
boat trips, rentals, sales, service, installation.

CBS DIVE SHOP
RR 10 COLUMBIA MO 65201

CAPT NEMO'S DIVE SHOP
2001A MISSOURI BLVD JEFFERSON CITY MO 65101

CAPT NEMO'S DIVE SHOP
BRIDGEPORT MARINA OSAGE BEACH MO 65065

DIVERS DOWN
2624 E 7TH ST JOPLIN MO 64801

DIVERS EQPT & REPAIR SERVICE
5800 BARRYMORE KANSAS CITY MO 64134

SKIN-N-SCUBA SHOP
12009 E 43RD ST KANSAS CITY MO 64133

THE DIVE SHOP
8135 N OAK KANSAS CITY MO 64118

WHEELER MARINE
1924 BURLINGTON N KANSAS CITY MO 64116

ACADEMY OF SCUBA TRAINING
437 BROADWAY CAPE GIRARDEAU MO 63701

ADVENTURE WORLD
12683 DORSETT ST LOUIS MO 63141

INNER WORLD DIVING CENTER
9953 LEWIS & CLARK ST LOUIS MO 63136

INNER WORLD DIVING II
11736 GRAVOIS RD ST LOUIS MO 63127

WEST END DIVING CENTER
11215 Natural Bridge Rd
St. Louis MO 63044
314/731-5003
Guided u/w tours of Bonne Terre Mine: 100'+
visibility, year-round 62° air temperature, 58°
water temperature.

WEST END DIVING CENTERS
11004 MANCHESTER ST LOUIS MO 63122

THE DIVE SHOP INC
9832 MANCHESTER RD ST LOUIS MO 63119

U/W SPORTS INC
8340 WATSON RD ST LOUIS MO 63119

BI-STATE U/W INC
3334 S GRAND ST LOUIS MO 63118

UNDERSEA SPORTS
230 MANCHESTER RD WINCHESER MO 63011

MONTANA

MOUNTAIN STATES DIVERS SUPPLY
1525 Central Ave
Billings MT 59102
406/252-7583
All major brands of equipment. Factory-trained
certified service. Diving school. Air station,
rentals.

REITERS MARINA
450 HIGHWAY 10 E BILLINGS MT 59102

THE DIVING FLAG
PO BOX 30316 HARDING RD BILLINGS MT 59107

DIVERS DEN
3711 3RD AVE N GREAT FALLS MT 59401

JIM'S DIVE SHOP
108 RIVERVIEW 3 E GREAT FALLS MT 59404

SCUBA CENTER
PO BOX 1334 BOZEMAN MT 59715

BIGHORN DIVERS
2521 West Babcock
Bozeman MT 59715
406/586-3252
Sales, rentals, instructions. Dive crystal-clear
mountain lakes. Convenient location to Yellowstone
National Park. Air available. Friendly guides,
area information.

WIRTZ DIVING SERVICE
2929 W BABCOCK BOZEMAN MT 59715

THE SPORTSMAN/SKI HAUS
40 E IDAHO ST KALISPELL MT 59901

NEBRASKA

FATHOM DIVING SCHOOLS
1620 E OVERLAND SCOTTSBLUFF NE 69361

BIG MAC SCUBA SHACK
HWY 61 & 92 PO BOX 713 OGALLALA NE 69153

AL ZIEGLER'S DIVING SERVICE
602 S MEYER N PLATTE NE 69101

U/W SPORTS OF LINCOLN
1630 Q ST PO BOX 80564 LINCOLN NE 68501

MID COAST DIVERS SUPPLY
7115 N 65TH AVE OMAHA NE 68152

ACTION SPORTS OMAHA
13463 W CENTER RD OMAHA NE 68104

NEVADA

S & B RECREATION
848 A E LAKE MEAD DR HENDERSON NV 89015

DIVE WEST INC
5831 E LAKE MEAD BLVD LAS VEGAS NV 89115

DESERT DIVERS SUPPLY
5720 E CHARLESTON BLVD LAS VEGAS NV 89122

SIERRA DIVING CENTER
104 E GROVE ST RENO NV 89502

FOUR SEASONS DIVING CENTER
315 SPOKANE ST #8 RENO NV 89512

NEW HAMPSHIRE

ALDEN ENGINEERING CO
RR1 BOX 56 MASON NH 03048

WATER SPORTS INC
352 S BROADWAY SALEM NH 03079

QUEEN CITY SCUBA SCHOOL
297 S WILLOW MANCHESTER NH 03103

DIVERS DEN DIVE SHOP
730 MAMMOTH RD MANCHESTER NH 03104

NORTH COUNTRY SCUBA DIVING
57 ELM ST LACONIA LAKEPORT NH 03246

U/W SPORTS OF NH
334 PARK AVE KEENE NH 03431

KEENE DIVERS SUPPLY
27 WATER KEENE NH 03431

UNDERSEA ENTERPRISES
46 STATE PORTSMOUTH NH 03801

NEW ENGLAND AQUATICS
522 SAGAMORE RD RYE NH 03801

ATLANTIC AQUA SPORT
522 SAGAMORE RD RYE NH 03870

NORTH COUNTRY SCUBA
1055 S MAIN ST WOLFEBORO NH 03894

NEW JERSEY

SUB-OCEAN SERVICES INC
340 BROADWAY BAYONNE NJ 07002

AQUANAUT VOYAGEUR INC
BOX 1583 WEST CALDWELL NJ 07007

U/W EXPLORATION
151 LOWELL ST CARTERET NJ 07008

CEDAR GROVE DIVER'S SUPPLY
492 POMPTON AVE RT 23 CEDAR GROVE NJ 07009

THE QUARRY DIVE SITE
RT 517 HAMBURG NJ 07419

BERGEN COUNTY SCUBA
181 E FRANKLIN TURNPIKE HOBOKUS NJ 07423

MARLIN SCUBA
506 RT 17 RAMSEY NJ 07448

UNDERWATER SPORTS OF NEW JERSEY Inc.
Rt 17 South
Rochelle Park NJ 07662
201/843-3340
New Jersey's oldest professional dive shop. Call
201/843-3340. Full services: instruction, travel,
repair, sales. Scubapro and other major brands.

U/W SPORTS OF NJ
RT 17 S ROCHELLE PARK NJ 07662

SKI & SCUBA SPORTS
32 WESTWOOD AVE WESTWOOD NJ 07675

DIVERS TWO INC
1 MAIN ST AVON NJ 07717

DOSIL'S SPORT CENTER
261 STATE HWY 36 E KEANSBURG NJ 07734

EAST COAST DIVING SERVICE
340 F SPRING VALLEY RD MORGANVILLE NJ 07751

PROFESSIONAL DIVERS
70 STATE HWY 35 NEPTUNE CITY NJ 07753

NEPTUNE'S DEN
RT 46 HACKETTSTOWN NJ 07840

U/W ADVENTURES INC
1152 ROUTE 10 RANDOLPH NJ 07869

LAKELAND SCUBA DIVERS INC
92 ROUTE 10 EAST HANOVER NJ 07936

TRITON DIVERS OF LBI
44TH & LONG BEACH BLVD BRANT BEACH NJ 08008

PRINCETON AQUA SPORTS
306 Alexander St
Princeton NJ 08540
609/924-4240
PADI training facility. Diving vacations our
specialty. Basic & advanced courses. Weekend
charters. Rentals, sales, service. Most major
brands.

THE DIVE SHOP OF NJ
RT 38 MAPLE SHADE NJ 08052

THE DIVE SHOP OF NJ
RD 1 #33 DELSEA DR HURFFVILLE NJ 08080

M & E MARINE SUPPLY
PO BOX 601 CAMDEN NJ 08101

EAST COAST DIVING SUPPLY
2603 NEW ROAD NORTHFIELD NJ 08225

BORDENTOWN AQUASPORTS
261 RT 130 BORDENTOWN NJ 08505

PRINCETON AQUA SPORTS
306 ALEXANDER ST PRINCETON NJ 08540

FOUR DIVERS INC
56 BROADWAY POINT PLEASANT BEACH NJ 08742

U/W DISCOVERY
2716 STATE HWY 37 TOMS RIVER NJ 08753

EDISON SKINDIVING CTR
1659 HWY 27 EDISON NJ 08817

DIVER HEAVEN
120 ROSE ST PHILLIPSBURG NJ 08865

DIVERS COVE
STATE HWY 35 LAWRENCE HARBOR NJ 08879

NEW MEXICO

NEW MEXICO DIVERS SUPPLY
625 AMHERST DR NE ALBUQUERQUE NM 87106

WATERSPORTS
4927 PROSPECT ALBUQUERQUE NM 87110

NEW MEXICO SCUBA SCHOOLS
11200-17 MONTGOMERY NE ALBUQUERQUE NM 87111

DIVERS DEN
1228B JUAN TABO BLVD NE ALBUQUERQUE NM 87112

NEW MEXICO SCHOOL OF DIVING
207 E MAIN ST FARMINGTON NM 87401

MAC'S DIVE SHOP
4101 CEDAR DR FARMINGTON NM 87401

FRONTIER SPORTS
6475 E MAIN FARMINGTON NM 87401

NORTHERN NEW MEXICO DIVING CTR
2427 CAMINO DE VIDA SANTA FE NM 87501

CLOVIS MARINE
2110 E MABRY DR CLOVIS NM 88101

RANDY'S SCUBA SALES INC
117 E 7TH ST CLOVIS NM 88101

NEW YORK

HARVEY'S DIVE CENTER
3179 EMMONS AVE BROOKLYN NY 11235

CENTRAL SKINDIVERS CENTER
160-09 JAMAICA AVE JAMAICA NY 11432

ISLAND SCUBA CENTERS
74 WOODGLEFT AVE FREEPORT NY 11520

SKIN DIVING SCHOOL OF LI
70 FREEPORT MALL FREEPORT NY 11520

INNERSPACE DIVE SHOP INC
57 FOREST AVE GLEN COVE NY 11542

DIVERS WAY
596 SUNRISE HWY BAY SHORE NY 11706

ISLAND DIVERS INC
110 W MAIN ST BAYSHORE NY 11706

SOUND WATERSPORTS
271 BAYVILLE AVE BAYVILLE NY 11709

CENTRAL SKINDIVERS
2608 MERRICK RD BELLMORE NY 11710

SUFFOLK DIVING CENTER
58 LARKFIELD RD E NORTHPORT NY 11731

DIVEMASTER CENTER
57 MILL LANE HUNTINGTON NY 11743

KELLY'S SCUBA TRAVEL
3 E ROGUES PATH HUNTINGTON STATION NY 11746

SOUTH BAY DIVING CENTER
3028 MERRICK RD WANTAGH NY 11753

THE DIVING CENTER
26 WOLCOTT RD LEVITTOWN NY 11756

UNDERSEA ADVENTURES
PO BOX 888 MILLER PLACE NY 11764

U/W SERVICES UNLTD
NINE QUIET COURT MILLER PLACE NY 11764

PORTHOLE DIVE SHOP
811 RT 25A PT JEFFERSON STATION NY 11776

SWIMKING DIVE SHOP
Rt 25-A
Rocky Point NY 11778
516/744-7707
(Next to McDonald's.) NASDS professional store
school. Lessons — basic, advanced, u/w
photography. Local wreck diving & Caribbean
trips — Christmas, midwinter, & Easter.

CHUGAI INTERNATIONAL
ONE AMES CT PLAINVIEW NY 11803

7 Z'S HAMPTON BAYS DIVERS
1140 FLANDERS RD RIVERHEAD NY 11901

DIVERS WORLD ENTERPRISES
1263 LOUDON RD RD 1 COHOES NY 12047

CAHILL'S SPORTING GOODS
26 4TH ST TROY NY 12180

HERMANS WORLD
20 WOLF RD ALBANY NY 12205

DIVING DISCOVERY
1629 CENTRAL AVE ALBANY NY 12205

NORTHEAST DIVERS INC
193 MORRIS RD SCHENECTADY NY 12303

MID HUDSON DIVING CENTER
BOICES LANE KINGSTON NY 12401

KING FOX DIVE & SPORT
206 ESOPUS AVE ULSTER PARK NY 12487

ADVENTURE WORLD SPORTS
RT 9 POUGHKEEPSIE NY 12601

MARSH SCUBA SUPPLY
19 LAUER RD POUGHKEEPSIE NY 12603

LAMB BROS
MAIN ST BOLTON LANDING NY 12814

MOBY DICK'S DIVE SHOP
BLOODY POND ROAD LAKE GEORGE NY 12845

AQUALUNG DIVING CENTER
LOUDEN RD SARATOGA SPRINGS NY 12866

CAHILL'S SPORTING GOODS
PYRAMID MALL PLATTSBURGH NY 12901

DIVING CENTER OF LIVERPOOL
504 OLD LIVERPOOL DR LIVERPOOL NY 13088

NATIONAL AQUATIC SERVICE
1732 ERIE BLVD E SYRACUSE NY 13210

BRICE'S DIVING EQPT
RD 1 FISH LANE RD MARCY NY 13403

CENTRAL NY SCHOOL OF SKINDIVING
1716 BURRSTONE RD NEW HARTFORD NY 13413

PRO DIVERS SUPPLY
103 MAIN ST WHITESBORO NY 13492

HUNT U/W SPECIALTIES
200 E MAIN ST WATERTOWN NY 13601

ST LAWRENCE DIVING SHOP
2 MAIN ST TASSENA NY 13662

DIVERS DEPOT
223 W MAIN ST SACKETS HARBOR NY 13685

CENTRAL NY SCHOOL OF SKINDIVING
27 N BROAD ST NORWICH NY 13815

CENTRAL NY SCHOOL OF SKINDIVING
28 ONEIDA ST ONEIDA NY 13820

NYPENN DIVERS SUPPLY
400 PROSPECT ST BINGHAMTON NY 13905

BENTHCO DIVING
7055 RIDGE RD LOCKPORT NY 14094

SKIN DIVING SCHOOL OF WEST NY
2048 NIAGARA ST BUFFALO NY 14207

DIP N DIVE INC
500 NIAGARA FALLS BLVD BUFFALO NY 14223

NORTHERN SCUBA
7708 BUFFALO AVE NIAGARA FALLS NY 14304

FINGER LAKES SCUBA
CITY PIER CANANDAIGUA NY 14424

PISCES SCHOOL OF DIVE
781 RAIRPORT RD E ROCHESTER NY 14445

THE DIVE PLAN
3320 1/2 E LAKE RD LIVONIA NY 14487

ROCHESTER DIVING CENTER INC
545 TITUS AVE ROCHESTER NY 14617

U/W WORLD
C/O YMCA BLDG 101 E 4TH ST JAMESTOWN NY 14701

MASTER DIVE SHOP
171 CHESTNUT ST CORNING NY 14830

EDS DIVE SHOP
92 OAKWOOD AVE ELMIRA HTS NY 14903

SCUBA PLUS
106 3RD AVE NY NY 10003

PARAGON SPORTING GOODS
867 BROADWAY NY NY 10003

ATLANTIS 2
498 AVENUE OF THE AMERICAS
NY NY 10011

JACK W FINE
121 E 79TH ST NY NY 10021

AQUA SCHOOL OF NY
1089 2ND AVE NY NY 10022

PAN AQUA DIVING SERVICE INC
10 E 85TH ST NY NY 10028

SPORTS HOLIDAYS INC
15 W 44TH ST NY NY 10036

RICHARD'S AQUALUNG CENTER
233 W 42ND ST NY NY 10036

AQUA ADVENTURES INC
PO BOX 1792 MURRAY HILL STATION NY NY 10156

EAST COAST DIVING INC
1500 HYLAN BLVD STATEN ISLAND NY 10305

PRO DIVING SCHOOL OF NY
222 FORDHAM ST BRONX NY 10464

COUGAR SPORTS
3470 WEBSTER AVE BRONX NY 10465

NANCY C
40 S HIGHLAND #9 OSSINING NY 10562

SEA VENTURES
84 RIDGEVIEW DR PLEASANTVILLE NY 10570

WESTCHESTER DIVE CENTER
62 WESTCHESTER AVE PORT CHESTER NY 10573

COUGAR SPORTS INC
590 CENTRAL PARK AVE SCARSDALE NY 10583

THE DIVE SHOP
I-40 Claremont Exit
Claremont NC 28610
704/459-7440 or 459-7286
PADI instruction. Sales, service, air, rentals.
Compare our low prices. Wreck dives, Florida
& Caribbean trips.

DIVE SHOP
218 1ST AVE W CONOVER NC 28613

DANE LANE ENTERPRISES
RT 9 BOX 329 HENDERSONVILLE NC 28739

OHIO

SUB-AQUATICS INC
8855 E BROAD REYNOLDSBURG OH 43008

KIRBY'S SCUBA SUPPLIES
7336 E MAIN ST REYNOLDSBURG OH 43068

U/W SPORTS OF OHIO
703 S MAIN ST URBANA OH 43078

CEN OH SCH OF DIVING
2355 W DUBLIN-GRANVILLE RD
WORTHINGTON OH 43085

ASK WATERSPORTS INC
80 W LONG ST COLUMBUS OH 43215

B G AQUA HUT INT INC
1002 S MAIN BOWLING GREEN OH 43402

AQUANETIC CENTER
203 BORNWELL NAPOLEON OH 43545

INNERSPACE EQUIPMENT
410 RYDER RD TOLEDO OH 43607

DUKE'S DIVE SHOP
844 CIRCLEVIEW DR TOLEDO OH 43607

U/W SPORTS
BARTON MANOR CAMBRIDGE OH 43725

U/W ENTERPRISES
832 LAKE AVE ELYRIA OH 44035

BOB'S AQUATIC SUPPLY
1766 ORKNEY R MADISON OH 44057

SUBAQUATICS INC
10333 NORTHFIELD NORTHFIELD OH 44067

ATWELLS
205 CHESTNUT ST PAINESVILLE OH 44077

ALMIRA DIVERS SUPPLY
9722 ALMIRA ST CLEVELAND OH 44102

AQUA SPECIALISTS INC
16604 MADISON AVE LAKEWOOD OH 44107

SCUBA WEST
17021 LORAIN AVE CLEVELAND OH 44111

BUCKEYE DIVING SCHOOLS
46 WARRENSVILLE CENTER RD BEDFORD OH 44146

DEEP SIX SPECIALIST
1074 BROWN AKRON OH 44311

BRIAN SCOTT SCUBA
7524 VAN NESS AVE HUBBARD OH 44425

TREASURE COVE SCUBA
1037 YOUNGSTOWN RD NILES OH 44446

GENE'S SCUBA SUPPLIES
220 E ERIE ST LORAIN OH 44452

SCUBA VENTURES
1481 SOUTH AVE YOUNGSTOWN OH 44502

MULLET SPORTING GOODS
RT 3 MILLERSBURG OH 44654

KA PUKA WAU U/W SCH OF DIVING
1506 WHIPPLE AVE NW CANTON OH 44708

DALE'S DIVING SHOP
302 MEIGS ST SANDUSKY OH 44870

DIVE INC
428 PARK AVE W MANSFIELD OH 44901

U/W TECHNOLOGIES
7962 JULIE MARIE DR W CHESTER OH 45069

CINCINNATI DIVING CENTER
8412 WINTON RD CINCINNATI OH 45231

SCUBA UNLIMITED
9290 KENWOOD RD CINCINNATI OH 45242

EASTGATE SCUBA
835 OHIO PIKE CINCINNATI OH 45245

C & J SCUBA SUPPLY
5825 N DIXIE DR DAYTON OH 45414

GREY LADY DOWN DIVERS
1210 BERNA LANE KETTERING OH 45429

AQUA SPORTS
3065 FAR HILLS DAYTON OH 45429

MIAMI VALLEY SCHOOL OF DIVING
873 E FRANKLIN RD CENTERVILLE OH 45459

REIFF SPORTS SUPPLY
1214 ALLENTOWN RD LIMA OH 45805

LONG LAKE SCUBA
3160 LONG RD LIMA OH 45807

JAQUA'S SPORTING GOODS
315 S MAIN ST FINDLAY OH 45840

OKLAHOMA

GENE'S AQUA PRO SHOP
RT 1 BOX 255G AQUA PARK GORE OK 74435

HEAD SCUBA
4405 S SHERIDAN TULSA OK 74145

CHARISMATIC DIVER CO
8177 S HARVARD #320 TULSA OK 74136

A-1 DIVING SERVICE
6530 SE 21 ST TULSA OK 74129

A & I SCUBA INC
6540 E 21ST ST TULSA OK 74129

A-1 DIVING SERVICE
10941 E 4TH PLACE TULSA OK 74128

INLAND DIVERS
1140 S 107TH E AVE TULSA OK 74128

CULLUM & BOREN
5345 E 41ST ST TULSA OK 74125

J RICH SPORTS
1726 UTICA SQ TULSA OK 74114

INLAND REEF
1615 S MEMORIAL DR TULSA OK 74112

POSEIDON ADVENTURES LTD
3402 S PEORIA TULSA OK 74105

BLUE HOLE DIVING SCHOOL
2724 E 15TH ST TULSA OK 74104

DEANS DIVING SHOP
4113 WISCONSIN BARTLESVILLE OK 74003

THE DIVE SHOP
804 W GORE LAWTON OK 73501

OKLAHOMA SCHOOL OF SCUBA
1015 1ST ST NW ARDMORE OK 73401

DIVERS WORLD INC
1324 SW 34TH OKLAHOMA CITY OK 73119

CHALET SPORTS CENTER
2822 COUNTRY CLUB W OKLAHOMA CITY OK 73116

DIVERS UNLIMITED
1705 S SUNNY LANE OKLAHOMA CITY OK 73115

H & B ENTERPRISES
4045 NW 33RD OKLAHOMA CITY OK 73112

FRANK'S U/W SPORTS SHOP
14TH & N MAY AVE OKLAHOMA CITY OK 73107

HUTTO'S DIVING
111 W MAIN ST WEATHERFORD OK 73096

OREGON

NEPTUNE'S DIVE & WATERSPORTS
12625 SW CANYON RD BEAVERTON OR 97005

COLUMBIA DIVING SCHOOL
679 E HARBOR ST WARRENTOWN OR 97146

KING NEPTUNE'S DIVE SHOP
3310 N LOMBARD PORTLAND OR 97217

FRED DEVINE DIVING & SALVAGE
6211 N ENSIGN PORTLAND OR 97217

VALLEY SCUBA
10803 SW BARBUR PORTLAND OR 97219

U/W WORKS
11299 SW HALL BLVD TIGARD OR 97223

DOLPIN AQUATIC SPORTS
11527 SW PACIFIC HWY PORTLAND OR 97223

TRI-WEST DIVING SCHOOL
13604 SE POWELL PORTLAND OR 97236

STREED'S SCUBA UNLTD
8450 SE 82ND AVE PORTLAND OR 97266

ANDERSONS SPORTING GOODS
340 COURT ST SALEM OR 97301

OREGON DIVING SCHOOL
1790 CENTER ST NE SALEM OR 97301

BEAVER WATER SPORTS LTD
919 C NW CIRCLE BLVD CORVALLIS OR 97330

DEEP SEA JOHN'S
PO BOX 1557 NEWPORT OR 97365

NEWPORT DIVERS SUPPLY
513 SW 9TH PO BOX 490 NEWPORT OR 97365

EUGENE SKIN DIVERS SUPPLY
1090 W 6TH AVE EUGENE OR 97402

NORTHWEST DIVERS SUPPLY
852 S BROADWAY COOS BAY OR 97420

QUIET WORLD
CHARLESTON BOAT BASIN COOS BAY OR 97420

OPEN WATER DIVING SYSTEMS
PO BOX 422 CRESWELL OR 97426

CAP'N FROGS
312 N CENTRAL ST MEDFORD OR 97501

DIVERS WORLD
255 HUMBERD LANE GRANTS PASS OR 97526

REESE'S DIVE SHOP
208 N MAIN ST PHOENIX OR 97535

DIVERS DEN
1349 SW 15TH ST REDMOND OR 97756

PENNSYLVANIA

SCUBA SCHOOL
MR 2 SUNSET DR BADEN PA 15005

SMILEY'S SCUBA SHOP INC
153 STATE ST BADEN PA 15005

DEWALTS SCUBA CENTER
1907 PENNSYLVANIA AVE WEST MIFFLIN PA 15122

PROFESSIONAL DIVING SERVICES
1135 PITTSBURGH ST SPRINGDALE PA 15144

SCUBA SWIM INC
10 HAWLEY AVE BELLEVUE PA 15202

PITTSBURGH SCUBA
314 N CRAIG ST PITTSBURGH PA 15213

SUB-AQUATICS
1428 BANKVILLE PITTSBURG PA 15216

INLAND RIVERS DIVING
316 HARDY DR PITTSBURG PA 15241

RANDY'S DIVE SHOP
RD 6 SANDYHILL RD IRWIN PA 15642

B&B MARINE SPECIALTIES
PO BOX 277 HILLSVILLE PA 16132

THOMPSON DIVE SHOP
RD 3 NEW BETHLEHEM PA 16242

DIVERS WORLD
1904 W 26TH ST ERIE PA 16508

J-S DIVE SHOP
4203 ALVIN ST ERIE PA 16510

M&S SCUBA
1502 HEMLOCK AVE CARLISLE PA 17013

HARRISBURG SCUBA CENTER
991-A PEIFFERS LANE HARRISBURG PA 17033

JOLLY ROGER DIVE SHOP
Rd 1 Millardsville Rd
Richland PA 17087
717/866-5535

Across from Willow Springs. Full service, fills, classes, on-site hydro, repairs, sales. Hours: January-March 10:30 am-7:00 pm, April-December 8:30 am-8:00 pm. Mon., Tues., Wed. by appointment.

JOLLY ROGER DIVE SHOP
Rt 441
Bainbridge PA 17502
717/866-5535
Full-service diving at Richland store location.

YORK DIVERS LTD
968 S GEORGE ST YORK PA 17403

BAINBRIDGE DIVE SHOP
RD 1 Box 23-1
Bainbridge PA 17502
717/426-2114
Full-service dive store. New & used equipment. PADI & NAUI. October to Decmber: weekends only. Call 717/426-2114.

BAINBRIDGE DIVE SHOP
RD 1 BOX 23-1 BAINBRIDGE PA 17502

SMOKEY'S DIVERS DEN
412 N DUKE ST LANCASTER PA 17602

DON COOKS SCUBA EQUIPMENT
940 MARKET ST WILLIAMSPORT PA 17701

SUNKEN TREASURE DIVE SHOP
RD 4 BOX 396 JERSEY SHORE PA 17740

THE SCUBA TANK
RT 512 RD 2 BETHLEHEM PA 18015

SEA-WORLD DIVERS
1113 Union Blvd
Allentown PA 18103
215/432-6866
Full service, air, PADI instruction, sales, service, rentals, repairs, island tours, rentals. Located only minutes from Dutch Springs diving facility.

POCONO NORTHEAST DIVERS
330 S MAIN ST SCRANTON PA 18504

SCUBA AMERICA
600 E DRINKER ST DUNMORE PA 18512

NORTHEAST DIVERS KINGSTON
338 PIERCE ST KINGSTON PA 18704

MID-ATLANTIC SCUBA CENTER
318 E BUTLER AVE AMBLER PA 19002

MID-ATLANTIC SCUBA CENTER
3540 STREET RD BENSALEM PA 19020

U/W WORLD INC
373 EASTON RD HORSHAM PA 19044

THE DIVING BELL
681 N BROAD ST PHILADELPHIA PA 19123

AQUA HUT PLUS
4327 MAIN ST PHILADELPHIA PA 19127

GILLIGANS ISLE INC
17 W CENTRAL AVE PAOLI PA 19301

DUDAS DIVING DUDS
101 BARTRAMS LANE WESTCHESTER PA 19380

Bainbridge Sportsmen's Club

27 acres of water, depth to 120', 60% less than 60', visibility 30-50', 100+ acres of woods for hiking and picnicking. Showers and changing rooms.
HRS: 9 a.m. to 7 p.m.
April 1st thru Oct. 1st;
Oct., Nov., Dec., weekends only
Between Harrisburg and Columbia off Rt. 441 — Call

717/426-2114

RHODE ISLAND

DIVERS WORLD
754 MAIN ST E GREENWICH RI 02818

JAMESTOWN SCUBA
7 CLINTON AVE JAMESTOWN RI 02835

OCEAN STATE SCUBA
NARRANGANSETT AVE JAMESTOWN RI 02835

NEWPORT DIVING CENTER
433 THAMES ST NEWPORT RI 02840

AQUIDNECK ISLAND DIVING
492 Thames St
Newport RI 02840
401/847-9293
Sales, service, rentals, instruction, commercial diving, 5000-psi air station.

VIKING DIVE SHOP
124 E MAIN MIDDLETOWN RI 02840

DIVERS DEN
5 HILL ST PAWTUCKET RI 02860

PISCES DIVING CENTER
983 MAIN RD TIVERTON RI 02878

356

GOB SHOP DIVE CENTER
465 MAIN ST WARREN RI 02885

DEMARCO DIVERS
11 VIREO ST NORTH PROVIDENCE RI 02904

RI DIVERS SUPPLY
209 ELMWOOD AVE PROVIDENCE RI 02907

BOB JOHNSON'S SCUBA
1180 PONTIAC AVE CRANSTON RI 02910

DIVERS WORLD
2060 SMITH ST N PROVIDENCE RI 02911

5 FATHOM DIVERS
307 TAUNTON AVE E PROVIDENCE RI 02914

SOUTH CAROLINA

U/W WORKS LTD
#7 BOARDWALK PLAZA COLUMBIA SC 29210

THE SCUBA SHOP

1274A Asheville Hwy

Spartanburg SC 29303

803/585-5694

**IDEA training facility with ratings to instructor.
Specialty salvage training. Group tours on our
own Greyhound bus. Scuba compressor sales.**

AQUA VENTURE DIVING SCHOOL
4357 FT JACKSON BLVD COLUMBIA SC 29405

THE WET SHOP
5121 RIVERS AVE CHARLESTON SC 29405

SUB-MARINER INC
405 MARINA DR GEORGETOWN SC 29440

OCEAN SCUBA
312 FARM RD GOOSE CREEK SC 29445

BUDDY LINE DIVERS

1035 Hwy 17 Bypass

Mt Pleasant SC 29464

803/884-3606

**Low Country's 5-star training facility. Instruction
and certification. Sales, equipment specialist,
rentals, air. Tours & charters. "Our Business is
Going Under."**

AQUA SHACK
2121 MIDDLE ST SULLIVANS ISLE SC 29482

OCEAN SPORTS
167 N IRBY ST FLORENCE SC 29501

MYRTLE BEACH DIVERS CO INC
PO BOX 2189 MYRTLE BEACH SC 29577

DIVERS WORLD
3225 AUGUSTA RD GREENVILLE SC 29605

SCUBA DIVERS
HWY 24 PO BOX 913 ANDERSON SC 29622

NEPTUNE DIVE & SKI
133 GEORGIA AVE N AUGUSTA SC 29841

SCUBA 3 SCHOOL OF DIVING
LADYS ISLAND BEAUFORT SC 29902

FORDHAM HARDWARE INC
PO BOX 568 BEAUFORT SC 29902

PALMETTO SCUBA
HWY 21 PO BOX 4743 BEAUFORT SC 29902

PALMETTO SCUBA
205 TRIANGLE SQ HILTON HEAD ISLAND SC 29938

SOUTH DAKOTA

LEWIS & CLARK SPORT & SSCUBA
325 DOUGLAS YANKTON SD 57078

LEWIS & CLARK SPORT & SCUBA
402 BROADWAY YANKTON SD 57078

SKIN & SCUBA-OAHE

455 South Pierre

Pierre SD 57501

605/224-4154

**Sales, service, rentals, instruction. Local diving
charters on Lake Oahe. Walleye spearfishing,
buffalo skull & artifact hunting. 605/224-4154.**

ANDYS SKI AND SAIL
4240 CANYON LAKE RD RAPID CITY SD 57701

SCUBA SUPPLY
1607 ST JOE RAPID CITY SD 57701

TENNESSEE

NEPTUNE EQUIPMENT CORP
2610 FRANKLIN RD NASHVILLE TN 37204

AQUATIC SPORTS & TRAVEL
105 EWING DR NASHVILLE TN 37207

THE SKI RACQUET
2160 BANDYWOOD DR NASHVILLE TN 37215

WOODS WATER SPORTS
RT 2 BOX 354 ENGLEWOOD TN 37329

CRIPPLE CREEK EXPEDITIONS
PO BOX 98 OCOEE TN 37361

LEISURE TIME DIVE CENTER
4157 RINGGOLD RD EAST RIDGE TN 37412

CHOO CHOO'S DIVE SHOP
3415 HIXSON PIKE CHATTANOOGA TN 37415

THE SCUBA LOCKER
1310 W MARKET ST JOHNSON CITY TN 37601

SMOKEY MT DIVERS
COLLEGE SQ SHPG CTR JEFFERSON CITY TN 37760

CURRINT ENTERPRISES
104 MITCHELL ST OAK RIDGE TN 37830

CURRINT INTERPRISES INC
600 MAGNOLIA AVE KNOXVILLE TN 37917

SKI/SCUBA CENTER INC
3521 SUTHERLAND AVE KNOXVILLE TN 37919

WEST KNOX SCUBA
342 TROY CIRCLE KNOXVILLE TN 37919

SCUBA VENTURES
8805 KINGSTON PARK KNOXVILLE TN 37923

WATERWORKS SKI & SCUBA
2008 MADISON AVE MEMPHIS TN 38104

DOWDLE SPORTING GOODS
5043 PARK AVE MEMPHIS TN 38111

DIVE SHOP
3149 POPLAR AVE MEMPHIS TN 38111

SCUBA & TRAVEL INC
PO BOX 38202 GERMANTOWN TN 38138

AQUA KNIGHTS INC
229 FIRST ST UNION CITY TN 38261

MID STATE DIVERS
PO BOX 710 COLUMBIA TN 38401

CRAWFORD'S SKINDIVE SHOP
1729 SPRING ST COOKVILLE TN 38501

TEXAS

ATLANTIS DIVERS INC
1234 ALLSTON HOUSTON TX 77008

DIVERS TRAINING CENTER INC
1709 N CENTRAL EXPY PLANO TX 75075

KING NEPTUNE INC
639 FREEPORT HOUSTON TX 77015

SKI & SCUBA INC
12505 HILLCROFT HOUSTON TX 77035

CUSTIES INTERNATIONAL INC
6607 FOXFERN HOUSTON TX 77049

PROFESSIONAL DIVING SERVICES
7402 DEARBORN HOUSTON TX 77055

ALL AMERICAN DIVERS
6383 WESTHEIMER HOUSTON TX 77057

SPORT DIVERS
2402 BAY AREA BLVD HOUSTON TX 77058

TEXAS SCUBA INC #1
8718 FM 1960 W HOUSTON TX 77070

HYDROSPACE
11635 ROWAN LN HOUSTON TX 77072

UNIVERSAL SCUBA DISTRIBUTORS
14230 WESTHEIMER HOUSTON TX 77077

HOUSTON SCUBA ACADEMY WEST
14609 KIMBERLY HOUSTON TX 77079

AQUAVENTURES SCUBA CENTER
1614 GESSNER HOUSTON TX 77080

KENLEE'S WEST
5705 GLENMONT HOUSTON TX 77081

RAINBOW DIVERS INC
8822 MOONLIGHT FOREST DR HOUSTON TX 77088

CHAMPIONS DIVE CENTER
1974 EM 1960 West
Houston TX 77090
713/444-7878
Sales, rentals, repairs. Local & international trips. U/w photography. PADI training facility.

TEXAS SCUBA #2
5414 KATY FREEWAY HOUSTON TX 77007

BLUE WATER DIVING SCHOOL
910 WESTHEIMER HOUSTON TX 77006

EQUIFIX SPORTING GOODS
1510 ANTOINE HOUSTON TX 77006

LONE STAR DIVING CO
5111 BUFFALO SPEEDWAY HOUSTON TX 77005

J RICH SPORTS LTD
2367 RICE BLVD HOUSTON TX 77005

SPORT DIVERS WORLD INC
2607 BISSONNET ST HOUSTON TX 77005

LAM'S PRO SKI & DIVE SHOP
1953 AUSTIN SAN ANGELO TX 76903

TEXAS DIVERS ASSOC INC
1529 WEST AVE N SAN ANGELO TX 76901

TRADEWIND DIVING ACADEMY
5215 Sanger Ave
Waco TX 76710
817/772-6674
PADI training facility. Sales, rentals, repairs, classes year-round. Dive trips. Six specialty ratings, master scuba diver trainer.

SCUBA SHOP
430 LAKE AIR WACO TX 76710

CAMPBELL'S DIVE SHOP
5219 SANGER ST WACO TX 76704

GULF DIVE SHOP
1905 JEFFERSON DR PT ARTHUR TX 76640

U/W WORLD OF TEXAS
RT 1 BOX 3339 KEMPNER TX 76539

CHARLES SPORTS
1019 S 33RD TEMPE TX 76501

PROFESSIONAL DIVERS INC
2700 LOOP 363 TEMPLE TX 76501

DEL MAR SPORTS STORE
2614 BUCHANAN ST WICHITA FALLS TX 76309

INLAND DIVERS
1704 N ELM DENTON TX 76201

SCUBA SPHERE
6709 CAMP BOWIE FT WORTH TX 76116

SCUBA DIVING SCHOOL
3807 SOUTHWEST BLVD FT WORTH TX 76116

RED'S LEO SALES
2400 H LUDELDE ST FT WORTH TX 76109

CULLUM & BOREN
2254 N E MALL FT WORTH TX 76103

DIVERS SUPPLY
3807 SW BLVD FT WORTH TX 76102

SCUBA SPHERE NE
102 S ECTOR DR EULESS TX 76040

ARLINGTON SCUBA CENTER
2414 W PARK ROW DR ARLINGTON TX 76013

SCUBA WEST INC
586 LINCOLN SQ ARLINGTON TX 76011

SCUBA DYNAMICS INC
2514 JEWEL ARLINGTON TX 76010

DIVERS ODYSSEY SCUBA
922 N COLLINS ARLINGTON TX 76010

DIVERS DEPOT
720 S ST NACOGDOCHES TX 75961

DIVERS PARADISE
1109 E DENMAN LUFKIN TX 75901

LONE PINE DIVE SHOP
ROUTE 6 BOX 117 PALESTINE TX 75801

EAST TEXAS AQUA SPORTS
PO BOX 162 RUSK TX 75785

DIVERS SUPPLY
325 S VINE ST TYLER TX 75702

THE SCUBA CENTER OF TYLER
107 W 6TH ST TYLER TX 75701

DICK'S SCUBA CENTER
201 E HAWKINS PKWY LONGVIEW TX 75601

SEA LYONS DIVING CO
9115 MEREDITH HIGHLANDS TX 75562

DIVERS COVE
425 S CHURCH ST PARIS TX 75460

MT PLEASANT PRO SCUBA
1506 W FIRST ST MT PLEASANT TX 75455

SCUBA WEST
14902 PRESTON #412 DALLAS TX 75240

SCUBA WEST
12801 MIDWAY RD #401 DALLAS TX 75234

THE SCUBA SHOP
3817 ELFLAND CIR DALLAS TX 75229

SPORTS ADVENTURES OF TEXAS
2152 West NW Hwy
Dallas TX 75220
214/556-0011
Full PADI training facility. Instruction. Equipment sales & repair. Rentals. Trips.

SCUBA PLACE
4920 MAPLE AVE DALLAS TX 75209

SCUBA WEST
5500 GREENVILLE AVE #901 DALLAS TX 75206

DOWN TIME DIVING
216 W FRANKLIN BOX 976 WAXAHACHIE TX 75165

SPORT SCUBA CENTER
4014 MEDITERRANEAN ROCKWALL TX 75087

DIVERS WORLD INC
632 S CENTRAL EXPWY RICHARDSON TX 75080

DIVERS TRAINING CENTER Inc.
1709 North Central Expwy
Plano TX 75075
214/424-6563
Equipment, instruction, travel, rentals, service. PADI 5-star training facility.

TUCKERS DIVE SHOP
2025 E MAIN ST GRAND PRAIRIE TX 75051

TOTAL SCUBA CENTER
PO BOX 1987 CONROE TX 77305

WATER WORLD ADVENTURES
140 N HOUSTON AVE HUMBLE TX 77338

SCUBA SCHOOLS OF HUNTSVILLE
1329-B UNIVERSITY AVE HUNTSVILLE TX 77340

H2 OPERATIONS
409 N WASHINGTON LIVINGSTON TX 77351

SCUBA TREK INT
2819 RED BLUFF PASADENA TX 77503

U/W ADVENTURES
4232D DECKER DR BAYTOWN TX 77521

W W DIVING CO
1511 INDIAN SHORES RD CROSBY TX 77532

LONE STAR DIVERS
8009 SPENCER HWY DEER PARK TX 77536

AQUA TREK
804 UNIVERSITY BLVD GALVESTON TX 77550

ISLAND DIVE SHOP
4708 SEAWALL BLVD GALVESTON TX 77550

AQUASPHERE INC
112 TREMONT GALVESTON TX 77550

LAKEWOOD YACHT MARINA
16 LAKEWOOD LN SEABROOK TX 77586

KENLEE'S AQUASPORT
PO BOX 806 S HOUSTON TX 77587

ALL AMERICAN DIVERS
123 BAY AREA BLVD WEBSTER TX 77598

GULF DIVE SHOP
901 N TWIN CITY HWY NEDERLAND TX 77627

AQUAVENTURES DIVE SHOP
1447 1/2 GRAND BEAUMONT TX 77701

SKI SCUBA ETC
6240 PHELAN BLVD BEAUMONT TX 77706

DAVY JONES LOCKER
6797 EASTEX FREEWAY BEAUMONT TX 77706

RECREATIONAL SERVICES
PO Box 3966 Bryan TX 77805
Scuba & u/w photographic equipment specializing in sales to the scientific community.
Gregory S. Boland owner; M.S. biological oceanography.

TRI-STATE SPORTING GOODS
2023 TEXAS AVE BRYAN TX 77802

THE DIVERS CONNECTION
5907 HALLETTSVILLE HWY VICTORIA TX 77904

FOUR SEASONS SPORTS CENTER
310 N VIRGINIA ST PT LAVACA TX 77979

EL CENTRO
920 ITURBIDE LAREDO TX 78040

TRIDENT DIVING EQUIPMENT
2110 WEST AVE IH10 SAN ANTONIO TX 78201

SCUBA DEN
111 STANFORD SAN ANTONIO TX 78212

DIVEMASTERS
447 MCCARTY RD SAN ANTONIO TX 78216

AQUASUN
12006 PERRIN BEITEL RD SAN ANTONIO TX 78217

DIVE WORLD
5712 Mobud Dr
San Antonio TX 78238
512/681-5423
A PADI 5-star facility. Travel, training, sales, & service. "Excellence our Motto, Fun our Goal!"

SCHEME A THINGS
9330 BIANCA DR SAN ANTONIO TX 78250

INTERNATIONAL MARINE SERVICE
4457 BALDWIN CORPUS CHRISTI TX 78403

COPELANDS
4041 S PADRE ISLAND DR CORPUS CHRISTI TX 78411

PADRE ISLAND DIVE SHOP
7336 S PADRE ISLAND DR CORPUS CHRISTI TX 78412

THE DIVE SHOP OF C C
6341 S PADRE ISL DR CORPUS CHRISTI TX 78412

MAGILL SPORTS SPECIALTIES
1333 ANNAPOLIS CORPUS CHRISTI TX 78415

B&B DIVE SHOP
PO BOX 3230 BROWNSVILLE TX 78520

SCUBA SHOP
311 GRFRUIT WAY BOX 233 PHARR TX 78577

L & L DIVERS SCUBA CTR
114 HWY 100 PT ISABEL TX 78578

SCUBA UNLIMITED
PO BOX 52 HWY 1431 KINGSLAND TX 78639

SCUBATEXAS!"IT'LL DIVEYA CRAZY"
RT 3 BOX 169P LAKE TRAVIS TX 78641

THE DIVE SHOP INC
1426 RANCH RD #12 SAN MARCOS TX 78666

SCUBA POINT TRAVIS
11401 RR 2222
Austin, Texas 78732
512-266-2406
PADI Instruction, basic, advanced, specialty. Prorated airfills. Equipment sales, service, repair. Dive travel, Caribbean charters. Boat storage. Wind Surfing.

SCUBA POINT AUSTIN
4032 S. Lamar Suite 100
Austin, Texas 78704
512-444-4946

SCUBA ETC
6808 RR 620 N AUSTIN TX 78732

ADVENTURE SPORTS Inc
5300 N. Lamar Blvd #103
Austin, Texas 78751
512-453-7676

THE PROFESSIONAL DIVING CENTER
— Instruction, Sales, Rentals, Travel, Repair, Local Activities, Air, Scubapro dealer.

SCUBA EDUCATION OF AUSTIN
1004 ROMERIA AUSTIN TX 78757

TOM'S DIVE & SKI Inc.
6407 Burnet Rd
Austin TX 78758
512/451-3225
Boat trips on Lake Travis. Rentals, sales, air, classes.

SPORT DIVER TOURS
PO BOX 9894 AUSTIN TX 78766

J. RICH SPORTS
420 NORTHCROSS MALL AUSTIN TX 78766

AMISTAD SCUBA DIVERS
SR 2 BOX 39 DEL RIO TX 78840

DEL RIO DIVING
1108 E GIBBS DEL RIO TX 78840

PROFESSIONAL SCUBA SCHOOL
BOX 989 STRATFORD TX 79084

SPORT DIVERS SUPPLY
1503 E CARDWELL BROWNFIELD TX 79316

THE AQUANAUT
1009 UNIVERSITY LUBBOCK TX 79401

SCHOOL OF SCUBA
942 WALNUT ST ABILENE TX 79601

KEY CITY DIVE SHOP
4249 DON JUAN ABILENE TX 79605

STOVALL'S DIVE SHOP
1308 S MIDKIFF #103-106 MIDLAND TX 79701

SPORT DIVING SERVICES INC
4606 W HWY 80 MIDLAND TX 79703

AQUATIC CENTER
1453 BRITTANY ODESSA TX 79760

SCUBA OF ODESSA INC
1514 GRANDVIEW ODESSA TX 79761

BO-TOMS DIVE SHOPPE INC
2209 W 83RD ODESSA TX 79764

INNER SPACE DIVERS OF EL PASO
4111 N MESA #2 EL PASO TX 79902

SUN CITY SCUBA
9348 MCCOMBS EL PASO TX 79924

SCUBA DIVING SCHOOL OF EL PASO
6130 MONTANA #216 EL PASO TX 79925

SOUTHWEST SCUBA DIVERS
1665 LOMALAND EL PASO TX 79935

International Buddy System

An international network of Scuba Divers with desire to meet, dive and visit with other divers from other cities, states, provinces and countries. An International buddy System member diver can now meet a "local" International Buddy at the dive destination, rather than being left "on your own."

The Purpose

An international organization designed to put the international diver in contact with other divers and dive shops/resorts world wide.

The International Buddy System functions on both an International and National basis. Regardless where a diver travels, within the diver's own country or abroad, the diver *knows someone locally long before arriving at the dive destination.*

The Objective

1) To create an international society of Scuba divers who have and enjoy similar diving habits and goals, and who are interested in meeting socially with local divers wherever one may dive.
2) To provide information and contacts on local dive shops and resorts wherever one may dive.
3) To coordinate advanced communications between members of the International Buddy System on diving schedules.

The Benefits

A) Meet and dive with a local International Buddy System diver who lives and dives within your dive destination area.
B) Receive first hand information about popular local dive sites as well as dive sites not normally available to general tourists.
C) Develop an extensive international association of friends, contacts and business associates.
D) Attend annual international conventions of the International Buddy System membership, held in a difference country each year.
E) Obtain International Buddy System membership T-Shirt and equipment decals for buddy identification.
F) Establish confidence and trust in dive shops, dive boats and resorts who are International Buddy System members as well as diving resources recommended by the local International Buddy System diver(s) you have talked with.

International Buddy System provides an opportunity to expand your Scuba Diving pleasure and experience to the **world's** maximum. To begin developing your International Buddies, send $5.00 to: International Buddy System
76 St. Stephens Rd.
Austin, TX 78746
and receive your membership application.

UTAH

CROSS INTERNATIONAL DIVING
155 W 800 N OREM UT 84057

WOLFE'S
250 S STATE ST E SALT LAKE CITY UT 84101

NEPTUNE DIVERS
2445 South 900 East
Salt Lake City UT 84106
801/466-9630
Scuba service, sales, & lessons. SSI & PADI training
facility. SSI instructor school. In-store pool.
Scuba skills updates available.

HWR CRUISING LTD
2345 LYNWOOD DR SALT LAKE CITY UT 84109

BANNER RECREATION
2150 MAJOR ST SALT LAKE CITY UT 84115

THUNDER ISLAND DIVERS
2520 W 4700 S SALT LAKE CITY UT 84118

SPECIALTY SPORTS
4921 S 1950 W TAYLORSVILLE UT 84118

SCUBA UTAH
2356 S REDWOOD RD SALT LAKE CITY UT 84119

WOLFE'S
6151 HIGHLAND DR SALT LAKE CITY UT 84121

INTERMOUNTAIN SCUBA
156 W UTOPIA SALT LAKE CITY UT 84121

MOUNTAIN DIVERS
59 E 100 N SMITHFIELD UT 84335

THE DIVE SHOP
1930 WALL AVE OGDEN UT 84401

WOLFE'S
23 WASHINGTON ST OGDEN UT 84401

THUNDER ISLAND DIVERS
444 N 200 W PROVO UT 84601

VERMONT

NORTHERN DIVERS
65 Main St
Burlington VT 05401
802/862-3881
NAUI, PADI training facility. Instruction, air,
rentals, repairs. Lake Champlain charters.

CHIOTT'S SCUBA EQUIPMENT
67 KING ST BURLINGTON VT 05401

LEISURE LINES REC EQIP
WOODSTOCK AVE RT 4E RUTLAND VT 05701

NORTHEASTERN DIVERS
BOX 6 AVERILL VT 05901

VIRGINIA

DIVE SHOP
9401 LITTLE RIVER TPKE FAIRFAX VA 22030

SEA VENTURES Inc.
9650 Main (Fair City Mall)
Fairfax VA 22031
703/425-7676
Northern Virginia's complete pro dive shop.
Sales & service, rentals, trips. Instruction: PADI,
NAUI, & YMCA. Open daily Mon.-Fri. 12-9
pm, Sat.-Sun. 12-6 pm.

THE DIVE SHOP
2841 ROGERS DR FALLS CHURCH VA 22042

AMERICAN WATERSPORTS OF VA
6775 WILSON BLVD FALLS CHURCH VA 22044

RICH WELL'S DIVE SHOP
2740 HUNTER RD OAKTON VA 22124

HERMANS WORLD
6787 SPRINGFIELD MALL SPRINGFIELD VA 22150

THE WET ONES
163 GLYNDON ST VIENNA VA 22180

UNIVERSAL DIVERS
14574 JEFF DAVIS WOODBRIDGE VA 22191

SKI & DIVE SHOP
1543 North Quaker Ln
Alexandria VA 22302
703/998-6140
Instruction: free introductory classes through
instructor rating. Quality travel from Florida
throught the Caribbean. Wreck, oyster, quarry
diving. Sales & service.

KATHYS SCUBA INC
896 N LIBERTY ST HARRISONBURG VA 22801

BLUE RIDGE DIVE SHOP
1726 ALLIED SY CHARLOTTESVILLE VA 22901

W & W DIVE SHOP
6029 MIDLOTHIAN TURNPIKE RICHMOND VA 23225

THE DIVE SHOP
1925 N HAMILTON ST RICHMOND VA 23230

SCUBA VENTURES INC
2247 N GREAT NECK RD VIRGINIA BEACH VA 23451

RUDD'S SPORTS EQUIPMENT INC
1604 HILLTOP WEST VIRGINIA BEACH VA 23454

LYNNHAVEN DIVE CENTER
3829 SHORE DR VIRGINIA BEACH VA 23455

AQUA LUNG DIVING CENTER
805 W LITTLE CREEK RD NORFOLK VA 23505

AQUA LUNG DIVING CENTER
9601 JEFFERSON AVE NEWPORT NEWS VA 23601

CHESAPEAKE DIVING CTR
1815 A W QUEEN PT HAMPTON VA 23666

SEASPRAY
167 GLENN COVE SEAFORD VA 23696

DIVER'S CORNER
1530 FIRST ST RADFORD VA 24141

AQUATICS INTERNATIONAL
710 POPLAR TERRACE DR LYNCHBURG VA 24502

WASHINGTON

HOUSE OF DIVING
31120 PACIFIC HWY S #7 FEDERAL WAY WA 98003

U/W SPORTS
12014 BELLEVUE-REDMOND NE BELLEVUE WA 98005

SILENT WORLD DIVERS
13600 NE 20TH BELLEVUE WA 98005

NEW ENGLAND DIVERS
14330 NE 20TH ST BELLEVUE WA 98007

EDMONDS SCUBA CENTER
264 RAILROAD AVE EDMONDS WA 98020

NEW ENGLAND DIVERS
24860 PAC HWY S KENT WA 98032

MARKAY SCHOOL OF DIVING
10248 65TH ST SEATTLE WA 98100

DIVERS INST OF TECHNOLOGY
1133 NW 45TH AVE SEATTLE WA 98107

HARRY TRUITT'S LIGHTHOUSE
DIVING CENTER Inc.
8215 Lake City Way NE
Seattle WA 98115
206/524-1633
Open seven days for sales, rentals, air, two-day
scuba review courses & u/w photography rentals
for Puget Sound diving.

HARRY TRUITT'S LIGHTHOUSE
DIVING CENTER Inc.
5421C 196th St SW
Lynnwood WA 98036
206/771-2679
Open seven days for sales, rentals, air, two-day
scuba review courses & u/w photography rentals
for Puget Sound diving.

SEATTLE SKINDIVING SUPPLY
1661 HARBOR AVE SW SEATTLE WA 98126

U/W SPORTS
10545 AURORA AVE N SEATTLE WA 98133

ANACORTES DIVING & SUPPLY
2818 COMMERCIAL AVE ANACORTES WA 98221

WASHINGTON DIVERS
903 N STATE ST BELLINGHAM WA 98225

BELLINGHAM SCUBA CTR
2720 W MAPLEWOOD ST BELLINGHAM WA 98225

DIVERS DEN
602 N DIVISION ST MT VERNON WA 98273

WHIDBEY DIVERS
PO BOX RR 80 NW OAK HARBOR WA 98277

SOUND DIVE CENTER
990 SYLVAN WAY BREMERTON WA 98310

THE SEA KING DIVE SHOP
4101 HARBORVIEW DR GIG HARBOR WA 98335

MIKES NAUTICAL HIDEAWAY
3302 HARBORVIEW DR GIG HARBOR WA 98335

SCUBA SUPPLIES
738 MARINE DR PT ANGELES WA 98362

NAUTILUS DIVE
1941 BAY ST PT ORCHARD WA 98366

GREBE DIVE SHOP
1049 CENTER ST PT TOWNSEND WA 98368

NORTHWEST DIVERS INC
1113 RIVER RD PUYALLUP WA 98371

PACIFIC REEF INC
7516 27TH ST W TACOMA WA 98466

U/W SPORTS
9608 40 AVE SW TACOMA WA 98499

EASON'S MARINE SERVICE
9020 MARTIN WAY OLYMPIA WA 98506

CAPITOL SKIN & SCUBA
107 E STATE ST OLYMPIA WA 98506

U/W INST & SPORTS
8513 HWY 99 VANCOUVER WA 98665

U/W INSTRUTORS
7207 NE HAZEL DELL VANCOUVER WA 98665

THE DIVE INN
3215 RIVER RD YAKIMA WA 98902

SCUBA CENTER OF SPOKANE
3607 N DIVISION SPOKANE WA 99207

WEST VIRGINIA

MOUNTAINEER II DIVE SHOP
600 CROSS DANES DR NITRO WV 25143

SCOTTIE'S DIVE WORLD
4300 MALDEN DR CHARLESTON WV 25306

REEF RAIDERS DIVE SHOP
4714 MACCORKLE AVE SW S CHARLESTON WV 25309

HUNTINGTON SPT & COMM DIV CTR
3234 WOODLAND DR HUNTINGTON WV 25705

DIVEALOT SCUBA CENTER
646 ABNEY RD COAL CITY WV 25823

WISCONSIN

NEPTUNE'S DIVE CENTER
RFD 2 BOX 10 CHILTON WI 53014

THE PORTHOLE SCUBA CTR
PO BOX 313 MENOMINEE FALLS WI 53051

THE U/W CNTN
16459 APPLETON AVE MENOMINEE FALLS WI 53051

AQUATIC WORLD SCUBA CENTER
131 N MAIN ST OCONOMOWOC WI 53066

ENTERPRISE SHIPWRECK CHARTERS
2602 EISNER AVE SHEBOYGAN WI 53081

ROY'S DIVING CENTER
721 S 27TH ST SHEBOYGAN WI 53081

BENNETT ACADEMY OF SCUBA
114 N MAIN ST THIENSVILLE WI 53092

WEST BEND AQUA SHOP
1829 N MAIN ST WEST BEND WI 53095

FONTANA OUTDOOR SPORTS
HWY 67 PO BOX 350 FONTANA WI 53125

ERV'S DIVING EQUIPMENT
10751 W PARNELL AVE HALES CORNER WI 53130

WATER WORLD
5025 6th AVE KENOSHA WI 53140

WISCONSIN STATE DIVERS ASSOCIATION
122 West Broadway
Waukesha WI 53186
414/547-1115
(West side of Milwaukee on I-94.) Equipment
sales, repairs, air refills. Instruction & complete
rentals. Mon.-Fri. 9 am-9 pm, Sat. 9 am-5 pm.

BENNETT ACADEMY OF SKI & SCUBA
6509 W NORTH AVE WAUWATOSA WI 53213

PIRATE'S COVE DIVING
1103 W OKLAHOMA AVE MILWAUKEE WI 53215

AIR POOL DIVERS EQUIPMENT
4201 S 68TH ST MILWAUKEE WI 53220

FONTANA ARMY-NAVY FONTANA II
949 E WASHINGTON AVE MADISON WI 53703

PETRIE'S SCUBALAB
1406 EMIL ST MADISON WI 53713

THREE LITTLE DEVILS
RT 4 HWY 123 BARABOO WI 53913

SWEETMAN'S SCUBA SALES
1006 N UNIVERSITY AVE BEAVER DAM WI 53916

SCUBA CENTER
RT 1 BOX 56 COLEMAN WI 54112

ADVENTURE SPORTS
114 S BROADWAY DE PERE WI 54115

ON THE ROCKS
849 WISCONSIN BAY RD ELLISON BAY WI 54210

HAROLD RUSCHE DIVING SERVICE
3893 CHERRY RD STURGEON BAY WI 54235

FANTA-SEAS INC
2790 UNIVERSITY AVE GREEN BAY WI 54302

AQUA CENTER
2680 S ASHLAND AVE GREEN BAY WI 54304

CENTRAL WI DIVING ACADEMY
13311 8TH ST S WISCONSIN RAPIDS WI 54494

SCUBA DEW'S DIVING
907 E WALL ST EAGLE RIVER WI 54521

BENNETT'S SPORT SHOP
HWY 51 MINOCQUA WI 54548

MARINELAND OF ONALASKA
412 CAMPBELL RD ONALASKA WI 54650

BLUE WATER DIVERS INC
1825 BRACKETT AVE EAU CLAIRE WI 54701

BLUE WATERS DIVERS
RT 3 NEW AUBURN WI 54747

LINDAHL'S STORE
132 N IOWA AVE HAYWARD WI 54843

THE SELF-PROPELLED SHOP
1813 W BAYFIELD ST WASHBURN WI 54891

ACEE DEUCEE DIVERS
1329 OREGON ST OSHKOSH WI 54901

MT BAY SKI & DIVE
1607 N RICHMOND ST APPLETON WI 54911

THE DEEP END SCUBA TRNG
RT 5 1703 FOREST AV FOND DU LAC WI 54935

INLAND SEAS DIVING ACADEMY
310 N COMMERCIAL ST NEENAH WI 54956

WYOMING

ROCKY MOUNTAINEERING LTD
211 S 2ND ST LARAMIE WY 82070

TETON AQUATIC SUPPLIES
365 N GLENWOOD PO BOX 3482 JACKSON WY 83001

INDEX

ALABAMA
Black Warrior River 119
Blue Water Park 119
Dry docks 119
Liberty Ships 119
Martin Lake 119
Pickwick 118
Smith Lake 119
Tennessee River 119
Wilson Lake 118

ALASKA
Amchitka 25
Chenega Island 24
Clara Nevada 23
Harding Lake 25
Kenai Peninsula 24
Ketchikan 21
Knight Island 24
Port Etches 24
Prince William Sound 24
Princess Kathleen 22
Princess Sophia 23
Revillagigedo Island 21
Rocky Point 24
Shrine of St. Teresa 22
Sitka Sound 21
Smitty's Cove 24
State of California 23
Sunshine Cove 22
Whittier 24

ARIZONA
Ashhurst Lake 99
Lake Mary 99
Lake Mead 99
Lake Powell 99
Saguaro Lake 99

ARKANSAS
Beaver Lake 137
Buffalo River 138
Bull Shoals Lake 137
Dam Site Area 1 137
Greer's Ferry Lake 137
Lake DeGray 138
Lake Ouachita 138
Mondel City 137
Norfork Lake 137
Robinson Point Island 137

CALIFORNIA
1000 Stairs 68
Albion 52
Aliso Beach 72
Alligator Head 74
Anchor Bay 52
Arch Rock 81,90
Arch Rocks 83
Arroyo Burro State Park 67
Avalon 70
Avila Beach 62
Barge 57
Barn Cove 61
Barn 73
Bat Ray Cove 81
Bathtub Rock 74
Beacon Reef 84
Bee Rock 83

Begg Rock 91
Big Fisherman Cove 86
Bird Rock 72,75
Bird Rock 88
Blue Cavern Point 87
Bolsa 55
Boomer Beach 75
Camel Beach 50
Cannery Row 56
Cape Mendocino 50
Capitola 56
Carlsbad State Beach 73
Carmel Point 59
Carmel River Mouth Beach 60
Carmel State Beach 59
Carmel Trench 60
Carpinteria Beach State Park 68
Casa Cove 75
Casino Point U/W Park 86
Casper Point 51
Castle Rock 93
Cat Rock 81
Cathedral Cove 81
Cathedral Rock 92
Chase Reef 59
China Point 94
Christmas Tree Cove 70
Cleone Beach 50
Cluster Point 83
Coal Oil Point 67
Copper Roof 59
Coral Beach 69
Cortes Bank 94
Crescent Bay 71
Crescent City 52
Crescent City 49
Crystal Cove 71
D.L. Bliss State Park 95
Dana Point 73
Dead Man's Reef 71
Descanso Cove 86
Devil's Jaws 63
Devil's Slides 74
Diablo Canyon 62
Diver's Cove 72
Doheny State U/W Park 73
Dutch Harbor 91
Eagle Rock 88
East End 91
East Fish Camp 81
East Point 83
Eel Point 94
El Capitan State Beach 67
Elk 52
Emerald Bay 95
Emerald Cove 88
Encino Power Plant 73
Equator 81
Escondido Beach 69
Farnsworth Bank 89
Fishhook 93
Fisk Mill 53
Fort Ross State Historical Park 54
Frazier Cove 83
Frenchy's Cove 81
Gerstle Cove 52
Golden Horn 83
Goldfish Bowl 81
Goldfish Point 74
Gosford 63

Greyhound Rock 55
Gull Island 83
Haggerty's 70
Half Moon Bay 55
Harbor Drive at Noyo 51
Heeser Drive 51
Hen Rock Reef 86
Hendry's 67
Hopkins Reef 57
Horse Pastures 71
Horseshoe Cove 52
Humboldt Bay 50
Hurricane Point 61
Indian Rock 88
Ironbound Cove 88
Isthmus Reef 87
Italian Gardens 87
J. P. Burns State U/W Park 61
Jade Cove National Monument 61
Jetty 49
John C. Butler 93
Johnson's Lee 83
La Jolla Canyon 75
La Jolla Cove 74
Lake Oroville 95
Lake Perris 95
Lake Shasta 95
Lake Tahoe 95
Las Tunas State Beach 69
Leo Carrillo Park 68
Lighthouse Point 56
Lighthouse Reef 81
Lighthouse 90
Little Farnsworth 87
Little Flower 93
Little River Beach 50
Long Point Light 87
Lover's Point 57
Macabee Beach 56
Main Beach 72
Malaga Cove 69
Malibu Beach 69
Margate 70
McKerricher Park 50
Mendocino Headlands 51
Mesa Lane 67
Mohawk Reef 67
Monastery Beach 60
Monterey Breakwater 56
Morro Bay 62
Morro Rock 62
Morse Point 83
Mosquito Cove 93
Moss Beach 55
Moss Street 72
Naples Reef 67
Natural Bridges Beach 56
New Hope Rock 76
Nine Fathom Reef 93
Ning Po 89
Norlina 54
Otter Cove 59
Painted Cave 81
Paradise Cove 69
Partington Cove 61
Patrick's Point State Park 50
Pebble Beach Drive 49
Pendleton artificial reef 73
Picnic Beach 72
Pigeon Point Lighthouse 55
Pinnacles 59
Pismo Beach 63
Point Arena Rock 52

Point Arguello 63
Point Buchon 62
Point Dume 68
Point Fermin Park 71
Point Lobos 60
Point Loma 76
Point Mugu State Park 68
Point Sal 63
Point San Luis 62
Point Vincente County Park 70
Potato Patch 83
Pothole 90
Princeton Jetty 55
Prisoner's Harbor 83
Pyramid Cove 92
Pyramid Head High Spot 92
Refugio State Beach Park 67
Richardson's Rock 85
Ripper's Cove 87
Rocky Beach 72
Rocky Point 61
Royal Palms State Beach 70
Russian Gulch State Park 51
S-37 submarine 76
Salt Creek 73
Salt Point State Park 52
San Elijo State Park 74
San Simeon 62
Sandy Point 83
Santa Cruz 56
Scorpion Anchorage 81
Scotchman's Cove 71
Scott Creek 55
Scripps Canyon 74
Seal Cove 94
Seven Fathom Reef 91
Shaw's Cove 72
Shell Beach 62
Shelter Cove 50
Shelter Cove 55
Ship Rock 88
Smuggler's Cove 83
Sonoma Coast State Beaches 54
St. George Reef 49
Stillwater Cove 59
Stump Beach 53
Sutil Island 90
Tajiquas Beach 64
Talcott Shoals 84
Tamarack 73
Tanner Bank 94
The Boiler 91
The Pinnacle 87
Three Mile Reef 91
Tide County Park 74
Timber Cove 54
Torrey Pines State Beach 74
Trinidad Head and Bay 50
USS Gregory 94
Valiant 86
Van Damme State Park 51
WWII Corsair fighter plane 71
Wagon Tracks 93
Westport 50
Westward Beach 68
Whale Rock 88
Whalers Cove 60
White's Point 71
Wilson's Creek 49
Wilson's Rock 85
Winfield Scott 81
Woods Cove 72
Wyckoff Ledge 85

Yankee Point 61
Yuba River 95
Zuma Beach 68

COLORADO

Blue Mesa Reservoir 100
Carter 99
Horsetooth Reservoir 100
Jefferson 99
Pearl Lake 100
Pueblo Reservoir 100
Redfeather 100
San Isabel 100
Tarryall Reservoir 100

CONNECTICUT

Black Rock Harbor 191
Candlewood Lake 193
Enders Island 191
G-2 submarine 191
Green Falls Pond 193
Hammonaset State Park 191
Harkness Memorial Park 191
Lake Mashapaug 193
Lake Waramaug 193
Middle Ground 191
Mount Tom State Park 193
Norwalk Light 189
Penfield Light 191
Pleasure Beach 191
Seaside Point 191
Sheffield Island 189
Sherwood Island State Park 189
Sherwood Point 189
Squantz Pond State Park 193
Stonington Breakwaters 193
Stratford Shoal 191

DELAWARE

Fenwich Shoals 216
Indian River Inlet 216
Lewes Breakwater 216

FLORIDA

12 Mile Wreck 256
Air transport plane 286
Ajax Reef 271
Alexander Springs 309
Alexander 285
Alligator Reef 279
Almirante 270
Amaryllis 259
Amazon 258
Amberjack Rocks 286
Aquanaut 283
Arida 269
Artificial reefs 295
B-29 plane 292
Barge Wreck 272
Barge 259,269
Barge 292
Barges 289
Barracuda Hole 294
Bathtub Reef 258
Bay Ronto 294
Beans 280
Becky's Ledge 266
Becton Spring 299
Benwood 276
Big Dismal Sink 302
Big Jack Hole 293
Big Rocks 286
Big Spring 301

Big Spring 311
Blackmar's Reef 255
Blowing Rocks Preserve 258
Blue Fire 270
Blue Grotto 309
Blue Hole Spring 306
Blue Hole 300
Blue Spring 299
Blue Springs 308,310,314
Blue Spring, Lafayette County 304
Boca Reef 265
Boynton Ledge 262
Bozell Springs 300
Breaker's Reef 261
Breconshire 257
Brewster Reef 270
Bridge rubble 289
Bridge 289
Buzzard Log 301
CO Reef 292
Cable Crossing 261
Cannabis Cruiser 279
Carlin Park 258
Carysfort Reef 272
Casa Blanca 255
Catfish Corner 313
Catfish Hotel 305
Cathedral Cave 276
Cathy II 295
Causeway Bridge 294
Challenge Sink 303
Charles Spring 304
Chassahowitzka River 313
Chaves 278
Chipola River 300
Christ of the Abyss 275
Christmas Tree Cave 276
Cisteen Sink 303
Clearwater Reef 292
Coal Barges 286
Coffin Patch 280
Commander 290
Conch Reef 277
Copenhagen 266
Crab Creek Springs 314
Crocker Reef 278
Crystal River 311
Crystal Springs 315
Cuda Reef 266
Cypress Spring 299,301
Davis Reef 277
Deep Freeze 269
Delray Ledge 265
Delray Wreck 264
Delta Shoals 281
Devil's Eye 308
Devil's Punch Bowl 314
Diver's Spring 311
Doc's Barge 293
Dogwood Spring 308
Dunedin Reef 292
East Eleven 256
East Ridge 256
Eastern Dry Rocks 284
Eastern Sambo 283
El Bargo 278
El Capitan 278
El Infante 278
Emerald Reef 269
Empire Mica 291
Fingers 258
First Reef 265
Fish Sink 301

Forty Fathom Sink 309
Four Barges 267
Fowey Rocks 270
French Reef 276
G Marker .292
Gator Hole 312
Gator Spring 300
Ginnie Springs 307
Grand Canyon Spring 312
Grecian Rocks 276
Grey Ghost 291
Grouper Hole 265
Gulf Pride 258
Gunsmoke 293
HMS Winchester 272
Halfway Heads 270
Hammerhead Reef 267
Harbor House Reef 268
Harrison's Cave 272
Hart Spring 304
Hellcat 292
Hens and Chickens 278
Herrera 278
Hogfish Reef 262
Hole in the Wall 277
Holmes Creek 299
Hopper Barge 269
Horseshoe Reef 261
Horseshoe 258
Horseshoe 276
Hospital Hole 315
House of Refuge 258
Houseboat Springs 314
Houseboat wreck 295
Houseboat 268
Ichetucknee River 306
Ichetucknee Spring 306
Idiot's Delight 312
Ignacio 281
Indian River Shores 257
Inlet Park .257
Islamorada Coral Gardens 278
Ivory Wreck 281
Jap Rock .265
Jaycee Beach 257
Jaycee Park 257
Jetties 289,294
July Spring 308
Juniper Creek 309
Juniper Springs 309
Jupiter Reef 258
Kelley Reef 289
Key Biscayne Wreck 269
King's Bay 311
Klem's Wreck 275
Koller's Reef 261
Labonte Reef 265
Lakeland .269
Leopard Reef 272
Lerri 278
Liberty Ship 256
Liberty Ship 286,289,290
Little Blue Spring 308
Little Conch Reef 277
Little Dismal Sink 302
Little Grecian 276
Little River Spring 302
Lobbster Ledges 293
Long Reef 270
Looe Key .281
Loss Pontoon 290
Lowrance .268
Lynn's Reef 262

Manatee Spring State Park 305
Masthead Ledge 292
Matecumbe Dropoff 280
Mecco's Barge 293
Merritt's Mill Pond 300
Mexican Pride 293
Middle Sambo 283
Minesweeper 295
Minnow Hole 276
Mizpah 259
Molasses Barge 294
Molasses Reef 277
Monomy .268
Morrison Spring 299
Mullet's Gullet 312
Naked Spring 308
Navy Trash Pile 290
Nine Mile Hill 256
Nine Mile Reef 254
No Name Reef 278
North Horseshoe 276
North Jetty Reef 258
North Jetty 256
Oak Ridge Blue Sink 301
Oakland Ridge 267
Old South Bridge 258
Old Toll Bridge 286
Olson Sink 303
Orange Grove Sink 304
Orion 269
Osborne Reef 268
Osgood Sink 301
Otter Spring 305
P.M. Reef .254
PCMI barge 290
PS Reef 292
Pacific Reef 271
Paddlewheeler 257
Patch Reefs 270
Patrol craft 259
Peace River 294
Peacock Springs 303
Pepper Park 257
Peppertree 289
Percy Payne 289
Phillips Inlet 289
Pickles Reef 277
Pinnacles .295
Ponce de Leon Spring 299
Ponce de Leon Springs 310
Ponte Vedra Ground 255
Pothole Sink 303
Punta Rasa 295
Quonset Hut 290
Rabbit's Lair 255
Racetrack Reef 272
Railroad trestle 294
Rainbow River 313
Rainbow Springs 313
Raspberry 280
Rio Bravo .268
River Sinks 301
Rock Bluff Springs 304
Rock Key .284
Rock Springs 310
Rock jetties 289
Rock ledges 294
Round Island Beach 257
Royal Spring 302
Sailboat 268
Salt Springs 309
Sambo Reefs 283
San Jose 278

San Pablo	286
San Pedro	278
Sand Key	284
Seashell City	261
Sebastian Inlet Recreation Area	257
Second Gully	260
Second Reef	266
Seven Mile Bridge Reef	281
Shangri-la Spring	300
Shark Sink	313
Shrimper	269
Silver Glen Springs	309
Snake Sink	304
Sombrero Reef	281
South Jack Hole	293
South Seas	269
Southeast 16-17	255
Spanish barge	289
Spiny Oyster Barge	278
Spotfin Reef	266
St. Mark's River	301
St. Petersburg Reef	293
Stage II	290
Stage I	290
Star Reef	270
Sun Spring	304
T-33 trainer jet	290
Table Top	293
Tarpon	290
Teepee Reef	278
Ten Fathom Bar	285
Ten Fathom Ledge #1	285
Ten Fathom Ledge #2	283
The Cave	260
The Caves	293
The City of Washington	272
The Coral Gardens	295
The Elbow	272
The Gullies	294
The Gully	295
The Mud Hole	295
The Rocks	278
The Rocks	294
The Valley	261
The Volcano	295
Third Pier	294
Third Reef	266
Three Peaks	278
Three Sisters	312
Tile wreck	284
Timberhole	289
Treasure Island Reef	293
Trench	261
Tres Puentes	278
Triumph Reef	270
Troy Springs	302
Turtle Mound	256
Turtle Reef	292
Twin Caves	300
Twin bombers	256
Two Freighters	258
USCG Blackthorn	292
USS Alligator	279
USS Massachusetts	286
USS Mindanao	255
Uncle John's Sink	314
Venice Ledges	294
Venice Public Beach	294
Vortex Blue Spring	299
W Reef	295
Wabasso Beach Park	257
Wacissa River	301
Wakulla River	300
Warsaw Hole	290
Watson's Reef	272
Weeki Wachee River	314
Wekiwa Springs State Park	310
West Hole Sink	301
Western Sambo	283
White Hill Reef	289
Wiggins Pass State Park	295
Windlass Wreck	277
Yana Spring	304

GEORGIA

A.B. Daniels	240
E.S. Nettleton	240
"G" Reef	240
Gray's Reef	240
"J" Reef	240
Lake Lanier	241
Snapper Banks	240
Tampa	240

HAWAII

Ahihi Bay	13
American fighter planes	7
Anaeho'omalu Bay Beach Park	16
Black Rock	12
City of Refuge	15
Fantasy Reef	7
First Cathedral	11
Five Caves	13
General Store	18
Hana Bay	13
Hanalei Bay	17
Hanauma Bay	4
apuna Beach State Park	16
Honokohau Bay	14
Honokohua Bay	16
Honolua Bay	12
Japanese Zeros	7
Kahalu'u Beach County Park	15
Kahe Point Beach Park	7
Kahoolawe	11
Kailua Kona	15
Kaiwi Point	16
Kapa'a Beach County Park	16
Kapalua Beach	12
Kauhako Bay	15
Kealakekua Bay	15
Knob Hill	11
La Perouse Bay	13
Lanai	11
Lava Flows	7
Magic Island	7
Mahukona Beach Harbor	16
Maili Cove	8
Makaha Beach Park	8
Makua Beach	8
McGregor Point	12
Moku Manu Islands	10
Mokuhooniki Rock	11
Mokule'ia Bay	12
Molokai	11
Molokini Shoal	10
Monolith Rock	11
Napili Bay	12
Nuu Bay	13
Old Koloa Landing	18
Old Kona Airport State Park	15
Olowalu	12
Palemano Point	15
Pine Trees	17
ohakunui Beach	8
Poipu Beach	18

Portlock Point 4
Puako Beach Park 16
Punaluu Beach Park 9
Pupukea Cove 9
Pyramid Rock 16
Rabbit Island 10
Redhill 16
Sea Village 17
Second Cathedral 11
Sergeant Major Reef 11
Shark Fin Rock 11
Sheraton Caverns 18
The Grotto 11
Three Tables 9
Ulua Beach 13
Ulua Ridge 11
Wai'anapanapa State Park 14
Wailea Beach 13
Waimea Bay 8
Wash Rock 11

IDAHO
Alturas 105
Blue Heart 105
Brownlee 105
Coeur d'Alene 104
Crystal Spring 105
Dierke's Lake 105
Diver's Point 104
Payette Lake 104
Pend Oreille Lakes 104
Redfish 105
Stanley Lakes 105

ILLINOIS
4-mile crib 151
Flora M. Hill 151
Iowa 151
Pearl Lake 151
Strip mines 151

INDIANA
Blue Springs 156
Fawn 157
Frances Park 152
J.D. Marshall 152
Lake Cicott 156
Pigeon 157
Shriner Lake 156
Tippecanoe 156
Washington Park 152

IOWA
Big Creek Lake 139
Big Spirit Lake 138
Brown's Bay 138
Cedar Valley Quarries 139
Gull Point 138
Lake Rathbun 139
Lake Yenrouge 139
Terrace Park 138
West Okoboji 138

KANSAS
Blue Hole 140
Strip mines 140

KENTUCKY
Cerulean Springs 182
Dale Hollow Lake 182
Hanover Quarry 182
Laurel Lake 182
Rock Island 182
Woods Creek Lake 183

LOUISIANA
Corney Lake 121
Grand Isle 120
Lake Bistineau 121
Lake Claiborne 121

MAINE
Acadia National Park 197
Anemone Cave 197
Annie 196
Benjamin River 197
Biddeford Pool 195
C. McGuire 196
Cobscook Bay 197
Dyer's Cove 195
Hallowell Quarry 197
Hendrick's Head 196
Hermit Island 196
Kennebec 198
Kettle Cove 195
Land's End 196
Lockenvar 196
Moosehead Lake 197
Nancy 196
Nubble Light 194
Pemaquid Light 196
Penobscot 198
Portland Head Light 196
Pott's Point 196
Richmond Island 195
Sagamore 195
Sebago Lake 197
Ship's Cove 196

MARYLAND
Bloomington Lake 221
Calvert Cliffs 217
Choptank River 221
Deep Creek Lake 221
Eastern Bay 221
Governor Run 217
Love Point 221
Ocean City Inlet 217
Point Lookout 217
Potomac River 221
Susquehanna River 221
West Ocean City 217

MASSACHUSETTS
27-mile obstruction 206
Albert Gallatin 205
Alva 201
Angela 199
Brant Rock Beach 203
Breakwater 201
Burt's Beach 203
California 207
Cape Higgon 200
Cat Island 204
Cathedral Rock 206
Charles S. Haight 207
Chatham 201
Chelsea 207
Chester A. Poling 206
City of Columbus 200
City of Salisbury 204
Cliffs 1 through 4 203
Cohasset Public Beach 203
Corporation Beach 202
Cuttyhunk 199
Devil's Bridge 200
Dry Salvages 207
Edward Rich 207

Folley's Cove	206
Gay Head	200
Gloucester Bay	206
Graves Lighthouse	204
Great Egg Rock	205
Green Island	204
Grouse	207
Gurnet Point	203
Halfway Rock	204
Harding's Beach	201
Hathaway's Pond	201
Henry J. Endicott	202
Herring Cove	201
John Dwight	199
Loblolly Cove	206
Lunet	199
Makoniky Head	200
Manomet Point	203
Mars	203
Maryann Rocks	203
Minot's Lighthouse	203
Monomoy Island	201
Naushon Island	199
Pebble Beach	206
Pendleton	201
Pigeon Cove	206
Pinthis	203
Port Hunter	199
Pottstown	203
Provincetown	201
Provincetown Harbor	201
Roaring Bulls	204
Rockport Breakwater	207
Sagamore	200
Sandwich Beach	202
Scusset Breakwater	202
Sengekontacket Pond	200
Strawberry Point	203
Tansy Bitters	199
Tarpaulin Cove	199
The Race	202
Triana	199
USS New Hampshire	205
Vineyard Lightship	200
West Stockbridge	207
Whitehorse Beach	203

MICHIGAN

Algoma	159
America	158
Ben Hur	164
Boardman River	166
C.R. Price	163
Chester A. Congdon	158
Coulborn	165
Cumberland	158
Dreadnaught	160
Emperor	158
Francis Morozan	166
George M. Cox	158
Glenlyon	159
Granada	160
Grecian	163
Gull Lake	167
Hartzell	166
Havana	165
Henry Chisholm	158
Henry Cort	165
Herman Hettler	160
Isle Royale	157
Johnson	163
Kiowa	161
Kumloops	160

M.E. Trembel	164
Manhattan	160
Menominee	166
Monahamphet	163
Monarch	158
Monrovia	163
Montana	163
Nordmeer	163
Oscar T. Flint	163
Otter Lake	167
Paw Paw Lake	167
Rock jetties	166
Smith Moore	160
St. Clair River	164
Stoney Lake	166
Superior	161
Union Lake	167
Walter Frost	166
Westmoreland	166
Whitney Bridge	165

MINNESOTA

Big Fish Lake	169
Big Watab Lake	170
Christmas Lake	169
Crosby-Ironton iron pits	170
Grindstone Lake	170
Lake Elmo	169
Madeira	168
Mille Lacs	170
Samuel P. Ely	168
Square Lake	169

MISSISSIPPI

Davis Lake	122
Lake Bogue Homa	122
Liberty Ships	121
Marguerite	121
Oil rigs	121
Walker	121

MISSOURI

Black Water Quarry	142
Bonne Terre Mine	142
Bull Creek	140
Bull Shoals	142
Casey's Hole	141
Current	141
Eleven Point River	142
Enchanted Forest	142
Jack's Fork River	141
Norfork Lake	142
North Fork River	142
Oronogo Circle Mine	142
Roubideaux Springs	142
Swan Creek	141
Table Rock	142

MONTANA

Alder Gold Dredge Pond	108
Apgar Lodge	106
Bearmouth Warm Springs	107
Bighorn Lake	109
Hyalite Reservoir	108
Blue Bay	107
Box Canyon	109
Canyon Ferry Reservoir	108
Cemetery Island	108
Chain Canyon	109
Cole's Cabins	109
Crystal Cave	109
Echo Lake	107
Flathead Lake	107

Fort Peck Reservoir 109
Gallatin River 108
Gold Creek Dredge Pond 107
Homestake Lake 107
Lake McDonald 106
Lewis and Clark Picnic Area 108
Loralie Picnic Area 108
Markley Bridge 108
McDonald Creek 106
McDonald Lake 107
Mystic Lake 108
Natural Bridge State Monument 109
Rock Creek Campground 109
Sprague Creek Campground 106
Trudau Lake 108
West Rosebud Lake 109

NEBRASKA
Crystal Cove Lake 145
Lake McConaughy 145
North Platte River 145
Sand pits 145

NEVADA
Boulder Beach 111
Donner Lake 110
Gold Lake 110
Kingman Wash 111
Lake Mead National
   Recreation Area 111
Lake Tahoe 110
Pyramid Lake 110
Ringbolt Rapids 111
Sand Harbor 110
Willow Beach 111

NEW HAMPSHIRE
Clark's Point Cliffs 209
Fort William and Mary 208
Governor Endicott 209
Great Island 208
Great Island Commons 208
Lady of the Lake 209
Lake Spofford 209
Lake Sunapee 208
Lake Winnipesaukee 209
Melvin Village 209
Meredith Bay 209

NEW JERSEY
19th Avenue Beach 225
Allenhurst T-jetty 225
Almirante 224
Barge 222
Chaparro 223
City of Athens 224
Delaware 224
Eighth Avenue 225
Great Isaac 223
Gulf Trade 223
Lana Carrol 223
Manasquan Inlet 225
Manasquan train bridge 225
Maurice Tracy 224
Mohawk 224
Pinta 222
Pliny 225
Quarry 226
R.P. Resor 224
Rock pile 224
Round Valley 226
San Jose 224
San Saba 223

Sea Hag 224
Shark River Inlet 225
Shrewsbury Rock 225
Spruce Run 226
Stolt Dagali 223
Tolten 224
Vizcaya 223

NEW MEXICO
Avalon 112
Blue Hole 112
Caballo 112
Cochiti 112
Conchas 112
Elephant Butte 112
Jackson 112
Lea 112
McMillan 112
Navajo Lake 112
Santa Rosa Lake 112
Sumner 112
Twin Lakes 112
Ute 112

NEW YORK
Acme 233
Adirondack mountain lakes 230
Alabama 233
Bare Hill 232
Barge 43 233
Blue Mountain Lake 230
Canandaigua Lake 232
Charity Shoals 231
Chautauqua Lake 233
City of Rome 233
Coin pile 233
Crane Neck Point 227
Dacotah 233
Deep Run Park 232
Delaware River 229
Diamond Island 230
Dome Island 230
Duck Pond Point 227
Eaton's Neck 227
Execution Rocks 227
Finger Lakes 21
Fire Island National Seashore 228
Fishers Island 227
Greenwood Lake 229
Gwendoline Steers 227
Hart Island 227
HMS Culloden 228
Huntington Harbor Light 227
Iberia 228
Keuka Lake 232
Lake Champlain 230
Lake George 230
Lake Minnewaska 229
Lake Ontario 231
Lake Placid 230
Lake Skaneateles 232
Lizzie D. 229
Long Island 226
Lower Niagara 233
Mailboat 232
Maine 227
Minne-Ha-Ha 230
Mirror Lake 230
Montauk Point jetties 228
Narrowsburg bridge 230
North Hill 228
Ohio 227
Oregon 228

Otter 233
Philadelphia 230
Phoenix 230
Pond Eddy 230
Raleigh Briton 233
Reeves Beach 227
Robert Fulton 233
Rogers Rock 230
Rye Breakwater 226
Sackets Harbor 231
San Diego 229
Seneca Lake 231
Shinnecock Inlet 228
Smithtown artificial reef 227
SS Olinda 227
St. Lawrence River 231
Stone barge 229
Stony Point 231
Taylor warehouse area 232
The Sore Thumb 228
Ticonderoga 230
Upper, "west" Niagara 232
USS Turner 229
Valcour Island 230
W.C. Richardson 233

NORTH CAROLINA
Ashkhabad 246
Atlas 246
Badin Lake 250
Benson 245
Caribe Sea 246
Cassimer 248
Ciltvaira 245
Goldston Quarry 250
Hutton 246
John D. Gill 248
Modern Greece 249
Naeco 247
Normannia 248
Norvana 245
Papoose 247
Portland 246
Proteus 245
Suloide 246
Tamaulipas 246
U-352 247
U-85 242
USS Shurz 247
USS Tarpon 246

OHIO
Adventure 171
America 171
F.H. Prince 171
Nelson Ledges Quarry Park 172
North Carolina 171
Portage Quarry 171
Salisbury Quarry 171
Sportsman Lake 172
White Star Park 171

OKLAHOMA
Fort Gibson Lake 146
Lake Eufaula 146
Lake Tenkiller 146
Strayhorn Landing 146

OREGON
3 Arch Rocks 28
Baltimore 26
Blue Lake 29
Brookings 26

Clear Lake 28
Coos Bay 27
Kilchis 29
Nehalem Bay 28
Nestucca 29
Newport Reefs 28
O'Dell Lake 29
Pirate's Cove 27
Port Orford 25
Simpson's Reef 26
Sunset Bay 26
Trask 29
Umpqua 29
USS Brush 27
Wallowa Lake 29
Wilson 29
Winchester Bay 27
Yaquina Lighthouse 27

PENNSYLVANIA
Bainbridge Sportsmen's Club . . . 234
Beaver Dam Quarry 234
Billmeyer Quarry 234
Dutch Springs 234
Fleetwing 235
Isolde 235
Lake Edinboro 235
Lake Erie 235
Lake Pleasant 235
Paper barge 235
Quarries 235
Quest 234
Susquehanna River 234
Willow Springs 234
Youghiogheny River 235
Youghiogheny River Lake 235

RHODE ISLAND
Beavertail Point 211
Belleville 212
Black Point 210
Block Island 211
Brenton Cove 212
Castle Hill 212
Fort Wetherill 211
Gooseberry Island 212
Green Bridge 212
Jamestown Harbor 213
King's Beach 212
Land's End 212
Larchmont 210
Lightburne 211
Lydia Skolfield 212
Montana 211
Pinnacle 211
Point Judith 210
Sachuest Point 213
Sakonnet Point 213
Seal Rock 212
Third Beach 213
U-853 210
USS Bass 211
Watch Hill 210

SOUTH CAROLINA
Betsy Ross 251
Caper's Island Reef 251
City of Richmond 252
Cooper River 252
Devil's Fork 252
Edisto River 252
Georgeanna 252
Hinton 251

Kiawah Island Reef (4KI) 251
Lake Hartwell 252
Lake Jocassee 252
Martin's Landing 252
R-8 251
Strawberry Landing 252
Sullivan's Landing 252

SOUTH DAKOTA
Alexandria Quarry 147
Lake Oahe 147
Pactola Reservoir 147
Tailwaters of Oahe Dam 147

TENNESSEE
Bear Hole Bend 184
Catfish Hole 184
Dale Hollow Lake 184
First Island 184
Norris Lake 184
Point 19 184
Smyrna Rock Quarry 184
Tennessee River 184
The School 184

TEXAS
3 Hickey Rocks 127
Arkansas Bend 130
Canyon Lake 130
Castle Canyon 128
Civil War gunboats 127
Comal Park 130
Comal River 131
Diablo East 128
Flower Gardens 125
Hersh Harbor 130
Indian Springs 128
Lake Amistad 128
Lake Balmorhea 129
Lake Meredith 131
Lake Sam Rayburn 132
Lake Travis 129
Lakeview Recreation Area 132
Landa Park 131
LCRA Park 129
Liberty Ships 125
Magnolia Beach 127
Medina Lake 130
North Park 130
Oil rigs 122
Paleface Park 130
Park Chalk Bluff 130
Possum Kingdom Lake 131
Red Hills Lake 132
San Marcos River 130
Scuba Point 131
Sometimes Island 130
Starne's Island 129
Stetson Bank 127
Sunken German submarine 127
Toledo Bend 132
Tom Hughes Park 129
Tyler Lake 132
V.A. Fogg 125
Windy Point 129

UTAH
Bear Lake 113
Blue Lake 114
Cisco Beach 113
Fish Lake 113
Flaming Gorge 113
Glen Canyon Dam 114

Logan River 113
Tony Grove Lake 113

VERMONT
Champlain 214
General Butler 214
Glen Ellis Falls 214
Lake Champlain 213
Lake Memphremagog 214
Marble quarries 214
Phoenix 1 214
Rouse's Point 213
Water Witch 214
White River 214

VIRGINIA
Buckroe Beach 236
Chesapeake Bay Bridge Tunnel 236
Chesapeake Light Tower 236
Dixie Girl 237
Dry River 238
Garrison 237
Gulf Hustler 237
Hampton Roads Tunnel 236
Havilon 237
Haymarket Quarry 237
James River 237
Kingston 236
Little Foxes Islands 236
Luckenbach 237
Morgan 237
Ocean View 236
Philpott Reservoir 238
Rappahannock River 236
Sherando Lake 237
Sontorre 236
Spring Cove 238
Tiger 236
Todd Lake 237
Trepka 237
Triangle Wrecks 237
Webster 237
York River 237

WASHINGTON
Abandoned Ferry Landing 33
Agate Pass 33
Alki Beach 31
Alki Pipeline 33
Alki Point 31
Bead Lake 42
Blake Island 33
Blakely Rocks 33
Boulevard Park 41
Center Reef 39
Columbia River 42
Crescent Lake 42
Danger Reef 39
Day Island 34
Dead Man's Bay 39
Deception Pass 39
Diamond Knot 38
Duncan Rock 38
Duwamish Head 31
Echo 40
Edmonds City Underwater Park 30
Edmonds Oil Docks 30

Fort Ward 33
Fort Worden 37
Fox Island 35
Frost Island 40
Gibson Point 35
Iceberg Point 40
James Island 40
Keystone 41
Kopachuck 35
Lake Chelan 42
Lake Merwin 42
Larabee State Park 41
Lewis River 42
Lime Kiln 39
Lover's Cove 39
Low Island 39
Matia 40
Neah Bay 38
Octopus Hole 37
Old Fox Island Ferry Landing 35
Orcas Island 39
Patos 40
Peapod Rocks 39
Point Wilson 37
Richmond Beach County Park 30
Rosario Beach 41
Salt Creek 38
Saltwater 34
San Juan County Park 35
Spokane River 42
Stuart Island 40
Sucia 40
Tacoma Narrows Bridge 34
Tatoosh Island 38
Titlow Beach 34
Tolmie State Park 36
Tongue Point 38
Union Wharf 37
West Beach Reef 39
Westhaven State Park 29

WEST VIRGINIA

Cheat Lake 185
Summersville Lake 185

WISCONSIN

Appomattox 174
Bailey's Harbor 174
Big Round Lake 179
Clear Lake 179
Devil's Lake State Park 179
Emeline 174
Fleetwing 175
Garrett Bay 175
Grindstone 179
H.P. Hill 176
Japan 175
Kate Kelly 174
Lady of the Lake 178
Lake Delevan 178
Lake Geneva 178
Lake Mendota 179
Lake Nashota 179
Lost Land 179
Louisiana 175
Lucius Newberry 178
Meridian 178
Milwaukee 173
Niagara 174
Norland 174
Pilot Island 176
Poverty Island 177

Prins Willem V 173
R.J. Hackett 177
Racine Quarry 178
Red Granite Quarry 179
Riverside 177
Roen Steam Barge 177
Sebastopol 174
Sparkling Lake 179
Spider Lake 179
Spread Eagle Chain of Lakes 179
Table Bluff 175
Upper Lake Namahbin 179
Whalesback Shoals 177
Wisconsin 173
Wisconsin Bay 175

WYOMING

Alcova Reservoir 115
Beartooth Lake 116
Buffalo Bill Reservoir 116
Cathedral Bay 115
Firehole River 116
Fremont Lake 115
Glendo Reservoir 115
Gull Point 116
Island Lake 116
Jackson Lake 1115
Lake Hattie 115
Lake Hotel Steamboat Landing 116
Little Thumb Creek 115
Long Lake 116
Pumice Point 2 116
Snake River 115
Spalding Bay 115
Yellowstone Lake 115